DUNGEONS & DRAGONS

ESSENTIALS™

MONSTER VAULT™

ROLEPLAYING GAME CORE RULES

Rodney Thompson • Logan Bonner • Matthew Sernett

CREDITS

Design
Rodney Thompson (lead),
Logan Bonner, Matthew Sernett

Development
Peter Schaefer

Additional Development
Andy Collins, Jeremy Crawford, Mike Mearls,
Stephen Schubert, Rodney Thompson

Editing
Greg Bilsland (lead), Jeremy Crawford,
Dawn J. Geluso, Ray Vallese

Managing Editing
Kim Mohan

D&D R&D/Book Publishing Director
Bill Slavicsek

D&D Creative Manager
Christopher Perkins

D&D Design Manager
James Wyatt

D&D Development and Editing Manager
Andy Collins

D&D Senior Creative Art Director
Jon Schindehette

D&D Brand Team
Liz Schuh, Jesse Decker, Kierin Chase,
Laura Tommervik, Shelly Mazzanoble,
Chris Lindsay, Hilary Ross

Art Director
Kate Irwin

Graphic Designers
Leon Cortez, Keven Smith, Emi Tanji,
Add'l Design by Jino Choi, Yasuyo Dunnett

Interior Illustrations
Dave Allsop, Steve Argyle, Daren
Bader, Zoltan Boros & Gabor Szikszai,
Chippy, Stephen Crowe, Julie Dillon,
Wayne England, Jason A. Engle,
Carl Frank, Lars Grant-West, David
Griffith, Fred Hooper, Michael Komarck,
Todd Lockwood, Warren Mahy, Raven
Mimura, Jim Nelson, William O'Connor,
rk post, Steve Prescott, Wayne Reynolds,
Marc Sasso, Ron Spears, Anne Stokes,
Sarah Stone, Arnie Swekel, Francis Tsai,
Udon, Pete Venters, Eva Widermann,
Sam Wood, Ben Wootten

Publishing Production Specialists
Angelika Lokotz, Erin Dorries

Prepress Manager
Jefferson Dunlap

Imaging Technician
Carmen Cheung, Ashley Brock

Production Manager
Cynda Callaway

D&D 4th Edition Design
Rob Heinsoo, Andy Collins, James Wyatt

Building on the Design of Previous Editions by
E. Gary Gygax, Dave Arneson,
David "Zeb" Cook, Jonathan Tweet,
Monte Cook, Skip Williams, Richard Baker,
Peter Adkison

U.S., CANADA, ASIA, PACIFIC,
& LATIN AMERICA
Wizards of the Coast LLC
P.O. Box 707
Renton WA 98057-0707
+1-800-324-6496

EUROPEAN HEADQUARTERS
Hasbro UK Ltd
Caswell Way
Newport, Gwent NP9 0YH
GREAT BRITAIN
Please keep this address for your records

WIZARDS OF THE COAST,
BELGIUM
Industrialaan 1
1702 Groot-Bijgaarden
Belgium
+32.070.233.277

620-24465000-001 EN   ISBN: 978-0-7869-5631-9

CONTENTS

CHIPPY

MONSTERS A-Z

They lurk in the shadows. They beat down the doors. They wrap their slimy tentacles around you and drag you down into a hole. They come with fire, axes, spells, and teeth. They are the creatures of DUNGEONS & DRAGONS®, and they are yours to command.

Monster Vault is a reference for Dungeon Masters that contains the essential monsters of the DUNGEONS & DRAGONS game. Inside the pages of this book, you'll find a codex of monsters and villains to throw at the heroes as they delve into dungeons or stage attacks on planar fortresses. You can use this book as a reference when running published adventures or as a tool when designing your own encounters.

Inside the pages of this book, you'll find monsters and villains to throw at the heroes. You can use this book as a reference or as a tool.

Most monster entries in this book begin with a two-page spread consisting of an illustration of a monster and some lore about its origin, habits, allies, and ecology. You'll also find information on how to run the monster in both combat and noncombat encounters, as well as details about adventure and campaign hooks related to a monster.

Following the illustration and lore is a series of monster statistics blocks representing different varieties of a type of monster. You can use these statistics blocks together or with other monsters described in a creature's lore. You might also mix and match monsters as appropriate for your campaign or adventure. The monsters have a variety of roles and levels, allowing you to utilize the creatures throughout the heroes' adventuring careers.

MONSTER STATISTICS BLOCKS

Monster statistics are presented in a format designed to be easy to use and reference. This section describes the typical components of a statistics block.

Name

Each statistics block begins with the creature's name. Most names include the general name of the monster type plus an additional descriptor, such as "gith-yanki warrior" or "deathpledged gnoll." In some cases, these descriptive names reflect titles adopted by the monsters themselves, perhaps reflecting a particular status in the monster's society. Many others are descriptions applied to the monster, often by its victims.

Level and Role

A monster's level and role are tools for you to use when building an encounter. The *Dungeon Master's Kit* explains how to use these tools.

Level: A monster's level summarizes how tough it is in an encounter. Level determines most of the monster's statistics as well as the experience point (XP) award the PCs earn for defeating it.

Role: A monster's role describes its preferred combat tactics, much as a character class's role suggests tactics for characters of that class. Monster roles are artillery, brute, controller, lurker, skirmisher, and soldier.

    A monster might have a second role: elite, solo, or minion. Elite monsters and solo monsters are tougher than standard monsters, and minions are weaker. For the purpose of encounter building, an elite monster counts as two standard monsters of its level, a solo monster counts as five, and four to six minions count as one—four at heroic tier (levels 1–10), five at paragon tier (levels 11–20), and six at epic tier (levels 21–30).

    In addition, a monster might have the leader subrole, indicating that it grants some sort of boon to its allies, such as a beneficial aura.

Size

A creature's size determines its space as well as its reach. A creature might have a greater reach depending on the characteristics of its body.

Monster Size	Space	Typical Reach
Tiny	1/2 × 1/2	0
Small	1 × 1	1
Medium	1 × 1	1
Large	2 × 2	1 or 2
Huge	3 × 3	2 or 3
Gargantuan	4 × 4 or larger	3 or 4

Space: This is the area (measured in squares) that a creature occupies on the battle grid.

Reach: Typically, the reach of a creature using a melee attack power is the same as the range entry of that power. If you need to determine a creature's reach for some other purpose, such as for a grab attack or an attempt to pick up an object, refer to the table above.

    Even if a creature's reach or melee range is greater than 1, the creature can't make opportunity attacks against targets that aren't adjacent to it.

    A creature that has a melee attack with a range of 0 must occupy at least 1 square of the space of its target to make the attack.

Origin

A monster's origin—aberrant, elemental, fey, immortal, natural, or shadow—describes its place in the DUNGEONS & DRAGONS cosmology. See the glossary for information about each origin.

Type

A creature's type—animate, beast, humanoid, or magical beast—summarizes some basic facts about its appearance and behavior. See the glossary for information about each type.

Keywords/Race   Some monsters have keywords that further define them. These keywords represent groups of monsters, such as demon, devil, dragon, and undead. See the glossary for information about monster keywords. This part of the entry might also include a monster's race if its race is not included in the monster's name.

XP Value

The experience point award for defeating this creature is given beneath its level and role.

HP/Initiative

The monster's maximum hit points, bloodied value, and modifier to initiative checks are on the top line of its statistics.

Defenses/Perception

All four defense scores are on the next line, along with the monster's Perception modifier (often used at the start of an encounter).

Senses

Some monsters have special senses, such as darkvision or tremorsense. Any such senses are noted below a monster's Perception modifier, and these terms are defined in the glossary.

Speed

A monster's speed represents the number of squares it can move when taking a move action to walk. If a monster has alternative movement modes, such as fly, climb, or swim, that fact is noted in its "Speed" entry. Special modes of movement are defined in the glossary.

Immune

If a monster is immune to a damage type (such as cold or fire), it doesn't take that type of damage. If a monster is immune to a condition or another effect (such as the dazed condition or forced movement), it is unaffected by that condition or effect. If a monster is immune to charm, fear, illusion, poison, or sleep, it is unaffected by the nondamaging effects of a power that has that keyword.

Immunity to one part of a power does not make a monster immune to other parts of the power. For example, a thunder power deals no thunder damage to a creature that is immune to thunder, but the power could still push the creature.

Resist

Resistance means a creature takes less damage from a specific damage type. For example, if a creature has resist 5 fire, the creature takes 5 less fire damage whenever it takes that type of damage.

Against Combined Damage Types: A creature's resistance is ineffective against combined damage types unless the creature has resistance to each of the damage types, and then only the weakest of the resistances applies.

For example, if a creature has resist 10 lightning and resist 5 thunder and an attack deals 15 lightning and thunder damage to it, the creature takes 10 damage, for the resistance to the combined damage types is limited by the lesser of the two resistances.

Not Cumulative: Resistances against the same damage type are not cumulative. Only the highest resistance applies. For example, if a creature has resist 5 cold and gains resist 10 cold, the creature has resist 10 cold, not resist 15 cold.

Vulnerable

Being vulnerable to a damage type means a creature takes extra damage from that damage type. For example, if a creature has vulnerable 5 fire, the creature takes 5 extra fire damage whenever it takes that type of damage.

Against Combined Damage Types: Vulnerability to a specific damage type applies even when that damage type is combined with another. For example, if a creature has vulnerable 5 fire, the creature takes 5 extra damage when it takes ongoing fire and radiant damage.

Not Cumulative: Vulnerabilities to the same damage type are not cumulative. Only the highest vulnerability applies. For example, if a creature has vulnerable 5 psychic and then gains vulnerable 10 psychic, the creature has vulnerable 10 psychic, not vulnerable 15 psychic.

Saving Throws

Some monsters have bonuses to saving throws. A monster adds its bonuses to its saving throw result to see if an effect ends.

Action Points

Elite and solo monsters typically have action points they can spend to take extra actions, just as player characters do. Unlike characters, a monster can spend more than 1 action point in an encounter, but only 1 per round.

Traits

The Traits section includes characteristics of the creature that are not powers. Many traits are always in effect, such as regeneration or the ability to deal extra damage on certain attacks. Others can be turned on or off, such as an aura or a benefit for a creature's mount or rider.

Aura An aura power creates an aura, which is a continuous effect that emanates from a creature. It's denoted by a special icon (✵), and the aura's size is noted to the right of its name. Unless noted otherwise, an aura uses the following rules.

Fills an Area: The aura fills each square that is both within a specified range of the creature and within line of effect of it. An aura 1 affects each square adjacent to the creature, for example. A creature is normally unaffected by its own aura.

Unaffected by the Environment: The aura is unaffected by environmental phenomena and terrain, although blocking terrain blocks an aura. For instance, an aura of fire is unaffected by an area of extreme cold.

Overlapping Auras: If auras overlap and impose penalties to the same roll or game statistic, a creature affected by the overlapping auras is subjected to the worst penalty; the penalties are not cumulative. For instance, if a creature is affected by three overlapping auras that each impose a -2 penalty to attack rolls, the creature takes a -2 penalty, not a -6 penalty.

Deactivating an Aura: A creature can take a minor action to deactivate or reactivate one of its auras.

Death or Unconsciousness Ends: A creature's auras end immediately when it falls unconscious or dies.

Action Type

A monster's standard, move, minor, and nontriggered free actions are organized by action type.

Powers A monster's powers are presented under their respective action type in order of frequency of usage, from at-will to recharge to encounter powers.

Icon/Type The name line of an attack power includes an icon (if applicable) that represents the power's type: melee (✦), ranged (✦), close (✦), or area (✦).

A basic attack has a circle around its icon, denoting a melee basic attack ⊕ or ranged basic attack ⊛.

Usage A monster power is usable at will, once per encounter (or rarely once per day), or it recharges in certain circumstances.

Recharge ⚁ ⚃ ⚅: The power has a random chance of recharging during each round of combat. At the start of each of the monster's turns, roll a d6. If the roll is one of the die results shown in the power description, the monster regains the use of that power. The power also recharges after a short rest.

Recharge if/when . . . : The power recharges in a specific circumstance, such as when the monster is first bloodied during an encounter. The power also recharges after a short rest.

Requirement Some powers have a precondition that must be met for a monster to use the power.

Attack A monster power that has an attack roll is usually an attack power. Sometimes an "Attack" entry includes special information about a component of that entry.

Type and Range A power's type and range are given first on the power's "Attack" entry. The types are melee, ranged, area, and close. Each type has rules for range and targeting, detailed in the *Rules Compendium*.

Targets In parentheses after the attack type and range is information that describes which or how many creatures a power targets.

Attack Bonus/Defense Usually, the last element in a power's "Attack" entry is the monster's attack bonus and the defense the power targets.

Hit This entry describes what happens to each target that a monster hits with a power's attack.

Miss This entry describes what happens to each target that a monster misses with a power's attack.

"Half damage" in this entry refers to rolled damage. Roll the damage specified in the "Hit" entry and deal half of that damage to each target the monster misses. "Half damage" does not apply to ongoing damage or any other damaging effects in the "Hit" entry.

Effect Anything that appears in an "Effect" entry occurs when the monster uses the power, whether or not it hits with it. Some "Effect" entries include range, type, and target information.

Secondary Attack
Some powers allow a monster to make secondary attack. A "Hit," a "Miss," or an "Effect" entry tells you if a monster makes a secondary attack. Unless otherwise noted, the attack type and the range of a secondary attack are the same as the power's, and the secondary attack doesn't require a separate action. As with normal attacks, the target of a secondary attack is identified after the attack's type and range.

Sustain
If a power has a "Sustain" entry, the monster can keep part of that power active by taking a specific type of action before the end of each of its turns. A monster can't take the sustaining action until the turn after it uses the power. The entry's name specifies the action type that must be taken—most often minor, move, or standard. See the *Rules Compendium* for more about sustaining powers.

Aftereffect
An aftereffect automatically occurs after another effect ends. In a power description, an "Aftereffect" entry follows the effect it applies to.

A target is sometimes subjected to an aftereffect after a save. If that save occurs when the target is rolling multiple saving throws, the aftereffect takes effect after the target has rolled all of them.

Failed Saving Throw
Sometimes an effect changes as a target fails saving throws against it. The new effect, specified in a "First Failed Saving Throw" or a "Second Failed Saving Throw" entry, takes effect after the target fails a saving throw against the previous effect at the end of the target's turn. A few effects also specify something that happens on "Each Failed Saving Throw." This is a new effect that is repeated whenever a target fails a saving throw against the effect during the end of its turn.

An effect doesn't change if the creature fails a saving throw against it at a time other than the end of its turn.

Special
Any unusual information about the use of a power appears in this entry. For example, some powers can be used as basic attacks, which is noted in a "Special" entry.

Triggered Actions
This section contains powers that have triggers. These powers have a few entries that other powers don't.

Trigger
A trigger defines when a monster is able to use a power. A monster must still be able to take the power's required action and meet any requirements.

(Action)
A triggered power's action type is given in parentheses at the start of its "Attack" entry or its "Effect" entry. The type might be an immediate reaction, an immediate interrupt, an opportunity action, or a free action. Some powers require no action to use; they simply occur in response to a trigger.

Skills

The skills section of a monster's statistics block includes only trained skills or skills for which the monster has an unusual modifier. A monster's Perception modifier isn't repeated here, even if Perception is trained.

Ability Scores

A monster's six ability scores are included toward the bottom of its statistics block. Following each score in parentheses is the adjusted ability score modifier, including one-half the monster's level, which is useful whenever the monster needs to make an untrained skill check or an ability check.

Alignment

A monster's most typical alignment is noted in its statistics block. The *Rules Compendium* contains information on the various alignments.

Languages

This entry gives the languages that a monster can speak and understand. An individual monster might know additional languages, such as Common or the languages of its companions. See the *Rules Compendium* for more information about the languages of the DUNGEONS & DRAGONS world.

Equipment

A monster's "Equipment" entry notes important items a monster is carrying. A monster might carry equipment that is not noted here. Equipment that is unimportant to a monster is left for the Dungeon Master to decide.

If a character gains a monster's equipment, he or she can use it as normal gear. A character does not gain the powers that a monster uses through a piece of equipment.

A piece of equipment that player characters use does not necessarily have the same properties for monsters. For example, a greataxe has the high crit property, but a monster using the item does not benefit from the property unless otherwise noted in its statistics.

Healing Surges

Monsters have healing surges. However, few monsters have powers that let them spend healing surges. The number of healing surges a monster has is based on its level: 1-10, one healing surge; 11-20, two healing surges; 21 or higher, three healing surges.

Because they rarely come into play, healing surges are not included in a monster's statistics block.

ANGEL

Beautiful and terrible, the bright sight of an angel strikes awe into the soul and drives onlookers to their knees in obeisance to the divine order. Yet angels can do more than deliver the miracles of the gods. They are destroyers, too, and the appearance of an angel is a harbinger of woe as often as it is a sign of hope.

As manifestations of divine will, angels involve themselves in mortal concerns far more often than do deities or exarchs. Angels act both openly and secretly, serving as emissaries, generals, or assassins. Although one ordinary mortal in ten thousand might count himself lucky to have his life touched by an angel, those who intrude into the affairs of the gods can expect to meet dozens of angels—most likely on the field of battle.

Offspring of the Astral Eternity: Angels serve the gods, leading some people to believe that they were created by the gods. In reality, angels are powerful astral beings that appeared during the first moments of the formation of the Astral Sea. Angels are made of the same spirit as the gods, created as part of the original compact of heaven. They exist as expressions of the Astral Sea, sentient energy in humanoid form. Perhaps the needs of the gods caused the astral stuff to spew angels forth, but it was not a conscious act of creation. Different types of angels have different callings; they are manifestations of celestial vocations, such as protection, battle, and vengeance. Although their appearances can vary, all angels are vaguely humanoid in form, with masculine or feminine features and lower bodies that trail off into flowing energy.

> *"Long ago, I swore an oath to Bahamut. That oath is the only thing keeping you alive."*
>
> —Andravar, angel of Vecna

Servants to the Divine Masters: During the Dawn War between the gods and the primordials, angels fought for the deities that best exemplified their callings. Today they serve as mercenaries for anyone willing to meet their price, be it wealth, power, or a cause worthy of their attention. In this way, the gods share angels with mortals. Most angels are nameless servitors that take pride in having scant personalities, which allows them to flow smoothly into the service of any god that calls them. The angels' mission is to perform the will of the deities, not to cling to one god and promote its cause above those of all others.

Not all angels adhere to these standard behaviors. Some feel suited for service to a single god, adapting elements of that deity's ornamentation and symbolism into neutral angelic dress. Other angels develop strong personalities and choose names. These forceful angels might become exarchs of the gods they serve or carve bizarre paths through the Astral Sea before they disappear, are destroyed, or fade from existence.

Constrained by Divine Laws: The gods and their servants often have conflicting goals. As a result, angels sometimes battle one another. Even so, they cannot be persuaded to lend their energy to rituals or sacrifices that would imperil a deity or eliminate a large number of rival angels. They will fight each other in single combat or in groups of a dozen at a time, if that is the wish of a god or other wielder of divine power, but they will not willingly destroy planar gates, shatter astral dominions, or slay deities. No angel can make a direct assault upon a god—at least, not without dire consequences for the angel and perhaps the compact of heaven.

An angel follows other rules and codes of conduct derived from the deity it serves. An angel of Kord must be forthright and valorous, whereas Vecna demands that his angels be circumspect and conniving. An angel might be bound by ancient oaths to one god while it serves another, and much can hinge on the angel's delicate balancing of conflicting obligations.

Angel of Protection	Level 14 Soldier
Medium immortal humanoid (angel)	XP 1,000

HP 141; **Bloodied** 70	**Initiative** +12
AC 30, **Fortitude** 26, **Reflex** 24, **Will** 25	**Perception** +11
Speed 6, fly 8 (hover)	
Immune fear; **Resist** 10 radiant	

TRAITS

✪ **Angelic Shield ✦ Aura 5**

While the angel is not bloodied and within 5 squares of its ward, squares in the aura are difficult terrain for enemies.

Angelic Presence

While the angel is not bloodied, attack rolls against it take a -2 penalty.

STANDARD ACTIONS

⊕ **Greatsword (radiant, weapon) ✦ At-Will**

Attack: Melee 1 (one creature); +19 vs. AC

Hit: 2d10 + 11 radiant damage.

Ward ✦ At-Will

Effect: Ranged 5 (one creature). The angel designates the target as its ward. While the angel is within 5 squares of the target, the target takes half damage from melee attacks and ranged attacks against it, and the angel takes an equal amount of damage. While the angel is adjacent to the target, the target gains a +2 bonus to AC. A creature can be the ward of only one angel at a time. If multiple angels designate the same creature as their wards, it becomes the ward of the last angel to designate it as such.

Skills Insight +16

Str 22 (+13)	**Dex** 17 (+10)	**Wis** 19 (+11)
Con 21 (+12)	**Int** 12 (+8)	**Cha** 14 (+9)

Alignment unaligned   **Languages** Supernal

Equipment greatsword

Angel of Battle

Large immortal humanoid (angel)

Level 15 Skirmisher

XP 1,200

HP 148; **Bloodied** 74

AC 29, **Fortitude** 27, **Reflex** 25, **Will** 28

Speed 8, fly 12 (hover)

Immune fear; **Resist** 10 radiant

Initiative +13

Perception +11

TRAITS

Angelic Presence

While the angel is not bloodied, attack rolls against it take a -2 penalty.

STANDARD ACTIONS

⊕ **Falchion** (weapon) ✦ **At-Will**

Attack: Melee 2 (one creature); +20 vs. AC

Hit: 3d10 + 5 damage, and the target grants combat advantage until the start of the angel's next turn.

† **Mobile Melee Attack** ✦ **At-Will**

Effect: The angel moves up to half its speed and uses *falchion* once at any point during the movement. The angel doesn't provoke opportunity attacks when moving away from the target of the attack.

⬅ **Storm of Blades** ✦ **Encounter**

Attack: Close burst 3 (enemies in the burst); +20 vs. AC

Hit: 6d8 + 7 damage.

Effect: The angel's fly speed changes to 2 (hover) until the end of the encounter.

Str 23 (+13)	Dex 19 (+11)	Wis 18 (+11)
Con 20 (+12)	Int 15 (+9)	Cha 25 (+14)

Alignment unaligned

Equipment falchion

Languages Supernal

(Left to right) angel of protection, angel of battle, angel of vengeance

JULIE DILLON

Angel of Valor Veteran

Level 16 Minion Soldier

Medium immortal humanoid (angel)

XP 350

HP 1; a missed attack never damages a minion.

AC 32, **Fortitude** 30, **Reflex** 27, **Will** 26

Initiative +12

Perception +10

Speed 6, fly 9 (hover)

Immune fear; **Resist** 10 fire, 10 radiant

Standard Actions

⊕ **Greatsword** (fire, weapon) ✦ **At-Will**

Attack: Melee 1 (one creature); +21 vs. AC

Hit: 11 fire damage.

Str 24 (+15)	Dex 18 (+12)	Wis 14 (+10)
Con 18 (+12)	Int 12 (+9)	Cha 16 (+11)

Alignment unaligned   **Languages** Supernal

Equipment chainmail, greatsword

Angel of Vengeance

Level 19 Elite Brute

Large immortal humanoid (angel)

XP 4,800

HP 426; **Bloodied** 213

AC 31, **Fortitude** 33, **Reflex** 29, **Will** 33

Initiative +13

Perception +16

Speed 8, fly 12 (hover)

Immune fear; **Resist** 15 cold, 15 fire, 15 radiant

Saving Throws +2; **Action Points** 1

Traits

Cloak of Vengeance (cold, fire)

While the angel is not bloodied, attack rolls against it take a -2 penalty, and any creature that hits the angel with a melee attack takes 10 cold and fire damage.

Standard Actions

⊕ **Longsword** (cold, fire, weapon) ✦ **At-Will**

Attack: Melee 2 (one creature); +24 vs. AC

Hit: 4d10 + 12 cold and fire damage.

† **Double Attack** ✦ **At-Will**

Effect: The angel uses longsword twice.

Minor Actions

Sign of Vengeance ✦ **Encounter**

Effect: Ranged sight (one creature). Until the end of the encounter, the angel can teleport adjacent to the target as a move action.

Triggered Actions

⬳ **Coldfire Pillar Transformation** (cold, fire, polymorph) ✦ **Encounter**

Trigger: The angel is first bloodied.

Effect (Free Action): The angel becomes a 6-square-high pillar until the start of its next turn. While in this form, it is immune to all damage. When the effect ends, the angel makes the following attack.

Attack: Close burst 2 (enemies in the burst); +22 vs. Reflex

Hit: 2d8 + 18 cold and fire damage.

Skills Insight +21

Str 27 (+17)	Dex 18 (+13)	Wis 25 (+16)
Con 13 (+10)	Int 19 (+13)	Cha 26 (+17)

Alignment unaligned   **Languages** Supernal

Equipment 2 longswords

ARCHON

Opposing the gods is the sole purpose of the archons. Highly intelligent elemental creatures, archons serve as soldiers and leaders in the armies of the primordials. They also act as mercenaries for those in need of elemental might.

When the gods brought their armies of angels, exarchs, and exalted beings to fight the primordials in the Dawn War, the primordials responded by creating their own soldiers from the elemental foundations of their home plane. The primordials already had great beasts and chaotic elementals that were being used as pure weapons, but they needed more reliable and inventive creatures to populate and lead their armies. Archons were gifted with a degree of cunning not found in other primordial creations. Each archon is a dangerous opponent, drawing on unrestrained combat prowess, the keen mind of a veteran soldier, and an elemental weapon that vanishes when its wielder falls.

"Finding a fire archon forge is a bit like finding a termite nest in your home. You feel a sense of dread that slowly dawns into gut-wrenching terror and then decays into despair."

—Baredd, Champion of Argent

Soldiers in an Elemental Army: Archons fight for the primordials, mainly as soldiers and officers in their armies but also as special agents and shock troops. In addition, archons turn up in the service of lesser elemental princes and powerful beings that roam the Elemental Chaos, including high-ranking demons of the Abyss. More than just mighty warriors, archons engage in unorthodox tactics to take down their enemies. For example, a squad of archon assassins might burst through a planar portal to ambush a target's carriage as it travels between towns, or a team of archons sent to intimidate the locals might appear during a violent earthquake or ride in on rushing floodwaters for greater effect. Although archons were created for battle, they also excel in leadership roles; would-be heroes might be surprised to find that the head of a band of elemental cultists is an archon put in place by a higher power. Regardless of whether archons are dispatched to fight or lead, they take full advantage of their elemental connections to get the job done.

Fighting for the Highest Bidder: Many primordials were slain or imprisoned after the Dawn War, leaving untold numbers of archons with no masters to serve. Some were quickly snatched up by formidable rulers of the Elemental Chaos; those that remained free drifted into a life of mercenary service on the roiling plane. Efreets, demon lords, giants, and other influential denizens of the Chaos employ archons as soldiers and bodyguards. Archons have their own needs and desires, as do other sentient creatures, but where mortals vie for riches and power, archons seek opportunities for destruction. The chance to commit violence and mayhem is a strong lure for archons—after all, the creatures were literally born to fight. It is difficult to bribe an archon with wealth, but presenting an intriguing destructive challenge (for example, bringing down fortress walls that have been reinforced with powerful arcane runes) is a sure way to get an archon's interest, if not its servitude.

Cunning Enemies and Tacticians: Unlike their lesser cousins, the elementals, archons work well together, and each kind brings its own strengths into play. Whereas earth archons are patient, inexorable defenders, fire archons are aggressive and highly effective when attacking enemy positions or laying siege. Water archons travel as easily through rivers and lakes as others do on land; they make excellent naval forces and can sneak into occupied territory before launching a surprise attack from behind enemy lines. Ice archons are brilliant, ruthless tacticians whose calculated plans are devoid of emotion. When united, archons of different kinds are more destructive than when they act separately, and the strongest groups are those that have diverse elemental affinities. For example, water archons might infiltrate a castle by means of an underground river, opening the gates so that fire archons can spill into the structure and attack. Earth archons fortify that position and hold the gates open, while ice archons ensure that no one escapes from the castle to warn nearby villages or seek reinforcements.

WAYNE ENGLAND

(Top, left to right) earth archon, ice archon, water archon, fire archon

Earth Archon

Level 12 Brute
Medium elemental humanoid (earth)
XP 700

HP 149; **Bloodied** 74
AC 25, **Fortitude** 26, **Reflex** 23, **Will** 21
Speed 6 (earth walk)
Immune disease, petrification, poison

Initiative +5
Perception +9
Tremorsense 5

TRAITS

Earth Walk
The archon ignores difficult terrain that is rubble, uneven stone, or an earthen construction.

Shattering Tremors
Whenever the archon takes thunder damage, it is slowed until the end of its next turn.

STANDARD ACTIONS

⊕ **Stony Warhammer** ✦ **At-Will**
Attack: Melee 1 (one creature); +17 vs. AC
Hit: 4d8 + 7 damage.

✦ **Avalanche Charge** ✦ **Recharge** when first bloodied
Effect: Before the attack, the archon moves up to its speed.
Attack: Melee 1 (one creature); +15 vs. Fortitude
Hit: 4d12 + 9 damage, and the archon pushes the target up to 2 squares and knocks it prone.
Miss: Half damage, and the target falls prone.

| Str 23 (+12) | Dex 9 (+5) | Wis 16 (+9) |
| Con 19 (+10) | Int 18 (+10) | Cha 11 (+6) |

Alignment chaotic evil **Languages** Primordial

Fire Archon

Level 13 Skirmisher
Medium elemental humanoid (fire)
XP 800

HP 130; **Bloodied** 65
AC 27, **Fortitude** 25, **Reflex** 26, **Will** 23
Speed 8
Immune disease, poison; **Resist** 20 fire

Initiative +14
Perception +9

TRAITS

Guttering Flames
Whenever the archon takes cold damage, it cannot shift until the end of its next turn.

STANDARD ACTIONS

⊕ **Fiery Scimitar** (fire) ✦ **At-Will**
Attack: Melee 1 (one creature); +18 vs. AC
Hit: 3d8 + 8 fire damage.

MOVE ACTIONS

Flickering Step ✦ **At-Will**
Effect: The archon shifts up to half its speed.

Blaze Step (fire) ✦ **Encounter**
Effect: The archon shifts up to its speed. Each square it shifts through fills with elemental flames that last until the end of the encounter. Each time a nonfire creature enters or starts its turn in a square filled with these flames, it takes 10 fire damage.

| Str 15 (+8) | Dex 22 (+12) | Wis 17 (+9) |
| Con 18 (+10) | Int 16 (+9) | Cha 9 (+5) |

Alignment chaotic evil **Languages** Primordial

Ice Archon
Medium elemental humanoid (cold)

Level 13 Soldier
XP 800

HP 135; **Bloodied** 67
AC 29, **Fortitude** 27, **Reflex** 25, **Will** 22
Speed 6
Immune disease, poison; **Resist** 20 cold

Initiative +8
Perception +9

TRAITS

☼ **Chilling Aura** ✦ **Aura** 2
Enemies cannot shift while in the aura.

Melting Ice
Whenever the archon takes fire damage, it takes a -2 penalty to all defenses until the end of its next turn.

STANDARD ACTIONS

⊕ **Frigid Mace** (cold) ✦ **At-Will**
Attack: Melee 1 (one creature); +18 vs. AC
Hit: 4d6 + 7 cold damage.
Effect: The archon marks each enemy within 2 squares of it until the end of the archon's next turn.

TRIGGERED ACTIONS

⚔ **Frozen Rebuke** ✦ **At-Will**
Trigger: An enemy marked by the archon makes an attack that doesn't include it as a target.
Attack (Opportunity Action): Melee 1 (triggering enemy); +18 vs. AC
Hit: 2d8 + 5 damage, and the target is weakened until the end of its next turn.

Str 15 (+8)	**Dex** 11 (+6)	**Wis** 17 (+9)
Con 23 (+12)	**Int** 18 (+10)	**Cha** 11 (+6)

Alignment chaotic evil   **Languages** Primordial

Water Archon
Medium elemental humanoid (aquatic, water)

Level 14 Controller
XP 1,000

HP 140; **Bloodied** 70
AC 28, **Fortitude** 26, **Reflex** 24, **Will** 28
Speed 6, swim 6
Immune disease, poison; **Resist** 20 acid

Initiative +11
Perception +8

TRAITS

Aquatic
The archon can breathe underwater. In aquatic combat, it gains a +2 bonus to attack rolls against nonaquatic creatures.

Frozen Waves
Whenever the archon takes cold damage, it is slowed until the end of its next turn.

STANDARD ACTIONS

⊕ **Cresting Staff** ✦ **At-Will**
Attack: Melee 1 (one creature); +19 vs. AC
Hit: 2d10 + 10 damage, and the target is slowed until the end of the archon's next turn.

⬳ **Whirlpool** ✦ **At-Will**
Attack: Close burst 3 (enemies in the burst); +17 vs. Fortitude
Hit: 4d6 + 7 damage, and the archon slides the target up to 3 squares.
Miss: The archon can slide the target 1 square.

Str 14 (+9)	**Dex** 18 (+11)	**Wis** 13 (+8)
Con 20 (+12)	**Int** 11 (+7)	**Cha** 22 (+13)

Alignment chaotic evil   **Languages** Primordial

BASILISK

The eyes of the basilisk glow with potent magic. Just a glance, and a victim is weakened, envenomed, or, worst of all, turned to stone. Averting your gaze will not save you, because a basilisk has teeth as well as eyes.

Rumors and legends shroud the enigmatic basilisk. Unlike many rampaging beasts, basilisks keep themselves concealed and are not spotted stomping through fields or tearing up towns. What's more, because the creature's gaze is so dangerous, few ordinary people have seen a basilisk and survived. The fates of basilisks' victims can seem mysterious. If a villager disappears and a stone sculpture that resembles the missing person is later found, people do not necessarily jump to the conclusion that a basilisk is nearby. They might consider the situation a sign of magic run rampant, a portent of imminent danger, or a trick of mischievous fey that kidnapped the victim and left a crude reproduction as a joke. Similarly, those slain by a venom-eye basilisk might look as though they fell to a strange plague or were struck down by the god Zehir.

Although wild basilisks live hidden in solitude, the creatures can be domesticated. A wise master takes no risks with a trained basilisk, recognizing that a simple slip-up could be deadly. Owners set basilisks as sentries in places where no allies are present or where servants are expendable. Some basilisk masters use the remains of victims who have been petrified as morbid decorations.

Statuaries of the Fallen: Surrounding the lair of a typical stone-eye basilisk, statues of humanoids and other creatures stand in awkward, fearful poses, frozen in the horror of their transformation into rock. These lifeless figures are the basilisk's victims, and the creature is capable of eating its petrified foes. A statue that displays large bite marks is a sure sign that a basilisk dwells nearby. (Other signs include patches of blackened grass and dead shrubs, since the

DAREN BADER

Mesmeric-Eye Basilisk

Large natural beast (reptile)

Level 10 Soldier

XP 500

HP 109; **Bloodied** 54
AC 26, **Fortitude** 22, **Reflex** 20, **Will** 24
Speed 4

Initiative +8
Perception +7

STANDARD ACTIONS

⊕ Bite ✦ At-Will

Attack: Melee 1 (one creature); +15 vs. AC
Hit: 2d12 + 5 damage.

↢ Mesmerizing Gaze (charm, psychic) ✦ At-Will

Attack: Close blast 3 (creatures in the blast); +13 vs. Will
Hit: 2d8 + 7 psychic damage, and the basilisk pulls the target up to 2 squares.
Effect: The basilisk marks the target until the end of the basilisk's next turn.

TRIGGERED ACTIONS

↢ Mesmeric Punishment (charm) ✦ At-Will

Trigger: An enemy marked by and within 5 squares of the basilisk makes an attack that does not include it as a target.
Attack (Immediate Interrupt): Close burst 5 (triggering enemy); +13 vs. Will
Hit: The target takes a -2 penalty to the triggering attack roll and is dazed (save ends).

Str 16 (+8)	**Dex** 13 (+6)	**Wis** 14 (+7)
Con 17 (+8)	**Int** 2 (+1)	**Cha** 8 (+4)

Alignment unaligned   **Languages** —

monster's noxious presence kills plant life near its lair.) The petrified victims are not dead and can be turned from stone to flesh once again. A rescue mission to free a petrified person might involve investigating methods of reversing the transformation, followed by a dangerous journey to the beast's lair.

Pack Predators of the Feywild: In the natural world, most basilisks dwell alone, living within isolated lairs and leaving only occasionally to hunt. The basilisks that inhabit the Feywild, however, hunt in packs that leave trails of desiccated foliage and dead animals in their wake. Reptilian eyes glowing from between the massive tree trunks of a dark Feywild forest are often the last sight an explorer sees. Like many creatures of the Feywild, basilisks wander where they wish. Strong-willed fey magicians can command the creatures, and the evil giants of the Feywild known as fomorians use basilisks to guard hidden tunnels that lead to their underground kingdoms.

Demonic Pets: Some greater demons feel a kinship with basilisks and keep the deadly creatures as pets; lesser demons that venture into the world use basilisks as guards or guides. A basilisk might stride fearlessly into a city as the precursor to a brutal demonic massacre. Although ordinary basilisks lead solitary lives—some can even be called timid—those that serve demons fight with the same ferocity and cruelty as the spawn of the Abyss. Long ago, a group of basilisks was taken to different layers of the Abyss, where they grew more deadly in the chaos of that evil place. Today, these transformed creatures, or perhaps their descendants, guard gates that the demons never want opened. No one knows what lies beyond such doors—perhaps the darkest secrets of the Abyss, or perhaps unimaginable horrors that even the demons fear.

Venom-Eye Basilisk — Level 10 Artillery
Large natural beast (reptile) — XP 500

HP 87; **Bloodied** 43 — **Initiative** +6
AC 24, **Fortitude** 23, **Reflex** 20, **Will** 22 — **Perception** +11
Speed 6
Resist 5 poison

STANDARD ACTIONS

⊕ **Bite** ✦ **At-Will**
Attack: Melee 1 (one creature); +15 vs. AC
Hit: 2d6 + 8 damage.

✸ **Venomous Gaze** (poison) ✦ **At-Will**
Attack: Area burst 1 within 10 (creatures in the burst); +15 vs. Fortitude
Hit: 2d8 + 5 poison damage, and ongoing 5 poison damage (save ends). While the target is taking ongoing poison damage from this attack, the target deals 2 poison damage to each creature adjacent to it at the start of each of its turns.
Effect: The target takes a -2 penalty to attack rolls until the end of the basilisk's next turn.

Skills Stealth +11
Str 19 (+9) — **Dex** 12 (+6) — **Wis** 13 (+6)
Con 21 (+10) — **Int** 2 (+1) — **Cha** 8 (+4)
Alignment unaligned — **Languages** –

"A basilisk makes a great sentry, if you don't mind cluttering your entry hall with ugly statues."

—Lathras, Mage of Saruun

Wilt-Eye Basilisk — Level 11 Controller
Large natural beast (reptile) — XP 600

HP 117; **Bloodied** 58 — **Initiative** +7
AC 25, **Fortitude** 25, **Reflex** 21, **Will** 23 — **Perception** +11
Speed 4

STANDARD ACTIONS

⊕ **Bite** ✦ **At-Will**
Attack: Melee 1 (one creature); +16 vs. AC
Hit: 2d8 + 10 damage.

✸ **Enervating Gaze** ✦ **At-Will**
Attack: Area burst 1 within 5 (creatures in the burst); +14 vs. Fortitude
Hit: The target takes a -2 penalty to attack rolls (save ends).
First Failed Saving Throw: The target falls unconscious (save ends).
Miss: The target takes a -2 penalty to attack rolls until the end of the basilisk's next turn.

Skills Stealth +12
Str 17 (+8) — **Dex** 14 (+7) — **Wis** 12 (+6)
Con 21 (+10) — **Int** 2 (+1) — **Cha** 8 (+4)
Alignment unaligned — **Languages** –

Basilisk — Level 12 Controller

Large natural beast (reptile)

XP 700

HP 126; **Bloodied** 63
AC 26, **Fortitude** 26, **Reflex** 22, **Will** 22
Speed 4
Immune petrification

Initiative +7
Perception +13

TRAITS

✷ Baleful Gaze ✦ Aura 5

Any enemy in the aura that attacks the basilisk is slowed until the end of that enemy's next turn.

STANDARD ACTIONS

⊕ Bite ✦ At-Will

Attack: Melee 1 (one creature); +17 vs. AC
Hit: 2d12 + 7 damage.

↤ Petrifying Gaze ✦ At-Will

Attack: Close blast 3 (creatures in the blast); +15 vs. Fortitude
Hit: The target is immobilized (save ends).
  First Failed Saving Throw: The target is restrained instead of immobilized (save ends).
  Second Failed Saving Throw: The target is petrified.
Miss: The target is slowed until the end of the basilisk's next turn.

Skills Stealth + 12

Str 20 (+11)	**Dex** 12 (+7)	**Wis** 14 (+8)
Con 22 (+12)	**Int** 2 (+2)	**Cha** 8 (+5)

Alignment unaligned   **Languages** —

Abyssal Basilisk — Level 13 Artillery

Large elemental beast (reptile)

XP 800

HP 106; **Bloodied** 53
AC 27, **Fortitude** 26, **Reflex** 23, **Will** 23
Speed 4

Initiative +7
Perception +13

STANDARD ACTIONS

⊕ Bite ✦ At-Will

Attack: Melee 1 (one creature); +18 vs. AC
Hit: 2d10 + 5 damage.

❉ Gaze of Abyssal Horror (charm, psychic) **✦ At-Will**

Attack: Area burst 1 within 10 (creatures in the burst); +18 vs. Will
Hit: 2d8 + 2 psychic damage, and ongoing 10 psychic damage (save ends).
  First Failed Saving Throw: The target makes a melee basic attack or a ranged basic attack against its nearest ally as a free action.
  Second Failed Saving Throw: The target takes ongoing 10 psychic damage and is dominated (save ends both).

Skills Stealth + 12

Str 19 (+10)	**Dex** 12 (+7)	**Wis** 14 (+8)
Con 22 (+12)	**Int** 2 (+2)	**Cha** 8 (+5)

Alignment chaotic evil   **Languages** —

BEHOLDER

Creatures of abhorrent shape and alien mind, beholders seek dominance over all they survey. The floating horrors enforce their will by firing rays of magic from their eyestalks.

When the unwholesome plane known as the Far Realm comes into tenuous contact with reality, terrible things boil across the boundary. Nightmares form the thunderhead of psychic storms that presage the arrival of warped beings and forces undreamt of by the maddest demon or the vilest devil. Many aberrant creatures stumble upon the world by accident, pushed in like chill wind through a door suddenly opened. Others crash into reality because it is as loathsome to them as their surreal homeland is to all sane natives of the rational planes. Beholders, however, come as conquerors. Each one seeks to claim all in its sight, and beholders see much indeed.

Beholders do not belong in the world or in any of the planes inhabited by immortal or elemental, primordial or god. Their home, the Far Realm, is so antithetical to rational thought that most who glimpse the plane go mad. Like other unsettling inhabitants of that place, beholders have forms unlike those of natural creatures.

Diverse and Horrible Powers: Beholders come in a bewildering variety, and many that escape the Far Realm emerge into the world altered by the passage. Each beholder projects a number of supernatural powers through its eyes, but the specific details and arrangement of those powers vary by beholder variety. Worse, the powers can change and improve over time, so that as a beholder grows older, it becomes more fearsome.

JIM NELSON

Ruled by Few: The only certainty when dealing with beholders is that they possess malignant intent and a desire for dominance. Indeed, beholders rarely tolerate subservience to other beings, and they shun the company of their own kind. When beholders work together or do the bidding of a more powerful master, the world is in peril.

Beholders serve only those creatures that they fear and from which they cannot escape. Formidable titans, mighty dragons, and legendary spellcasters can sometimes command a beholder's allegiance, but these would-be lords must be cautious of betrayal. As deceitful as it is malign, a beholder will submit to the authority of a strong leader if it believes it can one day claim that creature's power.

Masters of Many: Beholders believe that they deserve to rule all they see. Lesser beings that show obedience to these hungry and unpredictable horrors can find a place—albeit not a safe one—in their service. Beholders accept all manner of creatures as their attendants, lackeys, and minions. Such slaves must frequently prove themselves valuable, lest their masters decide that they would make better meals than they do servants.

Beholder Gauth	Level 5 Elite Artillery
Medium aberrant magical beast	XP 400

HP 102; **Bloodied** 51 **Initiative** +4
AC 17, **Fortitude** 16, **Reflex** 18, **Will** 19 **Perception** +10
Speed 0, fly 6 (hover) All-around vision, darkvision
Saving Throws +2; **Action Points** 1

Traits

All-Around Vision
Enemies can't gain combat advantage by flanking the gauth.

Standard Actions

⊕ **Bite ✦ At-Will**
Attack: Melee 1 (one creature); +10 vs. AC
Hit: 2d4 + 5 damage.

↗ **Eye Rays ✦ At-Will**
Effect: The gauth uses two *eye ray* powers chosen from the list below. Each *eye ray* must target a different creature. Using *eye rays* does not provoke opportunity attacks.
  1. *Fire Ray* (fire): Ranged 8; +10 vs. Reflex; 2d6 + 6 fire damage.
  2. *Exhaustion Ray* (necrotic): Ranged 8; +10 vs. Fortitude; 1d8 + 4 necrotic damage, and the target is weakened (save ends).
  3. *Sleep Ray* (charm): Ranged 8; +10 vs. Fortitude; the target is slowed (save ends).
     First Failed Saving Throw: The target is knocked unconscious instead of slowed (save ends).
  4. *Telekinesis Ray:* Ranged 8; +10 vs. Fortitude; the gauth slides the target up to 4 squares.

Minor Actions

↗ **Central Eye ✦ At-Will**
Attack: Ranged 5 (one creature); +10 vs. Will
Hit: The target is immobilized until the end of the gauth's next turn.

Str 12 (+3)	**Dex** 15 (+4)	**Wis** 16 (+5)
Con 15 (+4)	**Int** 18 (+6)	**Cha** 20 (+7)

Alignment evil **Languages** Deep Speech

Beholder — Level 9 Solo Artillery

Beholder	Level 9 Solo Artillery
Large aberrant magical beast	XP 2,000

HP 392; **Bloodied** 196   **Initiative** +9
AC 23, **Fortitude** 21, **Reflex** 22, **Will** 22   **Perception** +11
Speed 0, fly 4 (hover)   All-around vision, darkvision
Saving Throws +5; **Action Points** 2

TRAITS

All-Around Vision
Enemies can't gain combat advantage by flanking the beholder.

STANDARD ACTIONS

⊕ **Bite** ✦ At-Will
Attack: Melee 1 (one creature); 14 vs. AC
Hit: 2d8 + 8 damage.

⌁ **Eye Rays** ✦ At-Will
Effect: The beholder uses two of the following eye rays, using each against a different target. This attack does not provoke opportunity attacks.
1. *Charm Ray* (charm): Ranged 10; +14 vs. Will; the target is dominated until the end of its next turn.
2. *Wounding Ray* (necrotic): Ranged 10; +14 vs. Fortitude; 2d10 + 6 necrotic damage.
3. *Sleep Ray* (charm): Ranged 10; +14 vs. Will; the target is immobilized (save ends).
    First Failed Saving Throw: The target is knocked unconscious instead of immobilized (save ends).
4. *Telekinesis Ray*: Ranged 10; +14 vs. Fortitude; the beholder slides the target up to 4 squares.
5. *Slowing Ray* (necrotic): Ranged 10; +14 vs. Reflex; 3d6 + 5 necrotic damage, and the target is slowed (save ends).
6. *Brilliant Ray* (radiant): Ranged 10; +14 vs. Will; 1d6 + 5 radiant damage, and the target is blinded (save ends).
7. *Terror Ray* (fear, psychic): Ranged 10; +14 vs. Will; 2d8 + 5 psychic damage, and the beholder pushes the target its speed.
8. *Petrifying Ray*: Ranged 10; +14 vs. Fortitude; the target is petrified (save ends).
    Aftereffect: The target is immobilized (save ends).
9. *Death Ray* (necrotic): Ranged 10; +14 vs. Fortitude; 2d8 + 10 necrotic damage. If the target is bloodied before or after the attack, it is also dazed (save ends).
    First Failed Saving Throw: The target is dazed and weakened (save ends both).
    Second Failed Saving Throw: The target dies.
10. *Disintegrate Ray*: Ranged 10; +14 vs. Fortitude; 1d8 + 5 damage, and ongoing 10 damage (save ends).

⌁ **Eye Ray Frenzy** ✦ Recharge ⚅⚅
Requirement: The beholder must be bloodied.
Effect: As eye rays above, except the beholder makes three eye ray attacks.

MINOR ACTIONS

⟵ **Central Eye** ✦ At-Will (1/round)
Attack: Close blast 5 (enemies in the blast); +12 vs. Will
Hit: The target cannot use encounter or daily attack powers until the end of its next turn.

TRIGGERED ACTIONS

⌁ **Random Eye Ray** ✦ At-Will
Trigger: The beholder is conscious and an enemy starts its turn within 5 squares of it.
Effect (No Action): The beholder uses one random eye ray against the triggering enemy.

Str 18 (+8)	**Dex** 20 (+9)	**Wis** 15 (+6)
Con 18 (+8)	**Int** 19 (+8)	**Cha** 20 (+9)

Alignment evil   **Languages** Deep Speech

Beholder Eye Tyrant
Large aberrant magical beast

Level 19 Solo Artillery

XP 12,000

HP 720; **Bloodied** 360
AC 33, **Fortitude** 29, **Reflex** 31, **Will** 33
Speed 0, fly 4 (hover)
Saving Throws +5; **Action Points** 2

Initiative +16
Perception +17
All-around vision, darkvision

TRAITS

All-Around Vision

Enemies can't gain combat advantage by flanking the beholder.

STANDARD ACTIONS

⊕ **Bite** ✦ At-Will

Attack: Melee 1 (one creature); +24 vs. AC
Hit: 4d8 + 7 damage.

↗ **Eye Rays** ✦ At-Will

Effect: The beholder uses two of the following eye rays, using each against a different target. This attack does not provoke opportunity attacks.

1. *Searing Ray* (radiant): Ranged 10; +24 vs. Reflex; 3d10 + 11 radiant damage.
2. *Withering Ray* (necrotic): Ranged 10; +24 vs. Fortitude; 2d8 + 9 damage, and ongoing 10 necrotic damage (save ends).
3. *Sleep Ray* (charm): Ranged 10; +24 vs. Will; the target falls unconscious (save ends).
4. *Telekinesis Ray:* Ranged 10; +24 vs. Fortitude; the beholder slides the target up to 4 squares.
5. *Hold Ray:* Ranged 10; +24 vs. Reflex; the target is restrained (save ends).
6. *Confusion Ray* (charm): Ranged 10; +24 vs. Will; the target uses a free action to charge the nearest ally it is able to charge.
7. *Terror Ray* (fear, psychic): Ranged 10; +24 vs. Will; 2d12 + 8 psychic damage, and the target moves its speed as a free action. If it does not end this movement at least 4 squares farther from the beholder than it began, the target takes 2d12 + 8 psychic damage.
8. *Petrifying Ray:* Ranged 10; +24 vs. Fortitude; the target is slowed (save ends).
   First Failed Saving Throw: The target is immobilized instead of slowed (save ends).
   Second Failed Saving Throw: The target is petrified.
9. *Death Ray* (necrotic): Ranged 10; +24 vs. Fortitude; 4d10 + 6 necrotic damage. If the target is bloodied before or after the attack, it is also dazed (save ends).
   First Failed Saving Throw: The target is dazed and weakened (save ends both).
   Second Failed Saving Throw: The target dies.
10. *Disintegrate Ray:* Ranged 10; +24 vs. Fortitude; 2d10 + 9 damage, and ongoing 2d20 damage (save ends).

↗ **Eye Ray Frenzy** ✦ Recharge ⚅

Requirement: The beholder must be bloodied.
Effect: As *eye rays* above, except the eye tyrant makes four eye ray attacks.

MINOR ACTIONS

⇜ **Central Eye** ✦ At-Will (1/round)

Attack: Close blast 5 (enemies in the blast); +22 vs. Will
Hit: The target cannot use encounter or daily attack powers until the end of its next turn.

TRIGGERED ACTIONS

↗ **Random Eye Ray** ✦ At-Will

Trigger: The beholder is conscious and an enemy starts its turn within 5 squares of it.
Effect (No Action): The beholder uses one random eye ray against the triggering enemy.

Str 18 (+13)	**Dex** 24 (+16)	**Wis** 17 (+12)
Con 20 (+14)	**Int** 22 (+15)	**Cha** 28 (+18)
Alignment evil		**Languages** Deep Speech

BULETTE

An approaching furrow of rock and soil signals the arrival of a bulette. These massive, plated beasts spring from the ground and devour any fleshy creature they find.

Bulettes can appear anywhere and are always unwelcome. They move through earth the way a shark moves through water and pop up from the ground to attack. This behavior has earned them the nickname "land shark." Many people talk about land sharks as if they were mythical, but wiser heads realize that the creatures are real—and extremely dangerous. When signs of a bulette appear near a community, its leaders order the population to pull up stakes and relocate.

A bulette's thick armor plates let it shrug off attacks until it eats the attacker. This vaunted toughness gives land sharks a reputation as monsters that cannot be slain. Villagers who encounter one of these creatures without realizing its true nature might spread tales of an indestructible beast, a deadly creature made of stone, or a calamitous machine.

Bulettes live in burrows and underground caverns, and explorers of such areas might encounter the creatures there. Travelers might also run afoul of a bulette while it moves to new territory after exhausting all the resources of its former home. Land sharks rarely travel in groups, though sometimes a mated pair shares the same territory. These pairs eat for two, so they move from place to place more quickly than a single bulette would.

Stupid, Mean, and Fearless: It's easy to trick a bulette, and intelligent beings find clever ways to guide the monsters into areas they want to have destroyed. One of the few constants in the world is that a land shark will always want more food and will take the most direct route to get it. Although a bulette hunts when it's hungry, it might happen upon prey just after eating. This situation can bring out the beast's mean streak as it plays with its food by physically mauling or stalking and terrorizing the victim. To a land shark, any creature smaller than itself is prey (and anything the same size or larger is probably an enemy). As far as a bulette knows, smaller creatures can't harm it, so it doesn't hesitate to jump into battle and go straight after whatever it wants to eat.

Young Bulette
Medium natural beast

Level 7 Lurker

XP 300

HP 68; **Bloodied** 34
AC 21, **Fortitude** 20, **Reflex** 19, **Will** 16
Speed 6, burrow 6

Initiative +11
Perception +6
Darkvision, tremorsense 20

TRAITS

Ground Eruption

The squares of ground the bulette burrows into or emerges from become difficult terrain until the end of the encounter.

STANDARD ACTIONS

⊕ **Bite** ✦ **At-Will**

Attack: Melee 1 (one creature); +12 vs. AC
Hit: 1d10 + 4 damage.

Submerge in Earth ✦ **At-Will**

Requirement: The bulette must be aboveground.
Effect: The bulette shifts 1 square and then burrows up to its burrow speed.

✦ **Snapping Jaws** ✦ **Recharge** when the bulette uses *submerge in earth*

Requirement: The bulette must be underground.
Effect: The bulette burrows up to its burrow speed to a square aboveground. This movement does not provoke opportunity attacks. When it first enters a square aboveground during this movement, it makes the following attack.
Attack: Melee 1 (one creature); +12 vs. AC
Hit: 4d10 + 8 damage.

Str 22 (+9)	**Dex** 18 (+7)	**Wis** 16 (+6)
Con 20 (+8)	**Int** 2 (-1)	**Cha** 8 (+2)
Alignment unaligned	**Languages** —	

Eat First and Think Later: A bulette doesn't have much of a brain and is led around by its stomach. Once the creature finds a hunting ground, it devours any animal life living there. Ranch lands, fertile forest glades, and small communities become wastelands after land sharks move in. Only after an area has been devastated does a bulette move on to find a new territory. Since the beasts devour their victims entirely, leaving no bones behind, the most telling signs of a bulette's presence are uprooted trees, recent landslides, and wide furrows in the earth. An old wives' tale says that land sharks refuse to eat elves. Although this claim isn't true, a bulette might pass by an elf if a human or halfling can be obtained just as easily.

Wild Cards in Battle: The activity and noise of combat might draw a bulette from its subterranean burrow. When a land shark enters a battle, it usually joins as an independent combatant rather than taking one side or the other. Thus, all factions in a conflict might be devastated by a bulette moving through their ranks, gobbling up members of both sides. One group might be able to outsmart the hungry beast by maneuvering so that members of the other group become easier targets. However, there's no guarantee that a bulette won't continue eating the remaining warriors after one side has been eliminated.

BEN WOOTEN

Notoriously difficult to tame, bulettes rarely serve as subordinates to other creatures. Sometimes, those that have powerful mental abilities (such as mind flayers) can control land sharks, and brutal creatures (especially yuan-ti and hobgoblins) can condition bulettes into obedience with years of torture. The lives of many handlers are sacrificed in the process.

Bulette	Level 9 Elite Skirmisher
Large natural beast	XP 800

HP 200; **Bloodied** 100	**Initiative** +10
AC 24, **Fortitude** 22, **Reflex** 20, **Will** 19	**Perception** +7
Speed 6, burrow 6	Darkvision, tremorsense 20
Saving Throws +2; **Action Points** 1	

TRAITS

Ground Eruption
The squares of ground the bulette burrows into or emerges from become difficult terrain until the end of the encounter.

STANDARD ACTIONS

⊕ **Bite** ✦ **At-Will**
Attack: Melee 1 (one creature); +14 vs. AC
Hit: 3d6 + 7 damage, or 5d6 + 7 against a prone target.

↯ **Leaping Bite** ✦ **At-Will**
Effect: The bulette jumps up to 5 squares and then uses *bite*. This movement does not provoke opportunity attacks.

↩ **Rising Burst** ✦ **At-Will**
Requirement: The bulette must be underground.
Effect: The bulette moves up to its speed to a square aboveground. This movement does not provoke opportunity attacks. When it first enters a square aboveground during this movement, it makes the following attack.
Attack: Close burst 2 (creatures in the burst); +14 vs. AC
Hit: 2d8 + 5 damage.
Miss: Half damage.

MOVE ACTIONS

↯ **Earth Furrow** ✦ **At-Will**
Effect: The bulette burrows up to its speed at a depth of 1 square beneath the surface of the ground. This movement does not provoke opportunity attacks. Each time it moves beneath an enemy space for the first time during the movement, it makes the following attack against that enemy.
Attack: Melee 1; +12 vs. Fortitude.
Hit: The target falls prone.

Skills Athletics +15, Endurance +14		
Str 22 (+10)	**Dex** 18 (+8)	**Wis** 16 (+7)
Con 20 (+9)	**Int** 2 (+0)	**Cha** 8 (+3)
Alignment unaligned	**Languages** —	

Dire Bulette
Huge natural beast

Level 18 Elite Skirmisher

XP 4,000

HP 350; **Bloodied** 175
AC 33, **Fortitude** 31, **Reflex** 29, **Will** 28
Speed 8, burrow 8
Saving Throws +2; **Action Points** 1

Initiative +17
Perception +14
Darkvision, tremorsense 20

TRAITS

Ground Eruption
The squares of ground the bulette burrows into or emerges from become difficult terrain until the end of the encounter.

STANDARD ACTIONS

⊕ **Bite** ✦ **At-Will**
Attack: Melee 1 (one creature); +23 vs. AC
Hit: 3d10 + 10 damage, or 5d10 + 10 against a prone target.

✝ **Leaping Bite** ✦ **At-Will**
Effect: The bulette jumps up to 7 squares and can use *bite* at any point during the movement. This movement does not provoke opportunity attacks.

⬅ **Rising Burst** ✦ **At-Will**
Requirement: The bulette must be underground.
Effect: The bulette moves up to its speed to a square aboveground. This movement does not provoke opportunity attacks. When it first enters a square aboveground during this movement, it makes the following attack.
Attack: Close burst 3 (creatures in the burst); +23 vs. AC
Hit: 2d12 + 10 damage.
Miss: Half damage.

MOVE ACTIONS

✝ **Earth Furrow** ✦ **At-Will**
Effect: The bulette burrows up to its speed at a depth of 1 square beneath the surface of the ground. This movement does not provoke opportunity attacks. Each time it moves beneath an enemy space for the first time during the movement, it makes the following attack against that enemy.
Attack: Melee 1; +21 vs. Fortitude
Hit: The target falls prone.

Skills Athletics +22, Endurance +20

Str 26 (+17)	**Dex** 22 (+15)	**Wis** 20 (+14)
Con 23 (+15)	**Int** 5 (+6)	**Cha** 10 (+9)

Alignment unaligned   **Languages** —

Place a Large creature token inside this ring to create a Huge creature token.

"It's called a land shark for a reason, and it's not just about the fin on its back."

—Kathra, wizard of Haven

CARRION CRAWLER

Wriggling like giant, loathsome caterpillars, these aggressive beasts attack anything that invades their territory or disturbs their feasting on the dead. The crawlers paralyze victims with their tentacles before dragging the prey off to expire and rot.

Foul things feed on filth, and so it is that carrion crawlers squirm through all manner of death, rot, and offal. These bizarre creatures lurk in moist and dark places, seeking to scour putrid flesh from carcasses and gobble the slimy bones that remain.

Carrion Eaters: Like vultures, carrion crawlers follow the scent of death to their food. However, if they must travel great distances, it's likely that their intended meal will have been claimed by other scavengers by the time they arrive. Thus, carrion crawlers hunker down in territories where food is plentiful and other carrion-eaters have limited mobility. Caves, sewers, dungeons, and heavily forested marshes work best, but carrion crawlers are also drawn to battlefields and cemeteries. Woe to the city that has these monsters in its sewers in a time of siege or plague. In such places, a carrion crawler roams on the hunt, its tentacles feeling the air for the smell of blood or decay. Within structures, the repulsive creatures often scurry across the ceiling as they move toward food. In this way, they avoid contact with other dangerous inhabitants of the darkness, such as oozes and otyughs, and they can surprise trespassers who don't think to look up.

Carrion Crawler Scuttler	Level 5 Skirmisher
Large aberrant beast	XP 200

HP 63; Bloodied 31	Initiative +5
AC 19, Fortitude 18, Reflex 16, Will 17	Perception +3
Speed 8, climb 8 (spider climb)	Darkvision

STANDARD ACTIONS

⊕ **Bite ✦ At-Will**
Attack: Melee 1 (one creature); +10 vs. AC
Hit: 2d8 + 4 damage, or 3d8 + 4 against a stunned target.

↯ **Tentacles ✦ At-Will**
Attack: Melee 2 (one creature); +8 vs. Fortitude, or +10 vs. Fortitude against a prone target
Hit: The target is stunned (save ends). The carrion crawler shifts up to its speed, pulling the target with it.

MOVE ACTIONS

↯ **Unsettling Scuttle ✦ At-Will**
Effect: The carrion crawler shifts up to its speed. It can move through enemy spaces and climb during the shift. Each time the carrion crawler enters an enemy space for the first time during this movement, it makes the following attack against that enemy.
Attack: Melee 0; +8 vs. Reflex
Hit: The target falls prone.

Str 18 (+6)	Dex 13 (+3)	Wis 12 (+3)
Con 15 (+4)	Int 2 (–2)	Cha 14 (+4)
Alignment unaligned	**Languages** –	

Patient Predators: Carrion crawlers eat rotting flesh, but they don't always wait for a creature to die on its own. Despite their great size and poor instinct for stealth, crawlers can ambush victims by waiting around blind corners for prey to come to them. Since crawlers tend to live in subterranean darkness or hunt at night on the surface, light signals a potential meal, and a carrion crawler might follow a light source from a distance for hours, hoping to pick up the scent of blood.

Carrion Crawler	Level 7 Soldier
Large aberrant beast	XP 300

HP 81; Bloodied 40	Initiative +8
AC 23, Fortitude 19, Reflex 18, Will 17	Perception +5
Speed 6, climb 6 (spider climb)	Darkvision

STANDARD ACTIONS

⊕ **Tentacles** (poison) ✦ **At-Will**

Attack: Melee 2 (one creature); +10 vs. Fortitude

Hit: 2d4 + 5 damage, and the target takes ongoing 5 poison damage and is slowed (save ends both).

First Failed Saving Throw: The target is immobilized instead of slowed (save ends).

Second Failed Saving Throw: The target is stunned instead of immobilized (save ends).

Miss: The target is slowed until the end of the carrion crawler's next turn.

↓ **Bite** ✦ **At-Will**

Attack: Melee 1 (one creature); +12 vs. AC

Hit: 2d10 + 4 damage.

Str 20 (+8)	Dex 16 (+6)	Wis 14 (+5)
Con 17 (+6)	Int 2 (-1)	Cha 16 (+6)
Alignment unaligned	**Languages** —	

Carrion Crawler Putrefier	Level 15 Soldier
Large aberrant beast	XP 1,200

HP 148; Bloodied 74	Initiative +13
AC 31, Fortitude 28, Reflex 26, Will 25	Perception +9
Speed 6, climb 6 (spider climb)	Darkvision

TRAITS

✵ **Nauseous Stench** (poison) ✦ **Aura 3**

Any enemy that starts its turn in the aura takes 5 poison damage and is slowed (save ends both).

STANDARD ACTIONS

⊕ **Rotting Tentacles** (necrotic) ✦ **At-Will**

Attack: Melee 3 (one creature); +18 vs. Fortitude

Hit: 2d10 + 6 necrotic damage, the carrion crawler can pull the target 1 square, and the target is immobilized (save ends). If the target was already immobilized, it is instead stunned and takes ongoing 10 necrotic damage (save ends both).

↓ **Bite** ✦ **At-Will**

Attack: Melee 1 (one creature); +20 vs. AC

Hit: 2d12 + 10 damage.

Str 23 (+13)	Dex 18 (+11)	Wis 14 (+9)
Con 20 (+12)	Int 2 (+3)	Cha 16 (+10)
Alignment unaligned	**Languages** —	

When facing potential prey or intruders, a carrion crawler prefers to let its poison do the work. The beast strikes as many enemies as it can with its tentacles and saves its bite for poisoned foes who get too close for comfort. Once a victim becomes rigid with paralysis, the carrion crawler wraps it in tentacles and drags it away to a secure eating area, such as a high ledge or a hole in a wall. The crawler then looms over its meal and watches for signs of life, striking with a tentacle if it sees any. When the crawler believes the prey to be dead, it coats the victim's flesh with toxic saliva to disguise the stench as the corpse decays, and then it resumes patrolling its territory while waiting for the meal to ripen.

Horrors from Beyond: It has been suggested that a wizard's mad experiment gave birth to the first carrion crawlers. A wizard did introduce the revolting beasts to the world, but they were not created in a laboratory. A spellcaster whose

DAVE ALLSOP

name is lost to history opened a connection to the Far Realm in the hope of learning that plane's secrets. Her irresponsible act resulted in the slaughter of everyone in her city. Carrion crawlers were not the worst horrors to cross the bridge between dimensions that day—they came to devour those that other fell beings had already slain or driven mad. Since that ancient time, carrion crawlers have spread throughout the world, and they continue to cross over from the Far Realm whenever fools gain the power to breach that disturbing plane.

Foul Pets: Although they are wild and territorial, carrion crawlers can sometimes be manipulated or brought to heel. Kobolds, for example, leave offerings of rotten meat in particular tunnels, encouraging the crawlers to stake out a territory that acts as a buffer to the kobolds' lair. Goblins and similar creatures attempt to raise carrion crawlers and coach them for battle. The venom of young crawlers is too weak to paralyze prey, so they can be domesticated (after a fashion) and used as guard beasts. Some creatures train carrion crawlers as mounts, although riders must employ tentacle harnesses to keep from being paralyzed.

Enormous Carrion Crawler	Level 17 Elite Soldier
Huge aberrant beast	XP 3,200

HP 332; Bloodied 166	Initiative +14
AC 33, Fortitude 31, Reflex 30, Will 29	Perception +11
Speed 6, climb 6 (spider climb)	Darkvision
Saving Throws +2; Action Points 1	

TRAITS

Threatening Reach
The carrion crawler can make opportunity attacks against enemies within 3 squares of it.

STANDARD ACTIONS

⊕ **Tentacles** (poison) ✦ **At-Will**
Attack: Melee 3 (one creature); +20 vs. Fortitude
Hit: 2d6 + 8 damage, the carrion crawler can pull the target 1 square, and the target takes ongoing 10 poison damage and is slowed (save ends both).
First Failed Saving Throw: The target is immobilized instead of slowed (save ends).
Second Failed Saving Throw: The target is stunned instead of immobilized (save ends).

✦ **Bite** ✦ **At-Will**
Attack: Melee 1 (one creature); +22 vs. AC
Hit: 2d12 + 12 damage.

✦ **Hungry Assault** ✦ **At-Will**
Effect: The carrion crawler uses *tentacles* twice or uses *tentacles* once and *bite* once.

↤ **Tentacle Flurry** (poison) ✦ **Recharge when first bloodied**
Attack: Close blast 3 (creatures in the blast); 20 vs. Fortitude
Hit: 2d10 + 5 damage, and the target takes ongoing 10 poison damage and is slowed (save ends both).
First Failed Saving Throw: The target is immobilized instead of slowed (save ends).
Second Failed Saving Throw: The target is stunned instead of immobilized (save ends).

Str 25 (+15)	Dex 18 (+12)	Wis 16 (+11)
Con 22 (+14)	Int 4 (+5)	Cha 18 (+12)
Alignment unaligned	Languages —	

CYCLOPS

A towering giant with a single, evil eye, a cyclops is a creature of the Feywild—and a dangerous enemy. Cyclopses serve fomorians as soldiers and artisans, and they possess many of the same supernatural powers as their dark masters, combining physical might with magical ability.

Similar to the giants of the world, cyclopses act as bodyguards, enforcers, and foot soldiers for the tyrannical subterranean giants known as fomorians. Primarily found in the Feywild, cyclopses are thought to have originated as an echo of the world's ogres. Soon after the birth of their race, they came under the influence of the fomorians, who not only molded the cyclopses to suit their needs but also gifted them with the ability to master the evil eye. Since those ancient times, a nigh-unbreakable pact has existed between the fomorians and the cyclopses, creating a mighty force of giant creatures that terrorize denizens of the Feywild and the world alike. Despite this alliance, cyclopses are not as evil and depraved as their masters. They unfailingly honor their covenant as a matter of ritual and tradition, not out of any real pleasure in the acts they are ordered to undertake.

Loyal Servants: The cyclopses are the only allies that the fomorians trust completely. All others are considered prone to deception and betrayal. For a cyclops, honoring alliances and pacts is one of the most important requirements

Cyclops Crusher	Level 14 Brute
Large fey humanoid	XP 1,000

HP 171; Bloodied 85	Initiative +12
AC 26, Fortitude 27, Reflex 26, Will 25	Perception +16
Speed 8	

TRAITS

Truesight
The cyclops can see invisible creatures and objects.

STANDARD ACTIONS

⊕ **Spiked Greatclub** (weapon) ✦ At-Will
Attack: Melee 2 (one creature); +19 vs. AC
Hit: 3d12 + 8 damage.

⸸ **Tremor Smash** (weapon) ✦ Recharge ⚅ ⚏
Attack: Close blast 2 (enemies in the blast); 19 vs. AC
Hit: 5d12 + 12 damage, and the target falls prone.

MINOR ACTIONS

Evil Eye ✦ At-Will (1/round)
Effect: Ranged sight (one enemy). The target takes a -2 penalty to attack rolls and all defenses until the end of the encounter or until the cyclops uses this power again.

Skills Athletics +18
Str 23 (+13)	Dex 20 (+12)	Wis 19 (+11)
Con 21 (+12)	Int 10 (+7)	Cha 11 (+7)

Alignment unaligned   **Languages** Elven
Equipment scale armor, greatclub

(Left to right) cyclops crusher, cyclops rambler

of life. Once cyclopses have declared allegiance to a particular group, their dedication to maintaining that bond never falters in the face of adversity. Only outright betrayal could spur a cyclops to alter its allegiances. The race has remained steadfast allies of the fomorians since the dawn of time, even though the latter are reckless with the lives of their cyclops servants. The fomorians view this loyalty as a great strength, but it could be exploited and turned into a weakness by their enemies. If anyone managed to charm cyclopses or turn them against their dark masters, the Feywild might be thrown into chaos. Fomorians would look upon their trusted warriors with suspicion, and any cyclopses close to their masters could wreak terrible damage before being stopped.

Impressive Artisans: Cyclopses have a natural affinity for crafting, in particular the creation of magic items. Their reputation as highly skilled artisans extends well beyond the Feywild, and many sages and artificers in the world know that some of the most impressive magic devices, weapons, and armor come from cyclops forges. Meticulous workers toil endlessly to create interesting, beautiful, and powerful magic objects as tributes to their fomorian masters. In fact, their labor takes on a competitive element when cyclops tribes compete to see which one can produce the most lavish and impressive tributes. A cyclops artisan values quality above all else, and rather than crank out a large quantity of objects, he or she prefers to create one item at a time—something that is both remarkable and useful, such as a shield that can turn away a dragon's breath or a crown that can read the thoughts of others.

Cyclops Guard
Large fey humanoid

Level 14 Minion Brute

XP 250

HP 1; a missed attack never damages a minion.   **Initiative** +10
AC 26, **Fortitude** 28, **Reflex** 25, **Will** 25   **Perception** +15
Speed 6

STANDARD ACTIONS

⊕ **Battleaxe** (weapon) ✦ **At-Will**

Attack: Melee 2 (one creature); +19 vs. AC
Hit: 14 damage.

TRIGGERED ACTIONS

⚔ **Evil Eye** ✦ **At-Will**

Trigger: An enemy misses the cyclops with a melee attack.
Effect (Immediate Reaction): The cyclops uses *battleaxe* against the triggering enemy.

| Str 22 (+13) | Dex 16 (+10) | Wis 17 (+10) |
| Con 20 (+12) | Int 11 (+7) | Cha 11 (+7) |

Alignment unaligned   **Languages** Elven
Equipment hide armor, heavy shield, battleaxe

Cyclops Rambler
Large fey humanoid

Level 14 Skirmisher

XP 1,000

HP 141; **Bloodied** 70   **Initiative** +12
AC 28, **Fortitude** 28, **Reflex** 25, **Will** 26   **Perception** +16
Speed 8

TRAITS

Truesight

The cyclops can see invisible creatures and objects.

STANDARD ACTIONS

⊕ **Greatsword** (weapon) ✦ **At-Will**

Attack: Melee 2 (one creature); +19 vs. AC
Hit: 2d12 + 9 damage.

⚔ **Bounding Charge** (weapon) ✦ **Encounter**

Effect: Before and after the attack, the cyclops shifts up to 3 squares.
Attack: Melee 2 (one creature); +19 vs. AC
Hit: 4d12 + 7 damage.
Miss: Half damage.

MINOR ACTIONS

Evil Eye ✦ **At-Will** (1/round)

Effect: Ranged sight (one enemy). The target is affected by the cyclops's evil eye until the end of the encounter or until the cyclops uses this power again. While adjacent to the target, the cyclops can shift 1 extra square whenever it shifts.

TRIGGERED ACTIONS

Feywild Alacrity ✦ **Recharge** ⚁

Trigger: The cyclops hits a creature affected by its evil eye.
Effect (Free Action): The cyclops gains an extra move action that must be used before the end of its turn.

| Str 23 (+13) | Dex 16 (+10) | Wis 19 (+11) |
| Con 21 (+12) | Int 10 (+7) | Cha 12 (+8) |

Alignment unaligned   **Languages** Elven
Equipment chainmail, greatsword

Cyclops Hewer	Level 16 Soldier
Large fey humanoid	XP 1,400

HP 158; **Bloodied** 79	**Initiative** +13
AC 32, **Fortitude** 31, **Reflex** 27, **Will** 29	**Perception** +17
Speed 8	

Traits

Truesight
The cyclops can see invisible creatures and objects.

Standard Actions

⊕ **Battleaxe** (weapon) ✦ At-Will
Attack: Melee 2 (one creature); +21 vs. AC
Hit: 2d12 + 11 damage.

Triggered Actions

Evil Eye ✦ At-Will
Trigger: An enemy the cyclops can see misses one of the cyclops's allies with a melee attack.
Effect (Immediate Reaction): The cyclops uses *battleaxe* against the triggering enemy. In addition, until the end of the encounter or until the cyclops uses this power again, whenever the triggering enemy moves more than 2 squares away from the cyclops, the cyclops can shift 1 square closer to the target as an immediate reaction.

Str 25 (+15)	**Dex** 16 (+11)	**Wis** 19 (+12)
Con 22 (+14)	**Int** 10 (+8)	**Cha** 12 (+9)

Alignment unaligned	**Languages** Elven
Equipment chainmail, light shield, battleaxe	

Masters of the Evil Eye: The single, central eye of a cyclops–known as the evil eye–is just as dangerous as the creature's weapons. The eye serves as a focus of magical power that can hinder enemies and open them up to attack. The cyclopses owe their mastery of the evil eye to their fomorian allies, who have similar abilities, and some cyclopses develop different uses for this distinctive power. Many humanoid cultures have superstitions about the concept of the evil eye. Some invoke their version of an "evil eye" to place a curse on those who have wronged them, and others scrawl the image of an eye on the doors of their enemies' homes, hoping to draw misfortune down upon them. This tradition is based on a tale told by eladrin elders that, in ancient times, drow that had made a pact with a cyclops tribe would inscribe an arcane rune on the walls of certain dwellings to indicate where the cyclopses were supposed to attack. According to the tale, the cyclopses could attune their evil eyes to this rune, allowing them to see their targets (and put them under the effect of those evil eyes) before launching their assault.

"Trust me, there's nothing wrong with its vision for only having one eye. And you don't want to meet its gaze."

—Adrin of Tiri Kitor

DEATH KNIGHT

Among the most powerful of undead humanoids, death knights are warriors who chose to embrace undeath rather than pass on to the afterlife. They bind their souls into their weapons, fueling their necrotic powers as they marshal armies of undead.

A death knight wields fear like a weapon. It charges forward at the head of vast undead armies, shattering the courage of defenders. Gifted with undeath as a result of a ritual, a death knight is like the martial equivalent of a lich. In death, it retains its sentience and skill and gains the ability to shrug off wounds that would slay most mortals. A humanoid becomes a death knight through a profane ritual that strips away the emotional bonds of one's life, replacing them with cruelty and a perverse sense of honor. This ritual is often bestowed as a gift from high-ranking followers of Orcus, the Demon Prince of the Undead. When a warrior reaches a certain state of notoriety, Orcus's adherents approach the individual and try to tempt him or her with the promise of immortality. A warrior who accepts the offer turns into a dark reflection in the shattered mirror of undeath. Its armor becomes blackened and scarred, and its flesh becomes as withered and twisted as the person's corrupted soul.

Martial Champions: In life, most death knights were soldiers or warriors of great martial prowess, typically commanders or leaders who guided their people to many victories. In death, these warriors gain the strength and speed to match any living champion. A death knight can fight long after a mortal would have died. This characteristic allows a death knight to take on suicidal tasks, such as kidnapping a nobleman from a fortress. A death knight succeeds because it can ignore the arrows jutting from its body and can swat aside the swords of defenders. A death knight retains some of its personality from its former life, but its sense of honor becomes twisted in death. The creature might challenge an enemy commander to a duel rather than engaging in a pitched battle. The result of such a duel is almost always the death of the challenged foe. Alternatively, a death knight might give civilians time to clear out of a battle zone before marching its undead legions across the land, slaughtering any who stand against it.

Leaders of the Undead: A death knight often leads at the head of a column of undead, acting as an officer or a general for undisciplined undead, such as zombies and skeletons. Under a death knight's leadership, undead fight more efficiently and with greater skill. A death knight has magical talents of command as well as natural leadership. Strong-willed undead, such as vampires and liches, can resist a death knight's authority. These undead sometimes choose to work with a death knight, though. Slaying a death knight reduces the effectiveness of nearby undead, so an army facing a legion of skeletons or zombies might hire a group of mercenaries or assassins to take out a death knight before a large-scale assault begins.

"How does it feel, my dear, to know that you have brought pleasure to the damned? You have made my dreary realm of death interesting. Would that I had known you as a living man! But, my time is eternal. Perhaps I will wait for one who can share my throne."

—Lord Soth

Soul Weapons: The ritual that transforms a warrior into a death knight binds part of the subject's soul to one of his or her weapons. This weapon is not only a symbol of an individual's transformation, it is also the source of a death knight's power. A death knight jealously guards its soul weapon; humanoids sometimes try to steal this weapon, holding it for ransom or using it as leverage to bend a knight to their will. A death knight always keeps its soul weapon close, and such weapons are rarely left unattended. When a death knight is destroyed, its soul weapon crumbles to dust. A particularly powerful death knight could leave behind a mighty weapon that remains infused with part of the knight's soul. In such a case, the weapon might take on sentience of its own, even speaking to its wielder. A hero who slays a death knight and claims its weapon must be cautious, because many have been driven mad by the whispers of these weapons. Tales even recount how some people have become possessed by the souls of destroyed death knights.

Death Knight — Level 17 Elite Soldier

Medium natural humanoid (undead) — XP 3,200

HP 324; **Bloodied** 162
AC 33, **Fortitude** 31, **Reflex** 27, **Will** 29
Speed 5
Immune disease, poison; **Resist** 10 necrotic; **Vulnerable** 10 radiant
Saving Throws +2; **Action Points** 1

Initiative +11
Perception +8
Darkvision

TRAITS

☼ **Marshal Undead ✦ Aura 10**
Undead allies of level 17 or lower gain a +2 power bonus to attack rolls while in the aura.

STANDARD ACTIONS

⊕ **Soulsword** (necrotic, weapon) ✦ **At-Will**
Attack: Melee 1 (one creature); +22 vs. AC
Hit: 3d8 + 12 necrotic damage.
Effect: The death knight marks the target until the end of the death knight's next turn.

⊣ **Containing Strike** (necrotic, weapon) ✦ **At-Will**
Requirement: The death knight must be wielding a soulsword.
Attack: Melee 1 (one or two creatures); +22 vs. AC
Hit: 3d8 +12 necrotic damage, and the target is slowed until the end of the death knight's next turn.
Effect: The death knight marks the target until the end of the death knight's next turn.

⟡ **Unholy Flames** (fire, necrotic) ✦ **Recharge** ⚅ ⚄
Attack: Close burst 2 (living creatures in the burst); +20 vs. Reflex
Hit: 6d8 + 12 fire and necrotic damage.
Effect: Each undead ally in the burst deals 2d6 extra fire damage with melee attacks until the end of the death knight's next turn.

⊣ **Warrior's Challenge** (necrotic, weapon) ✦ **Encounter**
Requirement: The death knight must be wielding a soulsword.
Attack: Melee 1 (one or two creatures); +22 vs. AC
Hit: 4d8 + 19 necrotic damage, and the death knight pushes the target up to 2 squares. The death knight marks each enemy within 2 squares of the target until the end of the death knight's next turn.

TRIGGERED ACTIONS

⊣ **Combat Challenge ✦ At-Will**
Trigger: An enemy adjacent to and marked by the death knight shifts or makes an attack that doesn't include it as a target.
Effect (Opportunity Action): The death knight uses *soulsword* against the triggering enemy.

Implacable ✦ At-Will
Trigger: The death knight becomes marked, slowed, immobilized, dazed, or stunned by an effect.
Effect (Opportunity Action): The death knight makes a saving throw to end the triggering effect, even if the effect would not normally end on a save.

Str 20 (+13)	Dex 12 (+9)	Wis 11 (+8)
Con 18 (+12)	Int 13 (+9)	Cha 14 (+10)

Alignment evil — **Languages** Common
Equipment plate armor, heavy shield

Death Knight Blackguard — Level 18 Elite Skirmisher

Medium natural humanoid (undead) XP 4,000

HP 338; **Bloodied** 169	**Initiative** +17
AC 32, **Fortitude** 31, **Reflex** 29, **Will** 27	**Perception** +10
Speed 6	Darkvision

Immune disease, poison; **Resist** 10 necrotic; **Vulnerable** 10 radiant
Saving Throws +2; **Action Points** 1

TRAITS

✹ **Slayer of the Living** (fear) ✦ Aura 3
Whenever an enemy ends its turn in the aura, the death knight slides that enemy up to 3 squares.

STANDARD ACTIONS

⊕ **Soulsword** (necrotic, weapon) ✦ At-Will
Attack: Melee 1 (one creature); +23 vs. AC
Hit: 3d10 + 9 necrotic damage.
Effect: The death knight shifts up to 2 squares.

⊹ **Double Strike** ✦ At-Will
Requirement: The death knight must be wielding a soulsword.
Effect: The death knight uses *soulsword* twice, making each attack against a different enemy.

⊹ **Overpowering Attack** (necrotic, weapon) ✦ At-Will
Requirement: The death knight must be wielding a soulsword.
Attack: Melee 1 (one or two creatures); +23 vs. AC
Hit: 3d10 + 9 necrotic damage, and the death knight slides the target up to 2 squares.

⟵ **Abyssal Blast** (fire, necrotic) ✦ Encounter
Attack: Close burst 5 (enemies in the burst); +21 vs. Reflex
Hit: 5d6 + 13 fire and necrotic damage.
Miss: Half damage.

MINOR ACTIONS

Chilling Glare (fear) ✦ Recharge ⚄ ⚅
Effect: Close burst 5 (one enemy in the burst). The target grants combat advantage until the end of the death knight's next turn.

TRIGGERED ACTIONS

Implacable ✦ At-Will
Trigger: The death knight becomes marked, slowed, immobilized, dazed, or stunned by an effect.
Effect (Opportunity Action): The death knight makes a saving throw to end the triggering effect, even if the effect would not normally end on a save.

Str 24 (+16)	**Dex** 22 (+15)	**Wis** 13 (+10)
Con 17 (+12)	**Int** 14 (+11)	**Cha** 20 (+14)

Alignment evil   **Languages** Common
Equipment plate armor, light shield

"I have had centuries to reflect on my sins. They are all that sustain me."

—Kalaban, death knight of Nerath

DEMON

The monstrous demons spill out from the Abyss, spreading violence and destruction with every step they take. They tear down the strong, devour the weak, and despoil anything they touch with absolute evil.

The hateful agents of chaos known as demons come in a multitude of forms, each perverse and horrific. Their abilities and renown range from the stench of the weak, pitiful dretches to the crashing lightning and consuming flames of the immense, formidable balors. The only constant is the all-consuming wickedness that drives demons to slay and destroy until they meet their inevitable violent deaths. These fiendish creatures will never rest until they reduce the world to a blackened, flaming husk.

"Summoning a demon to help you in battle can be very effective, but never believe that the battle is over when your enemies are slain."

—Nimozaran, Septarch of Fallcrest

Demons' cruel impulses lead them to go wherever they can to cause the most pain and wreak the greatest destruction. Some days, they might join the raiding parties of vicious creatures such as gnolls or minotaurs. In truly dire times, entire war bands of demons might strike out from the Abyss, spreading like a wasting plague. Their armies (if these disorganized forces can truly be called such) roam from settlement to settlement, leaving no one alive except a small number of victims that they capture and then torture during the trip to their next destination.

Nearly everyone opposes demons, especially the fervent followers of gods and primal spirits. The desire of these faithful stalwarts to protect the world runs counter to the demons' need to rend it asunder. But even with so many forces

Dretch Lackey	Level 12 Minion Brute
Small elemental humanoid (demon)	XP 250
HP 1; a missed attack never damages a minion.	Initiative +9
AC 24, Fortitude 26, Reflex 24, Will 22	Perception +8
Speed 5	Darkvision

TRAITS

☼ **Sickening Miasma ✦ Aura 1**
Whenever an enemy in the aura takes a standard action or a move action, it takes 2 damage. Multiple *sickening miasma* auras stack, dealing up to 10 damage.

STANDARD ACTIONS

⊕ **Savage Claws ✦ At-Will**
Attack: Melee 1 (one creature); +17 vs. AC
Hit: 12 damage.

Str 20 (+11)	Dex 17 (+9)	Wis 12 (+7)
Con 16 (+9)	Int 5 (+3)	Cha 7 (+4)
Alignment chaotic evil	Languages Abyssal	

Babau — Level 13 Skirmisher

Babau	Level 13 Skirmisher
Medium elemental humanoid (demon)	XP 800

HP 127; **Bloodied** 63   **Initiative** +13
AC 26, **Fortitude** 23, **Reflex** 25, **Will** 24   **Perception** +10
Speed 7   Darkvision
Resist 5 acid

TRAITS

✦ **Protective Slime** (acid) ✦ **Aura** 1
  Any enemy in the aura that hits the babau with a melee attack takes 5 acid damage.

STANDARD ACTIONS

⊕ **Bite** (acid) ✦ **At-Will**
  Attack: Melee 1 (one creature); +18 vs. AC
  Hit: 2d6 + 3 damage. The target also takes ongoing 5 acid damage, or ongoing 10 acid damage if the babau is bloodied (save ends).

⊕ **Claws** ✦ **At-Will**
  Attack: Melee 1 (one creature); +18 vs. AC
  Hit: 2d6 + 3 damage, and the babau can shift 1 square.

✢ **Babau's Advantage** ✦ **At-Will**
  Effect: The babau uses *bite* and *claws* against a creature granting combat advantage to it.

MINOR ACTIONS

Murderous Abduction (teleportation) ✦ **Recharge** when the babau reduces an enemy to 0 hit points or fewer
  Effect: The babau teleports one creature adjacent to it up to 7 squares and then teleports to a square adjacent to that creature. The creature grants combat advantage to the babau until the end of the babau's next turn.

TRIGGERED ACTIONS

Variable Resistance ✦ **2/Encounter**
  Trigger: The babau takes acid, cold, fire, lightning, or thunder damage.
  Effect (Free Action): The babau gains resist 20 to the triggering damage type until the end of the encounter or until it uses *variable resistance* again.

Skills Athletics +14

Str 17 (+9)	Dex 21 (+11)	Wis 19 (+10)
Con 15 (+8)	Int 12 (+7)	Cha 14 (+8)

Alignment chaotic evil   **Languages** Abyssal

---

aligned against them, the demons could still win. They have nothing to lose, and their numbers could be endless—no one knows how many demons exist.

Blood and Violence: Demons live only to destroy, and whatever they can't destroy, they hate. A demon unleashed from the Abyss tears at the edifices of the world and rips apart anything it can, relishing bloodshed and brutality. The creatures have no concept of honor, mercy, or pity. The aftermath of a demon attack displays their cruelty. They leave behind villages burned to cinders, bodies torn limb from limb, and land forever corrupted by fiendish influence.

Abyssal Influences: The serpentine, six-armed marilith; the misshapen, wretched dretch; the blazing, winged balor; and the gaunt, vulturelike vrock are all evidence of how demons are warped and corrupted by their environment. An immeasurable number of horrific layers make up the swirling black vortex called the Abyss. Travelers there face not only the dangers of demons but also acidic pools of slime, storms of blood, and forests of razor-sharp foliage. The spreading

Vrock	Level 13 Skirmisher
Large elemental humanoid (demon)	XP 800

HP 132; **Bloodied** 66	**Initiative** +12
AC 27, **Fortitude** 25, **Reflex** 23, **Will** 23	**Perception** +13
Speed 6, fly 8	Darkvision

STANDARD ACTIONS

⊕ **Claw** ✦ **At-Will**

Attack: Melee 2 (one creature); +18 vs. AC

Hit: 3d8 + 8 damage.

↟ **Flyby Attack** ✦ **At-Will**

Effect: The vrock flies up to its speed and uses *claw* once during that
movement. It does not provoke opportunity attacks when moving away
from the target of the attack.

TRIGGERED ACTIONS

↢ **Spores of Madness** (poison) ✦ **Encounter**

Trigger: The vrock is first bloodied.

Attack (Free Action): Close burst 2 (enemies in the burst); +16 vs. Will

Hit: 3d10 + 6 poison damage, and the target is dazed (save ends).

Miss: Half damage.

Variable Resistance ✦ **2/Encounter**

Trigger: The vrock takes acid, cold, fire, lightning, or thunder damage.

Effect (Free Action): The vrock gains resist 10 to the triggering damage type until the end of the
encounter or until it uses *variable resistance* again.

Skills Bluff +15, Insight +13		
Str 23 (+12)	**Dex** 19 (+10)	**Wis** 15 (+8)
Con 20 (+11)	**Int** 12 (+7)	**Cha** 19 (+10)
Alignment chaotic evil	**Languages** Abyssal	

darkness spews corruption into the Elemental Chaos, and its malicious influence
creeps into the mortal world, bringing the demons with it.

Rule of Tooth and Claw: Enemies of all and allies of none, demons submit to
opponents only when the alternative is immediate death. The creatures have no
organized hierarchy, but the most powerful types order motley hordes of lesser
demons around. Since their greatest desire is to sow destruction, all demons
are quick to follow any orders that allow them to slaughter or raze. The mightiest leaders are the demon lords. These immensely powerful beings—including
Demogorgon, Orcus, Baphomet, Graz'zt, Lolth, and Yeenoghu—rule layers of
the Abyss and eternally contest one another's authority. Usually, these turf wars
involve conquering places of power on other planes rather than out-and-out conflict within the Abyss. The demon lords, unlike lesser demons, do have goals.
Many of them share a thirst for deicide, eager to murder the gods that created the
world the demons so fervently hate.

Summoning: Demons have such fearsome power that ambitious and evil
mortals desire to use it for their own ends. They summon and bind demons with
dark rituals, using the captive creatures as slaves or stripping away their elemental essence to fuel other magical endeavors. Few summoners truly understand
the nature of the diabolical forces they seek to conquer, and demons frequently
escape these would-be masters or use the magical conduit to bring more abyssal
spawn into the world.

Abyssal Eviscerator

Level 14 Brute

Medium elemental humanoid (demon)

XP 1,000

HP 173; **Bloodied** 86

Initiative +10

AC 26, **Fortitude** 28, **Reflex** 25, **Will** 24

Perception +9

Speed 6

Standard Actions

⊕ **Claw** ✦ At-Will

Attack: Melee 1 (one creature); +19 vs. AC

Hit: 3d10 + 5 damage.

↓ **Grab** ✦ At-Will

Attack: Melee 1 (one creature); +17 vs. Reflex

Hit: 4d6 + 4 damage, and the eviscerator grabs the target (escape DC 21) if it has fewer than two creatures grabbed.

Minor Actions

↓ **Eviscerating Talons** ✦ At-Will (1/round, or 3/round while the eviscerator is bloodied)

Effect: Melee 1 (one creature grabbed by the eviscerator). The target takes 6 damage.

Triggered Actions

Variable Resistance ✦ 2/Encounter

Trigger: The eviscerator takes acid, cold, fire, lightning, or thunder damage.

Effect (Free Action): The eviscerator gains resist 15 to the triggering damage type until the end of the encounter or until it uses *variable resistance* again.

Skills Athletics +18

Str 23 (+13)	**Dex** 17 (+10)	**Wis** 15 (+9)
Con 23 (+13)	**Int** 7 (+5)	**Cha** 11 (+7)

Alignment chaotic evil   **Languages** Abyssal

(Left to right) vrock, marilith, balor, hezrou

Hezrou
Level 22 Brute

Large elemental humanoid (demon) · XP 4,150

HP 254; **Bloodied** 127 · **Initiative** +17
AC 34, **Fortitude** 36, **Reflex** 33, **Will** 33 · **Perception** +17
Speed 6 · Darkvision

TRAITS
⛒ Noxious Stench (poison) ✦ **Aura** 2
Any enemy that makes an attack while in the aura takes 10 poison damage, or 20 poison damage while the hezrou is bloodied.

STANDARD ACTIONS
⊕ **Slam** ✦ **At-Will**
Attack: Melee 2 (one creature); +27 vs. AC
Hit: 4d10 + 10 damage.

⊹ **Bite** ✦ **Recharge** ⚅ ⚅ ⚅
Attack: Melee 2 (one creature); +27 vs. AC
Hit: 6d12 + 10 damage.

TRIGGERED ACTIONS
Variable Resistance ✦ **2/Encounter**
Trigger: The hezrou takes acid, cold, fire, lightning, or thunder damage.
Effect (Free Action): The hezrou gains resist 20 to the triggering damage type until the end of the encounter or until it uses *variable resistance* again.

Str 28 (+20)	**Dex** 23 (+17)	**Wis** 23 (+17)
Con 24 (+18)	**Int** 8 (+10)	**Cha** 16 (+14)

Alignment chaotic evil · **Languages** Abyssal

Marilith
Level 24 Elite Skirmisher

Large elemental humanoid (demon) · XP 12,100

HP 436; **Bloodied** 218 · **Initiative** +23
AC 38, **Fortitude** 35, **Reflex** 37, **Will** 35 · **Perception** +21
Speed 8 · Darkvision
Saving Throws +2; **Action Points** 1

STANDARD ACTIONS
⊕ **Scimitar** (weapon) ✦ **At-Will**
Attack: Melee 2 (one creature); +29 vs. AC
Hit: 3d10 + 12 damage.

⊹ **Shroud of Steel** (weapon) ✦ **At-Will**
Effect: The marilith uses *scimitar* twice and gains a +6 bonus to AC until the end of its turn.

⊹ **Weapon Dance** (weapon) ✦ **Recharge** when first bloodied
Effect: The marilith uses *scimitar* six times. Each time it hits, the marilith can shift 1 square.

TRIGGERED ACTIONS
⊹ **Hacking Blades** (weapon) ✦ **At-Will**
Trigger: An adjacent enemy misses the marilith with a melee attack.
Effect (Free Action): The marilith uses *scimitar* against the triggering enemy.

Variable Resistance ✦ **3/Encounter**
Trigger: The marilith takes acid, cold, fire, lightning, or thunder damage.
Effect (Free Action): The marilith gains resist 20 to the triggering damage type until the end of the encounter or until it uses *variable resistance* again.

Skills Bluff +24, Insight +21, Intimidate +24, Stealth +26

Str 25 (+19)	**Dex** 28 (+21)	**Wis** 19 (+16)
Con 18 (+16)	**Int** 14 (+14)	**Cha** 24 (+19)

Alignment chaotic evil · **Languages** Abyssal
Equipment 6 scimitars

Balor
Level 27 Elite Brute

Huge elemental humanoid (demon)   XP 22,000

HP 622; Bloodied 311	Initiative +20
AC 40, Fortitude 40, Reflex 37, Will 39	Perception +27
Speed 8, fly 12 (clumsy)	Blindsight 6, darkvision
Resist 20 fire	
Saving Throws +2; Action Points 1	

TRAITS

☼ **Flaming Body** (fire) ✦ **Aura** 2, or 3 while the balor is bloodied

Any enemy that starts its turn in the aura takes 10 fire damage, or 20 fire damage while the balor is bloodied.

STANDARD ACTIONS

⊕ **Lightning Sword** (lightning, weapon) ✦ **At-Will**

Attack: Melee 3 (one creature); +32 vs. AC

Hit: 6d10 + 11 lightning damage, or 3d10 + 71 lightning damage if the balor scores a critical hit.

† **Flaming Whip** (fire) ✦ **At-Will**

Attack: Melee 5 (one creature); +30 vs. Reflex

Hit: 2d10 + 10 fire damage, and ongoing 15 fire damage (save ends). The balor pulls the target up to 5 squares to a square adjacent to it.

† **Fire and Lightning** ✦ **At-Will**

Effect: The balor uses *lightning sword* once and *flaming whip* once.

⬔ **Beheading Blade** (lightning, weapon) ✦ **Recharge** when first bloodied

Attack: Close blast 3 (enemies in the blast); +32 vs. AC. The attack can score a critical hit on a roll of 15-20.

Hit: 5d12 + 14 lightning damage, or 3d12 + 74 lightning damage if the balor scores a critical hit.

TRIGGERED ACTIONS

⬔ **Death Burst** (fire)

Trigger: The balor drops to 0 hit points.

Attack (No Action): Close burst 10 (creatures in the burst); +30 vs. Reflex

Hit: 6d10 fire damage.

Miss: Half damage.

Effect: The balor is destroyed.

Variable Resistance ✦ **3/Encounter**

Trigger: The balor takes acid, cold, fire, lightning, or thunder damage.

Effect (Free Action): The balor gains resist 20 to the triggering damage type until the end of the encounter or until it uses *variable resistance* again.

Skills Bluff +20, Insight +27, Intimidate +20		
Str 30 (+23)	Dex 25 (+20)	Wis 29 (+22)
Con 31 (+23)	Int 12 (+14)	Cha 14 (+15)
Alignment chaotic evil	**Languages** Abyssal, Common	
Equipment lightning sword, flaming whip		

"Sages once believed that only six balors existed in the whole of the Abyss. If only that were true."

—Rhogar, paladin of Bahamut

DEVIL

Malevolent creatures from the Nine Hells, devils were once servants of the gods that rebelled and were cast out of their domains. Devils claim mortal souls to increase their power through temptation, betrayal, and manipulation.

Devils are infernal creatures whose once-luminous humanoid forms have been twisted and corrupted by their exile from the domains of the gods they once attended. They inhabit the burned-out husk of an astral dominion, now called the Nine Hells, as punishment for the slaying of a god by their dark master, Asmodeus. Cruel rulers and soldiers of a smoldering pit of anguish, devils delight in tormenting mortals and claiming their souls.

(**Left to right**) *pit fiend, succubus, imp, ice devil*

Fallen Servants of the Gods: The creatures that would become devils were once servants of the gods. Rallying behind their leader, Asmodeus, the devils helped to slay one of their divine masters. As a result, they were cursed and cast out into the devastated remains of that god's domain, which became the Nine Hells. The devils that now inhabit the Nine Hells are the same creatures that marched across astral battlefields, and though they have spent eons in their new home, the memories of their mutiny and subsequent exile remain fresh. These recollections fill devils with loathing and rage, and they burn with hatred for the gods—a hatred they have turned on the mortal races as well. Devils (particularly the ascended Asmodeus and his exarchs, the Lords of the Nine) seek to corrupt the creation of the gods by seizing the souls of mortals and bending them to their will. Each soul captured strengthens the armies of the Nine Hells. One day, the infernal legions say, the world will be so weakened and the devils will be so strong that they will march on the domains of the gods and seize control for themselves.

Imp	Level 3 Lurker
Small immortal humanoid (devil)	XP 150

HP 40; **Bloodied** 20	**Initiative** +8
AC 17, **Fortitude** 13, **Reflex** 17, **Will** 15	**Perception** +8
Speed 4, fly 6	Darkvision

STANDARD ACTIONS

⊕ **Bite** ✦ **At-Will**

Attack: Melee 1 (one creature); +8 vs. AC

Hit: 1d6 + 5 damage.

Vanish (illusion) ✦ **At-Will**

Effect: The imp becomes invisible until the end of its next turn or until it hits or misses with an attack.

⚔ **Tail Sting** (poison) ✦ **Recharge** when the imp uses *vanish*

Attack: Melee 1 (one creature); +8 vs. AC

Hit: 2d8 + 3 damage, and the target takes ongoing 10 poison damage and a -2 penalty to Will (save ends both).

Skills Arcana +9, Bluff +9, Stealth +9		
Str 12 (+2)	**Dex** 17 (+4)	**Wis** 14 (+3)
Con 16 (+4)	**Int** 16 (+4)	**Cha** 16 (+4)
Alignment evil	**Languages** Common, Supernal	

Tempters of Mortals: The followers of Asmodeus are, like their master, nothing if not cunning. Many devils prefer to capture the souls of mortals through nonviolent means, even convincing mortals to give up their souls of their own free will. For example, imps (small, red-skinned devils with leathery wings and stinger-tipped tails) whisper promises of power in mortals' ears, corrupting them with unholy contracts that divulge the secrets of arcane and divine magic. Succubi (bat-winged humanoids that appear as males and females of unparalleled beauty) use lust and greed as their tools, offering pleasure, wealth, or power in exchange for a mortal's eternal soul. Both of these types of devils are capable of fulfilling their promises, but everything comes with a price. A wizard who agrees to a contract with an imp might learn spells beyond imagination, but he is likely to sink slowly into madness as the dark magic erodes his sanity.

Soldiers of Hell: Not all devils are content to gain mortal souls through manipulation or seduction. Some vividly recall their struggles against the gods and have made themselves the champions of battle in the Nine Hells. In the old days, pit fiends (red-scaled, winged monsters that tower over humans) were commanders of the armies of the gods, viziers at the side of divine exarchs, or barons ruling over distant settlements in the astral domains. Now, they command dominions in the Nine Hells and all but explode with fury toward the gods and their mortal creations. Ice devils, from the frozen wastelands of the layer of the Nine Hells known as Cania, were once military commanders that have been twisted and corrupted. In a dark mockery of their former tactical prowess, they throw legions of lesser devils at their enemies with no care for the lives of their kin. Chain devils are jailers and torturers, using pain and suffering to extract information from the enemies of Asmodeus. The armies of the Nine Hells are largely made up of legion devils—cruel, pitiless warriors that gather in countless numbers from the scorched plains of Avernus to the deepest chasms of Nessus. All these kinds of devils are shadowy reflections of their former selves, made evil and vicious by their fall from grace.

Succubus	Level 9 Controller
Medium immortal humanoid (devil, shapechanger)	XP 400

HP 90; **Bloodied** 45   **Initiative** +8
AC 23, **Fortitude** 19, **Reflex** 21, **Will** 23   **Perception** +8
Speed 6, fly 6   Darkvision
Resist 10 fire

STANDARD ACTIONS

ⓐ **Corrupting Touch** ✦ **At-Will**
Attack: Melee 1 (one creature); +14 vs. AC
Hit: 3d6 + 6 damage.

⚔ **Charming Kiss** (charm) ✦ **At-Will**
Attack: Melee 1 (one creature); 12 vs. Will
Hit: The target cannot attack the succubus. The effect lasts until the succubus or one of its allies attacks the target, the succubus drops to 0 hit points, or the succubus uses this power again. If the target is affected by *charming kiss* at the end of the encounter, the effect lasts until the succubus fails to kiss the target during a 24-hour period. See also *loyal consort*.

⇗ **Dominate** (charm) ✦ **At-Will**
Attack: Ranged 5 (one creature); +12 vs. Will
Hit: The target is dominated until the end of the succubus's next turn.

MINOR ACTIONS

Change Shape (polymorph) ✦ **At-Will**
Effect: The succubus alters its physical form to appear as a Medium humanoid until it uses *change shape* again or until it drops to 0 hit points. To assume a specific individual's form, the succubus must have seen that individual. Other creatures can make a DC 30 Insight check to discern that the form is a disguise.

TRIGGERED ACTIONS

Loyal Consort (charm) ✦ **At-Will**
Trigger: A melee or a ranged attack targets the succubus while it is adjacent to a creature affected by its *charming kiss*.
Effect (Immediate Interrupt): The triggering attack instead targets the creature affected by the succubus's *charming kiss*.

Skills Bluff +15, Diplomacy +15, Insight +13

Str 11 (+4)	**Dex** 18 (+8)	**Wis** 19 (+8)
Con 10 (+4)	**Int** 15 (+6)	**Cha** 22 (+10)
Alignment evil	**Languages** Common, Supernal	

Chain Devil (Kyton)   Level 11 Skirmisher
Medium immortal humanoid (devil)   XP 600

HP 116; **Bloodied** 58   **Initiative** +14
AC 25, **Fortitude** 23, **Reflex** 25, **Will** 21   **Perception** +7
Speed 7   Darkvision
Resist 20 fire

STANDARD ACTIONS

⊕ **Spiked Chain** (weapon) ✦ **At-Will**
Attack: Melee 2 (one creature); +16 vs. AC
Hit: 2d4 + 5 damage.

⟊ **Double Attack** ✦ **At-Will**
Effect: The chain devil uses *spiked chain* twice.

⟊ **Hellish Chains** ✦ **At-Will**
Attack: Melee 2 (one creature); +14 vs. Reflex
Hit: 2d4 + 5 damage, and the target is restrained (save ends). The chain devil can restrain only one creature at a time.

MINOR ACTIONS

Dance of Battle ✦ **At-Will**
Effect: The chain devil shifts 1 square.

TRIGGERED ACTIONS

Dance of Defiance ✦ **Recharge** when first bloodied
Trigger: The chain devil is the target of a melee attack.
Effect (Immediate Interrupt): The chain devil shifts 1 square.

⟊ **Chains of Vengeance** ✦ **Encounter**
Trigger: The chain devil is first bloodied.
Effect (Free Action): The chain devil uses *spiked chain* twice.

Skills Intimidate +11
Str 19 (+9)	**Dex** 24 (+12)	**Wis** 15 (+7)
Con 20 (+10)	**Int** 14 (+7)	**Cha** 13 (+6)

Alignment evil   **Languages** Common, Supernal
Equipment spiked chain

Legion Devil Hellguard   Level 11 Minion Soldier
Medium immortal humanoid (devil)   XP 150

MINION

HP 1; a missed attack never damages a minion.   **Initiative** +8
AC 27, **Fortitude** 24, **Reflex** 23, **Will** 21   **Perception** +6
Speed 6, teleport 3   Darkvision

TRAITS

Squad Defense
The legion devil hellguard gains a +2 bonus to its AC while adjacent to another legion devil.

STANDARD ACTIONS

⊕ **Longsword** (fire, weapon) ✦ **At-Will**
Attack: Melee 1 (one creature); +16 vs. AC
Hit: 9 damage, and the target takes 4 fire damage if it willingly moves during its next turn.

Str 14 (+7)	**Dex** 12 (+6)	**Wis** 12 (+6)
Con 14 (+7)	**Int** 10 (+5)	**Cha** 12 (+6)

Alignment evil   **Languages** Supernal
Equipment longsword

Legion Devil Veteran — Level 16 Minion Soldier
Medium immortal humanoid (devil) — XP 350

MINION

HP 1; a missed attack never damages a minion. **Initiative** +11
AC 32, **Fortitude** 29, **Reflex** 28, **Will** 26 **Perception** +9
Speed 7, teleport 3 Darkvision

Traits
Squad Defense
The legion devil veteran gains a +2 bonus to AC while adjacent to another legion devil.

Standard Actions
⊕ **Longsword** (fire, weapon) ✦ At-Will
Attack: Melee 1 (one creature); +21 vs. AC
Hit: 12 damage, and the target takes 6 fire damage if it willingly moves during its next turn.

Str 14 (+10)	**Dex** 12 (+9)	**Wis** 12 (+9)
Con 14 (+10)	**Int** 10 (+8)	**Cha** 12 (+9)

Alignment evil **Languages** Supernal
Equipment longsword

Ice Devil (Gelugon) — Level 20 Soldier
Large immortal humanoid (devil) — XP 2,800

HP 195; **Bloodied** 97 **Initiative** +18
AC 36, **Fortitude** 33, **Reflex** 31, **Will** 29 **Perception** +13
Speed 8 Darkvision
Immune cold

Traits
☼ **Crippling Cold** (cold) ✦ Aura 2
Any enemy that starts its turn in the aura is slowed until the start of the ice devil's next turn.

Warming Weakness
When the ice devil takes fire damage, its *crippling cold* aura ends until the ice devil reactivates it.

Standard Actions
⊕ **Icy Longspear** (cold, weapon) ✦ At-Will
Attack: Melee 3 (one creature); +25 vs. AC
Hit: 2d12 + 15 cold damage.
Effect: The ice devil marks the target until the end of the ice devil's next turn.

↢ **Freezing Breath** (cold) ✦ Recharge ⚁ ⚂ ⚃
Attack: Close blast 5 (creatures in the blast); +23 vs. Fortitude
Hit: 4d8 + 18 cold damage.
Effect: The target is slowed (save ends).
First Failed Saving Throw: The target is immobilized instead of slowed (save ends).

Skills Endurance +23

Str 25 (+17)	**Dex** 22 (+16)	**Wis** 17 (+13)
Con 27 (+18)	**Int** 15 (+12)	**Cha** 19 (+14)

Alignment evil **Languages** Supernal
Equipment longspear

"Not all the hells are places of fire."

—Valthrun the Prescient

Pit Fiend — Level 26 Elite Soldier (Leader)

Large immortal humanoid (devil) XP 18,000

HP 486; **Bloodied** 243
AC 42, **Fortitude** 40, **Reflex** 36, **Will** 38
Speed 12, fly 12 (clumsy), teleport 10
Resist 30 fire, 15 poison
Saving Throws +2; **Action Points** 1

Initiative +22
Perception +23
Darkvision

Traits

⟳ **Aura of Fear** (fear) ✦ **Aura** 5
Any enemy in the aura at the start of the pit fiend's turn is marked by the pit fiend until the end of the pit fiend's next turn.

⟳ **Aura of Fire** (fire) ✦ **Aura** 5
Any enemy that enters the aura or starts its turn there takes 15 fire damage.

Standard Actions

⊕ **Flame-Touched Mace** (fire, weapon) ✦ **At-Will**
Attack: Melee 2 (one creature); +31 vs. AC
Hit: 2d10 + 11 fire damage, and the target takes ongoing 10 fire damage (save ends).

⳾ **Tail Sting** (poison) ✦ **At-Will**
Attack: Melee 2 (one creature); +29 vs. Fortitude
Hit: The target takes ongoing 25 poison damage and is weakened (save ends both).

⳾ **Pit Fiend Frenzy** ✦ **At-Will**
Effect: The pit fiend uses *flame-touched mace* and *tail sting*.

Move Actions

Tactical Teleport (teleportation) ✦ **Recharge** ⚃ ⚄ ⚅
Effect: Close burst 10 (one or two allies in the burst). The pit fiend teleports each target to a square in the burst.

Minor Actions

↗ **Point of Terror** (fear) ✦ **At-Will**
Attack: Ranged 5 (one creature); +29 vs. Will
Hit: The target takes a -5 penalty to all defenses until the end of the pit fiend's next turn.

Irresistible Command (charm, fire) ✦ **At-Will** (1/round)
Effect: Ranged 10 (one devil ally that is lower in level than the pit fiend). The pit fiend slides the target up to 5 squares, and the target drops to 0 hit points and is destroyed. Each creature within 2 squares of the target then takes 3d10 + 9 fire damage.

Triggered Actions

⳾ **Nightmarish Punishment** (fear, fire) ✦ **At-Will**
Trigger: An enemy marked by and within 2 squares of the pit fiend shifts or makes an attack that doesn't include it as a target.
Attack (Opportunity Action): Melee 2 (triggering enemy); +33 vs. AC
Hit: 2d10 + 11 fire damage, and the pit fiend slides the target up to 2 squares to a square adjacent to it.
Miss: Half damage.

Skills Bluff +27, Insight +23, Intimidate +27, Religion +24

Str 32 (+24)	**Dex** 24 (+20)	**Wis** 20 (+18)
Con 27 (+21)	**Int** 22 (+19)	**Cha** 28 (+22)

Alignment evil **Languages** Supernal
Equipment mace

DISPLACER BEAST

Seldom where they seem, displacer beasts mislead enemies by concealing their true location, which helps them evade the dangers of the Feywild where they live and hunt. They also prowl the forests and caverns of the natural world, where their glowing emerald eyes appear to change position constantly as they stare out from the darkness.

Displacer beasts look like enormous feline predators, but their barbed tentacles and powers of misdirection make them far deadlier. They quietly stalk their prey before bringing it down as quickly as possible in an ambush. The displacer beast's cunning, stealth, and ferocity have earned it a reputation as one of the most well-known predators of the Feywild. The creature's image is used in heraldry and literature to indicate a character or an organization that is elusive, tricky, or mysterious.

Some displacer beasts make their lairs behind dense foliage, in small caves, or within the boughs of massive trees. Others prowl from place to place, attacking prey where they can find it. Savvy explorers know to avoid locations where displacer beasts might dwell, but they also know that the creatures can spring out from anywhere. For any ordinary person or animal, a surprise attack by a displacer beast means a quick death. The beast's speed is so great, and its attacks so fierce, that it can swiftly drop anyone who is not prepared and trained for battle.

MICHAEL KOMARCK

Displacer Beast — Level 9 Skirmisher
Large fey magical beast XP 400

HP 97; **Bloodied** 48	**Initiative** +11
AC 23, **Fortitude** 21, **Reflex** 22, **Will** 20	**Perception** +12
Speed 12	Low-light vision

TRAITS

Displacement (illusion)
When a melee or a ranged attack hits the displacer beast, if the player rolled an odd number on the attack roll, the attack misses. If the player rolled an even number on the attack roll, the attack hits as normal, and the beast loses this trait until the start of its next turn.

Threatening Reach
The displacer beast can make opportunity attacks against enemies within 2 squares of it.

STANDARD ACTIONS

(+) **Tentacle** ✦ **At-Will**
Attack: Melee 2 (one creature); +14 vs. AC
Hit: 2d6 + 7 damage.

↓ **Bite** ✦ **At-Will**
Attack: Melee 1 (one creature); +14 vs. AC
Hit: 2d10 + 6 damage.

↓ **Cunning Blitz** ✦ **At-Will**
Effect: The displacer beast shifts up to half its speed. At any point during that movement, it uses *tentacle* once, or two times against different creatures.

TRIGGERED ACTIONS

Shifting Tactics ✦ **At-Will**
Trigger: An attack misses the displacer beast.
Effect (Free Action): The displacer beast shifts 1 square.

Skills Stealth +14

Str 18 (+8)	**Dex** 20 (+9)	**Wis** 17 (+7)
Con 17 (+7)	**Int** 4 (+1)	**Cha** 10 (+4)

Alignment unaligned   **Languages** —

Difficult to Pin Down: With their displacement ability and deft movement, displacer beasts can avoid most enemies, which means the creatures usually enter battle as the aggressors. They attack the weakest targets first, using their maneuverability to slip past tougher defenders. When hunted, displacer beasts spring ambushes in thick forests or other places where they can quickly escape from enemies that prove too strong. If they're outmatched or gravely wounded, the beasts nearly always try to retreat, unless starvation drives them to fight on in hopes of claiming a meal.

"I can't tell where it is! My sword keeps cutting empty air!"
—Douven Staul

Intelligent Predators: Displacer beasts hold a comfortable spot near the top of the food chain. Their predatory skill is unmatched, and they possess strong instincts and far greater intelligence than most ordinary animals. Displacer beasts set ambushes, track their prey by following clues (not just scents), and lure enemies into traps and hazards when fighting in a dangerous area. They're also capable of making relatively intricate plans. For example, they might remember which trade routes have seasonal traffic and return in the spring to plague travelers. It's rare to encounter more than two displacer beasts (usually a mated pair) at one time, but a beast might lead a pack of other wild predators. Because of their natural instinct to seek dominance within a pack, displacer beasts prefer to attack animals rather than humanoids.

Tough and Smart Pack Lords: Displacer beasts are rare as a species, and their pack lords number even fewer. These massive mutants have the same intelligence as ordinary people and sometimes lead groups of normal displacer beasts. Whereas standard beasts patrol large hunting grounds, pack lords terrorize entire regions. They maintain lairs that can handle their bulk, such as wide, moss-laden Feywild caverns or halls within crumbled ruins.

Savage Displacer Beast	Level 11 Brute
Large fey magical beast	XP 600
HP 136; Bloodied 68	Initiative +10
AC 23, Fortitude 23, Reflex 25, Will 21	Perception +8
Speed 8	Low-light vision

TRAITS

Displacement (illusion)
  When a melee or a ranged attack hits the displacer beast, if the player rolled an odd number on the attack roll, the attack misses. If the player rolled an even number on the attack roll, the attack hits as normal, and the beast loses this trait until the start of its next turn.

Threatening Reach
  The displacer beast can make opportunity attacks against enemies within 2 squares of it.

STANDARD ACTIONS

⊕ **Tentacle ✦ At-Will**
  Attack: Melee 2 (one creature); +16 vs. AC
  Hit: 4d8 + 3 damage, and the displacer beast can push the target 1 square.

↯ **Bite ✦ At-Will**
  Attack: Melee 1 (one creature); +16 vs. AC
  Hit: 3d10 + 8 damage.

TRIGGERED ACTIONS

Brutal Tactics ✦ At-Will
  Trigger: An enemy misses the displacer beast with a melee attack.
  Effect (Free Action): The displacer beast pushes the triggering enemy 1 square.

Skills Stealth +15		
Str 18 (+9)	Dex 21 (+10)	Wis 17 (+8)
Con 16 (+8)	Int 4 (+2)	Cha 10 (+5)
Alignment unaligned	Languages –	

Displacer Beast Pack Lord — Level 13 Elite Skirmisher

Huge fey magical beast   XP 1,600

HP 258; **Bloodied** 129	**Initiative** +14
AC 27, **Fortitude** 25, **Reflex** 26, **Will** 24	**Perception** +15
Speed 12	Low-light vision
Saving Throws +2; **Action Points** 1	

TRAITS

Displacement (illusion)

When a melee or a ranged attack hits the pack lord, if the player rolled an odd number on the attack roll, the attack misses. If the player rolled an even number on the attack roll, the attack hits as normal, and the beast loses this trait until the start of its next turn.

Nimble Stride

The pack lord ignores difficult terrain and speed penalties for squeezing.

Threatening Reach

The pack lord can make opportunity attacks against enemies within 3 squares of it.

STANDARD ACTIONS

⊕ **Tentacle ✦ At-Will**

Attack: Melee 3 (one creature); +18 vs. AC

Hit: 3d8 + 7 damage.

† **Bite ✦ At-Will**

Attack: Melee 1 (one creature); +18 vs. AC

Hit: 2d12 + 10 damage.

† **Cunning Blitz ✦ At-Will**

Effect: The pack lord shifts up to half its speed. At any point during that movement, it uses *tentacle* once, or two times against different creatures.

⬐ **Clear the Path ✦ Recharge** when first bloodied

Attack: Close burst 3 (enemies in the burst); +16 vs. Reflex

Hit: 2d6 + 7 damage, and the pack lord slides the target up to 3 squares.

Miss: Half damage, and the pack lord can slide the target 1 square.

TRIGGERED ACTIONS

Superior Shifting Tactics ✦ At-Will

Trigger: An attack misses the pack lord.

Effect (Free Action): The pack lord shifts 1 square. Before or after the movement, it uses *tentacle*.

Skills Stealth +17

Str 24 (+13)	**Dex** 23 (+12)	**Wis** 18 (+10)
Con 17 (+9)	**Int** 10 (+6)	**Cha** 12 (+7)
Alignment unaligned	**Languages** –	

Prized as Guards and Pets: Displacer beasts will follow more intelligent creatures, but only if they gain some benefit from the arrangement. Most often, displacer beasts guard secluded rooms in a palace or accompany wealthy or influential humanoids. Occasionally, they are captured and paraded about as status symbols, especially by callow young eladrin nobles. A displacer beast might serve a master in exchange for regular meals of fresh meat or out of loyalty to a creature that saved its life or kept it from harm. Despite their willingness to be trained in these circumstances, displacer beasts are smart enough to realize when a situation changes, and they might turn against their masters if necessary to protect their own lives.

DOPPELGANGER

Infiltrators, spies, and impersonators, doppelgangers are humanoid shapeshifters that take on the appearances of other humanoids. They are cunning opponents that lure in their victims or throw off pursuit with misdirection and disguise.

Few creatures spread fear, suspicion, and deceit better than doppelgangers do. Found in every land, with no true homeland of their own, doppelgangers transform their bodies to blend in with other races. They are much like humans in that they display a wide variety of personalities and dispositions. Doppelgangers as a whole are few in number, but when living among other races, they congregate in small groups. Three disguised doppelgangers might live together in a dwarven stronghold city, outwardly appearing to be stalwart dwarves while secretly plotting to bring down the city's defenses. Their knowledge of many cultures and their ability to manipulate others allow doppelgangers to walk about freely with little fear of detection.

Sowers of Paranoia: Unscrupulous people know that hiring a doppelganger (if they could afford to do so) is the surest way to slip an agent into the ranks of their enemies. With the ability to look like anyone, a doppelganger can launch an attack in one guise, duck around the corner and assume another appearance, and evade pursuit by looking like a dumbfounded bystander. With the right disguise, a doppelganger can stroll past sentries, coax secret information out of confidants, or walk out of a noble's manor carrying looted treasure in plain sight. Doppelgangers can get closer to an enemy than any other type of assassin can, taking on the visage of a trusted ally before planting a knife in

an unsuspecting back. Capturing a doppelganger can prove calamitous to a community, immediately casting suspicion on everyone–after all, if there could be one doppelganger, there might be more. As a result, some doppelgangers spend months or years infiltrating a town for the express purpose of revealing their deception when the time is right, then throwing suspicion onto others and letting the community destroy itself.

Doppelganger Sneak	Level 3 Skirmisher
Medium natural humanoid (shapechanger)	XP 150

HP 45; **Bloodied** 22
AC 17, **Fortitude** 14, **Reflex** 16, **Will** 15
Speed 6

Initiative +6
Perception +2

STANDARD ACTION

⊕ **Short Sword** (weapon) ✦ **At-Will**

Attack: Melee 1 (one creature); +8 vs. AC

Hit: 1d6 + 6 damage, or 2d6 + 6 if the doppelganger has combat advantage against the target.

MINOR ACTIONS

Change Shape (polymorph) ✦ **At-Will**

Effect: The doppelganger alters its physical form to appear as a Medium humanoid until it uses *change shape* again or until it drops to 0 hit points. To assume a specific individual's form, the doppelganger must have seen that individual. Other creatures can make a DC 30 Insight check to discern that the form is a disguise.

† **Shapeshifter Feint** ✦ **At-Will** (1/round)

Attack: Melee 1 (one creature); +6 vs. Reflex

Hit: The target grants combat advantage to the doppelganger until the end of the doppelganger's next turn.

Skills Bluff +8, Insight +7, Stealth +9

Str 11 (+1)	Dex 16 (+4)	Wis 12 (+2)
Con 13 (+2)	Int 10 (+1)	Cha 15 (+3)

Alignment unaligned
Equipment short sword

Languages Common

"I've been so many people I can hardly remember my own name. I was a male dwarf, stocky and strong, when I traveled to Vor Rukoth in search of the Rod of Kings. I was a female eladrin for a trip through the Feywild, lithe and full of laughter. I've been an orc, a minotaur, and a bugbear for different missions. Sometimes I wake up and have to touch my face to remember who I am that day. And sometimes I can't remember whether I'm supposed to woo you or kill you without glancing in the mirror first."

—Aunn, doppelganger spy

Doppelganger Infiltrator
Level 11 Lurker

Medium natural humanoid (shapechanger)
XP 600

HP 90; **Bloodied** 45
AC 25, **Fortitude** 21, **Reflex** 25, **Will** 23
Speed 6

Initiative +15
Perception +6

STANDARD ACTIONS

⊕ **Dagger** (weapon) ✦ **At-Will**
Attack: Melee 1 (one creature); +16 vs. AC
Hit: 2d4 + 6 damage.

Perfect Replica (illusion, polymorph) ✦ **At-Will**
Effect: Melee 1 (one Medium creature). The doppelganger takes on the form of the target and alters its clothing and gear to match those of the target. Until the end of the doppelganger's next turn, the target is immobilized and takes 6d8 extra damage from the doppelganger's *dagger* power. See also *replica switch*.

MINOR ACTIONS

Change Shape (polymorph) ✦ **At-Will**
Effect: The doppelganger alters its physical form to appear as a Medium humanoid until it uses *change shape* again or until it drops to 0 hit points. To assume a specific individual's form, the doppelganger must have seen that individual. Other creatures can make a DC 32 Insight check to discern that the form is a disguise.

TRIGGERED ACTIONS

Replica Switch ✦ **At-Will**
Requirement: The doppelganger must be adjacent to an enemy affected by its *perfect replica*.
Trigger: A melee or ranged attack from an enemy unaffected by the doppelganger's *perfect replica* targets the doppelganger.
Effect (Opportunity Action): The doppelganger and the enemy affected by its *perfect replica* swap places, and the triggering attack instead targets the enemy affected by the doppelganger's *perfect replica*.

Skills Bluff +14, Insight +11, Stealth +16

Str 12 (+6)	**Dex** 22 (+11)	**Wis** 13 (+6)
Con 18 (+9)	**Int** 10 (+5)	**Cha** 19 (+9)

Alignment unaligned   **Languages** Common
Equipment dagger

Dedicated Impersonators: When a doppelganger assumes another form, it can stay in that shape for prolonged periods of time. A doppelganger might spend weeks, months, or years in the guise of an eladrin wizard or a human soldier, maintaining the deception around the clock to keep from being discovered. Some doppelgangers find this effort stressful and revert to their natural forms when they believe that no one is looking. Still, their ability to hold a form over time allows doppelgangers to live among other races, developing relationships with neighbors and becoming a part of the community without raising suspicion. The farmer from down the road, the baker's wife, or a distant relative come to visit could be a doppelganger despite having been familiar to a person for years. A few particularly savvy doppelgangers have risen to great power by infiltrating other races, with ruinous results for those creatures.

Wielders of Many Powers: Doppelgangers use magic and other supernatural powers just as members of other races do, though often with more guile and finesse. Doppelgangers prefer magic that complements their natural shapeshifting ability and helps them infiltrate other groups; for example, they favor illusion magic, since it allows them to create distractions that can redirect suspicion. A few doppelgangers turn to the darker powers granted by shadow magic, augmenting their skill at blending in by adding the ability to vanish from sight. Some doppelgangers master psionic magic and can detect the surface thoughts of others, allowing them to assuage suspicions by providing the right answers to any questions put to them.

Doppelganger Master Assassin	Level 19 Lurker
Medium natural humanoid (shapechanger)	XP 2,400
HP 142; **Bloodied** 71	**Initiative** +20
AC 33, **Fortitude** 31, **Reflex** 32, **Will** 29	**Perception** +12
Speed 6	

TRAITS

Blend In
While the doppelganger is adjacent to at least one other creature, it can make a Stealth check to become hidden. The doppelganger remains hidden even if it does not have cover or concealment.

STANDARD ACTIONS

⊕ **Dagger** (weapon) ✦ **At-Will**
Attack: Melee 1 (one creature); +24 vs. AC
Hit: 3d4 + 6 damage.

† **Assassin's Strike** (necrotic, weapon) ✦ **Recharge** when the doppelganger uses *vanish*
Attack: Melee 1 (one creature); +24 vs. AC
Hit: 3d4 + 6 damage plus 4d10 + 16 necrotic damage.
Miss: 3d10 + 12 necrotic damage.

Vanish (illusion) ✦ **At-Will**
Effect: The doppelganger becomes invisible until the end of its next turn and shifts up to its speed.

MINOR ACTIONS

Alter Shape (illusion, polymorph) ✦ **At-Will**
Effect: The doppelganger alters its physical form to appear as a Medium humanoid and changes the appearance of its clothing and gear until it uses *alter shape* again or until it drops to 0 hit points. To assume a specific individual's form, the doppelganger must have seen that individual. Other creatures can make a DC 38 Insight check to discern that the form is a disguise.

Skills Bluff +20, Insight +17, Stealth +21
Str 11 (+9)	**Dex** 25 (+16)	**Wis** 16 (+12)
Con 22 (+15)	**Int** 13 (+10)	**Cha** 23 (+15)

Alignment unaligned   **Languages** Common
Equipment dagger

DRAGON

If any creature can claim to be an enlightened sage, a powerful tyrant, and a terrible monster, it is a dragon. Majestic and deadly, these creatures strike fear into the hearts of any who fall under the shadows of their enormous winged forms.

The size and majesty of dragons have shrouded them in myth. As ancient as the world, dragons are a living embodiment of legend. The oldest among them possess knowledge exceeding what most mortals can ever hope to attain. They hold the deepest secrets of the cosmos within their grasp. Dragons are no mere beasts ready to fall victim to a knight-errant or a treasure hunter. They are sages, oracles, and prophets; they are forces of nature capable of destruction and mayhem.

Fledgling White Dragon	Level 1 Solo Brute
Large natural magical beast (dragon)	XP 500

HP 128; **Bloodied** 64	**Initiative** +0
AC 15, **Fortitude** 15, **Reflex** 11, **Will** 13	**Perception** +7
Speed 6 (ice walk), fly 6	Darkvision
Resist 5 cold	
Saving Throws +5; **Action Points** 2	

TRAITS

Savage Blood
 While the dragon is bloodied, it can score a critical hit on a roll of 17-20.

STANDARD ACTIONS

⊕ **Bite** (cold) ✦ **At-Will**
 Attack: Melee 2 (one creature); +6 vs. AC
 Hit: 1d12 + 11 cold damage.

⊹ **Claws** ✦ **At-Will**
 Attack: Melee 2 (one or two creatures); +6 vs. AC. If the dragon targets only one creature, it can make this attack twice against that creature.
 Hit: 1d12 + 4 damage.

⬳ **Breath Weapon** (cold) ✦ **Recharge** ⚄ ⚅
 Attack: Close blast 5 (creatures in the blast); +4 vs. Reflex
 Hit: 2d8 + 4 cold damage, and the target is slowed (save ends).
 Miss: Half damage.

TRIGGERED ACTIONS

⊹ **Tail Slap** ✦ **At-Will**
 Trigger: An enemy hits the dragon while flanking it.
 Attack (Immediate Reaction): Melee 2 (triggering enemy); +4 vs. Fortitude
 Hit: 1d12 + 4 damage, and the dragon pushes the target up to 3 squares.

Bloodied Breath ✦ **Encounter**
 Trigger: The dragon is first bloodied.
 Effect (Free Action): Breath weapon recharges, and the dragon uses it.

Skills Athletics +9		
Str 18 (+4)	**Dex** 11 (+0)	**Wis** 15 (+2)
Con 16 (+3)	**Int** 8 (-1)	**Cha** 8 (-1)
Alignment evil	**Languages** Common, Draconic	

(Left to right) blue dragon, black dragon, green dragon

The Colors of Evil: The most famous and most feared dragons are part of the chromatic bloodline, including black, blue, green, red, and white dragons. Chromatic dragons have a penchant for evil and cruelty. They live to exert their dominance over other creatures through terror and violence.

Even among chromatic dragons, few share the cruelty of blacks. A black dragon does not hunt out of a need to survive or to protect its territory. Instead, a black dragon chases and tortures prey for the pleasure it gains from inspiring fear and causing pain. Black dragons are also among the most cowardly and cautious chromatic dragons. A black dragon waits in ambush or attacks from concealment. When a black dragon retreats, victims of its attack sometimes mistake its departure for a genuine withdrawal, not realizing until too late that the black is merely preparing for another assault.

Blue dragons are the most vain, proud, and arrogant of the chromatic dragons. A blue dragon delights in asserting its power over lesser creatures. A blue dragon will battle foes or preside over humanoids simply to exhibit its strength. When creatures venerate a blue dragon and respect its territorial claims, it can be the most reasonable of the chromatic dragons. Most blue dragons lair in areas where storms are fierce and frequent. As a result, many blues live along the coast, where they extort food and wealth from those who lack the strength to stand against them.

Few dragons are as reviled by humanoids as the sly, forest-dwelling green dragons. Although green dragons are weaker and less destructive than their chromatic kin, they are more cunning and deceptive. A green dragon tells lies as easily as other creatures breathe. A green relishes intrigue, preferring to achieve its goals through guile and betrayal rather than combat.

The savage white dragons lair in the coldest climes of the world, where they think of little more than their next meal and the contents of their treasure hoards. The oldest and most intelligent among them might seek to dominate other creatures, if only to feel assured of their power and superiority.

"Rapacious, cunning, and destructive, red dragons are Tiamat's favored children, embodying the worst that dragonkind has to offer. . . ."

When a legend or a fable tells of a dragon that laid kingdoms to waste, devoured virtuous maidens, or incinerated valiant heroes, then odds are the subject of the tale is a red dragon. The most voracious of the chromatic dragons, a red dragon consumes far more than it requires. All dragons are avaricious, but a red dragon possesses greed that far surpasses that of its kin. It is also a vindictive creature, dwelling on the smallest slights and delivering revenge tenfold for territorial intrusions, thefts, and insults. Reds are not mindless brutes, however. They are accomplished strategists that spend their idle time developing tactics and contingency plans for virtually any scenario.

Driven by Greed and Ego: The secret to understanding chromatic dragons is comprehending their worldview. One trait unites and informs their psychology: the belief that they are superior beings. Dragons consider themselves more powerful, intelligent, important, and worthy of being dominators than any other mortal creature. Chromatic dragons are born with this sense of superiority, and it is a cornerstone of their personalities and worldviews. Trying to humble any dragon is like trying to convince the wind to stop blowing. To chromatic dragons, humanoids are animals, fit to serve as prey or beasts of burden, unworthy of respect or acknowledgment.

". . . But stripped of life, of hunger, of the needs of the flesh, an undead dragon is simply evil incarnate."

—Jothan Ironspell

If one characteristic other than arrogance defines chromatic dragons, it's greed. Dragon hoards are the stuff of legend—enormous piles of gold, gleaming gems, and magic items, enough wealth to buy a kingdom. And yet dragons have no interest in commerce, despite the value of their hoards. They amass wealth for no other reason than to have it. A chromatic dragon's desire to create a hoard is a psychological need, or, arguably, a biological imperative. The source of this desire is a mystery, but it probably lies somewhere in a dragon's enjoyment of possessing what others lack.

Dangerous Lairs: One thing dragons and humanoids share is the desire to find permanent shelter. Humanoids want a place that offers comfort and a little security. A dragon, with its innate toughness, poor tactile senses, and tolerance for severe conditions, instead chooses a home that is defensible, has multiple ways to enter and leave, and that provides the utmost security for its hoard.

Chromatic dragons rarely construct lairs and instead find naturally occurring locations that can accommodate them. A blue dragon might lair within a sea cave that is occupied by subservient pirates. A red dragon could claim the caldera of an active volcano. After provoking a war, a green dragon might inhabit a city brought to ruin through the dragon's machinations.

Young White Dragon	Level 3 Solo Brute
Large natural magical beast (dragon)	XP 750

HP 200; **Bloodied** 100
AC 17, **Fortitude** 17, **Reflex** 13, **Will** 15   **Initiative** +1
Speed 6 (ice walk), fly 6   **Perception** +8
Resist 10 cold   Darkvision
Saving Throws +5; **Action Points** 2

TRAITS

Action Recovery
Whenever the dragon ends its turn, any dazing, stunning, or dominating effect on it ends.

Instinctive Rampage
On an initiative of 10 + the dragon's initiative check, the dragon can move up to its speed as a free action. The dragon can move through enemies' spaces and gains resist 5 to all damage during the move. Each time the dragon enters an enemy's space for the first time during the move, it can use *claw* against that enemy. If the attack hits, the target also falls prone. If the dragon cannot use a free action to take this move due to a dominating or stunning effect, then that effect ends instead of the dragon making this move.

Savage Blood
While bloodied, the dragon can score a critical hit on a roll of 17-20.

STANDARD ACTIONS

⊕ **Bite** (cold) ✦ **At-Will**
Attack: Melee 2 (one creature); +8 vs. AC
Hit: 3d10 + 4 cold damage.
Miss: 1d10 cold damage.

✦ **Claw** ✦ **At-Will**
Attack: Melee 2 (one creature); +8 vs. AC
Hit: 2d8 + 4 damage.

✦ **Dragon's Fury** ✦ **At-Will**
Effect: The dragon uses *claw* twice.

↞ **Breath Weapon** (cold) ✦ **Recharge** ⚄ ⚅
Attack: Close blast 5 (creatures in the blast); +6 vs. Reflex
Hit: 3d8 + 6 cold damage, and the target is slowed (save ends).
Miss: Half damage.

TRIGGERED ACTIONS

✦ **Tail Slap** ✦ **At-Will**
Trigger: An enemy hits the dragon while flanking it.
Attack (Free Action): Melee 2 (triggering enemy); +6 vs. Fortitude
Hit: 2d8 + 4 damage, and the dragon pushes the target up to 5 squares.

↞ **Bloodied Breath** ✦ **Encounter**
Trigger: The dragon is first bloodied.
Effect (Free Action): Breath weapon recharges, and the dragon uses it.

Skills Athletics +10

Str 18 (+5)	Dex 11 (+1)	Wis 15 (+3)
Con 18 (+5)	Int 8 (+0)	Cha 8 (+0)

Alignment evil   **Languages** Common, Draconic

Young Black Dragon — Level 4 Solo Lurker

Large natural magical beast (aquatic, dragon)   XP 875

HP 208; **Bloodied** 104   **Initiative** +11
AC 18, **Fortitude** 16, **Reflex** 18, **Will** 15   **Perception** +9
Speed 7 (swamp walk), fly 7, swim 7   Darkvision
Resist 10 acid
Saving Throws +5; **Action Points** 2

TRAITS

Acidic Blood (acid)

Whenever the dragon takes damage while it is bloodied, each creature adjacent to it takes 5 acid damage.

Aquatic

The dragon can breathe underwater. In aquatic combat, it gains a +2 bonus to attack rolls against nonaquatic creatures.

Instinctive Devouring

On an initiative of 10 + its initiative check, the dragon can use a free action to charge or to use *bite*. If the dragon cannot use a free action to make this attack due to a dominating or stunning effect, then that effect ends instead of the dragon making the attack.

Action Recovery

Whenever the dragon ends its turn, any dazing, stunning, or dominating effect on it ends.

STANDARD ACTIONS

⊕ **Bite** (acid) ✦ At-Will

Attack: Melee 2 (one creature); +9 vs. AC
Hit: 2d8 + 4 damage, and ongoing 5 acid damage (save ends).
Miss: 5 acid damage.

† **Claw** ✦ At-Will

Attack: Melee 2 (one or two creatures); +9 vs. AC. If the dragon targets only one creature, it can make this attack twice against that creature.
Hit: 2d6 + 5 damage.

↢ **Breath Weapon** (acid) ✦ Recharge ⁙ ⚃

Attack: Close blast 5 (enemies in the blast); +7 vs. Reflex
Hit: 2d8 + 3 acid damage, and ongoing 5 acid damage (save ends).
Miss: Half damage.

Shroud of Gloom ✦ Recharge ⚃

Effect: Close burst 5 (enemies in the burst). Each target gains vulnerable 5 acid and takes a -2 penalty to attack rolls until the end of the encounter. A character can use a standard action to attempt a DC 10 Heal check to end this effect on himself or herself or an adjacent ally.

TRIGGERED ACTIONS

† **Tail Sweep** ✦ At-Will

Trigger: An enemy misses the dragon with a melee attack.
Attack (Opportunity Action): Melee 3 (triggering enemy); +7 vs. Reflex
Hit: 1d6 + 2 damage, and the target falls prone. In addition, each of the target's allies adjacent to the target takes 5 damage.

↢ **Bloodied Breath** ✦ Encounter

Trigger: The dragon is first bloodied.
Effect (Free Action): Breath weapon recharges, and the dragon uses it.

Skills Stealth +12

Str 16 (+5)	**Dex** 20 (+7)	**Wis** 15 (+4)
Con 12 (+3)	**Int** 12 (+3)	**Cha** 10 (+2)

Alignment evil   **Languages** Common, Draconic

Young Green Dragon — Level 5 Solo Skirmisher

Large natural magical beast (dragon)
XP 1,000

HP 252; **Bloodied** 126
AC 19, **Fortitude** 17, **Reflex** 19, **Will** 17
Speed 8 (forest walk), fly 10
Resist 10 poison
Saving Throws +5; **Action Points** 2

Initiative +9
Perception +10
Darkvision

TRAITS

☼ Poisonous Wounds (poison) ✦ **Aura 1**

While the dragon is bloodied, any enemy that ends its turn in the aura takes ongoing 5 poison damage (save ends), or ongoing 10 poison damage (save ends) if that enemy is bloodied.

Action Recovery

Whenever the dragon ends its turn, any dazing, stunning, or dominating effect on it ends.

Instinctive Flyby

On an initiative of 10 + its initiative check, the dragon can use a free action to use *flyby attack*. During the movement from *flyby attack*, the dragon gains a +4 bonus to all defenses against opportunity attacks. If the dragon cannot use a free action to make this attack due to a dominating or stunning effect, then that effect ends instead of the dragon making the attack.

STANDARD ACTIONS

⊕ Bite (poison) ✦ **At-Will**

Attack: Melee 2 (one creature); +10 vs. AC
Hit: 2d10 + 4 damage, and ongoing 5 poison damage (save ends).
Miss: 5 poison damage.

† Claw ✦ **At-Will**

Attack: Melee 2 (one or two creatures); +10 vs. AC. If the dragon targets only one creature, it can make this attack twice against that creature.
Hit: 2d8 + 4 damage, and the dragon shifts up to 2 squares.

↤ Breath Weapon (poison) ✦ **Recharge** ⚃ ⚄

Attack: Close blast 5 (enemies in the blast); +8 vs. Fortitude
Hit: 2d10 + 3 poison damage, and the target is slowed and takes ongoing 5 poison damage (save ends both).
Aftereffect: The target is slowed (save ends).

† ↤ Flyby Attack ✦ **Recharge** ⚃ ⚄

Effect: The dragon flies up to its speed, ignoring slowing effects during the movement. The dragon can use *bite* or *breath weapon* (if the power is recharged) at any point during the move.

MINOR ACTIONS

↤ Luring Glare (charm) ✦ **At-Will**

Attack: Close blast 10 (one creature in the blast); +8 vs. Will
Hit: The dragon slides the target up to 3 squares.

TRIGGERED ACTIONS

↤ Bloodied Breath ✦ **Encounter**

Trigger: The dragon is first bloodied.
Effect (Free Action): Breath weapon recharges, and the dragon uses it.

Skills Bluff +15, Insight +10, Stealth +12

Str 17 (+5)	**Dex** 20 (+7)	**Wis** 16 (+5)
Con 15 (+4)	**Int** 15 (+4)	**Cha** 17 (+5)

Alignment evil   **Languages** Common, Draconic

Young Blue Dragon   Level 6 Solo Artillery

Large natural magical beast (dragon)   XP 1,250

HP 296; **Bloodied** 148	**Initiative** +5
AC 20, **Fortitude** 20, **Reflex** 17, **Will** 18	**Perception** +11
Speed 8, fly 10	Darkvision
Resist 10 lightning	
Saving Throws +5; **Action Points** 2	

TRAITS

⟡ Uncontained Lightning (lightning) ✦ **Aura** 5

While the dragon is bloodied, any enemy that ends its turn in the aura takes 5 lightning damage.

Action Recovery

Whenever the dragon ends its turn, any dazing, stunning, or dominating effect on it ends.

Instinctive Lightning

On an initiative of 10 + its initiative check, the dragon can use a free action to fly up to its speed and use *lightning burst*. This movement does not provoke opportunity attacks. If the dragon cannot use a free action to make this attack due to a dominating or stunning effect, then that effect ends instead of the dragon making the attack.

STANDARD ACTIONS

⊕ Gore (lightning) ✦ **At-Will**

Attack: Melee 2 (one creature); +11 vs. AC

Hit: 4d6 + 5 lightning damage.

⟊ Claw ✦ **At-Will**

Attack: Melee 2 (one or two creatures); +11 vs. AC. If the dragon targets only one creature, it can make this attack twice against that creature.

Hit: 2d6 + 5 damage.

⁜ Lightning Burst (lightning) ✦ **At-Will**

Attack: Area burst 2 within 20 (creatures in the burst); +11 vs. Reflex

Hit: 2d10 + 5 lightning damage.

Miss: Half damage.

⟻ Breath Weapon (lightning) ✦ **Recharge** ⚄ ⚅

Attack: Close blast 10 (up to three creatures in the blast); +11 vs. Reflex.

Hit: 3d8 + 8 lightning damage.

Miss: Half damage.

TRIGGERED ACTIONS

⟻ Wing Backblast ✦ **At-Will**

Trigger: An enemy hits the dragon with a melee attack.

Attack (Immediate Reaction): Close burst 2 (enemies in the burst); +9 vs. Reflex

Hit: The target falls prone.

Effect: The dragon flies up to half its speed. This movement does not provoke opportunity attacks.

⟻ Bloodied Breath ✦ **Encounter**

Trigger: The dragon is first bloodied.

Effect (Free Action): *Breath weapon* recharges, and the dragon uses it.

Skills Athletics +13, Insight +11

Str 21 (+8)	**Dex** 15 (+5)	**Wis** 17 (+6)
Con 18 (+7)	**Int** 12 (+4)	**Cha** 13 (+4)

Alignment evil   **Languages** Common, Draconic

A chromatic dragon doesn't rely only on the natural defenses of its lair. A dragon employs magical guardians, traps, and subservient humanoids to protect its treasures. A dragon that lacks such resources instead makes sure to place its lair in such a dangerous and remote location that none but the most audacious mortals could ever reach it. A white dragon might lair in a cave within a massive icicle on a frozen mountainside. A black dragon could hide its wealth deep underwater in the hull of a sunken ship.

Young Red Dragon	**Level 7 Solo Soldier**
Large natural magical beast (dragon)	XP 1,500

HP 332; **Bloodied** 166	**Initiative** +8
AC 23, **Fortitude** 21, **Reflex** 18, **Will** 18	**Perception** +11
Speed 6, fly 8	Darkvision
Resist 15 fire	
Saving Throws +5; **Action Points** 2	

TRAITS

Action Recovery
Whenever the dragon ends its turn, any dazing, stunning, or dominating effect on it ends.

Instinctive Assault
On an initiative of 10 + its initiative check, the dragon can use a free action to use *bite* or *claw*. If the dragon cannot use a free action to make this attack due to a dominating or stunning effect, then that effect ends instead of the dragon making the attack.

STANDARD ACTIONS

⊕ **Bite** (fire) ✦ **At-Will**
Attack: Melee 2 (one creature); +12 vs. AC.
Hit: 2d10 + 6 damage. The target is grabbed and takes ongoing 5 fire damage, or ongoing 10 fire damage if the dragon is bloodied, until the grab ends (escape DC 19).

↓ **Claw** ✦ **At-Will**
Attack: Melee 2 (one or two creatures); +12 vs. AC. If the dragon targets only one creature, it can make this attack twice against that creature.
Hit: 2d8 + 5 damage, and the dragon grabs the target (escape DC 16) if it has fewer than two creatures grabbed.

↤ **Breath Weapon** (fire) ✦ **Recharge** ⚄ ⚅
Attack: Close blast 5 (creatures in the blast); +10 vs. Reflex
Hit: 2d12 + 7 fire damage, or 2d12 + 17 fire damage while the dragon is bloodied.
Miss: Half damage.

TRIGGERED ACTIONS

↓ **Tail Strike** ✦ **At-Will**
Trigger: An enemy leaves a square within 2 squares of the dragon.
Attack (Immediate Reaction): Melee 3 (triggering enemy); +10 vs. Reflex
Hit: 1d6 + 5 damage, and the target falls prone.

↤ **Bloodied Breath** ✦ **Encounter**
Trigger: The dragon is first bloodied.
Effect (Free Action): Breath weapon recharges, and the dragon uses it.

Skills Bluff +11, Insight +11		
Str 22 (+9)	Dex 17 (+6)	Wis 16 (+6)
Con 19 (+7)	Int 11 (+3)	Cha 14 (+5)
Alignment evil	**Languages** Common, Draconic	

Deathbringer Dracolich — Level 12 Solo Controller

Large natural magical beast (dragon, undead) — XP 3,500

HP 492; **Bloodied** 246 — **Initiative** +10
AC 26, **Fortitude** 26, **Reflex** 24, **Will** 24 — **Perception** +14
Speed 6, fly 8 (clumsy) — Darkvision
Immune disease, poison, **Resist** 10 necrotic,
Vulnerable 10 radiant
Saving Throws +5; **Action Points** 2

TRAITS

Action Recovery
Whenever the dragon ends its turn, any dazing, stunning, or dominating effect on it ends.

Instinctive Domination
On an initiative of 10 + its initiative check, the dragon can use a free action to use *mesmerizing glance*. This attack does not provoke opportunity attacks. If the dragon cannot use a free action to make this attack due to a dominating or stunning effect, then that effect ends instead of the dragon making the attack.

STANDARD ACTIONS

⊕ **Bite** (necrotic) ✦ **At-Will**
Attack: Melee 2 (one creature); +17 vs. AC
Hit: 2d10 + 9 damage, and ongoing 10 necrotic damage (save ends).

↓ **Claws** ✦ **At-Will**
Attack: Melee 2 (one or two creatures); +17 vs. AC. If the dragon targets only one creature, it can make this attack twice against that creature.
Hit: 3d6 + 9 damage.
Effect: The dracolich slides the target up to 2 squares.

↩ **Breath Weapon** (necrotic) ✦ **Recharge** ⚄ ⚅
Attack: Close blast 5 (enemies in the blast); +15 vs. Reflex
Hit: 3d12 + 8 necrotic damage, and the target is weakened (save ends).
Miss: Half damage, and the target is weakened until the end of its next turn.

MINOR ACTIONS

⤳ **Mesmerizing Glance** (charm, psychic) ✦ **At-Will** (1/round)
Attack: Ranged 10 (one creature); +15 vs. Will
Hit: The target is dominated (save ends).
Miss: If the target willingly moves to a square nearer to or adjacent to the dracolich before the end of its next turn, it takes 15 psychic damage.
Effect: The dracolich slides the target up to 2 squares.

TRIGGERED ACTIONS

↩ **Bloodied Breath** ✦ **Encounter**
Trigger: The dragon is first bloodied.
Effect (Free Action): *Breath weapon* recharges, and the dragon uses it.

Skills Insight +14

Str 22 (+12)	**Dex** 19 (+10)	**Wis** 17 (+9)
Con 19 (+10)	**Int** 17 (+9)	**Cha** 18 (+10)

Alignment evil — **Languages** Common, Draconic

Elder White Dragon
Level 17 Solo Brute

Huge natural magical beast (dragon)

XP 8,000

HP 668; **Bloodied** 334

AC 31, **Fortitude** 30, **Reflex** 27, **Will** 28
Speed 8 (ice walk), fly 8
Resist 15 cold
Saving Throws +5; **Action Points** 2

Initiative +10
Perception +16
Darkvision

TRAITS

Action Recovery

Whenever the dragon ends its turn, any dazing, stunning, dominating effect on it ends.

Instinctive Rampage

On an initiative of 10 + the dragon's initiative check, the dragon can move up to its speed as a free action. The dragon can move through enemies' spaces and gains resist 5 to all damage during the move. Each time the dragon enters an enemy's space for the first time during the move, it can use *claw* against that enemy. If the attack hits, the target also falls prone. If the dragon cannot use a free action to take this move due to a dominating or stunning effect, then that effect ends instead of the dragon making this move.

Savage Blood

While the dragon is bloodied, it can score a critical hit on a roll of 17–20.

STANDARD ACTIONS

⊕ **Bite** (cold) ✦ **At-Will**

Attack: Melee 3 (one creature); +22 vs. AC
Hit: 5d12 + 14 cold damage.
Miss: 1d12 cold damage.

† **Claw** ✦ **At-Will**

Attack: Melee 3 (one creature); +22 vs. AC
Hit: 3d10 + 10 damage.

† **Dragon's Fury** ✦ **At-Will**

Effect: The dragon uses *claw* twice.

⌁ **Icy Tomb** (cold) ✦ **Recharge** ⚄ ⚅

Attack: Ranged 10 (one creature); +20 vs. Reflex
Hit: The target is stunned, cannot be pulled, pushed, or slid, and takes ongoing 45 cold damage (save ends all).
Aftereffect: The target is slowed and takes ongoing 20 cold damage (save ends both).

↩ **Breath Weapon** (cold) ✦ **Recharge** ⚄ ⚅

Attack: Close blast 5 (creatures in the blast); +20 vs. Reflex
Hit: 6d10 + 13 cold damage, and the target is slowed (save ends).
Miss: Half damage.

TRIGGERED ACTIONS

† **Tail Slap** ✦ **At-Will**

Trigger: An enemy hits the dragon while flanking it.
Attack (Free Action): Melee 3 (triggering enemy); +20 vs. Fortitude
Hit: 2d8 + 6 damage, and the dragon pushes the target up to 5 squares.

↩ **Bloodied Breath** ✦ **Encounter**

Trigger: The dragon is first bloodied.
Effect (Free Action): Breath weapon recharges, and the dragon uses it.

Skills Athletics +19

Str 22 (+14)	**Dex** 14 (+10)	**Wis** 16 (+11)
Con 23 (+14)	**Int** 13 (+9)	**Cha** 13 (+9)

Alignment evil

Languages Draconic

Elder Black Dragon — Level 18 Solo Lurker

Huge natural magical beast (aquatic, dragon)   XP 10,000

HP 676; **Bloodied** 338   **Initiative** +20
AC 32, **Fortitude** 30, **Reflex** 32, **Will** 28   **Perception** +17
Speed 8 (swamp walk), fly 8, swim 8   Darkvision
Resist 15 acid
Saving Throws +5; **Action Points** 2

TRAITS

Acidic Blood (acid)
  Whenever the dragon takes damage while it is bloodied, each creature adjacent to it takes 10 acid damage.

Aquatic
  The dragon can breathe underwater. In aquatic combat, it gains a +2 bonus to attack rolls against nonaquatic creatures.

Instinctive Devouring
  On an initiative of 10 + its initiative check, the dragon can use a free action to charge or to use *bite*. If the dragon cannot use a free action to make this attack due to a dominating or stunning effect, then that effect ends instead of the dragon making the attack.

Action Recovery
  Whenever the dragon ends its turn, any dazing, stunning, or dominating effect on it ends.

STANDARD ACTIONS

⊕ **Bite** (acid) ✦ **At-Will**
  Attack: Melee 3 (one creature); +23 vs. AC
  Hit: 4d8 + 11 damage, and ongoing 10 acid damage (save ends).
  Miss: 10 acid damage.

⊢ **Claw** ✦ **At-Will**
  Attack: Melee 3 (one or two creatures); +23 vs. AC. If the dragon targets only one creature, it can make this attack twice against that creature.
  Hit: 3d10 + 10 damage.

⤳ **Acid Gob** (acid) ✦ **At-Will**
  Attack: Ranged 10 (one creature); +21 vs. Reflex
  Hit: The target takes ongoing 30 acid damage and is blinded (save ends both).

⟵ **Breath Weapon** (acid) ✦ **Recharge** ⚄ ⚅
  Attack: Close blast 5 (enemies in the blast); +21 vs. Reflex
  Hit: 3d10 + 5 acid damage, and ongoing 15 acid damage (save ends).
  Miss: Half damage, and ongoing 10 acid damage (save ends).

Shroud of Gloom ✦ **Recharge** ⚅
  Effect: Close burst 5 (enemies in the burst). Each target gains vulnerable 10 acid and takes a -2 penalty to attack rolls until the end of the encounter. A character can use a standard action to attempt a DC 17 Heal check to end this effect on himself or herself or an adjacent ally.

TRIGGERED ACTIONS

⊢ **Tail Sweep** ✦ **At-Will**
  Trigger: An enemy misses the dragon with a melee attack.
  Attack (Opportunity Action): Melee 4 (triggering enemy); +21 vs. Reflex
  Hit: 2d8 + 2 damage, and the target falls prone. In addition, each of the target's allies adjacent to the target takes 10 damage.

⟵ **Bloodied Breath** ✦ **Encounter**
  Trigger: The dragon is first bloodied.
  Effect (Free Action): Breath weapon recharges, and the dragon uses it.

Skills Stealth +21

Str 21 (+14)	**Dex** 25 (+16)	**Wis** 16 (+12)
Con 17 (+12)	**Int** 16 (+12)	**Cha** 14 (+11)

Alignment evil   **Languages** Common, Draconic

Elder Green Dragon — Level 19 Solo Skirmisher

Huge natural magical beast (dragon)
XP 12,000

HP 720; **Bloodied** 360
AC 33, **Fortitude** 31, **Reflex** 33, **Will** 29
Speed 10 (forest walk), fly 14
Resist 15 poison
Saving Throws +5; **Action Points** 2

Initiative +18
Perception +17
Darkvision

TRAITS

☼ **Poisonous Wounds** (poison) ✦ **Aura** 1

While the dragon is bloodied, any enemy that ends its turn in the aura takes ongoing 10 poison damage (save ends). This damage increases to 20 if that enemy is bloodied.

Action Recovery

Whenever the dragon ends its turn, any dazing, stunning, or dominating effect on it ends.

Instinctive Flyby

On an initiative of 10 + its initiative check, the dragon can use a free action to use *flyby attack*. During the movement from *flyby attack*, the dragon gains a +4 bonus to all defenses against opportunity attacks. If the dragon cannot use a free action to make this attack due to a dominating or stunning effect, then that effect ends instead of the dragon making the attack.

STANDARD ACTIONS

⊕ **Bite** (poison) ✦ **At-Will**

Attack: Melee 3 (one creature); +24 vs. AC
Hit: 3d10 + 14 damage, and ongoing 10 poison damage (save ends).
Miss: 10 poison damage.

† **Claw** ✦ **At-Will**

Attack: Melee 3 (one or two creatures); +24 vs. AC. If the dragon targets only one creature, it can make this attack twice against that creature.
Hit: 3d8 + 13 damage, and the dragon shifts up to 2 squares.

↩ **Breath Weapon** (poison) ✦ **Recharge** ⚄ ⚅

Attack: Close blast 5 (enemies in the blast); +22 vs. Fortitude
Hit: 2d12 + 12 poison damage, and the target is slowed and takes ongoing 15 poison damage (save ends both).
Aftereffect: The target is slowed (save ends).

† ↩ **Flyby Attack** ✦ **Recharge** ⚄ ⚅

Effect: The dragon flies up to 10 squares and uses *bite* or *breath weapon* (if the power is recharged) at any point during the move.

MINOR ACTIONS

↩ **Luring Glare** (charm) ✦ **At-Will**

Attack: Close blast 10 (one creature in the blast); +22 vs. Will
Hit: The dragon slides the target up to 3 squares.

TRIGGERED ACTIONS

↩ **Cunning Glance** ✦ **At-Will**

Trigger: An enemy shifts to a square within 2 squares of the dragon.
Effect (Immediate Reaction): The dragon uses *luring glare* against the triggering enemy.

↩ **Bloodied Breath** ✦ **Encounter**

Trigger: The dragon is first bloodied.
Effect (Free Action): Breath weapon recharges, and the dragon uses it.

Skills Bluff +21, Insight +17, Stealth +21

Str 22 (+15)	**Dex** 25 (+16)	**Wis** 16 (+12)
Con 20 (+14)	**Int** 16 (+12)	**Cha** 14 (+11)

Alignment evil
Languages Common, Draconic

Elder Blue Dragon — Level 20 Solo Artillery

Huge natural magical beast (dragon)   XP 14,000

HP 756; **Bloodied** 378   **Initiative** +13
AC 34, **Fortitude** 33, **Reflex** 30, **Will** 30   **Perception** +18
Speed 10, fly 12   Darkvision
Resist 15 lightning
Saving Throws +5; **Action Points** 2

TRAITS

☼ Uncontained Lightning (lightning) ✦ **Aura 5**
While the dragon is bloodied, any enemy that ends its turn in the aura takes 10 lightning damage.

Action Recovery
Whenever the dragon ends its turn, any dazing, stunning, or dominating effect on it ends.

Instinctive Lightning
On an initiative of 10 + its initiative check, the dragon can use a free action to fly up to its speed and use *lightning burst*. This movement does not provoke opportunity attacks. If the dragon cannot use a free action to make this attack due to a dominating or stunning effect, then that effect ends instead of the dragon making the attack.

STANDARD ACTIONS

⊕ Gore (lightning) ✦ **At-Will**
Attack: Melee 3 (one creature); +25 vs. AC.
Hit: 4d12 + 16 lightning damage.

⊢ Claw ✦ **At-Will**
Attack: Melee 3 (one or two creatures); +25 vs. AC. If the dragon targets only one creature, it can make this attack twice against that creature.
Hit: 4d8 + 13 damage.

⚹ Lightning Burst (lightning) ✦ **At-Will**
Attack: Area burst 2 within 20 (creatures in the burst); +25 vs. Reflex
Hit: 3d12 + 13 lightning damage.
Miss: Half damage.

⬱ Breath Weapon (lightning) ✦ **Recharge ⚄ ⚅**
Attack: Close blast 20 (up to three creatures in the blast); +25 vs. Reflex.
Hit: 4d12 + 16 lightning damage, and the target is dazed (save ends).
Miss: Half damage.

⚹ Thunderclap (thunder) ✦ **Recharge ⚄ ⚅**
Attack: Area burst 3 within 20 (creatures in the burst); +25 vs. Fortitude
Hit: 4d6 + 12 thunder damage, and the target is stunned until the end of the dragon's next turn.
Miss: Half damage, and the target is dazed until the end of the dragon's next turn.

TRIGGERED ACTIONS

⬱ Wing Backblast ✦ **At-Will**
Trigger: An enemy hits the dragon with a melee attack.
Attack (Immediate Reaction): Close burst 3 (enemies in the burst); +23 vs. Reflex
Hit: The target falls prone.
Effect: The dragon flies up to half its speed. This movement does not provoke opportunity attacks.

⬱ Bloodied Breath ✦ **Encounter**
Trigger: The dragon is first bloodied.
Effect (Free Action): Breath weapon recharges, and the dragon uses it.

Skills Athletics +22, Insight +18

Str 25 (+17)	Dex 16 (+13)	Wis 17 (+13)
Con 21 (+15)	Int 15 (+12)	Cha 16 (+13)

Alignment evil   **Languages** Common, Draconic

Elder Red Dragon — Level 22 Solo Soldier

Huge natural magical beast (dragon) — XP 20,750

HP 832; **Bloodied** 416
AC 38, **Fortitude** 36, **Reflex** 33, **Will** 32
Speed 8, fly 10
Resist 20 fire
Saving Throws +5; **Action Points** 2

Initiative +18
Perception +19
Darkvision

TRAITS

Action Recovery
Whenever the dragon ends its turn, any dazing, stunning, or dominating effect on it ends.

Instinctive Assault
On an initiative of 10 + its initiative check, the dragon can use a free action to use *bite* or *claw*. If the dragon cannot use a free action to make this attack due to a dominating or stunning effect, then that effect ends instead of the dragon making the attack.

STANDARD ACTIONS

⊕ **Bite** (fire) ✦ **At-Will**
Attack: Melee 3 (one creature); +27 vs. AC.
Hit: 2d10 + 6 damage. The target is grabbed and takes ongoing 15 fire damage, or ongoing 25 fire damage if the dragon is bloodied, until the grab ends (escape DC 30).

† **Claw** ✦ **At-Will**
Attack: Melee 3 (one or two creatures); +27 vs. AC. If the dragon targets only one creature, it can make this attack twice against that creature.
Hit: 3d10 + 14 damage, and the dragon grabs the target (escape DC 27) if it has fewer than two creatures grabbed.

↗ **Immolate Foe** (fire) ✦ **Recharge** ⚄ ⚅
Attack: Ranged 20 (one creature); +25 vs. Reflex
Hit: 4d10 + 7 fire damage, and ongoing 20 fire damage (save ends).
Miss: Half damage, and ongoing 10 fire damage (save ends).

↩ **Breath Weapon** (fire) ✦ **Recharge** ⚄ ⚅
Attack: Close blast 5 (creatures in the blast); +25 vs. Reflex
Hit: 4d12 + 17 fire damage.
Miss: Half damage.

TRIGGERED ACTIONS

† **Tail Strike** ✦ **At-Will**
Trigger: An enemy leaves a square within 3 squares of the dragon.
Attack (Immediate Reaction): Melee 4 (triggering enemy); +25 vs. Reflex
Hit: 2d8 + 4 damage, and the target falls prone.

↩ **Bloodied Breath** ✦ **Encounter**
Trigger: The dragon is first bloodied.
Effect (Free Action): Breath weapon recharges, and the dragon uses it.

Skills Bluff +17, Insight +18
Str 26 (+19) **Dex** 21 (+16) **Wis** 17 (+14)
Con 24 (+18) **Int** 14 (+13) **Cha** 15 (+13)
Alignment evil **Languages** Common, Draconic

(Left to right) red dragon, white dragon, dracolich doomlord

Dracoliches: Long-lived though they are, dragons can die. Yet even when their heartbeats falter, some dragons remain in the world, active and malicious, fueled by necrotic energy instead of blood. Through a powerful ritual, a few dragons become dracoliches. Some dragons choose this fate rather than death, while others are subjected to the ritual by worshipers of Tiamat or Vecna who seek a powerful thrall that can champion their cause.

"The older they get, the more like their terrible god they become."

—Jothan Ironspell

A chromatic dragon that becomes a dracolich tends to pursue the same goals it possessed in life: destruction, dominance, and treasure. The process of becoming a dracolich can drive a dragon toward new evil, though. Not only is a dracolich an unholy terror, it is a fiendishly intelligent tyrant that lays complex webs of foul schemes. A dracolich employs loyal intermediaries motivated by greed and a lust for power. It is especially difficult to overcome, because aside from the normal challenges associated with killing a dragon or a lich, it often acts from the shadows and keeps an array of backup plans.

Dracolich Doomlord — Level 22 Solo Controller

Huge natural magical beast (dragon, undead)   XP 20,750

HP 840; **Bloodied** 420	**Initiative** +18
AC 36, **Fortitude** 35, **Reflex** 34, **Will** 32	**Perception** +21
Speed 8, fly 10 (clumsy)	Darkvision

Immune disease, poison; **Resist** 15 necrotic;
Vulnerable 10 radiant
Saving Throws +5; **Action Points** 2

Place a Large creature token inside this ring to create a Huge creature token.

TRAITS

✷ **Aura of Doom ✦ Aura 3**
Enemies cannot regain hit points or gain temporary hit points while in the aura.

Action Recovery
Whenever the dragon ends its turn, any dazing, stunning, or dominating effect on it ends.

Instinctive Domination
On an initiative of 10 + its initiative check, the dragon can use a free action to use *mesmerizing glance*. This attack does not provoke opportunity attacks. If the dragon cannot use a free action to make this attack due to a dominating or stunning effect, then that effect ends instead of the dragon making the attack.

STANDARD ACTIONS

⊕ **Bite** (necrotic) **✦ At-Will**
Attack: Melee 2 (one creature); +27 vs. AC
Hit: 2d8 + 8 damage, and ongoing 10 necrotic damage (save ends).

⊺ **Claws ✦ At-Will**
Attack: Melee 2 (one or two creatures); +27 vs. AC. If the dracolich targets only one creature, it can make this attack twice against that creature.
Hit: 3d8 + 16 damage.
Effect: The dracolich slides the target up to 2 squares.

⟵ **Breath Weapon** (necrotic) **✦ Recharge** ⚄ ⚅
Attack: Close blast 5 (enemies in the blast); +25 vs. Reflex
Hit: 5d12 + 14 necrotic damage, and the target is weakened (save ends).
Miss: Half damage, and the target is weakened until the end of its next turn.
Effect: Each target loses any necrotic resistance (save ends).

MINOR ACTIONS

⤳ **Mesmerizing Glance** (charm) **✦ At-Will (1/round)**
Attack: Ranged 5 (one creature); +25 vs. Will
Hit: The the target is dominated (save ends).
Effect: The dracolich slides the target up to 2 squares.

TRIGGERED ACTIONS

⟵ **Bloodied Breath ✦ Encounter**
Trigger: The dragon is first bloodied.
Effect (Free Action): Breath weapon recharges, and the dragon uses it.

Skills Insight +21

Str 27 (+19)	**Dex** 24 (+18)	**Wis** 20 (+16)
Con 26 (+19)	**Int** 18 (+15)	**Cha** 17 (+14)

Alignment evil   **Languages** Common, Draconic

DRAGONBORN

Dragonborn are humanoids that share physical features with dragons. The race once ruled over the Empire of Arkhosia, but its numbers have now dwindled. The dragonborn that live today are scattered throughout the towns and villages of other races.

Most dragonborn are honorable warriors or powerful spellcasters who share ties to dragons. Despite having no communities of their own, dragonborn retain strong cultural traditions.

Honor Bound: A dragonborn lives by a code of honor that influences all aspects of his or her life. This code promotes loyalty to one's family and clan, so a dragonborn is very protective of allies and clan members. The code doesn't demand virtue, but it does encourage respect for one's enemies and victory through honorable combat.

Draconic Affinity: Dragonborn share a connection to dragons beyond just their physical appearance. Most dragonborn consider their draconic heritage a fundamental part of what makes their race unique. As a result, a dragonborn often has a personality that reflects the characteristics of dragons, such as being strong-willed, confident, independent, proud, or fearless.

Dragonborn Mercenary	Level 2 Skirmisher
Medium natural humanoid	XP 125

HP 38; **Bloodied** 19	**Initiative** +6
AC 16, **Fortitude** 13, **Reflex** 14, **Will** 14	**Perception** +2
Speed 6	

TRAITS

Skirmish
If the dragonborn ends a move on its turn at least 4 squares from where it started the move, it deals 1d6 extra damage with melee attacks until the start of its next turn.

STANDARD ACTIONS

⊕ **Battleaxe** (weapon) ✦ **At-Will**
Attack: Melee 1 (one creature); +7 vs. AC, or +8 vs. AC while the dragonborn is bloodied.
Hit: 1d10 + 4 damage, and the dragonborn shifts up to 2 squares.

† **Overwhelming Strike** (weapon) ✦ **Encounter**
Attack: Melee 1 (one creature); +7 vs. AC
Hit: 2d10 + 4 damage, and the target grants combat advantage (save ends).
Miss: Half damage.

MINOR ACTIONS

⟵ **Dragon Breath** (lightning) ✦ **Encounter**
Attack: Close blast 3 (creatures in the blast); +5 vs. Reflex
Hit: 1d6 + 2 lightning damage.

TRIGGERED ACTIONS

Tactical Withdrawal ✦ **Encounter**
Trigger: The dragonborn is bloodied.
Effect (Immediate Reaction): The dragonborn shifts up to 3 squares.

Str 18 (+5)	Dex 16 (+4)	Wis 13 (+2)
Con 14 (+3)	Int 8 (+0)	Cha 10 (+1)

Alignment unaligned   **Languages** Common, Draconic
Equipment hide armor, battleaxe

Dragonborn Soldier
Medium natural humanoid

Level 5 Soldier
XP 200

HP 63; **Bloodied** 31
AC 21, **Fortitude** 18, **Reflex** 16, **Will** 15
Speed 5

Initiative +6
Perception +3

STANDARD ACTIONS

⊕ **Longsword** (weapon) ✦ **At-Will**

Attack: Melee 1 (one creature); +10 vs. AC, or +11 vs. AC while the dragonborn is bloodied.
Hit: 1d8 + 9 damage.

MINOR ACTIONS

↢ **Dragon Breath** (cold) ✦ **Encounter**

Attack: Close blast 3 (creatures in the blast); +8 vs. Reflex
Hit: 1d6 + 4 cold damage.

TRIGGERED ACTIONS

⭝ **Impetuous Spirit** (weapon) ✦ **At-Will**

Trigger: An enemy leaves a square adjacent to the dragonborn.
Effect (Immediate Interrupt): The dragonborn uses *longsword* against the triggering enemy.

⭝ **Martial Recovery** ✦ **Recharge** when the dragonborn uses *impetuous spirit*

Trigger: The dragonborn misses an enemy with *longsword*.
Effect (Free Action): The dragonborn uses *longsword* against the triggering enemy again.

Str 16 (+5)	**Dex** 15 (+4)	**Wis** 12 (+3)
Con 15 (+4)	**Int** 11 (+2)	**Cha** 9 (+1)

Alignment unaligned   **Languages** Common, Draconic
Equipment scale armor, light shield, longsword

CHIPPY

DRAKE

Whether wild or domesticated, drakes are fierce and clever foes. They come in many shapes and sizes, and they sometimes serve as guards for those who have the patience and resilience to train them.

Drakes are reptilian beasts that have claws, fangs, and tails. They're similar to domesticated mammals but have a reputation for toughness and ferocity that few tame animals share. Although a guard drake might seem as threatening as a wolf, its disposition is more alien and unpredictable. People fear drakes because their appearance is reminiscent of dragons. A drake lunges at anything that threatens it or its master, and a drake never backs down from a fight.

"Most drakes aren't naturally vicious. Ferocious hunters, yes, but not mean. But it's hard to train a drake without also teaching it to be something far worse than it was in nature."

—Vadania, druid of the Harkenwood

Part of Civilization: Trappers collect drakes to sell or train, bringing the creatures into settlements. Drakes are more expensive than other domesticated beasts, but most buyers believe the drakes' ferocity and power merits the extra cost. Drakes usually appear in communities that border wilderness or in the camps of tribal humanoids such as goblins, orcs, lizardfolk, elves, and shifters. Only physically weak drakes, such as pseudodragons, serve as pets. Other drakes require more discipline and are best treated as pack animals or guardians.

Guard drakes, pseudodragons, and bloodseeker drakes are the most common types of drakes in humanoid communities. A guard drake lives up to its name by serving as a sentinel or an attack animal. A pseudodragon might be pampered as the pet of a wealthy noble or as the familiar of a spellcaster. One might also

Guard Drake	Level 2 Brute
Small natural beast (reptile)	XP 125

HP 48; Bloodied 24	Initiative +3
AC 15, Fortitude 15, Reflex 13, Will 12	Perception +7
Speed 6	

STANDARD ACTIONS

⊕ **Bite ✦ At-Will**
  Attack: Melee 1 (one creature); +7 vs. AC
  Hit: 1d10 + 3 damage, or 1d10 + 9 while the drake is within 2 squares of an ally.

Str 16 (+4)	Dex 15 (+3)	Wis 12 (+2)
Con 18 (+5)	Int 3 (−3)	Cha 12 (+2)
Alignment unaligned	**Languages** —	

Spitting Drake

Level 3 Artillery

Medium natural beast (reptile) — XP 150

HP 38; **Bloodied** 19
AC 17, **Fortitude** 14, **Reflex** 16, **Will** 14
Speed 7
Resist 10 acid

Initiative +5
Perception +3

STANDARD ACTIONS

⊕ **Bite** ✦ **At-Will**

Attack: Melee 1 (one creature); +8 vs. AC

Hit: 1d6 + 4 damage.

↗ **Caustic Spit** (acid) ✦ **At-Will**

Attack: Ranged 10 (one creature); +8 vs. Reflex

Hit: 2d6 + 4 acid damage.

Str 14 (+3)	Dex 18 (+5)	Wis 14 (+3)
Con 14 (+3)	Int 3 (-3)	Cha 12 (+2)

Alignment unaligned	**Languages** —

Pseudodragon

Level 3 Lurker

Small natural beast (reptile) — XP 150

HP 40; **Bloodied** 20
AC 17, **Fortitude** 14, **Reflex** 15, **Will** 14
Speed 4, fly 8 (hover)

Initiative +9
Perception +8

STANDARD ACTIONS

⊕ **Bite** ✦ **At-Will**

Attack: Melee 1 (one creature); +8 vs. AC

Hit: 1d8 + 4 damage.

Effect: The pseudodragon flies up to 4 squares. This movement does not provoke opportunity attacks.

⊕ **Sting** (poison) ✦ **At-Will**

Attack: Melee 1 (one creature that cannot see the pseudodragon); +6 vs. Fortitude

Hit: 1d8 + 4 damage, and ongoing 5 poison damage (save ends).

Invisibility (illusion) ✦ **Recharge** when the pseudodragon takes damage

Effect: The pseudodragon becomes invisible until it hits or misses with an attack.

Skills Insight +8, Stealth +10

Str 8 (+0)	Dex 18 (+5)	Wis 15 (+3)
Con 16 (+4)	Int 9 (+0)	Cha 17 (+4)

Alignment unaligned	**Languages** Common, Draconic

---

encounter a pseudodragon on the outskirts of a town, scavenging for scraps of food. A bloodseeker drake performs the task of a bloodhound. They are prized by trackers and lawbringers who use them to hunt down quarry.

Wild at Heart: The most powerful drakes are difficult to tame and rarely show up in captivity. These drakes live in dens and hunt in the surrounding regions. One example is the rage drake, which is violent and hostile to most creatures. A rage drake attacks any creature that intrudes in its lair or stumbles into its hunting grounds. Although a rage drake can be domesticated when raised from an early age, even then the creature is unstable and dangerous. Ambush drakes roam the plains, setting upon caravans, travelers, and sometimes small settlements. They lust for the taste of humanoid flesh and will gnaw on victims while the creatures are still conscious.

Bloodseeker Drake
Level 4 Soldier

Medium natural beast (reptile) — XP 175

HP 53; **Bloodied** 26   **Initiative** +7
AC 20, **Fortitude** 15, **Reflex** 17, **Will** 15   **Perception** +7
Speed 6

STANDARD ACTIONS

⊕ **Bite** ✦ At-Will

Attack: Melee 1 (one creature); +9 vs. AC

Hit: 1d10 + 5 damage, or 1d10 + 10 against a bloodied target.

TRIGGERED ACTIONS

↯ **Blood Frenzy** ✦ At-Will

Trigger: A bloodied enemy adjacent to the drake shifts.

Effect (Opportunity Action): The drake uses *bite* against the triggering enemy.

Str 13 (+3)	**Dex** 17 (+5)	**Wis** 10 (+2)
Con 13 (+3)	**Int** 2 (−2)	**Cha** 13 (+3)

Alignment unaligned   **Languages** —

Rage Drake
Level 5 Brute

Large natural beast (mount, reptile) — XP 200

HP 77; **Bloodied** 38   **Initiative** +3
AC 17, **Fortitude** 18, **Reflex** 15, **Will** 16   **Perception** +4
Speed 8

TRAITS

Raging Mount (mount)

While the drake is bloodied, its rider gains a +2 bonus to attack rolls and damage rolls with melee attacks.

STANDARD ACTIONS

⊕ **Bite** ✦ At-Will

Attack: Melee 1 (one creature); +10 vs. AC, or +12 vs. AC while the drake is bloodied

Hit: 2d10 + 5 damage, or 2d10 + 7 while the drake is bloodied.

↯ **Raking Charge** ✦ At-Will

Effect: The drake charges and makes the following attack twice against the target of its charge in place of a melee basic attack.

Attack: Melee 1 (one creature); +10 vs. AC, or +12 vs. AC while the drake is bloodied

Hit: 1d6 + 4 damage, or 1d6 + 6 while the drake is bloodied.

Str 19 (+6)	**Dex** 13 (+3)	**Wis** 14 (+4)
Con 17 (+5)	**Int** 3 (−2)	**Cha** 12 (+3)

Alignment unaligned   **Languages** —

Social Creatures: Drakes are social creatures that prefer the company of other drakes. Drakes form packs with their kin or submit to the dominance of a master they regard as the pack leader. Although a drake can't speak, it might attempt to communicate by growling, chirping, roaring, purring, or hissing. A more intelligent drake, such as a pseudodragon, can convey complex messages through sounds and movement. A lone drake might seek friendship from anyone who happens upon it. Although drakes desire companionship, none are truly loyal. If a drake grows too hungry, it might devour a packmate or its master.

(Top, left to right) rage drake, spitting drake, pseudodragon

Ambush Drake	Level 6 Skirmisher
Medium natural beast (reptile)	XP 250

HP 71; **Bloodied** 35	**Initiative** +7
AC 20, **Fortitude** 19, **Reflex** 18, **Will** 16	**Perception** +3
Speed 6, fly 4 (clumsy)	

STANDARD ACTIONS

⊕ **Claws** ✦ **At-Will**

Attack: Melee 1 (one creature); +11 vs. AC

Hit: 2d6 + 7 damage.

⸽ **Shifting Strike** ✦ **At-Will**

Attack: Melee 1 (one creature); +11 vs. AC

Hit: 2d6 + 7 damage.

Effect: The drake can shift 1 square before or after the attack.

MINOR ACTIONS

Ravenous ✦ **At-Will**

Requirement: The drake must be bloodied.

Effect: The drake shifts up to 2 squares to a square closer to a bloodied enemy.

Skills Stealth +10		
Str 16 (+6)	**Dex** 14 (+5)	**Wis** 11 (+3)
Con 15 (+5)	**Int** 3 (–1)	**Cha** 6 (+1)
Alignment unaligned	**Languages** –	

DRIDER

Foul creatures of the Underdark, driders are half drow and half spider. They are devoted servants of the dark goddess Lolth, who elevated them from drow and gave them new physical forms to resemble her own.

Driders have the torso and upper body of a drow, and many retain their drow traits, such as the power to create clouds of darkness and to outline their foes in fire. A drider's lower body is that of a massive spider, giving the creature the ability to climb walls and spin webs. A drow warrior considers the presence of a drider to be a good omen. Most warriors believe that becoming a drider is the pinnacle of one's life. The transformation into a drider infuses a warrior with a bloodthirsty and savage nature, leading it to be even more violent and pitiless than drow already are.

Champions of the Drow: Among the drow, driders are highly honored and have their own social caste outside drow society. They are both respected and feared; drow view them as manifestations of Lolth's will that function as champions, spies, and assassins. Before its transformation, a drider is already a powerful warrior who has proved fearless and deadly in battle. A renowned drow warrior might disappear one day, to emerge the next as a drider. Despite the driders' near-mythical status within drow society, all these creatures remain beholden to

ANNE STOKES

Drider   Level 14 Soldier

Large fey humanoid (spider), drow   XP 1,000

HP 138; Bloodied 69	Initiative +13
AC 30, Fortitude 27, Reflex 25, Will 26	Perception +7
Speed 8, climb 8 (spider climb)	Darkvision

TRAITS

Threatening Reach

The drider can make opportunity attacks against all enemies within 2 squares of it.

STANDARD ACTIONS

⊕ **Scimitar** (weapon) ✦ **At-Will**

Attack: Melee 2 (one creature); +19 vs. AC

Hit: 3d8 + 9 damage.

Effect: The drider marks the target until the end of the drider's next turn.

MINOR ACTIONS

↗ **Darkfire** ✦ **Encounter**

Attack: Ranged 10 (one creature); +17 vs. Reflex

Hit: The target grants combat advantage and cannot benefit from invisibility or concealment until the end of the drider's next turn.

TRIGGERED ACTIONS

Servant's Rebuke (necrotic, poison) ✦ **At-Will**

Trigger: An enemy marked by the drider shifts or makes an attack that doesn't include it as a target.

Effect (Opportunity Action): Close burst 10 (triggering enemy in the burst). The target takes 15 necrotic and poison damage.

Skills Stealth +16		
Str 23 (+13)	Dex 18 (+11)	Wis 11 (+7)
Con 18 (+11)	Int 8 (+6)	Cha 20 (+12)
Alignment evil	**Languages** Elven	
Equipment leather armor, scimitar		

priestesses of Lolth. Many driders chafe at the control the priestesses exert, but none yet have had the power and the following to defy them.

Spider Affinity: Driders have an affinity for spiders, as evidenced by their half-spider bodies. This affinity goes beyond physical similarity, though. Some driders can communicate with spiders through a kind of telepathy, and they might use spiders as spies, scouts, or combat troops. Many driders feel at home more among spiders than among drow. A drider might become a recluse that lives in the caves outside a drow city, emerging only at the command of Lolth's priestesses. A drider's lair consists of narrow tunnels, each barely wide enough for the drider to squeeze through. The webs of thousands of spiders fill these tunnels. A drider relies on the spiders to incapacitate prey or to alert it of intruders. Although most spiders lack the intelligence to perform complex tasks, driders who have mastered arcane magic can summon intelligent spiders from other planes, such as the Demonweb Pits, the layer of the Abyss where Lolth dwells.

Drider Shadowspinner   Level 14 Skirmisher

Large fey humanoid (spider), drow   XP 1,000

HP 134; **Bloodied** 67   **Initiative** +12
AC 28, **Fortitude** 24, **Reflex** 27, **Will** 26   **Perception** +14
Speed 8, climb 8 (spider climb)   Darkvision

TRAITS

Combat Advantage (necrotic)

The drider deals 2d6 extra necrotic damage against any target granting combat advantage to it.

Shifting Shadows

If the drider ends a move on its turn at least 3 squares from where it started the move, it gains partial concealment until the end of its next turn.

STANDARD ACTIONS

⊕ **Short Sword** (necrotic, weapon) ✦ **At-Will**

Attack: Melee 1 (one creature); +19 vs. AC

Hit: 3d8 + 9 necrotic damage, and the drider ends any mark on it and can shift 1 square.

⤢ **Slashing Darkness** (necrotic) ✦ **At-Will**

Attack: Ranged 5 (one creature); +17 vs. Reflex

Hit: 3d8 + 7 necrotic damage.

⤢ **Web** ✦ **Recharge** ⚁ ⚃ ⚅

Attack: Ranged 5 (one creature); +17 vs. Reflex

Hit: The target is restrained until it escapes (DC 21) or teleports.

MINOR ACTIONS

⤢ **Cloud of Darkness** (zone) ✦ **Encounter**

Effect: Close burst 1. The burst creates a zone that lasts until the end of the drider's next turn. The cloud blocks line of sight for all creatures except the drider. Any creature other than the drider is blinded while entirely within the cloud.

⤢ **Darkfire** ✦ **Encounter**

Attack: Ranged 10 (one creature); +17 vs. Reflex

Hit: The target grants combat advantage and cannot benefit from invisibility or concealment until the end of the drider's next turn.

Skills Dungeoneering +14, Stealth +15

Str 13 (+8)	**Dex** 17 (+10)	**Wis** 14 (+9)
Con 14 (+9)	**Int** 12 (+8)	**Cha** 17 (+10)

Alignment evil   **Languages** Elven

Equipment leather armor, short sword

"Cursed? I'm afraid not. In this form, I wield more power than I could have imagined before the Test. As you shall soon see, Lolth has blessed me richly."

—Azarax, drider of Erelhei-Cinlu

Drider Fanglord
Large fey humanoid (spider), drow

Level 14 Brute
XP 1,000

HP 172; **Bloodied** 86
AC 26, **Fortitude** 27, **Reflex** 25, **Will** 23
Speed 8, climb 8 (spider climb)

Initiative +12
Perception +15
Darkvision

STANDARD ACTIONS

⊕ **Greatsword** (weapon) ✦ **At-Will**
Attack: Melee 1 (one creature); +19 vs. AC
Hit: 3d12 + 8 damage.

⌇ **Web** ✦ **Recharge** ⚅ ⚄ ⚃
Attack: Ranged 5 (one creature); +17 vs. Reflex
Hit: The target is restrained until it escapes (DC 21) or teleports.

MINOR ACTIONS

✦ **Quick Bite** (poison) ✦ **At-Will**
Attack: Melee 1 (one creature granting combat advantage to the drider); +17 vs. Reflex
Hit: 1d4 damage, and ongoing 10 poison damage (save ends).

⌇ **Darkfire** ✦ **Encounter**
Attack: Ranged 10 (one creature); +17 vs. Reflex
Hit: The target grants combat advantage and cannot benefit from invisibility or concealment until the end of the drider's next turn.

Skills Dungeoneering +15, Stealth +17

Str 24 (+14)	**Dex** 21 (+12)	**Wis** 16 (+10)
Con 22 (+13)	**Int** 13 (+8)	**Cha** 9 (+6)

Alignment evil **Languages** Elven
Equipment leather armor, greatsword

The Test of Lolth: After a drow warrior has proven himself or herself to possess exemplary prowess and bravery, a priestess of Lolth allows the warrior to undertake the Test of Lolth—a grueling and painful magical ritual that transforms the drow into a drider. Many drow don't survive this process, succumbing to the mental or physical torment. The details of the Test of Lolth are carefully guarded by the priestesses. Although a renegade drow might, on occasion, attempt to steal or record the secrets of the ritual, no one has yet managed to survive the wrath of the priestesses. Many factions within drow society covet the knowledge of this test. They hope to unlock its secrets and, in doing so, gain the ability to create legions of drider warriors that could upset the balance of power and break the priestesses' control. For their part, driders have little to say about the test, preferring to keep its secret so that they continue to be rare and honored within drow culture.

DRYAD

Normally shy and reclusive, dryads live in out-of-the-way, untouched forests, appearing only when intruders from civilization threaten their homes. When that happens, these temperamental creatures lash out with primal magic and the strength of oaks.

As unpredictable and inscrutable as the weather, dryads live only in the wild and refuse to make homes in cities or other settlements. Even an eladrin city, which is entwined within trees, frightens or angers a dryad. Dryads prefer to live in dark, thickly forested areas. They can merge with great trees, and each dryad has one tree that it calls home. It's not always easy to identify a dryad's tree or grove, though. Some people say dryads' groves are darker than other nearby areas of the forest; others claim that the sky turns green when you near one of them.

"As beautiful and welcoming as a sunlit glade in high summer, as terrifying and deadly as a winter gale sweeping through a barren forest—that's a dryad. In the space of moments."
—Galados of Celduilon

A dryad is deeply protective of its home. A dryad will die fighting to protect the forest, though sometimes it is driven away by forces it cannot vanquish. Other times, a dryad awakens after a long, deep slumber to discover that its forest is being ravaged by lumbering. A

Dryad Recluse

Level 5 Lurker

Medium fey humanoid (plant) XP 200

HP 50; **Bloodied** 25	**Initiative** +10
AC 19, **Fortitude** 16, **Reflex** 18, **Will** 17	**Perception** +10
Speed 8 (forest walk)	

STANDARD ACTIONS

⊕ **Claw ✦ At-Will**

Attack: Melee 1 (one creature); +10 vs. AC

Hit: 2d6 + 6 damage.

⌁ **Sylvan Charm** (charm) **✦ At-Will**

Attack: Ranged 5 (one creature); +8 vs. Will

Hit: The dryad pulls the target up to 5 squares to a square adjacent to it. The target is charmed until it is no longer adjacent to the dryad or until the dryad uses this power again. A charmed creature is immobilized and can't attack the dryad. When an enemy's melee or ranged attack hits the dryad, it deals half damage to the dryad and half damage to the charmed creature. If the attacker is adjacent to the charmed creature, the charmed creature must make a melee basic attack (of the dryad's choice) against the enemy as a free action.

MOVE ACTIONS

Treestride (teleportation) **✦ At-Will**

Requirement: The dryad must be adjacent to a tree or a Large plant.

Effect: The dryad teleports up to 8 squares to a square adjacent to a tree or a Large plant. Any creature charmed by the dryad teleports with the dryad to a square adjacent to it.

MINOR ACTIONS

Deceptive Veil (illusion) **✦ At-Will**

Effect: The dryad disguises itself to appear as a Medium humanoid (usually a beautiful elf or eladrin) until it uses *deceptive veil* again or until it drops to 0 hit points. Other creatures can make a DC 27 Insight check to discern that the form is an illusion.

Str 12 (+3)	**Dex** 19 (+6)	**Wis** 16 (+5)
Con 14 (+4)	**Int** 12 (+3)	**Cha** 13 (+3)
Alignment unaligned	**Languages** Elven	

dryad that undergoes such trauma can become a heartless creature intent only on inflicting pain on any who trespass in its demesne.

Fey Magic: Dryads wield the ancient and unfathomable magic of the Feywild, which gives them power over plants and mortals alike. A dryad has the ability to influence the mind of its foe, luring the prey into a dangerous patch of flora or off a deadly precipice. Most dryads have some talent for illusion. Using its *deceptive veil,* a dryad can appear as an elf or an eladrin maiden who has hair like orange autumn leaves or green spring blossoms. Anyone who draws close to the veiled creature soon discovers that the dryad's disguised thorny claws are very real.

Fear and Allure: The dichotomy of nature—its capacity for both sublime beauty and violent destruction—echoes in the form of dryads. When calm and serene, or when masked by its *deceptive veil,* a dryad is a creature of beauty and grace. When angered, though, a dryad can be a deadly deceiver or a storm of claws. When one townsperson recounts seeing a beautiful maiden in the forest and another describes being chased from the woods by a shrieking tree-creature, it is possible that the two describe the same dryad. A dryad's ability to both captivate and frighten has gained the creature a reputation throughout the land as being both a blessing and a curse.

Quick to Anger: Fey are often characterized as fickle creatures. A dryad, however, is better characterized as rash or impulsive. The smallest threat or slight can anger a dryad. When intruders approach a dryad's glade or grove, the creature uses any means to drive off or kill the trespassers. A dryad might provide misleading directions, lead the interlopers into traps, or misdirect them to the den of nearby monsters. Other dryads simply charge forward and attack, nourishing the tree roots with the blood of their victims. Once a dryad decides an intruder must die, nothing can dissuade it. Nonetheless, it's possible to reason with a dryad and prevent combat. Anyone who wants to speak with a dryad must approach a grove slowly and avoid harming the forest. Once they are confronted, those wishing to speak to the dryad must make their intentions clear. A dryad might accept offerings as a sign of good faith, including nature rituals or the saplings or seeds of rare trees.

Friends of the Wild: Dryads fight alongside other plant creatures and forest denizens. They share an innate bond with natural flora and fauna. A dryad can quickly learn about a disturbance in the forest, even one that occurred many miles away. A dryad sometimes fights alongside eladrin or other civilized races, but only when it believes a danger to the forest merits such an allegiance. Although most dryads are solitary creatures, they exhibit great unity in times of war. If a group of dryads is aiding in a battle, it might leave if even one of the group finds the actions of its civilized allies to be offensive.

Dryad Hunter	Level 7 Skirmisher
Medium fey humanoid (plant)	XP 300

HP 82; **Bloodied** 41	**Initiative** +9
AC 21, **Fortitude** 20, **Reflex** 20, **Will** 18	**Perception** +10
Speed 8 (forest walk)	

STANDARD ACTIONS

⊕ **Claw** ✦ At-Will
  Attack: Melee 1 (one creature); +12 vs. AC
  Hit: 2d8 + 6 damage, or 3d8 + 8 if no other enemy is adjacent to the dryad.

⊦ **Luring Feint** ✦ At-Will
  Effect: The dryad uses *claw*. If the attack hits, the dryad shifts up to 4 squares, pulling the target with it. If the attack misses, the dryad shifts up to its speed.

MOVE ACTIONS

Treestride (teleportation) ✦ At-Will
  Requirement: The dryad must be adjacent to a tree or a Large plant.
  Effect: The dryad teleports up to 8 squares to a square adjacent to a tree or a Large plant.

MINOR ACTIONS

Deceptive Veil (illusion) ✦ At-Will
  Effect: The dryad disguises itself to appear as a Medium humanoid (usually a beautiful elf or eladrin) until it uses *deceptive veil* again or until it drops to 0 hit points. Other creatures can make a DC 28 Insight check to discern that the form is an illusion.

Str 16 (+6)	**Dex** 18 (+7)	**Wis** 15 (+5)
Con 18 (+7)	**Int** 10 (+3)	**Cha** 13 (+4)
Alignment unaligned	**Languages** Elven	

Dryad Witch
Level 8 Controller

Medium fey humanoid (plant)

XP 350

HP 84; **Bloodied** 42
AC 22, **Fortitude** 18, **Reflex** 20, **Will** 22
Speed 8 (forest walk)

Initiative +7
Perception +14

STANDARD ACTIONS

⊕ **Thorny Vine** ✦ **At-Will**

Attack: Melee 2 (one creature); +13 vs. AC

Hit: 2d8 + 7 damage.

Effect: The dryad can slide the target 1 square.

↭ **Beguiling Verdure** (charm) ✦ **At-Will**

Attack: Ranged 5 (one dazed creature); +11 vs. Will

Hit: The dryad slides the target up to the target's speed, and the target must then make a basic attack as a free action against a creature of the dryad's choice.

↞ **Soporific Fragrance** (charm) ✦ **Recharge** ⚃ ⚄ ⚅

Attack: Close blast 3 (enemies in the blast); +11 vs. Will

Hit: The target is dazed (save ends).

MOVE ACTIONS

Treestride (teleportation) ✦ **At-Will**

Requirement: The dryad must be adjacent to a tree or a Large plant.

Effect: The dryad teleports up to 8 squares to a square adjacent to a tree or a Large plant.

MINOR ACTIONS

Deceptive Veil (illusion) ✦ **At-Will**

Effect: The dryad disguises itself to appear as a Medium humanoid (usually a beautiful elf or eladrin) until it uses *deceptive veil* again or until it drops to 0 hit points. Other creatures can make a DC 29 Insight check to discern that the form is an illusion.

Str 11 (+4)	**Dex** 17 (+7)	**Wis** 20 (+9)
Con 12 (+5)	**Int** 12 (+5)	**Cha** 16 (+7)

Alignment unaligned **Languages** Elven

Bough Dryad
Level 15 Minion Skirmisher

Medium fey humanoid (plant)

XP 300

HP 1; a missed attack never damages a minion.
AC 29, **Fortitude** 28, **Reflex** 28, **Will** 26
Speed 8 (forest walk)

Initiative +16
Perception +17

STANDARD ACTIONS

⊕ **Claw** ✦ **At-Will**

Attack: Melee 1 (one creature); +20 vs. AC

Hit: 11 damage, or 13 if no other enemy is adjacent to the dryad.

TRIGGERED ACTIONS

Boon of Life

Trigger: The dryad drops to 0 hit points.

Effect (No Action): Close burst 5 (one ally in the burst). The target gains 5 temporary hit points.

Str 21 (+12)	**Dex** 24 (+14)	**Wis** 21 (+12)
Con 24 (+14)	**Int** 11 (+7)	**Cha** 17 (+10)

Alignment unaligned **Languages** Elven

DUERGAR

The duergar are slavers that dwell in volcanic regions of the Underdark. They were once the thralls of mind flayers, but they turned to devils to help escape from bondage. Now, they acquire their own slaves by making raids into the surface world.

The dwarves that suffered generations of servitude under the brutal mind flayers became duergar after they turned to the devils to help them gain their freedom. Believing that Moradin had abandoned them, the dwarves swore dark oaths to the powers of the Nine Hells, who were only too happy to offer aid in exchange for loyalty.

Built on the Backs of Slaves: Duergar have a well-earned reputation as slavers. They rarely perform exhausting or risky tasks, relying instead on the work of slaves. A duergar recognizes the value of slaves, though, rarely tasking them with jobs that are deadly or unlikely to yield a high reward. Most duergar slavers capture only those who exhibit physical prowess or exceptional skill. A duergar has no interest in enslaving the young, the sick, or the elderly; such individuals are often left dead as a result of duergar raids.

Duergar Scout	Level 4 Lurker
Medium natural humanoid, dwarf	XP 175

HP 48; **Bloodied** 24	**Initiative** +8
AC 18, **Fortitude** 18, **Reflex** 16, **Will** 16	**Perception** +9
Speed 5	Darkvision
Resist 5 fire, 5 poison	

TRAITS

Shadow Attack
  The duergar scout's attacks deal 4d6 extra damage when the scout hits a target that cannot see it.

STANDARD ACTIONS

⊕ **Warhammer** (weapon) ✦ At-Will
  Attack: Melee 1 (one creature); +9 vs. AC
  Hit: 1d10 + 4 damage.

⊙ **Crossbow** (weapon) ✦ At-Will
  Attack: Ranged 20 (one creature); +9 vs. AC
  Hit: 1d8 + 5 damage.

Underdark Sneak ✦ At-Will
  Effect: The scout becomes invisible until the end of its next turn or until it hits or misses with an attack.

MINOR ACTIONS

⊙ **Infernal Quills** (poison) ✦ Encounter
  Attack: Ranged 3 (one creature); +9 vs. AC
  Hit: 1d8 + 4 damage, and the target takes a -2 penalty to attack rolls and ongoing 5 poison damage (save ends both).

Skills Dungeoneering +9, Stealth +9		
Str 13 (+3)	**Dex** 15 (+4)	**Wis** 14 (+4)
Con 18 (+6)	**Int** 10 (+2)	**Cha** 8 (+1
Alignment evil	**Languages** Common, Deep Speech, Dwarven	
Equipment chainmail, warhammer, crossbow		

Duergar Guard — Level 4 Soldier
Medium natural humanoid — XP 175

HP 58; **Bloodied** 29
AC 20, **Fortitude** 17, **Reflex** 15, **Will** 15
Speed 5
Resist 5 fire, 5 poison

Initiative +6
Perception +4
Darkvision

STANDARD ACTIONS

⊕ **Warhammer** (weapon) ✦ At-Will
Attack: Melee 1 (one creature); +9 vs. AC
Hit: 1d10 + 6 damage.
Effect: The duergar guard marks the target until the end of the target's next turn.

MINOR ACTIONS

Infernal Anger (fire) ✦ Recharge ⚄ ⚅
Effect: Until the start of the guard's next turn, its melee attacks deal 4 extra fire damage, and if an enemy adjacent to the guard moves, the guard can shift 1 square as an immediate reaction.

⊙ **Infernal Quills** (poison) ✦ Encounter
Attack: Ranged 3 (one creature); +9 vs. AC
Hit: 1d8 + 3 damage, and the target takes a -2 penalty to attack rolls and ongoing 5 poison damage (save ends both).

Skills Dungeoneering +9
Str 14 (+4)   **Dex** 15 (+4)   **Wis** 15 (+4)
Con 18 (+6)   **Int** 10 (+2)   **Cha** 8 (+1)
Alignment evil   **Languages** Common, Deep Speech, Dwarven
Equipment chainmail, warhammer

(Left to right) duergar scout, guard, and infernal consort

EVA WIDERMANN

Duergar Thug · Level 4 Minion Brute
Medium natural humanoid   XP 44

HP 1; a missed attack never damages a minion. | **Initiative** +4
AC 16, **Fortitude** 17, **Reflex** 15, **Will** 14 | **Perception** +4
Speed 5 | Darkvision
Resist 5 fire, 5 poison

STANDARD ACTIONS

⊕ **Warhammer** (weapon) ✦ **At-Will**
Attack: Melee 1 (one creature); +9 vs. AC
Hit: 8 damage.

MINOR ACTIONS

⊙ **Infernal Quills** (poison) ✦ **Encounter**
Attack: Ranged 3 (one creature); +9 vs. AC
Hit: 6 damage, and ongoing 2 poison damage (save ends).

| **Str** 14 (+4) | **Dex** 15 (+4) | **Wis** 15 (+4) |
| **Con** 18 (+6) | **Int** 10 (+2) | **Cha** 8 (+1) |

Alignment evil **Languages** Common, Deep Speech, Dwarven
Equipment chainmail, warhammer

Duergar Raid Leader · Level 5 Artillery (Leader)
Medium natural humanoid   XP 200

HP 51; **Bloodied** 25 | **Initiative** +3
AC 19, **Fortitude** 17, **Reflex** 19, **Will** 15 | **Perception** +4
Speed 5 | Darkvision
Resist 5 fire, 5 poison

STANDARD ACTIONS

⊕ **Warhammer** (weapon) ✦ **At-Will**
Attack: Melee 1 (one creature); +10 vs. AC
Hit: 1d10 + 5 damage.

⊙ **Crossbow** (weapon) ✦ **At-Will**
Attack: Ranged 20 (one creature); +12 vs. AC
Hit: 1d8 + 8 damage.

Raid Leader's Command ✦ **At-Will**
Effect: Ranged 5 (one ally). The target can make a basic attack as a free action.

MINOR ACTIONS

⊙ **Infernal Quills** (poison) ✦ **Encounter**
Attack: Ranged 3 (one creature); +12 vs. AC
Hit: 1d8 + 4 damage, and the target takes a -2 penalty to attack rolls and ongoing 5 poison damage (save ends both).

Skills Dungeoneering +9

| **Str** 11 (+2) | **Dex** 13 (+3) | **Wis** 14 (+4) |
| **Con** 15 (+4) | **Int** 18 (+6) | **Cha** 8 (+1) |

Alignment evil **Languages** Common, Deep Speech, Dwarven
Equipment chainmail, warhammer, crossbow

Duergar Infernal Consort — **Level 17 Controller**
Medium natural humanoid — XP 1,600

HP 164; **Bloodied** 82 — **Initiative** +8
AC 31, **Fortitude** 30, **Reflex** 28, **Will** 30 — **Perception** +9
Speed 5 — Darkvision
Resist 10 fire, 10 poison

Standard Actions

Warhammer (weapon) ✦ **At-Will**
Attack: Melee 1 (one creature); +22 vs. AC
Hit: 3d10 + 9 damage, and the duerger infernal consort pushes the target up to 3 squares. The target is slowed until the end of the consort's next turn.

Devil Possession (charm, fire) ✦ **Recharge** ⚄ ⚅
Attack: Ranged 3 (one creature); +20 vs. Will
Hit: The target is dominated until the end of the consort's next turn. While the target is dominated, any ally of the target that ends its turn adjacent to the target takes 10 fire damage.
Effect: At the start of the target's next turn, the consort slides the target up to 3 squares as a free action.

Infernal Summons (fire, zone) ✦ **At-Will**
Attack: Area burst 1 within 5 (creatures in the burst); +20 vs. Reflex
Hit: 4d6 + 6 fire damage.
Effect: The burst creates a zone of difficult terrain that lasts until the start of the consort's next turn. Any creature that enters the zone or ends its turn there takes 10 fire damage.

Minor Actions

Infernal Quills (poison) ✦ **Encounter**
Attack: Ranged 3 (one creature); +22 vs. AC
Hit: 2d8 + 6 damage, and the target takes a -2 penalty to attack rolls and ongoing 10 poison damage (save ends both).

Skills Dungeoneering +17, Religion +17

Str 11 (+8)	**Dex** 10 (+8)	**Wis** 13 (+9)
Con 20 (+13)	**Int** 19 (+12)	**Cha** 21 (+13)

Alignment evil — **Languages** Common, Deep Speech, Dwarven
Equipment leather armor, warhammer

A duergar retains a vestige of its dwarven heritage. Other Underdark denizens often call upon duergar to build keeps, castles, and other structures of stone. A duergar also employs its slaves to mine valuable substances, such as gold, platinum, and gems. Usually, a large number of slaves are overseen by a small number of duergar taskmasters. When the slaves are not working, they are treated like prisoners. A duergar keeps its slaves in defensible structures, discouraging outsiders from attempting to rescue them.

Consorting with Devils: The duergar embrace their mutually beneficial agreement with the infernal forces. Many of the fortresslike cities that duergar inhabit have places that serve as embassies for devils. Throughout these cities, devils travel openly in the streets. Humanoid devils, particularly succubi, are the most common visitors. Sometimes a powerful devil ascends to power in a duergar settlement, taking an active hand in the compact with its residents and granting boons in exchange for service.

Devil-Bred Duergar	Level 18 Minion Soldier
Medium natural humanoid	XP 500

HP 1; a missed attack never damages a minion.   **Initiative** +13
AC 34, **Fortitude** 32, **Reflex** 28, **Will** 30   **Perception** +11
Speed 5   Darkvision

STANDARD ACTIONS

⊕ **Warhammer** (weapon) ✦ **At-Will**
   Attack: Melee 1 (one creature); +23 vs. AC
   Hit: 13 damage.

TRIGGERED ACTIONS

Punishing Hammer (fire, weapon) ✦ **At-Will**
   Trigger: An enemy adjacent to the duergar makes an attack that doesn't include it as a target.
   Attack (Opportunity Action): Melee 1 (triggering enemy); +23 vs. AC
   Hit: 13 fire damage.

Str 20 (+14)	**Dex** 14 (+11)	**Wis** 14 (+11)
Con 22 (+15)	**Int** 10 (+9)	**Cha** 8 (+8)
Alignment evil	**Languages** Common, Deep Speech, Dwarven	
Equipment chainmail, warhammer		

A duergar outpost near the surface might host a significant tiefling population. A tiefling who embraces his or her infernal heritage often allies with duergar, who use the tiefling as an agent on the surface. A tiefling might become a member of a surface settlement, identifying choice victims for duergar slavers.

Surface Raiders: A duergar that lives in an outpost near the surface tends to actively raid settlements. Duergar are commonly sighted in borderland regions, where few patrols or militias can stand up to their attacks. A duergar living near the surface usually sells its slaves to markets in the Underdark or trades the slaves to duergar living deeper underground, where the slaves are more useful. A duergar slaver often learns the traditions and routines of surface-dwellers, putting those lessons to practice in its raiding techniques. A duergar raider might wait until fall harvest to attack, taking advantage of the large number of isolated, able-bodied workers in the fields.

Fortresses of the Deep: Deep-dwelling duergar make their homes in highly defensible areas of the Underdark, such as on islands in the middle of underground seas, in caverns surrounded by moats of lava, or on the edges of deep chasms. Duergar are typically slow to trust outsiders; an endorsement from a powerful devil is one of the few ways to gain the trust of a duergar. Duergar are always wary of attacks from mind flayers, aboleths, and other creatures that threaten to enslave them once again. Squads of a half-dozen or more soldiers patrol duergar strongholds, sometimes accompanied by devils or by duergar that have the psychic talent to detect mind flayers or aboleths. Duergar might seem defensive or cautious, but they quickly take advantage of their enemies' weaknesses, whether in combat or in social encounters.

Duergar Underlord   Level 20 Elite Skirmisher (Leader)

Medium natural humanoid   XP 5,600

HP 364; **Bloodied** 182   **Initiative** +20
AC 34, **Fortitude** 32, **Reflex** 33, **Will** 31   **Perception** +15
Speed 7   Darkvision
Resist 10 fire, 10 poison
Saving Throws +2; **Action Points** 1

Traits

Infernal Animation (healing)

  While the duergar underlord is conscious, whenever it starts its turn and no allies within 20 squares of it have at least 1 hit point, one ally within 20 squares returns to life with 1 hit point and can stand up as a free action. The ally acts immediately after the underlord's turn. The ally automatically drops to 0 hit points at the end of the encounter.

Standard Actions

⊕ **Warhammer** (weapon) ✦ **At-Will**

  Attack: Melee 1 (one creature); +25 vs. AC

  Hit: 3d10 + 12 damage.

  Effect: Any marking effects on the underlord end, and it shifts up to 3 squares.

⨎ **Battlecrazed Frenzy** (weapon) ✦ **Recharge** ⸬ ⸬

  Attack: Melee 1 (one creature); +25 vs. AC

  Hit: 3d10 + 12 damage, and the underlord shifts up to 2 squares and repeats this attack against an enemy it has not yet attacked during this turn.

Minor Actions

⊛ **Infernal Quills** (poison) ✦ **Encounter**

  Attack: Ranged 3 (one creature); +25 vs. AC

  Hit: 3d10 + 5 damage, and the target takes a -2 penalty to attack rolls and ongoing 10 poison damage (save ends both).

Underlord's Command ✦ **At-Will** (1/round)

  Effect: Close burst 10 (one ally in the burst). The target can use a free action to shift up to 3 squares and make a basic attack.

Skills Dungeoneering +20

Str 22 (+16)	**Dex** 26 (+18)	**Wis** 20 (+15)
Con 14 (+12)	**Int** 14 (+12)	**Cha** 16 (+13)

Alignment evil   **Languages** Common, Deep Speech, Dwarven
Equipment chainmail, warhammer

"Don't call them dwarves. They're not, not any more than a succubus is a human. They're fiends through and through, and don't ever forget it."

—Boldrik of Hammerfast

DWARF

The industrious and honorable dwarves carve kingdoms from the mountains, creating glimmering points of light in the darkness of the world. Their realms are strong and vast, though not all are welcoming of outsiders.

A dwarf lives for the ring of the smith's hammer and the chink of a chisel on stone. A dwarf exults in the gush of ale and the clink of coins. A dwarf speaks solemn oaths and bellows great battle cries. To the din of these sounds, dwarves live and work.

Masters of Mountains: Long ago, with the aid of their god Moradin, dwarves freed themselves from the dominion of the giants. Today, dwarven citadels guard mountain passes against giants and other denizens of the wilderness. These outposts are important waypoints for trade and travel; they allow dwarves to import simple products and export fine goods, such as weapons, armor, sculptures, and ales.

Sworn to the Clan: A dwarf tends to practice his or her clan's traditions wherever he or she might dwell. A dwarf living in a human city might forge armor, operate a tavern or brewery, or become a soldier. A dwarf warrior might shed blood alongside members of another humanoid race, so long as those people never make enemies of that dwarf's clan.

Dwarf Warrior	Level 1 Minion Artillery
Medium natural humanoid	XP 25

HP 1; a missed attack never damages a minion.	Initiative +3
AC 15, Fortitude 14, Reflex 12, Will 14	Perception +2
Speed 5	Low-light vision

TRAITS

Dwarf Solidarity
The dwarf gains a +4 bonus to AC and Reflex while adjacent to a dwarf ally.

Stand the Ground
The dwarf can move 1 square fewer than the effect specifies when subjected to a pull, a push, or a slide.

Steady-Footed
The dwarf can make a saving throw to avoid falling prone when an attack would knock it prone.

STANDARD ACTIONS

⊕ **Warhammer** (weapon) ✦ At-Will
Attack: Melee 1 (one creature); +6 vs. AC
Hit: 4 damage, or 6 while the dwarf is adjacent to a dwarf ally.

⊗ **Crossbow** (weapon) ✦ At-Will
Attack: Ranged 30 (one creature); +8 vs. AC
Hit: 4 damage, or 6 against a target that doesn't have cover.

Str 13 (+1)	Dex 16 (+3)	Wis 15 (+2)
Con 15 (+2)	Int 10 (+0)	Cha 10 (+0)

Alignment unaligned   **Languages** Common, Dwarven
Equipment chainmail, warhammer, crossbow, 20 bolts

Dwarf Clan Guard
Medium natural humanoid

Level 1 Soldier
XP 100

HP 33; **Bloodied** 16
AC 17, **Fortitude** 15, **Reflex** 13, **Will** 15
Speed 5

Initiative +3
Perception +8
Low-light vision

TRAITS

Stand the Ground
The dwarf can move 1 square fewer than the effect specifies when subjected to a pull, a push, or a slide.

Steady-Footed
The dwarf can make a saving throw to avoid falling prone when an attack would knock it prone.

STANDARD ACTIONS

(+) **Warhammer** (weapon) ✦ At-Will
Attack: Melee 1 (one creature); +6 vs. AC
Hit: 1d10 + 3 damage, and the dwarf can push the target 1 square. The dwarf can then shift 1 square to a square the target vacated.
Effect: The dwarf marks the target until the end of the dwarf's next turn.

↗ **Throwing Hammer** (weapon) ✦ At-Will
Attack: Ranged 10 (one creature); +6 vs. AC
Hit: 1d6 + 4 damage, and the dwarf marks the target until the end of the dwarf's next turn.

✝↗ **Double Hammer Strike** (weapon) ✦ Recharge ⚄ ⚅ ⚃
Effect: The dwarf uses *warhammer* and then uses *throwing hammer*. The dwarf does not provoke opportunity attacks for this use of *throwing hammer*.

Str 16 (+3)	**Dex** 12 (+1)	**Wis** 17 (+3)
Con 17 (+3)	**Int** 10 (+0)	**Cha** 10 (+0)

Alignment unaligned   **Languages** Common, Dwarven
Equipment plate armor, heavy shield, warhammer, 4 throwing hammers

(Left to right) dwarf clan guard, dwarf warrior

EFREET

These burning elemental lords enslave weaker humanoids, which they put to use in an effort to expand their dominion. Despite their tyrannical tendencies, efreets adhere to strict laws and customs, making their settlements rare havens of order within the Elemental Chaos.

Every efreet has a title—Glorious Sultan of the Eternal Fires, Caliph of the Burning Thunder, Pasha of the Gilded Flame, Maharaja of the Ruby Palace—and each has dozens of slaves. Efreets consider themselves the nobility of the Elemental Chaos. Their intellect and ambition have helped them to amass great wealth and to create great demesnes, where they can lord over mortals.

Fiery Potentates: Efreets are the self-proclaimed princes of the Elemental Chaos, and they are the strongest force of order in the tumultuous plane. Efreets believe they are the firstborn of the primordials and thus inheritors of the Elemental Chaos and creation. Despite this claim, an efreet exhibits scant loyalty to its progenitors. An efreet rarely worships a higher being, and it owes fealty only to the Lord of the Efreets, who accepts no master and honors only himself. Although few in number, efreets rule over vast numbers of slaves and soldiers, many of whom are loyal unto death. Many creatures of the Elemental Chaos see service to an efreet as a great honor, even when such bondage includes punishment.

There are no "efreet commoners." Every efreet belongs to a noble house. These houses ruthlessly plot and scheme against each other, and from time to time they muster enormous armies to battle one another. A house might contain only

(Left to right) efreet flamestrider, efreet fireblade, and efreet cinderlord

Efreet Fireblade
Large elemental humanoid (fire)

Level 22 Soldier
XP 4,150

HP 206; **Bloodied** 103
AC 38, **Fortitude** 36, **Reflex** 35, **Will** 33
Speed 6, fly 8 (hover)
Immune fire

Initiative +19
Perception +18

TRAITS

✧ Blazing Soul (fire) ✦ **Aura** 1
Any enemy that takes ongoing fire damage while in the aura takes 5 extra fire damage.

Frozen Fire
Whenever the efreet takes cold damage, it is slowed until the end of its next turn.

STANDARD ACTIONS

⊕ Scimitar (weapon) ✦ **At-Will**
Attack: Melee 2 (one creature); +27 vs. AC
Hit: 3d10 + 14 damage.
Effect: The efreet marks the target until the end of the efreet's next turn.

⤳ Flying Scimitar (weapon) ✦ **Recharge** ⚄ ⚅
Attack: Ranged 20 (one creature or two creatures within 5 squares of each other); +27 vs. AC
Hit: 3d10 + 14 damage.
Effect: The efreet marks each target until the end of the efreet's next turn.

⬅ Whirling Firesteel Strike (fire, weapon) ✦ **Recharge** ⚄ ⚅
Attack: Close burst 2 (enemies in the burst); +27 vs. AC
Hit: 3d10 + 14 damage, and ongoing 10 fire damage (save ends).

Skills Bluff +20, Insight +18

Str 24 (+18)	Dex 22 (+17)	Wis 15 (+13)
Con 22 (+17)	Int 18 (+15)	Cha 18 (+15)

Alignment evil **Languages** Primordial
Equipment scimitar

---

a small number of efreets, but through power and intimidation, those house members preside over many other elementals. Their control is not limited to fire creatures; the most cunning and powerful efreets keep creatures of many kinds. On rare occasions, an efreet might bind a demon to servitude. An efreet is shrewd enough not to rely too much on such bound servants, though.

Masters Who Hate Slavery: As creatures of nobility and self-importance, efreets fear and loathe servitude to others. Sometimes when two efreet houses clash, the losing side must surrender a junior member of its house to the victor for a certain amount of time. This loss is far more humiliating and punishing than lost goods or slain soldiers. An efreet considers being bound to serve a mortal the worst form of punishment. It burns with resentment against its erstwhile master, hoping for an opportunity to exact vengeance.

Citadels of Fire and Gold: Efreets use enslaved creatures and spellcasters to craft stunning citadels of metal and flames. These citadels become beacons of stability and trade in the wild and ever-changing furor of the plane. The greatest jewel among these fortresses is the glittering City of Brass, the seat of the efreets' power. Unchanging and eternal, the City of Brass occupies a permanent place in the roiling chaos, and it is there that the Lord of the Efreets rules with absolute authority.

Efreet Cinderlord — Level 23 Artillery

Large elemental humanoid (fire) — XP 5,100

HP 169; **Bloodied** 84 — **Initiative** +19
AC 37, **Fortitude** 34, **Reflex** 35, **Will** 33 — **Perception** +15
Speed 6, fly 8 (hover)
Immune fire

TRAITS

☼ Blazing Soul (fire) ✦ Aura 1

Any enemy in the aura that takes ongoing fire damage takes 5 extra fire damage.

Frozen Fire

Whenever the efreet takes cold damage, it is slowed until the end of its next turn.

STANDARD ACTIONS

⊕ Scimitar (fire, weapon) ✦ At-Will

Attack: Melee 2 (one creature); +28 vs. AC

Hit: 2d10 + 7 damage, and ongoing 5 fire damage (save ends).

⟶ Fire Bolt (fire) ✦ At-Will

Attack: Ranged 10 (one creature); +28 vs. Reflex

Hit: 3d6 + 10 damage, and ongoing 10 fire damage (save ends).

✳ Fan the Flames (fire) ✦ At-Will

Effect: Close burst 20 (one creature taking ongoing fire damage). The target takes 2d6 + 7 fire damage, and the efreet makes the following attack centered on the target.

Attack: Area burst 1 within 20 (creatures in the burst); +28 vs. Reflex

Hit: 2d6 + 7 fire damage.

⟶ Curse of the Efreet (fire) ✦ Recharge when first bloodied

Attack: Ranged 10 (one creature); +30 vs. AC

Hit: 3d10 + 15 fire damage, and ongoing 15 fire damage (save ends). The target cannot benefit from fire resistance until the end of the encounter.

Miss: Half damage, and ongoing 5 fire damage (save ends).

Skills Bluff +22, Insight +20

Str 24 (+18)	Dex 27 (+19)	Wis 18 (+15)
Con 25 (+18)	Int 16 (+14)	Cha 22 (+17)

Alignment evil — **Languages** Primordial
Equipment scimitar

"At the point where an efreet offers to grant your wish, you're in real trouble. You can refuse, but you'll offend the efreet's strange sense of hospitality and maybe make a powerful enemy. Or you can accept, and watch everything you've ever dreamed of come within your grasp . . . and then crumble into ash."

—Obanar, guardian of Argent

Efreet Flamestrider — Level 23 Skirmisher
Large elemental humanoid (fire) — XP 5,100

HP 217; **Bloodied** 108
AC 37, **Fortitude** 36, **Reflex** 35, **Will** 34
Speed 6, fly 8 (hover)
Immune fire

Initiative +20
Perception +15

Traits

☼ **Blazing Soul** (fire) ✦ **Aura 1**
Any enemy in the aura that takes ongoing fire damage takes 5 extra fire damage.

Frozen Fire
Whenever the efreet takes cold damage, it is slowed and can teleport only 5 squares using *fire step* until the end of its next turn.

Standard Actions

⊕ **Quarterstaff** (fire, weapon) ✦ **At-Will**
Attack: Melee 2 (one creature); +28 vs. AC
Hit: 2d10 + 10 damage, and ongoing 10 fire damage (save ends).

⤢ **Fiery Grasp** (fire) ✦ **At-Will**
Attack: Ranged 5 (one creature); +26 vs. Reflex
Hit: 2d6 + 8 fire damage, and the target is immobilized and takes ongoing 10 fire damage (save ends both).

Move Actions

Fire Step (teleportation) ✦ **At-Will**
Effect: The efreet teleports up to 20 squares to a square adjacent to a fire or a fire creature.

Skills Bluff +22, Insight +20

Str 27 (+19)	**Dex** 24 (+18)	**Wis** 18 (+15)
Con 25 (+18)	**Int** 16 (+14)	**Cha** 22 (+17)

Alignment evil   **Languages** Primordial
Equipment chainmail, quarterstaff

Evil Excursions and Dire Diversions: An efreet house sometimes sponsors an excursion in which a few nobles of the house venture out of the Elemental Chaos into the world or another plane. They might hunt mortals or a dangerous creature for sport, bringing home any trophies to place in their house's mansion. Members of these hunting parties challenge each other to see who can take the most slaves or who can foist the best deception upon a mortal. An efreet might take advantage of the common misconception among mortals that it can grant wishes. Efreets in fact have no power to grant wishes, but they are not averse to bargaining with weaker mortals. An efreet released from servitude might grant its liberator a "wish," but sometimes the wish can have unforeseen consequences.

Efreets engage in battle or start wars of conquest for entertainment. An efreet might have a goal in mind and be infuriated by even the smallest failures, but ultimately its long life and its desire for pleasure give it reason to care little about the consequences of its actions. Disappointment is temporary, and an efreet feels assured it will get what it wants in the end.

ELEMENTAL

Chaotic creatures formed from the fundamental building blocks of creation, elementals have brief, capricious lives. They embody the untamed nature of the Elemental Chaos and act without logic.

A fragment of creation given form and sapience, an elemental is a being of air, earth, fire, or water. Like the plane that birthed them, elementals are untamed and unpredictable; they wreak havoc wherever they go. An elemental has only a vague physical form. It appears as a shard of raw elemental energy that threatens to break apart at any moment.

"They might be small and fairly weak, but make no mistake: They're the front line of an army that would tear the world apart given half a chance."

—Shemeshka the Marauder

(Left to right) water elemental, earth elemental, air elemental, fire elemental

WAYNE ENGLAND

The Elemental Chaos constantly creates more elementals. When such creatures collide, the results are predictable. Water elementals quench their fiery kin; fire elementals fuse with creatures of air to produce columns of spinning, roiling flame; earth elementals stand firm as their watery counterparts smash against their stony forms. Of course, all these interactions do not preclude elementals from unconsciously working together to tear apart a settlement or a trespasser.

Creatures of Destruction: With nothing to govern their actions, elementals act randomly, burning, tearing, or smashing whatever they come across. Some sages speculate that the Elemental Chaos spits out elemental creatures to serve as agents of entropy that revert creation back to its most basic form. The energy and destructive power of elementals is coveted by spellcasters who hope to harness it for their own purposes. Elementals are sometimes captured and bound into service, allowing a spellcaster to funnel their elemental energy into spells or devices. Attempts to control elementals often end in disaster when the binder loses control, allowing the elementals to run amok.

Invaders from the Elemental Chaos: An elemental that is not summoned might enter the world through a planar event in which the Elemental Chaos intrudes on the natural world. These events are often unpredictable and can result in catastrophic destruction. If a settlement is near the location of such an event, an elemental incursion could cost many lives and undo years of work. Fire elementals might burn the fields of farmers; water elementals could cause flooding along riverbanks; earth elementals might smash through walls and buildings; air elementals could tear off roofs or bring rockslides crashing down. If a region isn't equipped to put down a group of rogue elementals, it might destroy numerous villages until someone comes along to stop it.

Weapons of Primordial Power: Some scholars believe that elementals, belying their chaotic nature, act under the guidance of higher powers. These sages assert that the primordials, the undisputed masters of elemental power, use elementals as tools in the world because they are unable to act from their prisons. An elemental attack on a distant outpost might seem like an isolated occurrence until someone realizes that each outpost along the border has suffered a similar attack. Perhaps the realm contains an ancient secret to help free one of the primordials, or perhaps it is a beacon of light and order in an otherwise dark and chaotic world. Alternatively, a spellcaster might find the summoning and binding of many powerful elementals to be a simple task, only to later discover that the elementals allowed themselves to be bound in order to later escape and sabotage a planar ritual, throwing open a portal to the Elemental Chaos. Regardless of whether the speculation of scholars holds true, elementals seem built to be weapons and tools. They lack intelligence and ambition, making them the perfect servants of those who want to act in secrecy and without fear of betrayal.

Lesser Air Elemental
Small elemental magical beast (air)

Level 1 Lurker
XP 100

HP 23; **Bloodied** 11
AC 15, **Fortitude** 12, **Reflex** 14, **Will** 13
Speed 0, fly 6 (hover)
Vulnerable 5 fire

Initiative +7
Perception +0

TRAITS

Phantom on the Wind

The lesser air elemental becomes invisible whenever it starts its turn without an enemy adjacent to it. The invisibility lasts until the end of its next turn or until it hits or misses with an attack.

STANDARD ACTIONS

⊕ **Slam ✦ At-Will**

Attack: Melee 1 (one creature); +6 vs. AC
Hit: 1d6 + 3 damage.

⸸ **Grasp of Storms ✦ At-Will**

Attack: Melee 1 (one creature that can't see the elemental); +4 vs. Reflex
Hit: 2d6 + 4 damage, and the elemental grabs the target (escape DC 12) if it does not have a creature grabbed. Until the grab ends, the target takes ongoing 5 damage, and any ranged or melee attacks that hit the elemental deal half damage to the target.

Skills Stealth +8

Str 16 (+3)	**Dex** 17 (+3)	**Wis** 11 (+0)
Con 11 (+0)	**Int** 5 (-3)	**Cha** 8 (-1)

Alignment unaligned   **Languages** understands Primordial

Lesser Earth Elemental
Small elemental magical beast (earth)

Level 2 Soldier
XP 125

HP 42; **Bloodied** 21
AC 17, **Fortitude** 15, **Reflex** 12, **Will** 13
Speed 5, burrow 5

Initiative +1
Perception +1
Tremorsense 5

TRAITS

Earth Glide

The elemental can pass through earth and rock as if it were phasing.

Brittle Skin

Whenever the elemental takes thunder damage, it takes a -2 penalty to all defenses until the end of its next turn.

STANDARD ACTIONS

⊕ **Slam ✦ At-Will**

Attack: Melee 1 (one creature); +7 vs. AC
Hit: 1d8 + 5 damage, and the target cannot shift until the end of the elemental's next turn.

TRIGGERED ACTIONS

Overwhelming Stone ✦ Recharge when first bloodied

Trigger: An enemy hits one of the elemental's allies with a melee attack.
Effect (Immediate Reaction): Melee 1 (triggering enemy). The target falls prone.

Str 17 (+4)	**Dex** 6 (-1)	**Wis** 11 (+1)
Con 18 (+5)	**Int** 5 (-2)	**Cha** 6 (-1)

Alignment unaligned   **Languages** understands Primordial

Lesser Fire Elemental
Level 1 Skirmisher

Small elemental magical beast (fire)

XP 100

HP 27; **Bloodied** 13	**Initiative** +6
AC 14, **Fortitude** 12, **Reflex** 14, **Will** 13	**Perception** +1
Speed 8, fly 4 (clumsy)	

TRAITS

Frozen in Place

Whenever the elemental takes cold damage, it cannot shift until the end of its next turn.

Heart of Flame (fire)

Whenever an enemy adjacent to the elemental misses it with a melee attack, that enemy takes 3 fire damage.

STANDARD ACTIONS

⊕ **Slam** (fire) ✦ At-Will

Attack: Melee 1 (one creature); +4 vs. Reflex

Hit: Ongoing 5 fire damage (save ends).

MINOR ACTIONS

Flickering Flame ✦ At-Will

Effect: The elemental shifts 1 square.

Str 10 (+0)	**Dex** 19 (+4)	**Wis** 13 (+1)
Con 11 (+0)	**Int** 5 (-3)	**Cha** 6 (-2)
Alignment unaligned	**Languages** understands Primordial	

Lesser Water Elemental
Level 1 Controller

Small elemental natural beast (aquatic, water)

XP 100

HP 29; **Bloodied** 14	**Initiative** +2
AC 15, **Fortitude** 14, **Reflex** 13, **Will** 12	**Perception** +0
Speed 6, swim 6	

TRAITS

Aquatic

The elemental can breathe underwater. In aquatic combat, it gains a +2 bonus to attack rolls against nonaquatic creatures.

Sensitive to Cold

Whenever the elemental takes cold damage, it gains vulnerable 5 against the next attack that hits it before the end of its next turn.

STANDARD ACTIONS

⊕ **Slam** ✦ At-Will

Attack: Melee 1 (one creature); +4 vs. Reflex

Hit: 1d6 damage, and ongoing 5 damage (save ends).

⟵ **Whelm** ✦ Encounter

Attack: Close blast 3 (enemies in the blast); +4 vs. Fortitude

Hit: 2d6 + 2 damage, and the elemental pushes the target up to 2 squares and knocks it prone.

MINOR ACTIONS

Drowning Essence ✦ At-Will (1/round)

Effect: The elemental slides each creature taking ongoing damage from its *slam* 1 square.

Str 16 (+3)	**Dex** 14 (+2)	**Wis** 11 (+0)
Con 13 (+1)	**Int** 5 (-3)	**Cha** 8 (-1)
Alignment unaligned	**Languages** understands Primordial	

ELF

Members of a lithe and agile race as old as the world, elves are fey humanoids who can be friend or foe to the other humanoid races. Three types of these creatures exist: elves, eladrin, and drow.

Like humans, elves come in many varieties, but they share a few characteristics. Although great gulfs exist between the three types of elves, they share their slim builds, pointed ears, long life spans, and smooth facial features. Most elves are skilled in many disciplines as a result of centuries of practice and training.

Elf Archer	Level 2 Artillery
Medium fey humanoid	XP 125

HP 32; Bloodied 16	Initiative +5
AC 16, Fortitude 12, Reflex 16, Will 14	Perception +9
Speed 7	Low-light vision

TRAITS

Archer's Mobility
If the elf moves at least 4 squares from the square where it started its move, it gains a +2 bonus to ranged attack rolls until the start of its next turn.

Wild Step
The elf ignores difficult terrain whenever it shifts.

STANDARD ACTIONS

⊕ **Short Sword** (weapon) ✦ At-Will
Attack: Melee 1 (one creature); +7 vs. AC
Hit: 1d6 + 4 damage.

⊙ **Longbow** (weapon) ✦ At-Will
Attack: Ranged 30 (one creature); +9 vs. AC
Hit: 1d10 + 4 damage.

TRIGGERED ACTIONS

Elven Accuracy ✦ Encounter
Trigger: The elf makes an attack roll.
Effect (Free Action): The elf rerolls the triggering attack roll and uses the second result.

⨪ **Not So Close** ✦ Encounter
Trigger: An enemy makes a melee attack against the elf.
Effect (Immediate Reaction): The elf can shift 1 square and then use *longbow* against the triggering enemy.

Skills Nature +9, Stealth +10

Str 13 (+2)	Dex 18 (+5)	Wis 16 (+4)
Con 14 (+3)	Int 12 (+2)	Cha 11 (+1)

Alignment unaligned   **Languages** Common, Elven
Equipment leather armor, short sword, longbow, 20 arrows

High Elves: Eladrin, also known as high elves, are residents of the Feywild and are the longest-living of the elf subraces. They are graceful warriors and potent wizards, commonly mixing swordplay with spells during battle. Eladrin share many of the traits, ambitions, and vices of other civilized races, and they tend to consider themselves above others' problems. This aloofness leads many eladrin to regard shorter-lived humanoids as tools or fodder, easily discarded when they outlive their usefulness.

Most eladrin live in shining cities created with the aid of arcane magic. Eladrin build cities within nature, fusing civilization with primal beauty to create magnificent structures that rise high into the treetops. Many eladrin cities have fallen into ruin, though, reclaimed by the land as a result of the collapse of their once-great empire. Some ancient eladrin fortresses remain untouched, protected for centuries by arcane wards. A few factions among the eladrin want to reclaim these abandoned lands and restore the power of the eladrin. Other factions believe that the time of the eladrin has passed. The two philosophies rarely clash in the world, but in the Feywild this conflict simmers.

> *"Your empire no longer claims these woods, human, and you are no longer welcome under its branches."*
> —Janic of the Harkenwood

Wood Elves: In the distant past, the race of elves broke away from the eladrin and settled into the forests of the world. These elves, commonly referred to as wood elves, live in areas of verdant forests. Since they make their homes on the surface of the world and not in the Feywild or the Underdark, wood elves frequently live among other humanoids. Unlike an eladrin, a wood elf is likely to

(Left to right) eladrin battle dancer, elf archer, drow arachnomancer

become involved in the affairs of other races, usually in defense of its home or as an ally against a great threat. A wood elf can also be an enemy to other humanoids, though. A militant elf clan might use violence to drive back those who encroach on its forest. Elves have a reputation as unparalleled archers. A few elf tribes even hire out as artillery for humans and other races.

Dark Elves: An ancient rebellion against their kin drove the drow into the depths of the Underdark where they now make their homes. Also called dark elves, drow serve the dark goddess Lolth, who bestows venomous blessings upon the priestesses who rule drow society.

Drow are consummate assassins and raiders. Their attacks on surface settlements leave few alive. Deep within the Underdark, drow cities boil over with manipulation and betrayal. The drow would be a potentially overwhelming force to surface-dwellers if they could stop fighting each other long enough to unify. Although some charismatic drow have attempted to overcome their race's tendencies, in the end, drow alliances fall apart as they are beset by a series of assassinations and betrayals.

Elf Scout	Level 2 Skirmisher
Medium fey humanoid	XP 125
HP 39; Bloodied 19	Initiative +7
AC 16, Fortitude 13, Reflex 15, Will 13	Perception +8
Speed 7	Low-light vision

TRAITS

Combat Advantage
The elf deals 1d6 extra damage against any creature granting combat advantage to it.

Wild Step
The elf ignores difficult terrain whenever it shifts.

STANDARD ACTIONS

⊕ **Longsword** (weapon) ✦ **At-Will**
Attack: Melee 1 (one creature); +7 vs. AC
Hit: 1d8 + 6 damage.

⊕ **Short Sword** (weapon) ✦ **At-Will**
Attack: Melee 1 (one creature); +7 vs. AC
Hit: 1d6 + 5 damage.

✦ **Two-Weapon Rend** ✦ **Encounter**
Effect: The elf uses *longsword* and *short sword* against the same target. If both attacks hit, the target takes 4 extra damage.

TRIGGERED ACTIONS

Elven Accuracy ✦ **Encounter**
Trigger: The elf makes an attack roll.
Effect (Free Action): The elf rerolls the triggering attack roll and uses the second result.

Skills Nature +8, Stealth +10		
Str 12 (+2)	Dex 18 (+5)	Wis 14 (+3)
Con 15 (+3)	Int 10 (+1)	Cha 12 (+2)
Alignment unaligned	Languages Common, Elven	

Equipment hide armor, longsword, short sword

Elf Hunter
Medium fey humanoid

Level 2 Minion Skirmisher

XP 31

HP 1; a missed attack never damages a minion | **Initiative** +6
AC 16, **Fortitude** 13, **Reflex** 15, **Will** 14 | **Perception** +7
Speed 7 | Low-light vision

TRAITS

Wild Step

The elf ignores difficult terrain whenever it shifts.

STANDARD ACTIONS

⊕ **Short Sword** (weapon) ✦ At-Will

Attack: Melee 1 (one creature); +7 vs. AC

Hit: 5 damage, and the elf shifts up to 2 squares.

Miss: The elf can shift 1 square.

| **Str** 14 (+3) | **Dex** 17 (+4) | **Wis** 12 (+2) |
| **Con** 12 (+2) | **Int** 14 (+3) | **Cha** 14 (+3) |

Alignment unaligned **Languages** Common, Elven

Equipment hide armor, short sword

Elf Noble Guard
Medium fey humanoid

Level 3 Soldier

XP 150

HP 46; **Bloodied** 23 | **Initiative** +6
AC 19, **Fortitude** 15, **Reflex** 17, **Will** 13 | **Perception** +3
Speed 7 | Low-light vision

TRAITS

Wild Step

The elf ignores difficult terrain whenever it shifts.

STANDARD ACTIONS

⊕ **Longsword** (weapon) ✦ At-Will

Attack: Melee 1 (one creature); +8 vs. AC

Hit: 1d8 + 7 damage.

Effect: The elf marks the target until the end of the elf's next turn.

⊕ **Hobbling Strike** (weapon) ✦ Recharge ⚄ ⚅

Attack: Melee 1 (one creature); +8 vs. AC

Hit: 2d8 + 7 damage, and the target is immobilized until the end of the elf's next turn.

Miss: Half damage, and the target is slowed until the end of the elf's next turn.

TRIGGERED ACTIONS

Elven Accuracy ✦ Encounter

Trigger: The elf makes an attack roll.

Effect (Free Action): The elf rerolls the triggering attack roll and uses the second result.

⫪ **Engaging Strike** (weapon) ✦ At-Will

Trigger: An enemy that is marked by the elf and is adjacent to it shifts or makes an attack that doesn't include it as a target.

Attack (Immediate Interrupt): Melee 1 (triggering enemy); +8 vs. AC

Hit: 1d8 + 7 damage, and the target is immobilized until the end of its turn.

Skills Athletics +6, Acrobatics +9

| **Str** 11 (+1) | **Dex** 16 (+4) | **Wis** 14 (+3) |
| **Con** 14 (+3) | **Int** 11 (+1) | **Cha** 10 (+1) |

Alignment unaligned **Languages** Common, Elven

Equipment chainmail, longsword

Eladrin Bow Mage

Level 7 Minion Artillery

Medium fey humanoid

XP 75

HP 1; a missed attack never damages a minion.	Initiative +7
AC 21, Fortitude 18, Reflex 21, Will 19	Perception +10
Speed 6	Low-light vision

Standard Actions

⊙ **Force Arrow** (force, weapon) ✦ At-Will

Attack: Ranged 20 (one creature); +14 vs. AC

Hit: 7 force damage, and the eladrin can push the target 1 square.

Move Actions

Fey Step (teleportation) ✦ Encounter

Effect: The eladrin teleports up to 5 squares.

Str 12 (+4)	Dex 18 (+7)	Wis 14 (+5)
Con 13 (+4)	Int 14 (+5)	Cha 11 (+3)

Alignment unaligned   **Languages** Common, Elven

Eladrin Fey Knight

Level 7 Soldier (Leader)

Medium fey humanoid

XP 300

HP 77; Bloodied 38	Initiative +11
AC 23, Fortitude 19, Reflex 21, Will 17	Perception +4
Speed 5	Low-light vision
Saving Throws +5 against charm effects	

Traits

☼ **Feywild Tactics** ✦ Aura 5

Fey allies can score critical hits on rolls of 19–20 while in the aura.

Standard Actions

⊕ **Longsword** (weapon) ✦ At-Will

Attack: Melee 1 (one creature); +12 vs. AC

Hit: 2d8 + 6 damage.

⊕ **Stab of the Wild** (weapon) ✦ Recharge ⚃ ⚅

Attack: Melee 1 (one creature); +12 vs. AC

Hit: 3d8 + 8 damage, and the target is restrained until the end of the eladrin's next turn.

Minor Actions

Feywild Challenge (radiant) ✦ At-Will

Effect: Close burst 5 (one enemy in the burst). The eladrin marks the target until the end of the encounter or until the eladrin uses this power again. While the enemy is marked by the eladrin, it takes 4 radiant damage whenever it ends its turn without attacking the eladrin.

Move Actions

Fey Step (teleportation) ✦ Encounter

Effect: The eladrin teleports up to 5 squares.

Triggered Actions

↯ **Harvest's Sorrow** ✦ At-Will

Trigger: An attack damages an ally.

Effect (Immediate Interrupt): Close burst 5 (triggering ally in the burst). The target takes half damage from the triggering attack, and the eladrin takes an equal amount of damage.

Skills Athletics +12, Nature +9

Str 18 (+7)	Dex 22 (+9)	Wis 13 (+4)
Con 13 (+4)	Int 14 (+5)	Cha 16 (+6)

Alignment unaligned   **Languages** Common, Elven

Equipment chainmail, light shield, longsword

Eladrin Twilight Incanter

Level 8 Controller

Medium fey humanoid

XP 350

HP 82; **Bloodied** 41
AC 22, **Fortitude** 18, **Reflex** 20, **Will** 22
Speed 6
Saving Throws +5 against charm effects

Initiative +7
Perception +5
Low-light vision

STANDARD ACTIONS

⊕ **Spear** (weapon) ✦ **At-Will**
Attack: Melee 1 (one creature); +13 vs. AC
Hit: 2d8 + 4 damage, and the target is slowed until the end of the eladrin's next turn.

⟐ **Binding Bolt** (force) ✦ **Encounter**
Attack: Ranged 5 (one creature); +11 vs. Reflex
Hit: 2d8 + 7 force damage, and the target is immobilized until the end of the eladrin's next turn.
Miss: The target is slowed until the end of the eladrin's next turn.

⟐ **Teleporting Bolt** (force, teleportation) ✦ **At-Will**
Attack: Ranged 5 (one creature); +11 vs. Reflex
Hit: 2d10 + 5 force damage, and the eladrin teleports the target up to 3 squares.
Miss: The eladrin can teleport the target 1 square.

⟡ **Dazzling Blast** (radiant) ✦ **Recharge** ⚅ ⚃
Attack: Close blast 3 (enemies in the blast); +11 vs. Will
Hit: 4d6 + 2 radiant damage, and the target is blinded until the end of the eladrin's next turn.

MOVE ACTIONS

Fey Step (teleportation) ✦ **Encounter**
Effect: The eladrin teleports up to 5 squares.

Str 12 (+5)	Dex 16 (+7)	Wis 12 (+5)
Con 10 (+4)	Int 20 (+9)	Cha 16 (+7)
Alignment unaligned	**Languages** Common, Elven	
Equipment robes, spear		

Eladrin Battle Dancer

Level 9 Skirmisher

Medium fey humanoid

XP 400

HP 94; **Bloodied** 47
AC 23, **Fortitude** 21, **Reflex** 22, **Will** 20
Speed 6
Saving Throws +5 against charm effects

Initiative +11
Perception +5
Low-light vision

STANDARD ACTIONS

⊕ **Dancing Blade** (weapon) ✦ **At-Will**
Attack: Melee 1 (one creature); +14 vs. AC
Hit: 2d8 + 8 damage, and the eladrin becomes invisible to the target until the end of the eladrin's next turn.

⫟ **Battle Dance** (weapon) ✦ **Encounter**
Effect: The eladrin shifts up to its speed. Each time the eladrin enters a square adjacent to an enemy for the first time during the move, it makes a melee basic attack against that enemy.

MOVE ACTIONS

Surprise Fey Step (teleportation) ✦ **Recharge** ⚃ ⚅ ⚃
Effect: The eladrin teleports 5 squares. Until the end of its turn, the eladrin gains combat advantage against each enemy adjacent to its destination square.

Str 17 (+7)	Dex 20 (+9)	Wis 13 (+5)
Con 14 (+6)	Int 15 (+6)	Cha 16 (+8)
Alignment unaligned	**Languages** Common, Elven	
Equipment chainmail, longsword		

Drow Stalker — Level 12 Minion Lurker

Medium fey humanoid · XP 175

HP 1; a missed attack never damages a minion. · Initiative +15
AC 26, Fortitude 22, Reflex 25, Will 25 · Perception +7
Speed 6 · Darkvision

TRAITS

Stalker Ambush
When the drow hits a creature that cannot see it, the drow's attack deals 5 extra damage.

STANDARD ACTIONS

⊕ **Longsword** (weapon) ✦ At-Will
Attack: Melee 1 (one creature); +17 vs. AC
Hit: 10 damage.

⌁ **Hand Crossbow** (poison, weapon) ✦ Encounter
Attack: Ranged 10 (one creature); +17 vs. AC
Hit: 5 damage, and ongoing 5 poison damage (save ends).

MINOR ACTIONS

Cloud of Darkness (zone) ✦ Encounter
Effect: Close burst 1. The burst creates a zone that lasts until the end of the drow's next turn. The cloud blocks line of sight for all creatures except the drow. While entirely within the cloud, any creature other than the drow is blinded.

Str 16 (+9)	Dex 20 (+11)	Wis 13 (+7)
Con 14 (+8)	Int 16 (+9)	Cha 11 (+6)

Alignment evil · **Languages** Common, Elven

Drow Venomblade — Level 13 Skirmisher

Medium fey humanoid · XP 800

HP 124; Bloodied 62 · Initiative +13
AC 27, Fortitude 23, Reflex 25, Will 22 · Perception +13
Speed 6 · Darkvision

STANDARD ACTIONS

⊕ **Longsword** (poison, weapon) ✦ At-Will
Attack: Melee 1 (one creature); +18 vs. AC
Hit: 2d8 + 7 damage, and ongoing 5 poison damage (save ends).

⊕ **Short Sword** (poison, weapon) ✦ At-Will
Attack: Melee 1 (one creature); +18 vs. AC
Hit: 2d6 + 7 damage, and ongoing 5 poison damage (save ends).

⸸ **Blade Mastery** ✦ Recharge ⚄ ⚅
Effect: The drow uses *longsword* once and *short sword* once.

MINOR ACTIONS

Cloud of Darkness (zone) ✦ Encounter
Effect: Close burst 1. The burst creates a zone that lasts until the end of the drow's next turn. The cloud blocks line of sight for all creatures except the drow. While entirely within the cloud, any creature other than the drow is blinded.

Skills Acrobatics +16, Stealth +16

Str 16 (+9)	Dex 21 (+11)	Wis 14 (+8)
Con 12 (+7)	Int 12 (+7)	Cha 12 (+7)

Alignment evil · **Languages** Common, Elven
Equipment longsword, short sword, hide armor

Drow Arachnomancer
Level 13 Artillery (Leader)

Medium fey humanoid

XP 800

HP 94; **Bloodied** 47
AC 27, **Fortitude** 23, **Reflex** 25, **Will** 25
Speed 6

Initiative +8
Perception +13
Darkvision

TRAITS

Lolth's Judgment

Whenever the drow hits an enemy with an attack, any spiders within sight of the drow gain a +2 bonus to attack rolls against that enemy until the end of the drow's next turn.

STANDARD ACTIONS

⊕ **Scourge** (weapon) ✦ **At-Will**

Attack: Melee 1 (one creature); +18 vs. AC

Hit: 2d6 + 5 damage, and the target is immobilized (save ends).

⤙ **Venom Ray** (poison) ✦ **At-Will**

Attack: Ranged 10 (one creature); +18 vs. Reflex

Hit: 2d6 + 4 poison damage, and ongoing 10 poison damage (save ends).

⤙ **Spider Curse** (necrotic) ✦ **Encounter**

Attack: Ranged 20 (one creature); +18 vs. Will

Hit: 2d10 + 5 necrotic damage, and the target is weakened and takes ongoing 10 necrotic damage (save ends both).

Miss: Half damage, and ongoing 5 necrotic damage (save ends).

⟵ **Venom Blast** (poison) ✦ **Encounter**

Attack: Close blast 5 (enemies in the blast); +16 vs. Fortitude

Hit: 3d6 + 10 poison damage.

Miss: Half damage.

MINOR ACTIONS

Cloud of Darkness (zone) ✦ **Encounter**

Effect: Close burst 1. The burst creates a zone that lasts until the end of the drow's next turn. The cloud blocks line of sight for all creatures except the drow. While entirely within the cloud, any creature other than the drow is blinded.

Skills Arcana +14, Dungeoneering +13

Str 10 (+6)	**Dex** 15 (+8)	**Wis** 14 (+8)
Con 10 (+6)	**Int** 16 (+9)	**Cha** 11 (+6)

Alignment evil

Languages Common, Elven

Equipment robes, scourge

"Lolth will savor your exquisite pain as my poison courses through your veins."

—Matron Urlvrain of Phaervorul

ETTIN

The two-headed ettin presents a double threat for any who are unfortunate enough to encounter one as it tramples through the hills in search of food and treasure. Even with two brains, though, an ettin's intellect is limited.

Although kin to the giants, a two-headed ettin lives like an ogre and eats like a troll. Two puny minds drive the creature's powerful body to kill anything that comes across its path. Only spells and swords can reason with these savage humanoids.

Quarrelsome Heads: Each ettin has two ugly heads, and the small brains in each thick skull feud over control of its body. An ettin is constantly at war with itself. Each head's personality strives to assert control. The heads often squabble with the same selfishness and rancor as a pair of young siblings. Because an ettin cannot survive without both heads, though, it avoids self-destructive behavior and manages to achieve a tenuous degree of teamwork. In combat and under stress, the two heads achieve surprising cooperation as each drives the ettin's body to take actions twice as fast as a normal giant.

Ettin Thug — Level 8 Brute
Large natural humanoid (giant) — XP 350

HP 110; **Bloodied** 55 — **Initiative** +5
AC 20, **Fortitude** 21, **Reflex** 17, **Will** 19 — **Perception** +11
Speed 6

TRAITS

Double Actions

The ettin makes two initiative checks and takes a full turn on each initiative result. The ettin can take two immediate actions per round but only one between one turn and the next.

STANDARD ACTIONS

⊕ Smash ✦ At-Will

Attack: Melee 2 (one creature); +13 vs. AC
Hit: 1d12 + 3 damage.

MOVE ACTIONS

⵮ Kick ✦ At-Will

Attack: Melee 1 (one creature); +11 vs. Fortitude
Hit: The ettin pushes the target up to 2 squares. The ettin then moves up to half its speed.

Str 20 (+9)	Dex 12 (+5)	Wis 15 (+6)
Con 20 (+9)	Int 8 (+3)	Cha 9 (+3)

Alignment chaotic evil — **Languages** Giant

Ettin Wrath Chanter — Level 8 Elite Controller (Leader)
Large natural humanoid (giant) — XP 700

HP 184; **Bloodied** 92 — **Initiative** +5
AC 22, **Fortitude** 21, **Reflex** 17, **Will** 20 — **Perception** +11
Speed 6
Saving Throws +2; **Action Points** 1

TRAITS

Rage Song ✦ Aura 5

Enemies take a -2 penalty to attack rolls and gain a +2 bonus to damage rolls while in the aura. Allies gain a +2 bonus to attack rolls and damage rolls while in the aura.

Double Actions

The ettin makes two initiative checks and takes a full turn on each initiative result. The ettin can take two immediate actions per round but only one between one turn and the next.

Dual Brain

At the end of each of its turns, the ettin automatically ends any dazing, stunning, or charm effect on itself.

STANDARD ACTIONS

⊕ Smash ✦ At-Will

Attack: Melee 2 (one creature); +13 vs. AC
Hit: 2d8 + 7 damage, and the target falls prone.

Invoke Fury ✦ At-Will

Effect: Close burst 5 (one enemy in the burst). The target must use a free action to charge or make a basic attack against a target of the ettin's choice. The movement for this charge does not provoke opportunity attacks.

Str 20 (+9)	Dex 12 (+5)	Wis 15 (+6)
Con 20 (+9)	Int 8 (+3)	Cha 17 (+7)

Alignment chaotic evil — **Languages** Giant

Vicious Hunters: A small tribe of ettins can carve a path of destruction through borderlands. A lone ettin could be less destructive but might instead build a savage fiefdom by bullying weaker humanoids to bring it tributes of wealth and food. An ettin will hunt, kill, and eat any creature—even other ettins, if they are vulnerable. The creature's tremendous strength and voracious appetite means that little remains of a victim, not even bones. Smashed caravans, collapsed houses, and churned earth are often the only evidence of an ettin attack.

"Stay here, next to squishy wizard!"
"No, elf's arrows hurt! Smash elf!"
—Gurgnash, ettin (to himself)

An ettin is a sinister creature driven by instinct to seek dominance, inflict pain, and cause terror. Power pleases an ettin, and it enjoys victimizing those it sees as weak or defenseless. Warriors take advantage of this trait, using vulnerable bait to set ambushes for ettins. Usually, livestock doesn't suffice to lure an ettin out. The terrified screams of a potential victim are the surest way to draw an ettin into the open.

Ettin Hunter	Level 10 Artillery
Large natural humanoid (giant)	XP 500

HP 86; **Bloodied** 43	**Initiative** +6
AC 24, **Fortitude** 23, **Reflex** 19, **Will** 20	**Perception** +12
Speed 6	

TRAITS

Double Actions
The ettin makes two initiative checks and takes a full turn on each initiative result. The ettin can take two immediate actions per round but only one between one turn and the next.

STANDARD ACTIONS

⊕ **Javelin** (weapon) ✦ **At-Will**
Attack: Melee 2 (one creature); +15 vs. AC
Hit: 1d6 + 6 damage.

⊛ **Javelin** (weapon) ✦ **At-Will**
Attack: Ranged 20 (one creature); +17 vs. AC
Hit: 1d6 + 6 damage.

⊛ **Pinion** (weapon) ✦ **Recharge** ⚄ ⚅
Attack: Ranged 20 (one creature); +17 vs. AC
Hit: 2d6 + 7 damage, and the target is restrained until it escapes (DC 18) or teleports.

Str 20 (+10)	**Dex** 12 (+6)	**Wis** 15 (+7)
Con 20 (+10)	**Int** 8 (+4)	**Cha** 9 (+4)

Alignment chaotic evil	**Languages** Giant
Equipment 10 javelins	

Primordial Demonism: Legend says that ettins arose from the blood of Storralk, a mighty primordial of earth and stone. In ancient times, this primordial set upon Demogorgon when the demon lord was nearly split in two by the god Amoth. Demogorgon defeated Storralk and, as punishment, entombed the primordial beneath his throne in the Abyss. After the battle concluded, Demogorgon's two heads gazed into the pools of Storralk's blood, and from those pools arose ettins. Demogorgon cast most of the giants out of the Elemental Chaos and into the world, knowing that as manifestations of Storralk's blood, any pain the ettins suffered would be inflicted upon the bound primordial.

Few ettins of the world know this story. An ettin that is aware of the tale, typically one living in the Elemental Chaos, tends to regard Demogorgon as the father of its race. An ettin respects strength, and it prefers to be associated with Demogorgon, since he was triumphant in the battle against Storralk. Ettins that know the story of their creation often worship other demons in addition to Demogorgon. Such ettins believe that demons are a closer representation of their kin than giants are. Tribes of these demon-worshiping ettins are more savage and evil than other tribes, and many of their members are possessed by demons or maddened by abyssal power.

Ettin Marauder	Level 10 Elite Soldier
Large natural humanoid (giant)	XP 1,000

HP 222; **Bloodied** 111	
AC 26, **Fortitude** 24, **Reflex** 20, **Will** 20	**Initiative** +8
Speed 6	**Perception** +12
Saving Throws +2; **Action Points** 1	

TRAITS

Double Actions

The ettin makes two initiative checks and takes a full turn on each initiative result. The ettin can take two immediate actions per round but only one between one turn and the next.

Dual Brain

At the end of each of its turns, the ettin automatically ends any dazing, stunning, or charm effect on itself.

STANDARD ACTIONS

⊕ **Smash** ✦ **At-Will**

Attack: Melee 2 (one creature); +15 vs. AC
Hit: 1d12 + 12 damage, and the ettin can push the target 1 square.
Effect: The ettin marks the target until the end of the ettin's next turn.

TRIGGERED ACTIONS

⥮ **Swat** ✦ **At-Will**

Trigger: An enemy enters a square where it flanks the ettin.
Attack (Immediate Reaction): Melee 2 (one creature flanking the ettin); +13 vs. Fortitude
Hit: The ettin pushes the target up to 3 squares.

Str 28 (+14)	**Dex** 12 (+6)	**Wis** 15 (+7)
Con 23 (+11)	**Int** 8 (+4)	**Cha** 9 (+4)
Alignment chaotic evil	**Languages** Giant	

GARGOYLE

A gargoyle is a vicious, stealthy creature that disguises itself as a statue by turning to stone. It waits for a potential victim to pass by and then swoops down to attack.

Gargoyle Rake	Level 5 Lurker
Medium elemental humanoid (earth)	XP 200

HP 52; **Bloodied** 26	**Initiative** +8
AC 19, **Fortitude** 17, **Reflex** 15, **Will** 15	**Perception** +9
Speed 6, fly 8	Darkvision

STANDARD ACTIONS

⊕ **Claw** ✦ At-Will
Attack: Melee 1 (one creature); +10 vs. AC
Hit: 1d10 + 4 damage plus 2 extra damage for each one of the gargoyle's allies adjacent to the target.

↓ **Swoop Attack** ✦ At-Will
Effect: The gargoyle flies up to its fly speed and uses *claw* at the end of the move. This movement does not provoke opportunity attacks.

Stone Form ✦ At-Will
Effect: The gargoyle enters stone form until it ends the effect as a minor action. While in this form, it gains tremorsense 10 and resist 20 to all damage, gains 5 temporary hit points at the start of each of its turns, and cannot take actions except to end the effect. When the gargoyle ends the effect, it gains a +15 bonus to its next damage roll before the end of its next turn.

Skills Stealth +9
Str 19 (+6)   **Dex** 15 (+4)   **Wis** 15 (+4)
Con 16 (+5)   **Int** 5 (-1)   **Cha** 13 (+3)
Alignment evil   **Languages** Primordial

Gargoyle	Level 9 Lurker
Medium elemental humanoid (earth)	XP 400

HP 77; **Bloodied** 38	**Initiative** +11
AC 23, **Fortitude** 21, **Reflex** 19, **Will** 19	**Perception** +12
Speed 6, fly 8	Darkvision

STANDARD ACTIONS

⊕ **Claw** ✦ At-Will
Attack: Melee 1 (one creature); +14 vs. AC
Hit: 2d6 + 5 damage.

↓ **Swoop Attack** ✦ At-Will
Effect: The gargoyle flies up to its fly speed and uses *claw* at the end of the move. This movement does not provoke opportunity attacks.

Stone Form ✦ At-Will
Effect: The gargoyle enters stone form until it ends the effect as a minor action. While in this form, it gains tremorsense 10 and resist 25 to all damage, gains 5 temporary hit points at the start of each of its turns, and cannot take actions except to end the effect. When the gargoyle ends the effect, it gains a +20 bonus to its next damage roll before the end of its next turn.

Skills Stealth +12
Str 21 (+9)   **Dex** 17 (+7)   **Wis** 17 (+7)
Con 17 (+7)   **Int** 5 (+1)   **Cha** 17 (+7)
Alignment evil   **Languages** Primordial

Gargoyle Rock Hurler

Level 11 Artillery

Medium elemental humanoid (earth)

XP 600

HP 87; **Bloodied** 43
AC 25, **Fortitude** 21, **Reflex** 19, **Will** 19
Speed 6, fly 8

Initiative +9
Perception +13
Darkvision

Traits

Stone Defense

The gargoyle has resist 10 to all damage from attacks originating at least 5 squares away from it.

Standard Actions

⊕ **Claw ✦ At-Will**

Attack: Melee 1 (one creature); +16 vs. AC

Hit: 2d8 + 8 damage.

⊛ **Hurled Stone ✦ At-Will**

Attack: Ranged 20 (one creature); +18 vs. AC

Hit: 3d6 + 9 damage.

⊛ **Hail of Hurled Stone ✦ At-Will**

Attack: Area burst 1 within 10 (creatures in the burst); +18 vs. AC

Hit: 2d6 + 7 damage, or 2d6 + 12 against a target in the burst's origin square.

Miss: Half damage.

Skills Stealth +14

Str 22 (+11)	**Dex** 18 (+9)	**Wis** 17 (+8)
Con 15 (+7)	**Int** 5 (+2)	**Cha** 17 (+8)

Alignment evil

Languages Primordial

Equipment 10 stones

Gargoyles take on grotesque, statuelike forms, lurking in these guises for days or weeks until prey comes near. A gargoyle might keep itself entertained by attacking birds or rodents, but what it really wants are sentient creatures. A gargoyle revels in ripping apart its enemies with its claws. Although a gargoyle might easily slay a normal humanoid with a single blow, it prefers to enjoy the kill by harrying its prey and delivering several raking attacks that leave a victim alive but incapacitated. A gargoyle will eventually kill and devour a victim after the monster has had its fun.

R SPEARS

A gargoyle lives in any environment where stone is common, whether it's an area of buildings, mountains, cliffs, or underground caves. Statues of gargoyles appear on buildings throughout the world, and many gargoyles hide among these features. A gargoyle's reputation for cruelty has transformed its visage into a sign of warning against intruders.

Boasts and Torture: Crude creatures that operate on base desires, gargoyles derive amusement from taunting and threatening foes. A gargoyle singles out an enemy that is physically weak, mocking the opponent as it swoops down to claw at the creature. A gargoyle issues dire threats of torture and pain, attempting to foster fear in its foe and cause the creature to bolt. Gargoyles don't require sustenance, but most enjoy gnawing on their still-living foes. A gargoyle roost is often adorned with the fresh corpses of victims. By the time a traveler spots such signs, though, a gargoyle is usually swooping down to attack.

The Element of Surprise: A gargoyle's stone form doesn't necessarily look like its natural form. The creature hides along high precipices and among statues, maintaining a humanoid, demonic, or reptilian shape to mislead observers. In their natural form, gargoyles have horns, wings, rocky flesh, and red eyes. When a gargoyle charges down to deliver a surprise attack, its adopted features melt away and are replaced by its natural appearance.

Nabassu Gargoyle	Level 18 Lurker
Medium elemental humanoid (earth)	XP 2,000

HP 131; **Bloodied** 65	**Initiative** +18
AC 32, **Fortitude** 30, **Reflex** 28, **Will** 28	**Perception** +14
Speed 6, fly 8	Darkvision

TRAITS

⟡ **Bloodfire** (fire, necrotic) ✦ **Aura** 3
While the gargoyle is affected by *stone form*, whenever any enemy ends its turn in the aura, the gargoyle gains 10 temporary hit points and the enemy takes 10 fire and necrotic damage.

STANDARD ACTIONS

⊕ **Claw** ✦ **At-Will**
Attack: Melee 1 (one creature); +23 vs. AC
Hit: 2d8 + 7 damage.

† **Abyssal Bite** ✦ **At-Will**
Attack: Melee 1 (one creature); +23 vs. AC
Hit: 2d12 + 8 damage.

Stone Form (fire, necrotic) ✦ **At-Will**
Effect: The gargoyle gains tremorsense 10 and resist 35 to all damage until it uses a minor action to end this effect. When the gargoyle ends this effect, each enemy within 3 squares of it takes 2d10 + 10 fire and necrotic damage.

Skills Stealth +19		
Str 25 (+16)	**Dex** 21 (+14)	**Wis** 21 (+14)
Con 17 (+12)	**Int** 5 (+6)	**Cha** 18 (+13)
Alignment evil	**Languages** Primordial	

Rocktempest Gargoyle

Level 23 Elite Lurker

Large elemental humanoid (earth)

XP 10,200

HP 330; **Bloodied** 165
AC 37, **Fortitude** 37, **Reflex** 36, **Will** 34
Speed 6, fly 8 (hover)
Immune petrification
Saving Throws +2; **Action Points** 1

Initiative +23
Perception +14
Darkvision

STANDARD ACTIONS

⊕ **Claw** ✦ At-Will

Attack: Melee 1 (one creature); +28 vs. AC
Hit: 2d8 + 6 damage, and ongoing 15 damage (save ends).

↯ **Tempest Claws** ✦ At-Will

Effect: The gargoyle uses *claw* two times. If both attacks hit the same target, the target is also dazed (save ends).

Stone Form ✦ At-Will

Effect: The gargoyle enters stone form until it ends the effect as a minor action. While in this form, it gains tremorsense 10 and resist 30 to all damage, gains 10 temporary hit points at the start of each of its turns, and cannot take actions except to end the effect. When the gargoyle ends the effect, it gains a +10 bonus to all damage rolls before the end of its next turn.

↯ **Flying Strike** ✦ Recharge when the gargoyle uses *stone form*

Effect: The gargoyle flies up to 8 squares. At any point during its move, it makes the following attack three times, but only once against any creature. This movement does not provoke opportunity attacks.
Attack: Melee 1 (one creature); +26 vs. Fortitude
Hit: 4d8 + 12 damage, and the gargoyle slides the target up to 3 squares.

Str 26 (+19)	**Dex** 27 (+19)	**Wis** 17 (+14)
Con 24 (+18)	**Int** 15 (+13)	**Cha** 21 (+16)

Alignment chaotic evil

Languages Primordial

The Chaos and the Abyss: Gargoyles live throughout the planes, from perches on ruined gates of Shadowfell cities to fortresses within the domains of dead gods in the Astral Sea. Home for most gargoyles is the churning landscape of the Elemental Chaos. There, gargoyles rarely pose as statues and instead hunt on the wing, often alongside other elemental creatures. Within and near the Abyss, deadly nabassu gargoyles join the ranks of demons to wage war or to capture creatures that elude the abyssal hordes.

Reluctant Guardians: Gargoyles sometimes serve demons or powerful spellcasters as guardians, keeping watch over gates and walls. A gargoyle rarely performs this service willingly; it is usually bound by magic or cowed by threats. A gargoyle might possess a key or a password to open a locked door or gate. A traveler who answers a riddle or provides the proper identification might be allowed to pass through the barrier unscathed. Gargoyles use the smallest mistake as an excuse to attack, though. Such guardian gargoyles are usually more intelligent than their untamed kin, but just as cruel and vicious.

GHOUL

Haunting graveyards, battlefields, and crypts, ghouls hunger for the flesh of living or recently dead creatures. They were once cannibalistic humanoids, but their actions caused them to be cursed in death with ravenous appetites that cannot be sated.

When an intelligent humanoid resorts to cannibalism or lives a life of gluttony and greed, it can be cursed to transform into a ghoul upon its death. Unlike a zombie or a skeleton, a ghoul retains sentience and many of the memories of its life. The creature's perspective is twisted by its death, though, and as a result, it recalls with torment a time when it was not driven by a gnawing hunger for living flesh. A ghoul has a humanoid appearance, but its skin sloughs away or turns a sickly cast of gray or green. The transformation causes a ghoul to grow sharp fangs and claws to tear at flesh. A ghoul dwells anyplace where bodies are discarded or left unattended, so a group of them might congregate in a cemetery or a battlefield. Clerics must often be called in to repel the creatures while bodies are gathered or sanctified for protection.

"Endless hunger for the flesh of the living, never sated, no matter how much it consumes—that is the dismal unlife of a ghoul."
—Verinn, paladin of the Raven Queen

Ghoul	Level 5 Soldier
Medium natural humanoid (undead)	XP 200

HP 63; **Bloodied** 31	**Initiative** +8
AC 21, **Fortitude** 17, **Reflex** 19, **Will** 16	**Perception** +2
Speed 8, climb 4	Darkvision
Immune disease, poison; **Resist** 10 necrotic	

TRAITS

Weakened Paralysis
Whenever the ghoul takes radiant damage, one creature immobilized or stunned by the ghoul can make a saving throw against one of those effects.

STANDARD ACTIONS

⊕ **Claws** ✦ **At-Will**
Attack: Melee 1 (one creature); +10 vs. AC
Hit: 2d6 + 6 damage, and the target is immobilized (save ends).

⊣ **Ghoulish Bite** ✦ **At-Will**
Attack: Melee 1 (one immobilized, restrained, stunned, or unconscious creature); +10 vs. AC
Hit: 4d6 + 6 damage, and the target is stunned (save ends).

Skills Stealth +11

Str 14 (+4)	**Dex** 19 (+6)	**Wis** 11 (+2)
Con 15 (+4)	**Int** 10 (+2)	**Cha** 12 (+3)

Alignment chaotic evil   **Languages** Common

Hunger for Flesh: A ghoul's hunger for flesh is its primary motivator, and it drives the ghoul to desperation when food is not in abundance. Although ghouls tend to lurk in graveyards and charnel houses, they sometimes attack settlements when food is scarce. Such attacks leave few survivors, for a group of ghouls will kill and eat anyone in its path. A pack of ghouls might even resort to attacking a well-defended settlement or keep, especially when it can gain entrance through sewers, tunnels, or gaps in the walls. Even in desperation, ghouls are cunning attackers. A horde of ghouls might wait until nightfall before slinking through a drainage tunnel to get inside a city's walls. Once the feeding begins, though, ghouls enter a ravenous frenzy. They pursue weak targets to sate their hunger quickly, but they gang up on tougher defenders if necessary.

Abyssal Blessings: Most ghouls are wretched, cursed beings that dwell in the dark places of the world, but some retain enough memories of life to yearn for a purpose. Many ghouls turn to Doresain, an exarch of Orcus, to find that purpose. The so-called Ghoul King commands his servants to empower some ghouls with additional strength, speed, and durability. The ghouls that receive these abyssal blessings are more powerful and are beholden to Doresain and his demonic master. Although these abyssal ghouls still possess a ravenous hunger, they work toward a greater end by focusing their violence against enemies of Orcus.

The White Kingdom: In the Abyss lies the White Kingdom, the seat of Doresain's power and a domain populated almost entirely by ghouls and other flesh-eating undead. The buildings in the White Kingdom are made from bones left over from devoured creatures. Doresain's palace, the largest of these buildings, is built from the remains of a massive primordial. The Ghoul King calls abyssal ghouls here to receive instructions. Although few living creatures see the

White Kingdom and live to tell about it, rumors tell of a ritual that can temporarily transform a living being into a facsimile of undeath. It is said that the ritual was crafted by one of Doresain's rivals, perhaps a demon lord, in the hope of infiltrating the White Kingdom. Anyone hoping to obtain such a ritual would be required to pay a terrible price, though.

Ravenous Ghoul	Level 5 Brute
Medium natural humanoid (undead)	XP 200

HP 76; Bloodied 38	Initiative +4
AC 17, Fortitude 18, Reflex 17, Will 15	Perception +1
Speed 8, climb 4	Darkvision
Immune disease, poison; Resist 10 necrotic; Vulnerable 5 radiant	

STANDARD ACTIONS

⊕ **Claws ✦ At-Will**
  Attack: Melee 1 (one creature); +10 vs. AC
  Hit: 3d8 + 4 damage.

⸸ **Ravenous Bite ✦ Recharge** ⸬ ⸿
  Attack: Melee 1 (one creature); +10 vs. AC
  Hit: 3d8 + 6 damage, and ongoing 5 damage (save ends).

Skills Stealth +9

Str 18 (+6)	Dex 14 (+4)	Wis 8 (+1)
Con 16 (+5)	Int 8 (+1)	Cha 13 (+3)

Alignment chaotic evil   **Languages** Common

Abyssal Ghoul	Level 16 Skirmisher
Medium elemental humanoid (undead)	XP 1,400

HP 156; Bloodied 78	Initiative +16
AC 30, Fortitude 30, Reflex 28, Will 25	Perception +10
Speed 8, climb 4	Darkvision
Immune disease, poison; Resist 10 necrotic	

TRAITS

✧ **Sepulchral Stench ✦ Aura** 3
  Enemies take a -2 penalty to all defenses while in the aura.

Hindering Light
  Whenever the ghoul takes radiant damage, it cannot shift until the end of its next turn.

STANDARD ACTIONS

⊕ **Bite ✦ At-Will**
  Attack: Melee 1 (one creature); +20 vs. AC
  Hit: 3d8 + 10 damage, plus 1d8 + 3 damage if the target is immobilized, restrained, stunned, or unconscious. In addition, the target is immobilized (save ends).
  Effect: The ghoul shifts up to 3 squares.

TRIGGERED ACTIONS

↢ **Dead Blood** (necrotic)
  Trigger: The ghoul drops to 0 hit points.
  Effect (No Action): Close burst 1 (enemies in the burst). Each target takes 10 necrotic damage.

Skills Stealth +19

Str 24 (+15)	Dex 22 (+14)	Wis 15 (+10)
Con 20 (+13)	Int 16 (+11)	Cha 10 (+8)

Alignment chaotic evil   **Languages** Common

Abyssal Ghoul Devourer — Level 16 Lurker
Medium elemental humanoid (undead)   XP 1,400

HP 118; **Bloodied** 59   **Initiative** +17
AC 30, **Fortitude** 29, **Reflex** 28, **Will** 26   **Perception** +13
Speed 8, climb 4   Darkvision
Immune disease, poison; **Resist** 10 necrotic; **Vulnerable** 5 radiant

TRAITS

Sepulchral Stench ✦ Aura 3

Enemies take a -2 penalty to all defenses while in the aura.

Unhindered

When the ghoul moves on its turn, it pulls with it any creature grabbed by it. The creature remains grabbed, and this movement does not provoke an opportunity attack from the grabbed creature.

STANDARD ACTIONS

⊕ **Grasping Claws ✦ At-Will**

Attack: Melee 1 (one creature); +21 vs. AC

Hit: 2d8 + 3 damage.

Effect: The ghoul grabs the target (escape DC 22) if it has fewer than two creatures grabbed. The ghoul then shifts up to half its speed. Until the grab ends, any melee or ranged attack that hits the ghoul deals half damage to the ghoul and half its damage to the target.

⊹ **Devour ✦ At-Will**

Attack: Melee 1 (one creature grabbed by the ghoul); +21 vs. AC

Hit: 3d10 + 5 damage, and the target is no longer grabbed by the ghoul. In addition, the target takes ongoing 10 damage (save ends).

Miss: Half damage, and the target is no longer grabbed by the ghoul. In addition, the target takes ongoing 5 damage (save ends).

Skills Stealth +18
Str 24 (+15)   **Dex** 21 (+13)   **Wis** 20 (+13)
Con 16 (+11)   **Int** 11 (+8)   **Cha** 7 (+6)
Alignment chaotic evil   **Languages** Common

Abyssal Ghoul Hungerer — Level 18 Minion Soldier
Medium elemental humanoid (undead)   XP 1,400

HP 1; a missed attack never damages a minion.   **Initiative** +18
AC 27, **Fortitude** 24, **Reflex** 23, **Will** 21   **Perception** +14
Speed 8, climb 4   Darkvision
Immune disease, poison; **Resist** 10 necrotic

STANDARD ACTIONS

⊕ **Claws ✦ At-Will**

Attack: Melee 1 (one creature); +23 vs. AC

Hit: 13 damage, and the target is immobilized (save ends).

TRIGGERED ACTIONS

⟵ **Dead Blood** (necrotic)

Trigger: The ghoul drops to 0 hit points.

Effect (No Action): Close burst 1 (creatures in the burst). Each target takes 10 necrotic damage.

Skills Stealth +22
Str 26 (+17)   **Dex** 25 (+16)   **Wis** 17 (+12)
Con 23 (+15)   **Int** 19 (+13)   **Cha** 13 (+10)
Alignment chaotic evil   **Languages** Abyssal

GIANT

These massive humanoids once ruled the world beside the primordials. Now, they dominate petty kingdoms and crush any who oppose their tyrannical reign.

Shortly after the world emerged from the smoldering forges of the primordials, titans stepped forth to help explore and shape the new creation. They walked atop the world's still-cooling crust and swam through its churning seas, yet even in their immensity, the titans were too few to explore the vast world. They created giants as a servant race, modeling them to resemble the titans' own elemental natures. With the aid of the giants, the titans spread out across the world. In time, the giants enslaved some of the nascent races of the gods, most notably the dwarves. Under the giants' steady gazes and heavy hands, these industrious slaves brought beauty and refinement to the world.

A Shattered Legacy: When the Dawn War began, titans and giants joined the side of their creators in the battle against the gods. Although often outnumbered by their foes, titans and giants possessed nearly unmatched strength. For a while, the giants were victorious, and they filled their halls with the spoils of their victories. Over time, the resolve of the giants was weakened as many of the great titans and mighty citadels began to fall and the gods slew or trapped some of the primordials. The blow that finally crippled the giants came from a source the creatures never predicted. The dwarves, who had maintained their secret devotion to Moradin for many years, rose up against their masters, unleashing the fury of a hundred generations of repression.

The giants and titans still covet the power they once possessed, and they have never forgiven the dwarves' betrayal. Although giants exist only in small, scattered colonies across the planes, many scheme to reclaim their former glory. They aspire to knock down the gods and bring the dwarves and other humanoid races under their heel. Few giants still serve the primordials or work together as once they did, yet even divided, they remain a powerful and dangerous threat.

Born from Furor: Giants stride about the planes, crafting castles in the highest clouds and building citadels in the darkest stretches of the Underdark. The most common types of giants in the world are hill giants, fire giants, and frost giants.

Dim-witted and bullying, a hill giant lives like a savage. With others of its kind, a hill giant builds crude log forts and mud-wattle huts in the hills and mountain valleys. Although brutish by nature, a hill giant possesses more cunning than an ogre. A hill giant might attempt to ape the traditions of a realm it destroys, anointing itself king and demanding a daily tribute of pumpkins and cows. Hill giants are the weaker branch of the family of earth giants, which all share connections to the primordial elements of earth and stone. Earth titans, towering brutes that appear to be made of living rock and soil, are the mightiest of these giants.

(Left to right) frost giant, fire giant, hill giant

Militaristic and domineering, a fire giant has a fiery body and a temper to match. The fire giants' mastery of metalwork is legendary, and many weapons of renown have been struck from their forges. A fire giant prefers to dwell in or around volcanoes and other areas of molten rock. If such areas are unavailable, fire giants will often build fortresses in rocky mountains. Behind the burning iron walls of these citadels, fire giants keep slaves—particularly dwarves—to mine ore or attend to mundane tasks.

Frost giants live in the frozen wastes, where they carve fortresses from the ice. In these chill domains, skalds sing of the giants' victories and of the bravery of their warriors. When food runs low or warriors grow bold, these fearsome giants leave their realms to raid along the borders, seeking glory, carnage, and wealth.

Titanic Leaders: Titans believe themselves to be the firstborn of creation, and they seek to emulate their primordial creators. They shape imitations of the world from the raw pieces of the Elemental Chaos. Unlike efreets, they do not try to impose order on the regions they control. Instead, the titans revel in the entropic jumble of elemental forces.

A titan realm might contain places where the Elemental Chaos erupts into the world, spilling into the heart of an active volcano, into the midst of a permanent storm, or into the deepest reaches of a frozen wasteland. In the world, these areas are usually populated by giants. Through these natural planar connections, giants and titans can wreak havoc upon nearby realms, conquering vast tracts of land until someone stops them by closing the portal or slaying their chief.

SAM WOOD

Hill Giant — Level 13 Brute
Large natural humanoid (earth, giant) — XP 800

HP 159; **Bloodied** 79
AC 25, **Fortitude** 27, **Reflex** 23, **Will** 25
Speed 8

Initiative +5
Perception +7

STANDARD ACTIONS

⊕ **Greatclub** (weapon) ✦ **At-Will**
Attack: Melee 2 (one creature); +18 vs. AC
Hit: 3d10 + 11 damage.

⌁ **Hurl Rock** (weapon) ✦ **At-Will**
Attack: Ranged 10 (one creature); +18 vs. AC
Hit: 2d10 + 8 damage.

† **Sweeping Club** (weapon) ✦ **Encounter**
Attack: Melee 2 (one or two creatures); +18 vs. AC
Hit: 3d10 + 11 damage, and the giant pushes the target up to 2 squares and knocks it prone.

Str 21 (+11)	**Dex** 8 (+5)	**Wis** 12 (+7)
Con 19 (+10)	**Int** 7 (+4)	**Cha** 9 (+5)

Alignment chaotic evil   **Languages** Giant
Equipment greatclub, 5 rocks

"Don't be fooled by its brutish appearance. A hill giant is as close to the earth beneath your feet as a storm giant is to the thunderhead above you."

—Noldir of Hammerfast

Hill Giant Hunter — Level 13 Artillery
Large natural humanoid (earth, giant) — XP 800

HP 103; **Bloodied** 51
AC 27, **Fortitude** 26, **Reflex** 23, **Will** 23
Speed 8

Initiative +5
Perception +12

STANDARD ACTIONS

⊕ **Javelin** (weapon) ✦ **At-Will**
Attack: Melee 2 (one creature); +18 vs. AC
Hit: 2d8 + 7 damage.

⌖ **Javelin** (weapon) ✦ **At-Will**
Attack: Ranged 20 (one creature); +20 vs. AC
Hit: 2d8 + 12 damage.

⌁ **Hurl Rock** (weapon) ✦ **Recharge** ⚅ ⚅
Attack: Ranged 20 (one creature); +20 vs. AC
Hit: 4d8 + 12 damage, and the giant can push the target 1 square and knocks it prone.

Str 21 (+11)	**Dex** 8 (+5)	**Wis** 12 (+7)
Con 19 (+10)	**Int** 7 (+4)	**Cha** 9 (+5)

Alignment chaotic evil   **Languages** Giant
Equipment 6 javelins, 4 rocks

Hill Giant Earth Shaman — Level 13 Controller (Leader)

Large natural humanoid (earth, giant)   XP 800

HP 131; **Bloodied** 65   **Initiative** +6
AC 27, **Fortitude** 25, **Reflex** 23, **Will** 23   **Perception** +8
Speed 8

STANDARD ACTIONS

ⓘ Earthgrip Slam ✦ At-Will

Attack: Melee 2 (one creature); +18 vs. AC

Hit: 2d8 + 10 damage, and the target is restrained until the end of the giant's next turn.

⤳ Earthen Chains (healing) **✦ Encounter**

Attack: Ranged 10 (one creature); +16 vs. Reflex

Hit: 1d8 + 5 damage, and the target is stunned (save ends). If the target is flying, it falls. The first time one of the giant's allies hits the target while it is stunned by this power, that ally regains 15 hit points.

↞ Earth Wave ✦ Recharge ⚄ ⚅

Attack: Close blast 5 (enemies in the blast); +16 vs. Fortitude

Hit: 1d10 + 4 damage, and the giant pushes the target up to 2 squares.

Effect: The target falls prone. Each ally in the blast can use a free action to shift up to 3 squares and make a basic attack.

Str 21 (+11)	Dex 10 (+6)	Wis 14 (+8)
Con 19 (+10)	Int 7 (+4)	Cha 16 (+9)

Alignment chaotic evil   **Languages** Giant

Earth Titan — Level 16 Elite Brute

Huge elemental humanoid (earth, giant)   XP 2,800

HP 384; **Bloodied** 192   **Initiative** +7
AC 30, **Fortitude** 31, **Reflex** 25, **Will** 26   **Perception** +9
Speed 6
Immune petrification
Saving Throws +2; **Action Points** 1

STANDARD ACTIONS

ⓘ Slam ✦ At-Will

Attack: Melee 3 (one creature); +21 vs. AC

Hit: 4d10 + 8 damage.

✝ Double Attack ✦ At-Will

Effect: The titan uses *slam* twice.

⤳ Hurl Rock ✦ At-Will

Attack: Ranged 20 (one creature); +21 vs. AC

Hit: 2d8 + 10 damage, and the target is dazed (save ends).

✳ Earth Shock ✦ Encounter

Attack: Close burst 2 (enemies in the burst); +19 vs. Fortitude

Hit: 3d12 + 6 damage, and the target is stunned until the end of the titan's next turn.

Miss: Half damage.

Skills Athletics +19

Str 23 (+14)	Dex 8 (+7)	Wis 12 (+9)
Con 22 (+14)	Int 10 (+8)	Cha 13 (+9)

Alignment chaotic evil   **Languages** Giant, Primordial
Equipment 5 rocks

Frost Giant
Level 17 Brute

Large elemental humanoid (cold, giant)
XP 1,600

HP 201; **Bloodied** 100
AC 29, **Fortitude** 32, **Reflex** 27, **Will** 28
Speed 8 (ice walk)
Resist 15 cold

Initiative +11
Perception +13

TRAITS

Icebound Footing
When an effect pulls, pushes, or slides the giant, it can choose to move 2 squares less than the effect specifies. The giant can make a saving throw to avoid falling prone when an attack would knock it prone.

STANDARD ACTIONS

⊕ **Icy Greataxe** (cold, weapon) ✦ At-Will
Attack: Melee 2 (one creature); +22 vs. AC
Hit: 3d12 + 11 cold damage, or 2d12 + 47 cold damage if the giant scores a critical hit.

↟ **Chilling Strike** (cold, weapon) ✦ Recharge ⚅ ⚃
Attack: Melee 2 (one creature); +22 vs. AC
Hit: 5d12 + 15 cold damage, and the target gains vulnerable 10 cold (save ends).

Skills Athletics +19
Str 23 (+14)　　**Dex** 16 (+11)　　**Wis** 20 (+13)
Con 21 (+13)　　**Int** 10 (+8)　　**Cha** 12 (+9)
Alignment evil　　　　**Languages** Giant
Equipment hide armor, greataxe

Frost Giant Marauder
Level 17 Skirmisher

Large elemental humanoid (cold, giant)
XP 1,600

HP 168; **Bloodied** 84
AC 31, **Fortitude** 31, **Reflex** 28, **Will** 27
Speed 8 (ice walk)
Resist 15 cold

Initiative +14
Perception +11

TRAITS

Icebound Footing
When an effect pulls, pushes, or slides the giant, it can choose to move 2 squares less than the effect specifies. The giant can make a saving throw to avoid falling prone when an attack would knock it prone.

STANDARD ACTIONS

⊕ ⊘ **Icy Handaxe** (cold, weapon) ✦ At-Will
Attack: Melee 2 or Ranged 10 (one creature); +22 vs. AC
Hit: 2d6 + 6 cold damage.
Effect: The giant shifts up to 2 squares.

↟ **Twin Strike** ✦ At-Will
Effect: The giant uses *icy handaxe* twice and can shift up to 2 squares between the attacks.

⌁ **Hurling Charge** ✦ Encounter
Effect: The giant uses *icy handaxe* twice as ranged attacks and then charges one of the targets.

Skills Athletics +18
Str 21 (+13)　　**Dex** 19 (+12)　　**Wis** 17 (+11)
Con 24 (+15)　　**Int** 10 (+8)　　**Cha** 12 (+9)
Alignment evil　　　　**Languages** Giant
Equipment 8 handaxes

Frost Titan **Level 20 Elite Brute**
Huge elemental humanoid (cold, giant) XP 5,600

HP 466; **Bloodied** 233 **Initiative** +14
AC 32, **Fortitude** 34, **Reflex** 29, **Will** 33 **Perception** +16
Speed 8 (ice walk)
Immune cold
Saving Throws +2; **Action Points** 1

TRAITS

Winter's Breath (cold) ✦ **Aura** 2
Squares in the aura are difficult terrain for enemies. In addition, any enemy that starts its turn in the aura takes 5 cold damage.

Icebound Footing
When an effect pulls, pushes, or slides the titan, it can choose to move up to 4 squares less than the effect specifies. The titan can make a saving throw to avoid falling prone when an attack would knock it prone.

Melting Flesh
When the titan takes fire damage, it takes a -2 penalty to AC until the end of its next turn.

STANDARD ACTIONS

Icy Greataxe (cold, weapon) ✦ **At-Will**
Attack: Melee 3 (one creature); +25 vs. AC
Hit: 4d8 + 7 cold damage, and ongoing 10 cold damage (save ends). If the titan scores a critical hit, the damage is 4d8 + 39 cold damage, and ongoing 10 cold damage (save ends).

Blast of Winter (cold) ✦ **Encounter**
Attack: Close blast 5 (creatures in the blast); +23 vs. Reflex
Hit: 3d12 + 12 cold damage, and ongoing 10 cold damage (save ends). In addition, the target is immobilized until the end of the titan's next turn.
Miss: Half damage.

MINOR ACTIONS

Cold-Blooded Kick ✦ **At-Will** (1/round)
Attack: Melee 3 (one creature); +23 vs. Reflex
Hit: 4d10 + 8 damage, and the titan pushes the target up to 2 squares and knocks it prone.

TRIGGERED ACTIONS

Furious Swipe ✦ **At-Will**
Trigger: The titan is first bloodied or drops to 0 hit points.
Effect (Immediate Interrupt): The titan uses *icy greataxe*.

Skills Athletics +24
Str 28 (+19) **Dex** 19 (+14) **Wis** 23 (+16)
Con 23 (+16) **Int** 10 (+10) **Cha** 16 (+13)
Alignment evil **Languages** Giant, Primordial
Equipment greataxe

"They prefer to live in the world's coldest places, but anywhere a frost giant decides to live becomes wintry soon enough."

—Moorin of Fallcrest

Fire Giant Flamecrusher — Level 17 Brute

Fire Giant Flamecrusher	Level 17 Brute
Large elemental humanoid (fire, giant)	XP 1,600

HP 204; **Bloodied** 102   **Initiative** +8
AC 29, **Fortitude** 30, **Reflex** 27, **Will** 27   **Perception** +10
Speed 8
Resist 15 fire

STANDARD ACTIONS

⊕ **Searing Maul** (fire, weapon) ✦ **At-Will**
  Attack: Melee 2 (one creature); +22 vs. AC
  Hit: 5d8 + 9 fire damage.

↓ **Overhead Smash** (fire, weapon) ✦ **At-Will**
  Attack: Melee 2 (one creature); +22 vs. AC
  Hit: 4d8 + 14 fire damage, and the target falls prone.

↢ **Battering Blows** (fire, weapon) ✦ **Recharge** if the power misses every target
  Requirement: The giant must be bloodied.
  Attack: Close burst 2 (enemies in the burst); +22 vs. AC
  Hit: 6d8 + 9 fire damage, and the giant pushes the target up to 2 squares.

Str 27 (+16)	**Dex** 11 (+8)	**Wis** 14 (+10)
Con 24 (+15)	**Int** 8 (+7)	**Cha** 11 (+8)

Alignment evil   **Languages** Giant
Equipment maul

"They live in volcanoes and tame hell hounds, but nothing is as hot as a fire giant's temper."

—Kristryd, paladin of Moradin

Fire Giant — Level 18 Soldier

Fire Giant	Level 18 Soldier
Large elemental humanoid (fire, giant)	XP 2,000

HP 174; **Bloodied** 87   **Initiative** +11
AC 34, **Fortitude** 34, **Reflex** 28, **Will** 28   **Perception** +14
Speed 8
Resist 15 fire

STANDARD ACTIONS

⊕ **Searing Greatsword** (fire, weapon) ✦ **At-Will**
  Attack: Melee 2 (one creature); +23 vs. AC
  Hit: 2d12 + 13 fire damage.
  Effect: The giant marks the target until the end of the giant's next turn.

↢ **Sweeping Sword** (fire, weapon) ✦ **At-Will**
  Attack: Close blast 2 (enemies in the blast); +23 vs. AC
  Hit: 2d12 + 13 fire damage.
  Effect: The giant marks the target until the end of the giant's next turn.

Str 23 (+15)	**Dex** 11 (+9)	**Wis** 10 (+9)
Con 22 (+15)	**Int** 10 (+9)	**Cha** 11 (+9)

Alignment evil   **Languages** Giant
Equipment chainmail, greatsword

Fire Giant Forgecaller — Level 18 Artillery

Large elemental humanoid (fire, giant)   XP 2,000

HP 136; **Bloodied** 68   **Initiative** +11
AC 32, **Fortitude** 33, **Reflex** 29, **Will** 30   **Perception** +17
Speed 8
Resist 15 fire

STANDARD ACTIONS

⊕ **Smoldering Mace** (fire, weapon) ✦ **At-Will**
Attack: Melee 2 (one creature); +23 vs. AC
Hit: 2d10 + 11 fire damage.

↗ **Fire Pillar** (fire) ✦ **At-Will**
Attack: Ranged 20 (one creature); +23 vs. Reflex
Hit: 3d10 + 10 fire damage.

❈ **Flaming Burst** (fire) ✦ **Recharge** ⚅
Attack: Area burst 2 within 10 (creatures in the burst); +23 vs. Reflex
Hit: 2d10 + 10 fire damage, and ongoing 10 fire damage (save ends).
Miss: Half damage, and ongoing 5 fire damage (save ends).

Str 23 (+15)	**Dex** 15 (+11)	**Wis** 16 (+12)
Con 22 (+15)	**Int** 10 (+9)	**Cha** 11 (+9)

Alignment evil   **Languages** Giant
Equipment mace

Fire Titan — Level 21 Elite Soldier

Huge elemental humanoid (fire, giant)   XP 6,400

HP 398; **Bloodied** 199   **Initiative** +18
AC 37, **Fortitude** 34, **Reflex** 31, **Will** 31   **Perception** +21
Speed 8
Immune fire
Saving Throws +2; **Action Points** 1

STANDARD ACTIONS

⊕ **Fiery Greatsword** (fire, weapon) ✦ **At-Will**
Attack: Melee 3 (one creature); +26 vs. AC
Hit: 6d6 + 9 fire damage, and the titan pushes the target
up to 2 squares.
Effect: The titan marks the target until the end of the titan's
next turn.

✢ **Double Attack** ✦ **At-Will**
Effect: The titan uses *fiery greatsword* twice.

↗ **Hurl Lava** (fire) ✦ **Recharge** ⚄ ⚅
Attack: Ranged 20 (one creature); +24 vs. Reflex
Hit: 6d6 + 15 fire damage, and the target is immobilized until the end of the titan's next turn. If
the target is flying, it falls.
Miss: Half damage, and the target is slowed until the end of the titan's next turn.

⇐ **Burning Wave** (fire) ✦ **At-Will**
Attack: Close burst 5 (creatures in the burst); +24 vs. Reflex
Hit: 2d8 + 3 fire damage, and ongoing 10 fire damage (save ends).

Str 29 (+19)	**Dex** 23 (+16)	**Wis** 23 (+16)
Con 23 (+16)	**Int** 10 (+10)	**Cha** 21 (+15)

Alignment evil   **Languages** Giant, Primordial
Equipment greatsword

GITHYANKI

Pirates, raiders, and soldiers of the Astral Sea, githyanki are bloodthirsty and ruthless in pursuit of their goals. Githyanki raiders use astral vessels to stage incursions, both on their home plane and in the world, pillaging their targets.

The githyanki are fierce psychic warriors that ply the Astral Sea and fight with silver swords. They were once members of a race known as the gith which spent countless years enslaved by mind flayers. After winning their freedom, a faction of gith fled to the Astral Sea and became xenophobic and militaristic. There, the githyanki built citadels and armies, and then set out to conquer everything in their path.

> *"It's almost as though the githyanki feel that the entire universe owes them reparations for the years of slavery they endured under the mind flayers."*
> —Philaster of Hestavar

Astral Pirates: Arguably the most skilled navigators of the Astral Sea, githyanki appear suddenly, seemingly out of nowhere, to launch surprise attacks on their victims. Githyanki use raids to obtain wealth both to sustain their ships and to provide their capital, Tu'narath, with supplies for the githyanki military machine. Githyanki pirate ships act at the discretion of their captains,

Githyanki Warrior	Level 12 Soldier
Medium natural humanoid	XP 700
HP 118; **Bloodied** 59	**Initiative** +11
AC 28, **Fortitude** 25, **Reflex** 23, **Will** 22	**Perception** +12
Speed 5	

STANDARD ACTIONS

⊕ **Silver Greatsword** (psychic, weapon) ✦ At-Will
Attack: Melee 1 (one creature); +17 vs. AC
Hit: 2d10 + 8 psychic damage, plus 3d6 psychic damage against an immobilized target.
Effect: The githyanki marks the target until the end of the githyanki's next turn. The penalty to attack rolls imposed by this mark is -4 instead of the normal -2.

⌁ **Telekinetic Grasp** ✦ Recharge ⚄ ⚅
Attack: Ranged 5 (one Medium or smaller creature); +15 vs. Fortitude
Hit: The target is immobilized (save ends).

MOVE ACTIONS

Telekinetic Leap ✦ Encounter
Effect: The githyanki flies up to 5 squares, or one ally within 10 squares of it can fly up to 5 squares as a free action.

Skills History +9, Insight +12		
Str 21 (+11)	**Dex** 17 (+9)	**Wis** 12 (+7)
Con 14 (+8)	**Int** 12 (+7)	**Cha** 13 (+7)
Alignment evil	**Languages** Common, Deep Speech	
Equipment plate armor, silver greatsword		

Githyanki Mindslicer — Level 13 Artillery
Medium natural humanoid — XP 800

HP 98; **Bloodied** 49 — **Initiative** +9
AC 27, **Fortitude** 24, **Reflex** 26, **Will** 23 — **Perception** +12
Speed 6

STANDARD ACTIONS

⊕ **Silver Longsword** (psychic, weapon) ✦ At-Will
Attack: Melee 1 (one creature); +18 vs. AC
Hit: 3d8 + 5 psychic damage.

⤙ **Mind Slice** (psychic) ✦ At-Will
Attack: Ranged 10 (one creature); +18 vs. Will
Hit: 3d8 + 8 psychic damage.

✸ **Psychic Barrage** (psychic) ✦ Recharge ⚅
Attack: Area burst 1 within 20 (creatures in the burst); +18 vs. Will
Hit: 2d8 + 8 psychic damage, and the target takes ongoing 10 psychic damage and can't use daily or encounter attack powers (save ends both).

MOVE ACTIONS

Telekinetic Leap ✦ Encounter
Effect: The githyanki flies up to 5 squares, or one ally within 10 squares of it can fly up to 5 squares as a free action.

Skills History +11, Insight +12
Str 14 (+8) — **Dex** 16 (+9) — **Wis** 12 (+7)
Con 14 (+8) — **Int** 17 (+9) — **Cha** 11 (+6)
Alignment evil — **Languages** Common, Deep Speech
Equipment robes, overcoat, silver longsword

(Left to right) githyanki mindslicer, githyanki warrior, githyanki raider

yet some githyanki raids are more than just grabs for plunder; they are part of a larger plan hatched by the githyanki leadership.

Githyanki are ruthless in their raids. They restrain themselves only enough to leave their prey with a bit to survive on. The githyanki know that a target can be harvested more than once only if the target isn't completely crushed, and they might return months or years later to plunder a target again.

Invaders from Another Plane: Githyanki incursions into the world are rare, but when they do occur, they can be devastating. Most of them are major military initiatives that feature fleets of planar ships and legions of githyanki warriors. They take advantage of complex military strategies, including establishing beachheads, securing defensive fortifications, dispatching advance scouts, and planning sorties into enemy territories.

Githyanki Raider	Level 13 Skirmisher
Medium natural humanoid	XP 800
HP 126; **Bloodied** 63	**Initiative** +11
AC 27, **Fortitude** 23, **Reflex** 25, **Will** 27	**Perception** +9
Speed 6	

TRAITS

Combat Advantage (psychic)
The githyanki deals 2d8 extra psychic damage against any creature granting combat advantage to it.

STANDARD ACTIONS

⊕ **Silver Longsword** (psychic, weapon) ✦ **At-Will**
Attack: Melee 1 (one creature); +18 vs. AC
Hit: 2d8 + 12 psychic damage.

↯ **Raider's Strike** (psychic, weapon) ✦ **At-Will**
Attack: Melee 1 (one creature); +18 vs. AC
Hit: 2d8 + 12 psychic damage.
Effect: The githyanki shifts up to 2 squares.

↯ **Slash and Dash** (psychic, weapon) ✦ **Encounter**
Attack: Melee 1 (one or two creatures); +18 vs. AC. The githyanki can shift up to its speed before making the second attack.
Hit: 4d8 + 14 psychic damage.
Miss: Half damage.

MOVE ACTIONS

Raider's Step ✦ **At-Will**
Effect: The githyanki shifts up to 2 squares.

Telekinetic Leap ✦ **Encounter**
Effect: The githyanki flies up to 5 squares, or one ally within 10 squares of it can fly up to 5 squares as a free action.

Skills History +7, Insight +14		
Str 22 (+12)	**Dex** 17 (+9)	**Wis** 16 (+9)
Con 14 (+8)	**Int** 9 (+5)	**Cha** 8 (+5)

Alignment evil   **Languages** Common, Deep Speech
Equipment leather armor, silver longsword

Githyanki Legionary

Githyanki Legionary	**Level 13 Minion Soldier**	
Medium natural humanoid	XP 175	

HP 1; a missed attack never damages a minion.   **Initiative** +10
AC 29, **Fortitude** 26, **Reflex** 23, **Will** 25   **Perception** +9
Speed 5

STANDARD ACTIONS

⊕ **Silver Short Sword** (psychic, weapon) ✦ At-Will
   Attack: Melee 1 (one creature); +18 vs. AC
   Hit: 10 damage, plus 5 psychic damage if the target is immobilized.

⟆ **Telekinetic Grasp** ✦ Encounter
   Attack: Ranged 5 (one creature); +16 vs. Fortitude
   Hit: The target is immobilized (save ends).

Str 16 (+9)	**Dex** 14 (+8)	**Wis** 16 (+9)
Con 12 (+7)	**Int** 12 (+7)	**Cha** 10 (+6)

Alignment chaotic evil   **Languages** Common, Deep Speech
Equipment chainmail, silver short sword

Once a githyanki incursion has begun, the githyanki sometimes seek allies among the natives of the area. It is rare for any natives to side with them, but occasionally the githyanki do find collaborators who seek protection, advantage, or both. Particularly cunning githyanki commanders dispatch emissaries to the world prior to an invasion, either to sabotage their targets' defenses or to identify potential collaborators. A greedy noble might be promised a kingdom captured by the githyanki in exchange for information and aid, or a wizard might be intimidated into providing assistance in return for the githyanki's promise to leave the wizard's tower untouched during the incursion. Additionally, githyanki often retain the service of red dragons, which serve them as mounts in battle.

Denizens of Tu'narath: Despite the fact that many of them spend their days wandering the Astral Sea, githyanki call the fortress-city Tu'narath their home and capital. Built atop the remains of a long-dead god, Tu'narath is the seat of power of the githyanki lich-queen Vlaakith.

Tu'narath serves as the focal point for githyanki navigational charts, the supply point for their mobile shipyards, and the center of githyanki culture. The city is also the basis for the githyanki method of navigation in the Astral Sea. Long ago, githyanki cartographers learned to read the echoes of magical energy created by Tu'narath, using the city as a central location around which other objects in the sea can be found. The navigators aboard githyanki vessels possess magic maps that remotely receive the latest navigational data from the capital's cartographers each day.

GNOLL

Gnolls are feral, demon-worshiping marauders. They attack communities along the borderlands without warning and slaughter without mercy, all in the name of the demon lord Yeenoghu.

Gnolls drive fear into the souls of many. These mad humanoids know nothing of mercy and think of little but bloodletting. For most, to see a gnoll's hyenalike face is to see one's death.

A Demon's Dogs: The Destroyer, the Beast of Butchery, and the Ruler of Ruin—Yeenoghu has many names, but the most famous among them is Demon Prince of Gnolls. Yeenoghu appears like a massive gnoll and has acted as a patron to the race for as long as any can remember.

As the mortal instruments of Yeenoghu, gnolls constantly perform atrocities. They follow the demon lord's edicts and the orders of his demons without question. When not marauding in Yeenoghu's name, gnolls fight among themselves and participate in ceremonies that involve acts of depravity and self-mutilation. Some gnolls are known to mate with demons or perform rituals that bind their bodies or souls to demonic forces.

Nomadic Destroyers: Gnolls rarely stay in one place for long. Their tribes rove en masse, laying waste when they can. When gnolls attack and pillage a settlement, they leave little behind but razed buildings, gnawed corpses, and befouled land.

Gnoll Huntmaster	Level 5 Artillery
Medium natural humanoid	XP 200
HP 50; **Bloodied** 25	**Initiative** +4
AC 19, **Fortitude** 17, **Reflex** 18, **Will** 15	**Perception** +11
Speed 8	Low-light vision

TRAITS

Pack Attack
The gnoll's attacks deal 5 extra damage to any enemy that has two or more of the gnoll's allies adjacent to it.

STANDARD ACTIONS

⊕ **Handaxe** (weapon) ✦ **At-Will**
Attack: Melee 1 (one creature); +10 vs. AC
Hit: 2d6 + 3 damage, or 2d6 + 5 while the gnoll is bloodied.

⤳ **Longbow** (weapon) ✦ **At-Will**
Attack: Ranged 30 (one creature); +12 vs. AC
Hit: 1d10 + 8 damage, or 1d10 + 10 while the gnoll is bloodied.

Skills Stealth +11

Str 16 (+5)	**Dex** 19 (+6)	**Wis** 14 (+4)
Con 14 (+4)	**Int** 8 (+1)	**Cha** 7 (+0)

Alignment chaotic evil   **Languages** Abyssal, Common
Equipment leather armor, handaxe, longbow, 30 arrows

(Left to right) deathpledged gnoll, gnoll pack lord, gnoll blood caller, gnoll huntmaster

Gnolls rarely build permanent structures and craft little of lasting value. Indeed, they see such permanence as an affront to the Destroyer. Their only sense of art manifests itself as grisly displays of past victories. Gnolls decorate their armor and encampments with the bones of their victims. Impatient and unskilled artisans, they wear patchwork armor and wield weapons taken from the dead.

Insatiable Bloodlust: Nothing pleases a gnoll more than wanton slaughter. Because of that fact, gnolls don't bargain or parley, and they can't be bribed. Nothing stops gnolls from killing except for overwhelming opposition, and even then, gnolls try to kill many foes before fleeing. Fortunately for other creatures, the gnolls' warmongering makes them an enemy to all. Even orcs avoid allying with gnolls.

Savage Slavers: Gnolls detest physical labor and often use slaves to perform menial chores. Slaves follow behind their raiders to haul their tents and the few goods that the gnolls deign to carry with them. Guarded by merciless gnoll youths, the slaves' only hope of living to the next day is to show strength and to obey.

The life of a slave in a gnoll camp is brutal and short. That said, slaves who show physical endurance and savagery might be indoctrinated into the gnoll vanguard. Such creatures are usually broken in mind and spirit, having become as cruel and ruthless as their masters.

STEVE PRESCOTT

Deathpledged Gnoll

Level 5 Brute

Medium natural humanoid

XP 200

HP 74; **Bloodied** 37
AC 18, **Fortitude** 18, **Reflex** 16, **Will** 16
Speed 8

Initiative +4
Perception +4
Low-light vision

TRAITS

Pack Attack

The gnoll's attacks deal 5 extra damage to any enemy that has two or more of the gnoll's allies adjacent to it.

STANDARD ACTIONS

⊕ **Longspear** (weapon) ✦ At-Will

Attack: Melee 1 (one creature); +10 vs. AC

Hit: 2d6 + 9 damage, or 2d6 + 11 while the gnoll is bloodied.

TRIGGERED ACTIONS

Claws of Yeenoghu (healing)

Trigger: The gnoll first drops to 0 hit points.

Effect (No Action): The gnoll regains 5 hit points, gains 1 action point, and gains resist 15 to all damage. At the end of its next turn, the gnoll drops to 0 hit points.

Str 18 (+6)	**Dex** 15 (+4)	**Wis** 15 (+4)
Con 14 (+4)	**Int** 9 (+1)	**Cha** 7 (+0)

Alignment chaotic evil   **Languages** Abyssal, Common

Equipment leather armor, light shield, longspear

Gnoll Blood Caller

Level 6 Soldier

Medium natural humanoid

XP 250

HP 70; **Bloodied** 35
AC 22, **Fortitude** 19, **Reflex** 18, **Will** 17
Speed 8

Initiative +8
Perception +5
Low-light vision

TRAITS

Pack Attack

The gnoll's attacks deal 5 extra damage to any enemy that has two or more of the gnoll's allies adjacent to it.

STANDARD ACTIONS

⊕ **Claws** ✦ At-Will

Attack: Melee 1 (one creature); +11 vs. AC

Hit: 2d6 + 7 damage, or 2d6 + 9 while the gnoll is bloodied.

Effect: The gnoll marks the target until the end of the gnoll's next turn.

↤ **Blood Call** (charm, psychic) ✦ At-Will

Effect: The gnoll shifts up to 3 squares.

Attack: Close burst 5 (each creature marked by the gnoll in the burst); +9 vs. Will

Hit: 1d10 + 9 psychic damage, and the gnoll pulls the target up to 3 squares.

MINOR ACTIONS

↤ **Blood Frenzy** ✦ At-Will (1/round)

Requirement: The gnoll must be bloodied.

Effect: Close burst 1 (enemies in the burst). Each target takes 5 damage and is marked by the gnoll until the end of the gnoll's next turn.

Str 19 (+7)	**Dex** 16 (+6)	**Wis** 15 (+5)
Con 14 (+5)	**Int** 9 (+2)	**Cha** 7 (+1)

Alignment chaotic evil   **Languages** Abyssal, Common

Equipment leather armor

Fang of Yeenoghu   Level 7 Skirmisher (Leader)
Medium natural humanoid, gnoll   XP 300

HP 77; **Bloodied** 38   **Initiative** +9
AC 21, **Fortitude** 18, **Reflex** 19, **Will** 18   **Perception** +3
Speed 8   Low-light vision

TRAITS
Pack Attack
The gnoll's attacks deal 5 extra damage to any enemy that has two or more of the gnoll's allies adjacent to it.

STANDARD ACTIONS
⊕ **Cudgel of Bloody Teeth** (weapon) ✦ **At-Will**
Attack: Melee 1 (one creature); +12 vs. AC
Hit: 2d6 + 8 damage, or 2d6 + 10 while the gnoll is bloodied. The target takes ongoing 5 damage (save ends).

† **Relentless Push** (weapon) ✦ **At-Will**
Effect: Before the attack, the gnoll shifts up to 2 squares.
Attack: Melee 1 (one creature); +12 vs. AC
Hit: 1d10 + 10 damage, or 1d10 + 12 while the gnoll is bloodied. The gnoll can push the target 1 square.
Effect: One ally within 5 squares of the gnoll can shift 1 square as a free action.

⟵ **Howl of the Demon** ✦ **Recharge** ⚅
Effect: Close burst 5 (allies in the burst). Each target can make a melee basic attack as a free action.

Str 16 (+6)	**Dex** 19 (+7)	**Wis** 11 (+3)
Con 13 (+4)	**Int** 10 (+3)	**Cha** 16 (+6)

Alignment chaotic evil   **Languages** Abyssal, Common
Equipment leather armor, cudgel of bloody teeth (greatclub)

Gnoll Gorger   Level 7 Brute
Medium natural humanoid   XP 300

HP 96; **Bloodied** 48   **Initiative** +6
AC 19, **Fortitude** 20, **Reflex** 18, **Will** 18   **Perception** +3
Speed 7   Low-light vision

TRAITS
Pack Attack
The gnoll's attacks deal 5 extra damage to any enemy that has two or more of the gnoll's allies adjacent to it.

STANDARD ACTIONS
⊕ **Bite** ✦ **At-Will**
Attack: Melee 1 (one creature); +12 vs. AC
Hit: 3d6 + 8 damage, or 3d6 + 10 while the gnoll is bloodied.

MINOR ACTIONS
Gorge (healing) ✦ **At-Will** (1/round)
Effect: Melee 1 (one ally). The target takes 5 damage, and the gnoll regains 5 hit points.

Skills Intimidate +11, Stealth +11

Str 20 (+8)	**Dex** 17 (+6)	**Wis** 11 (+3)
Con 16 (+6)	**Int** 9 (+2)	**Cha** 17 (+6)

Alignment chaotic evil   **Languages** Abyssal, Common
Equipment leather armor

Demon-Eye Gnoll

Medium natural humanoid

Level 7 Lurker
XP 300

HP 62; **Bloodied** 31
AC 21, **Fortitude** 20, **Reflex** 20, **Will** 18
Speed 8

Initiative +11
Perception +10
Low-light vision

TRAITS

☼ **Abyssal Mind** (charm, psychic) ✦ **Aura** 3

While the gnoll is bloodied, any enemy that ends its turn in the aura and can see the gnoll takes 5 psychic damage. If the enemy is dazed, it must also make a basic attack against its nearest ally as a free action.

Pack Attack

The gnoll's attacks deal 5 extra damage to any enemy that has two or more of the gnoll's allies adjacent to it.

STANDARD ACTIONS

⊕ **Glaive** (weapon) ✦ **At-Will**

Attack: Melee 2 (one creature); +12 vs. AC

Hit: 4d4 + 5 damage, or 6d4 + 15 if the target cannot see the gnoll.

↤ **Stare into the Abyss** ✦ **At-Will**

Attack: Close burst 3 (enemies in the burst that can see the gnoll); +10 vs. Will

Hit: The target is dazed until the end of the gnoll's next turn.

Effect: The gnoll becomes invisible to the targets until the end of its next turn.

Str 18 (+7)	**Dex** 18 (+7)	**Wis** 15 (+5)
Con 14 (+5)	**Int** 9 (+2)	**Cha** 7 (+1)

Alignment chaotic evil   **Languages** Abyssal, Common
Equipment leather armor, glaive

Gnoll Far Fang

Medium natural humanoid

Level 8 Artillery
XP 350

HP 68; **Bloodied** 34
AC 22, **Fortitude** 20, **Reflex** 22, **Will** 19
Speed 8

Initiative +9
Perception +11
Low-light vision

TRAITS

Pack Attack

The gnoll's attacks deal 5 extra damage to any enemy that has two or more of the gnoll's allies adjacent to it.

STANDARD ACTIONS

⊕ **Handaxe** (weapon) ✦ **At-Will**

Attack: Melee 1 (one creature); +13 vs. AC

Hit: 2d6 + 7 damage, or 2d6 + 9 while the gnoll is bloodied.

➹ **Fang Bow** (weapon) ✦ **At-Will**

Attack: Ranged 30 (one or two creatures); +15 vs. AC

Hit: 2d10 + 5 damage, or 2d10 + 7 while the gnoll is bloodied.

✸ **Hungry Arrows** (weapon) ✦ **Encounter**

Attack: Area burst 2 within 10 (enemies in the burst); +15 vs. AC

Hit: 2d10 + 5 damage, or 2d10 + 7 while the gnoll is bloodied. The target takes ongoing 5 damage (save ends).

Skills Stealth +14

Str 17 (+7)	**Dex** 21 (+9)	**Wis** 15 (+6)
Con 14 (+6)	**Int** 9 (+3)	**Cha** 7 (+2)

Alignment chaotic evil   **Languages** Abyssal, Common
Equipment leather armor, handaxe, fang bow (longbow)

Gnoll Pack Lord — Level 8 Controller (Leader)

Medium natural humanoid — XP 350

HP 90; Bloodied 45 — Initiative +6
AC 22, Fortitude 21, Reflex 19, Will 22 — Perception +6
Speed 8 — Low-light vision

Traits

Pack Attack
The gnoll's attacks deal 5 extra damage to any enemy that has two or more of the gnoll's allies adjacent to it.

Standard Actions

⊕ **Flail** (weapon) ✦ **At-Will**
Attack: Melee 1 (one creature); +13 vs. AC
Hit: 1d10 + 11 damage.

⊁ **Demonic Frenzy** (charm) ✦ **Recharge when an ally drops to 0 hit points**
Attack: Ranged 10 (one creature); +11 vs. Will
Hit: The target takes a -2 penalty to attack rolls until the end of its next turn. In addition, the target uses a free action to make two basic attacks against a target or targets of the gnoll's choice.
Effect: The target is dazed until the end of its next turn.

※ **Feed on the Weak** ✦ **At-Will**
Attack: Area burst 1 within 5 (enemies in the burst); +11 vs. Will
Hit: The target grants combat advantage until the start of its next turn.
Effect: One ally in the burst can make a basic attack as a free action.

Minor Actions

⇐ **Pack Cackle** ✦ **Recharge** 🎲 🎲
Effect: Close burst 5 (allies in the burst). Each target can shift up to 2 squares as a free action.

Str 17 (+7)	Dex 15 (+6)	Wis 15 (+6)
Con 18 (+8)	Int 10 (+4)	Cha 20 (+9)

Alignment chaotic evil — **Languages** Abyssal, Common
Equipment leather armor, flail

Gnoll Demon Spawn — Level 9 Brute

Large natural humanoid — XP 900

HP 120; Bloodied 60 — Initiative +7
AC 21, Fortitude 23, Reflex 21, Will 20 — Perception +6
Speed 8 — Low-light vision

Traits

Pack Attack
The gnoll's attacks deal 5 extra damage to any enemy that has two or more of the gnoll's allies adjacent to it.

Standard Actions

⊕ **Claws** ✦ **At-Will**
Attack: Melee 2 (one creature); +14 vs. AC
Hit: 3d10 + 5 damage.

Minor Actions

⊕ **Hungry Bite** ✦ **At-Will** (1/round)
Requirement: The gnoll must be bloodied.
Attack: Melee 2 (one creature); +14 vs. AC
Hit: 1d6 + 6 damage, and the gnoll gains 5 temporary hit points.

Str 22 (+10)	Dex 17 (+7)	Wis 15 (+6)
Con 20 (+9)	Int 8 (+3)	Cha 6 (+2)

Alignment chaotic evil — **Languages** Abyssal, Common

GNOME

Many believe that the gnomes are in decline, and some even think them long extinct. As with most things gnomish, the truth hides behind these illusions. Gnomes live in a culture of slyness and subtlety, so it is with good reason that they are known as the hidden people.

Long ago, gnomes fell under the sway of the giants of the Feywild known as fomorians. Sages say that this was when gnomes first mastered the magic of illusions. With the help of the eladrin—some say with their unwitting aid—gnomes escaped the yoke of their hideous masters and fled to the world. Now gnomes live in great numbers on both planes, although few know this fact.

Secretive and Cautious: Gnomes live in secret places. They are unobtrusive by nature and avoid confrontation when they can. In the forests of the Feywild and the world, communities of gnomes live among the roots of trees and within gigantic fallen trunks. Gnomes embed their structures in the forest floor, and their camouflaged chambers often have hidden passages.

Gnome Spy	Level 5 Lurker
Small fey humanoid	XP 200

HP 51; Bloodied 25	Initiative +10
AC 19, Fortitude 16, Reflex 18, Will 17	Perception +8
Speed 5	Low-light vision

TRAITS

Reactive Stealth
If the gnome has cover or concealment when it rolls initiative, it can make a Stealth check to become hidden.

STANDARD ACTIONS

⊕ **Short Sword** (weapon) ✦ **At-Will**
Attack: Melee 1 (one creature); +10 vs. AC
Hit: 2d6 + 4 damage, or 4d6 + 4 if the gnome was invisible to the target when it attacked.

⊙ **Dagger** (weapon) ✦ **At-Will**
Attack: Ranged 10 (one creature); +10 vs. AC
Hit: 2d4 + 5 damage, or 4d4 + 5 if the gnome was invisible to the target when it attacked.

Vanish from Sight (illusion) ✦ **At-Will**
Effect: The gnome becomes invisible until it hits or misses with an attack or until the end of its next turn.

TRIGGERED ACTIONS

Fade Away (illusion) ✦ **Encounter**
Trigger: The gnome takes damage.
Effect (Immediate Reaction): The gnome becomes invisible until it hits or misses with an attack or until the end of its next turn.

Skills Bluff +10, Stealth +11		
Str 10 (+2)	Dex 18 (+6)	Wis 13 (+3)
Con 15 (+4)	Int 11 (+2)	Cha 17 (+5)
Alignment unaligned	Languages Common, Elven	
Equipment leather armor, short sword, dagger		

Gnome Illusionist — Level 6 Artillery

Small fey humanoid   XP 250

HP 57; **Bloodied** 28
AC 20, **Fortitude** 15, **Reflex** 17, **Will** 18
Speed 5

Initiative +5
Perception +4
Low-light vision

Standard Actions

⊕ **Gnarled Staff** (weapon) ✦ At-Will
Attack: Melee 1 (one creature); +11 vs. AC
Hit: 1d8 + 6 damage.

✵ **Bedazzle** (illusion, implement, radiant) ✦ At-Will
Attack: Area burst 1 within 10 (enemies in the burst); +11 vs. Will
Hit: 2d6 + 5 radiant damage, and the target grants combat advantage (save ends).

↢ **See Me Not** (illusion, implement, psychic) ✦ Recharge ⚄ ⚅
Attack: Close blast 3 (enemies in the blast); +9 vs. Will
Hit: 2d6 + 10 psychic damage, and the target cannot see the gnome (save ends).

Move Actions

There, Not There (illusion, teleportation) ✦ Encounter
Effect: The gnome teleports up to 5 squares and creates two duplicates of itself within 5 squares of its destination space. The duplicates last until the gnome attacks or until they are destroyed. Each duplicate has 1 hit point and the same ability scores and defenses as the gnome. The gnome can use its actions to have a duplicate act in any way it could, except that the duplicates cannot use powers and cannot flank.

Minor Actions

Veil (illusion) ✦ At-Will
Effect: The gnome can disguise itself and up to three allies within 5 squares of it to appear as any Small or Medium creatures. A creature can see through the disguise with a successful Insight check opposed by the gnome's Bluff check.

Skills Bluff +13, Stealth +12

Str 10 (+3)	**Dex** 14 (+5)	**Wis** 13 (+4)
Con 15 (+5)	**Int** 18 (+7)	**Cha** 20 (+8)

Alignment unaligned   **Languages** Common, Elven
Equipment robes, gnarled staff (quarterstaff)

When gnomes must dwell outside forests, they use the same ingenuity and instinct to hide. A gnome in a big city might dwell in the hidden space between the walls of two buildings and use sewers and alleys to move about. A gnome merchant might hide his traveling goods in secret compartments built into his wagons.

Gnomes are similarly circumspect in their interpersonal interactions. They prefer to go unnoticed and to watch and learn, but when directly approached, they offer friendly smiles, a rapier wit, and as little reason to take offense as possible. Yet even after years of such amiable interactions, a gnome might still consider another person a rival or a foe. A gnome's pleasantries might camouflage his or her true intentions, just as foliage hides gnomish homes.

Masters of Illusion: Gnomes enjoy illusion and trickery, and they regularly use magical means to distract and deceive. Gnomes often study arcane or shadow magic and have many wizards and warlocks among them. Even without formal study, a typical gnome can turn invisible, and many gnomes have other magical abilities of deception.

"It's not so much that we like keeping secrets as that we hate being discovered. We prefer to live our lives beneath notice, because when we're noticed, it's usually much bigger and much meaner creatures that notice us."
—Egeira of Moonstair

Gnome Assassin	Level 7 Skirmisher
Small fey humanoid	XP 300
HP 78; **Bloodied** 39	**Initiative** +9
AC 21, **Fortitude** 18, **Reflex** 20, **Will** 19	**Perception** +9
Speed 5	Low-light vision

STANDARD ACTIONS

⊕ **Katar** (weapon) ✦ **At-Will**

Attack: Melee 1 (one creature); +12 vs. AC

Hit: 2d6 + 8 damage, or 4d6 + 8 if the attack ended the gnome's *shade form*.

MOVE ACTIONS

Shadow Step (teleportation) ✦ **At-Will**

Requirement: The gnome must be adjacent to a creature.

Effect: The gnome teleports up to 3 squares to a square adjacent to a different creature, and any mark on the gnome ends.

MINOR ACTIONS

Shade Form ✦ **Recharge** when first bloodied

Effect: The gnome assumes a shadowy form that lasts until it makes an attack roll or until the end of its next turn. While in this form, it is insubstantial and has vulnerable 5 radiant. In addition, it can make Stealth checks to become hidden if it has any cover or concealment.

Sustain Minor: The shadowy form persists until the end of the gnome's next turn.

Skills Stealth +12		
Str 10 (+3)	**Dex** 19 (+7)	**Wis** 13 (+4)
Con 14 (+5)	**Int** 14 (+5)	**Cha** 16 (+6)

Alignment unaligned	**Languages** Common, Elven
Equipment leather armor, 2 katars	

RAVEN MIMURA

Gnome Entropist	Level 8 Artillery
Small fey humanoid	XP 350

HP 71; **Bloodied** 35   **Initiative** +7
AC 22, **Fortitude** 19, **Reflex** 19, **Will** 21   **Perception** +3
Speed 5   Low-light vision

TRAITS

Illusory Defenses
The gnome gains a +2 bonus to all defenses against ranged attacks.

STANDARD ACTIONS

⊕ **Touch of Chaos** (acid, weapon) ✦ **At-Will**
Attack: Melee 1 (one creature); +13 vs. AC
Hit: 3d6 + 4 acid damage.

⌁ **Entropic Arc** (implement) ✦ **At-Will**
Attack: Ranged 10 (one creature); +13 vs. Reflex
Hit: 2d8 + 7 damage, and the target cannot take immediate actions or opportunity actions until the end of the gnome's next turn.

⁂ **Chaos Flare** ✦ **Recharge** if the power misses every target
Attack: Area burst 1 within 15 (enemies in the burst); +13 vs. Will
Hit: 3d8 + 5 damage, and the target is blinded (save ends).

TRIGGERED ACTIONS

Disappearing Act (illusion) ✦ **Encounter**
Trigger: The gnome takes damage from an attack.
Effect (Immediate Reaction): The gnome becomes invisible until the end of its next turn.

Str 10 (+4)	**Dex** 17 (+7)	**Wis** 8 (+3)
Con 17 (+7)	**Int** 12 (+5)	**Cha** 20 (+9)

Alignment unaligned   **Languages** Common, Elven
Equipment dagger

Disguises—both mundane and magical—cloak gnome communities. Many potential foes have passed through a gnome community without ever knowing it. When enemies manage to find a gnome settlement, the gnomes use illusions to draw them off and then move through secret passages to surround and attack them.

Gnomes also employ traps to safeguard themselves and their prized possessions. A gnome's dwelling might contain misleading passages that lead only to entrapment. The coin purse on a gnome's belt might hold a hand trap to catch would-be thieves. Through the use of traps and trickery, gnomes have earned a reputation for being more dangerous than they appear.

A Dark Side: The gnomish penchant for secrecy and deception leads some gnomes to be exceedingly suspicious. Others are drawn to professions where they can make careers out of duplicity. Gnomes are known to work for the eladrin as spies or burglars. Some gnomes worship Vecna, the keeper of secrets. Others go so far as to aid the fomorians, their former masters, acting as double agents in eladrin courts or as informers about the affairs of the world. Far from their traditional forest homes, gnomes also form their own guilds of thieves.

GOBLIN

Goblins live for conquest and seek to rule all they can through the might of blade or spell.

Aggressive and cruel, goblins range in disposition from outright savage to rigidly disciplined. Accompanied by their trained beasts, goblins go to war for conquest, not mere destruction.

Three Types: Goblins come in three distinct types: goblins, bugbears, and hobgoblins. All three have common physical characteristics: large and pointed ears, a prominent jaw filled with sharp teeth, a small nose, and dark hair. Their skin might be any shade of green, yellow, or orange, with goblins tending toward yellow-green, bugbears yellow-brown, and hobgoblins orange that can be nearly red. Although these types are frequently thought of as separate species that share a common ancestor, interbreeding is possible and results in offspring of either parent's type.

> *"Goblins might be pathetic if they weren't so habitually vicious."*
> —Anastrianna of Mithrendain

Goblins are the most common type of goblin and the ones that give name to the whole race. These small, ill-tempered, and wicked creatures are well known for their treacherous nature and infamous for their wolf-riding raiders.

Goblin Sniper	Level 1 Minion Artillery
Small natural humanoid	XP 25

HP 1; a missed attack never damages a minion.	**Initiative** +3
AC 13, **Fortitude** 12, **Reflex** 14, **Will** 12	**Perception** +1
Speed 6	Low-light vision

TRAITS

Sniper
If the goblin misses with a ranged attack while hidden, it remains hidden.

STANDARD ACTIONS

⊕ **Short Sword** (weapon) ✦ At-Will
Attack: Melee 1 (one creature); +8 vs. AC
Hit: 4 damage.

⊙ **Shortbow** (weapon) ✦ At-Will
Attack: Ranged 20 (one creature); +8 vs. AC
Hit: 4 damage.

TRIGGERED ACTIONS

Goblin Tactics ✦ At-Will
Trigger: The goblin is missed by a melee attack.
Effect (Immediate Reaction): The goblin shifts 1 square.

Skills Stealth +8, Thievery +8

Str 13 (+1)	Dex 17 (+3)	Wis 12 (+1)
Con 13 (+1)	Int 8 (-1)	Cha 8 (-1)

Alignment evil	**Languages** Common, Goblin

Equipment leather armor, short sword, shortbow, 20 arrows

Goblin Beast Rider
Level 1 Skirmisher

Small natural humanoid
XP 100

HP 29; **Bloodied** 14 | **Initiative** +5
AC 15, **Fortitude** 13, **Reflex** 15, **Will** 13 | **Perception** +1
Speed 6 | Low-light vision

Traits

Perfect Position

If the goblin is mounted and its mount ends its turn at least 4 squares from where it started, the mounted goblin's attacks deal 1d6 extra damage until the start of the mount's next turn.

Standard Actions

⊕ **Javelin** (weapon) ✦ At-Will

Attack: Melee 1 (one creature); +6 vs. AC

Hit: 1d6 + 6 damage.

⟩ **Javelin** (weapon) ✦ At-Will

Attack: Ranged 10 (one creature); +6 vs. AC

Hit: 1d6 + 5 damage.

Triggered Actions

Mounted Goblin Tactics ✦ At-Will

Requirement: The goblin must be mounted.

Trigger: The goblin or its mount is missed by a melee attack.

Effect (Immediate Reaction): The goblin's mount shifts 1 square.

Skills Stealth +8, Thievery +8

Str 13 (+1)	**Dex** 17 (+3)	**Wis** 12 (+1)
Con 13 (+1)	**Int** 8 (-1)	**Cha** 8 (-1)

Alignment evil | **Languages** Common, Goblin

Equipment leather armor, 6 javelins

(Left to right) bugbear thug, goblin cutthroat, hobgoblin spear soldier

JIM NELSON

Bugbears weigh in as the largest and burliest of the goblins. Despite their power, the brutes often possess astonishing skill in stealth. Whatever they can't bully out of weaker goblins, they can often gain through theft and assassination.

The bellicose and militaristic hobgoblins are the most civilized and intelligent of the goblin types, and they often rule over goblins and bugbears. After receiving training from hobgoblins, a savage goblin tribe known to raid caravans might become disciplined cavalry for an invading army of hobgoblins.

"That Urthok think he so smart. Hah! Next time he turn his back … shhhhkkt!"

—Grukik, goblin cutthroat

Beast Masters: Goblins possess a mysterious knack for beast mastery. They might not always tame the beasts they capture, but they often achieve success in channeling the creatures' aggression. Goblins frequently ride wolves or giant spiders into battle, and hobgoblins have used manticores and wyverns as mounts. Goblins train drakes like others train dogs, goad carrion crawlers into serving them as battle beasts, and put basilisks in wagons to act as war machines. The truly wild monsters they capture find their way into fighting pits where bold warriors or captives battle them to the death in front of cheering crowds.

Goblin Cutthroat	Level 1 Skirmisher
Small natural humanoid	XP 100

HP 30; Bloodied 15	Initiative +5
AC 15, Fortitude 13, Reflex 14, Will 13	Perception +2
Speed 6	Low-light vision

STANDARD ACTIONS

⊕ **Short Sword ✦ At-Will**
Attack: Melee 1 (one creature); +6 vs. AC
Hit: 1d6 + 5 damage, or 2d6 + 5 if the goblin has combat advantage against the target. In addition, the goblin can shift 1 square.

⟫ **Dagger ✦ At-Will**
Attack: Ranged 10 (one creature); +6 vs. AC
Hit: 1d4 + 5 damage.

MOVE ACTIONS

Deft Scurry ✦ At-Will
Effect: The goblin shifts up to 3 squares.

TRIGGERED ACTIONS

Goblin Tactics ✦ At-Will
Trigger: The goblin is missed by a melee attack.
Effect (Immediate Reaction): The goblin shifts 1 square.

Skills Stealth +8, Thievery +8		
Str 13 (+1)	Dex 17 (+3)	Wis 14 (+2)
Con 14 (+2)	Int 8 (-1)	Cha 8 (-1)

Alignment evil	Languages Common, Goblin

Equipment leather armor, light shield, short sword, 2 daggers

Goblin Hex Hurler
Small natural humanoid

Level 3 Controller (Leader)

XP 150

HP 46; **Bloodied** 23
AC 17, **Fortitude** 14, **Reflex** 15, **Will** 16
Speed 6

Initiative +3
Perception +2
Low-light vision

STANDARD ACTIONS

⊕ **Staff** (weapon) ✦ **At-Will**

Attack: Melee 1 (one creature); +8 vs. AC

Hit: 1d6 + 7 damage, and the goblin can slide the target 1 square.

⟳ **Blinding Hex** ✦ **At-Will**

Attack: Ranged 10 (one creature); +6 vs. Fortitude

Hit: 2d6 + 1 damage, and the target is blinded until the end of the goblin's next turn.

⟳ **Stinging Hex** ✦ **Recharge** ⚄ ⚅

Attack: Ranged 10 (one creature); +6 vs. Will

Hit: The target takes 3d6 + 1 damage if it moves during its turn (save ends).

❈ **Vexing Cloud** (zone) ✦ **Encounter**

Effect: Area burst 3 within 10. The burst creates a zone that lasts until the end of the goblin's next turn. Enemies take a –2 penalty to attack rolls while in the zone.

Sustain Minor: The zone persists until the end of the goblin's next turn, and the goblin can move it up to 5 squares.

TRIGGERED ACTIONS

Goblin Tactics ✦ **At-Will**

Trigger: The goblin is missed by a melee attack.

Effect (Immediate Reaction): The goblin shifts 1 square.

Lead from the Rear ✦ **At-Will**

Trigger: An enemy hits the goblin with a ranged attack.

Effect (Immediate Interrupt): The goblin can change the attack's target to an adjacent ally of the goblin's level or lower.

Skills Stealth +10, Thievery +10

Str 10 (+1)	**Dex** 15 (+3)	**Wis** 13 (+2)
Con 14 (+3)	**Int** 9 (+0)	**Cha** 18 (+5)

Alignment evil   **Languages** Common, Goblin
Equipment leather robes, staff

An Ancient Empire: The goblin tradition of beast mastery might have originated in the legendary empire the goblins once controlled. Stories of this realm often conflict, but accounts agree on three points: Hobgoblins built it up through conquest in the name of the god Bane, it stretched into the Feywild, and it fell due to internal strife, which was stoked by the fey. To this day, goblins loathe fey and often make special efforts to harm them, particularly elves and eladrin.

Diverse and Widespread Tribes: Goblins share a common history, a vicious nature, beast-taming traditions, and the worship of Bane. Beyond these features, each tribe of goblins might differ radically in culture. Spider-riding goblin savages might dwell in nests within the web-strewn crowns of trees, sharing space with allied ettercaps. Another goblin tribe might live constantly on the move with a pack of wolves, wearing wolf pelts and howling to communicate. A tribe of bugbears and goblins might live in the sewers of a city and act as a thieves' guild of sorts. Hobgoblins might live in a grand city-state of their own

Hobgoblin Beast Master — Level 3 Controller (Leader)

Medium natural humanoid — XP 150

HP 47; **Bloodied** 23	**Initiative** +3
AC 17, **Fortitude** 17, **Reflex** 15, **Will** 15	**Perception** +1
Speed 6	Low-light vision

Traits

Beast Master's Exhortation
When an allied beast or magical beast that is adjacent to the hobgoblin hits with an attack, that beast gains 5 temporary hit points.

Standard Actions

⊕ **Goad** (weapon) ✦ **At-Will**
Attack: Melee 1 (one creature); +8 vs. AC
Hit: 1d8 + 6 damage.

⸸ **War Whip** (weapon) ✦ **At-Will**
Attack: Melee 3 (one creature); +8 vs. AC
Hit: 2d4 + 5 damage, and the target falls prone.
Effect: The hobgoblin can slide the target 1 square.

Attack Command ✦ **At-Will**
Effect: Melee 1 (one beast or magical beast ally). The target can make a basic attack as a free action.

Move Actions

Phalanx Movement ✦ **At-Will**
Effect: Close burst 1 (allies in the burst). The hobgoblin and each target can shift 1 square as a free action. The target must shift to a square adjacent to the hobgoblin.

Str 19 (+5)	**Dex** 14 (+3)	**Wis** 10 (+1)
Con 15 (+3)	**Int** 10 (+1)	**Cha** 15 (+3)

Alignment evil — **Languages** Common, Goblin
Equipment leather armor, goad (war pick), whip

---

and war with nearby realms. Other hobgoblins might be ruthless headhunters who ride behemoths through the jungle.

Many goblins still dwell in the Feywild, where their cultures take on even stranger forms. Goblins in the Feywild dominate sentient plants and fey beasts, and they harness the magical energy of the fey realm. Hobgoblins might cruise through forests on floating crystals, hunting with pet will-o'-wisps.

These disparate tribes often battle one another just as readily as they do other races, but strong leaders can bring them together. Typically a charismatic hobgoblin warlord uses might and legends of the goblins' fallen empire to inspire unity. Then the traditions of wildly different tribes become the deadly tactics of military divisions.

Hobgoblin Battle Guard

Level 3 Soldier

Medium natural humanoid

XP 150

HP 49; **Bloodied** 24
AC 19, **Fortitude** 17, **Reflex** 15, **Will** 15
Speed 6

Initiative +5
Perception +8
Low-light vision

STANDARD ACTIONS

⊕ **Flail** (weapon) ✦ At-Will

Attack: Melee 1 (one creature); +8 vs. AC

Hit: 1d10 + 5 damage, and the hobgoblin marks the target until the start of the hobgoblin's next turn.

MOVE ACTIONS

Phalanx Movement ✦ At-Will

Effect: Close burst 1 (allies in the burst). The hobgoblin and each target can shift 1 square as a free action. The target must shift to a square adjacent to the hobgoblin.

TRIGGERED ACTIONS

Share Shield ✦ At-Will

Trigger: An adjacent ally is hit by an attack against AC or Reflex.

Effect (Immediate Interrupt): The ally gains a +2 bonus to AC and Reflex against the triggering attack.

Str 19 (+5)	**Dex** 14 (+3)	**Wis** 15 (+3)
Con 17 (+4)	**Int** 10 (+1)	**Cha** 10 (+1)

Alignment evil **Languages** Common, Goblin

Equipment chainmail, heavy shield, flail

Hobgoblin Spear Soldier

Level 3 Skirmisher

Medium natural humanoid

XP 150

HP 48; **Bloodied** 24
AC 17, **Fortitude** 17, **Reflex** 15, **Will** 15
Speed 6

Initiative +5
Perception +3
Low-light vision

TRAITS

Threatening Reach

The hobgoblin can make opportunity attacks against enemies within its weapon's reach (2 squares).

STANDARD ACTIONS

⊕ **Longspear** (weapon) ✦ At-Will

Attack: Melee 2 (one creature); +8 vs. AC

Hit: 1d10 + 6 damage.

⌐ **Javelin** (weapon) ✦ At-Will

Attack: Ranged 20 (one creature); +8 vs. AC

Hit: 2d6 + 4 damage.

MOVE ACTIONS

Phalanx Movement ✦ At-Will

Effect: The hobgoblin and each ally adjacent to it can shift 1 square as a free action. The allies must end adjacent to the hobgoblin.

TRIGGERED ACTIONS

Tactical Withdrawal ✦ At-Will

Trigger: An enemy enters a square adjacent to the hobgoblin.

Effect (Immediate Reaction): The hobgoblin shifts up to 3 squares.

Str 19 (+5)	**Dex** 15 (+3)	**Wis** 14 (+3)
Con 16 (+4)	**Int** 11 (+1)	**Cha** 10 (+1)

Alignment evil **Languages** Common, Goblin

Equipment chainmail, longspear, 6 javelins

Hobgoblin Warmonger — Level 4 Artillery (Leader)
Medium natural humanoid — XP 175

HP 46; **Bloodied** 23
AC 18, **Fortitude** 15, **Reflex** 17, **Will** 16
Speed 6

Initiative +6
Perception +4
Low-light vision

Standard Actions

⊕ **Mace** (weapon) ✦ **At-Will**
Attack: Melee 1 (one creature); +9 vs. AC
Hit: 1d8 + 6 damage.

⊰ **Longbow** (weapon) ✦ **At-Will**
Attack: Ranged 30 (one creature); +11 vs. AC
Hit: 1d10 + 7 damage, and the target grants combat advantage until the start of the hobgoblin's next turn.

⚜ **Battle Cry** (charm) ✦ **Recharge when first bloodied**
Target: Area burst 1 within 10 (enemies in the burst); +9 vs. Will
Hit: The target makes a basic attack as a free action against a creature of the hobgoblin's choice.
Effect: Each ally in the burst can charge or make a basic attack as a free action. If an ally hits with the attack granted by this power, that ally gains 5 temporary hit points.

Move Actions

Phalanx Movement ✦ **At-Will**
Effect: The hobgoblin and each ally adjacent to it can shift 1 square as a free action. The allies must end adjacent to the hobgoblin.

Str 15 (+4)	**Dex** 19 (+6)	**Wis** 14 (+4)
Con 16 (+5)	**Int** 11 (+2)	**Cha** 17 (+5)

Alignment evil **Languages** Common, Goblin
Equipment chainmail, mace, longbow, 20 arrows

Hobgoblin Commander — Level 5 Soldier (Leader)
Medium natural humanoid — XP 200

HP 64; **Bloodied** 32
AC 21, **Fortitude** 21, **Reflex** 18, **Will** 19
Speed 5

Initiative +6
Perception +5
Low-light vision

Traits

Lead from the Front
When the hobgoblin hits an enemy with a melee attack, the hobgoblin's allies gain a +2 bonus to attack rolls and damage rolls against that enemy until the end of the hobgoblin's next turn.

Standard Actions

⊕ **Spear** (weapon) ✦ **At-Will**
Attack: Melee 1 (one creature); +10 vs. AC
Hit: 2d8 + 4 damage.
Effect: The hobgoblin marks the target until the end of the hobgoblin's next turn.

Minor Actions

⟵ **Tactical Deployment** ✦ **Recharge** ⁙ ⚄
Effect: Close burst 5 (allies in the burst). Each target can shift up to 3 squares.

Triggered Actions

Hobgoblin Resilience ✦ **Encounter**
Trigger: The hobgoblin is subject to an effect that a save can end.
Effect (Immediate Reaction): The hobgoblin can make a saving throw against the triggering effect.

Str 20 (+7)	**Dex** 14 (+4)	**Wis** 16 (+5)
Con 16 (+5)	**Int** 12 (+3)	**Cha** 10 (+2)

Alignment evil **Languages** Common, Goblin
Equipment scale armor, heavy shield, spear

Bugbear Thug
Medium natural humanoid

Level 4 Brute
XP 175

HP 65; **Bloodied** 32
AC 16, **Fortitude** 15, **Reflex** 15, **Will** 11
Speed 6

Initiative +7
Perception +8
Low-light vision

TRAITS

Bushwhack
The bugbear gains a +4 bonus to attack rolls against a creature that has no allies adjacent to it.

STANDARD ACTIONS

⊕ **Morningstar** (weapon) ✦ At-Will
Attack: Melee 1 (one creature); +9 vs. AC
Hit: 2d8 + 6 damage, or 3d8 + 6 if the bugbear has combat advantage against the target.

⊁ **Handaxe** (weapon) ✦ At-Will
Attack: Ranged 10 (one creature); +9 vs. AC
Hit: 1d6 + 6 damage.

Skills Stealth +12

Str 20 (+7)	**Dex** 20 (+7)	**Wis** 13 (+3)
Con 15 (+4)	**Int** 8 (+1)	**Cha** 10 (+2)

Alignment evil   **Languages** Common, Goblin
Equipment leather armor, morningstar, 2 handaxes

Bugbear Backstabber
Medium natural humanoid

Level 5 Skirmisher
XP 200

HP 63; **Bloodied** 31
AC 19, **Fortitude** 18, **Reflex** 18, **Will** 15
Speed 6

Initiative +9
Perception +8
Low-light vision

TRAITS

Bushwhack
The bugbear gains a +4 bonus to attack rolls against a creature that has no allies adjacent to it.

Expert Ambusher
If the bugbear is hidden from its target when it makes an attack, the attack deals 5 extra damage.

STANDARD ACTIONS

⊕ **Greatsword** (weapon) ✦ At-Will
Attack: Melee 1 (one creature); +10 vs. AC
Hit: 1d10 + 6 damage.

⊁ **Handaxe** (weapon) ✦ At-Will
Attack: Ranged 10 (one creature); +10 vs. AC
Hit: 2d6 + 5 damage.

MOVE ACTIONS

Stealthy Positioning ✦ At-Will
Effect: The bugbear shifts up to its speed. If it has any cover at the end of the move, it can make a Stealth check to become hidden, with no penalty for movement.

Skills Stealth +12

Str 20 (+7)	**Dex** 20 (+7)	**Wis** 13 (+3)
Con 15 (+4)	**Int** 8 (+1)	**Cha** 10 (+2)

Alignment evil   **Languages** Common, Goblin
Equipment leather armor, greatsword, 4 handaxes

GOLEM

Golems might be made from humble stuff–stone, iron, or flesh and bones–but they possess astonishing power and durability. These automatons obey their creators above all else. Not even the threat of destruction can affect their obedience.

Golems have no wants, need no sustenance, require no rest, feel no pain, and know no remorse. No secrets pass their lips. No thoughts of betrayal fester in their simple minds. They seek only to follow their creators' commands. Golems protect or attack whomever or whatever their creators demand.

Created by Others: Only those who cannot trust living servants or who require ageless guardians go to the great expense and effort of creating golems. Dwarves who would see their tombs protected for eternity, a wizard who wants to work his will upon a frightened populace, a general who desires an unstoppable soldier, a queen who needs an enforcer and guard beyond reproach–such are the people who craft golems.

Flesh Golem	Level 12 Elite Brute
Large natural animate (construct)	XP 1,400
HP 304; Bloodied 152	Initiative +4
AC 24, Fortitude 26, Reflex 21, Will 21	Perception +5
Speed 6 (cannot shift)	Darkvision
Resist 10 cold	
Saving Throws +2; Action Points 1	

TRAITS

Primal Fear
When the golem takes fire damage from an attack, it takes a free action to move up to its speed, and each square it moves must place it farther from the attacker. If it cannot move at least half its speed, it grants combat advantage until the end of its next turn.

Life-Giving Jolt
When the golem takes lightning damage, it can make a basic attack as a free action.

STANDARD ACTIONS

⊕ **Slam** ✦ **At-Will**
Attack: Melee 2 (one creature); +17 vs. AC, or +19 vs. AC while the golem is bloodied
Hit: 3d10 + 9 damage.

✣ **Double Attack** ✦ **At-Will**
Effect: The golem uses *slam* twice. Each attack knocks the target prone if it hits.

✣ **Golem Rampage** ✦ **Recharge** ⚄ ⚅
Effect: The golem moves up to its speed + 2. During this movement, the golem can move through enemies' spaces, and when the golem first enters a creature's space, it uses *slam* against that creature.

TRIGGERED ACTIONS

✣ **Berserk Attack** ✦ **At-Will**
Trigger: An attack damages the golem while it is bloodied.
Effect (Immediate Reaction): The golem uses *slam* against a random target within its reach.

Str 20 (+11)	Dex 7 (+4)	Wis 8 (+5)
Con 22 (+12)	Int 3 (+2)	Cha 3 (+2)
Alignment unaligned	**Languages** –	

(Left to right) iron golem, flesh golem, stone golem

Painstakingly Crafted: The construction of a golem begins with the building of its body. This work requires great command of the craft, whether it's stonecutting, ironworking, or surgery. Sometimes a golem's creator is the master of the art, but often the individual who desires a golem must hire highly skilled artisans to do the work. If the artisans won't do the work for pay, they are sometimes kidnapped and forced into it.

Once a golem's body has been constructed, a ritual must be performed to give it life. There are many versions of such rituals, but all require a sacrifice of both wealth and blood or spirit. The vilest of these rituals are the least expensive in gold and the most expensive in life. All of them result in the establishment of a connection to the Elemental Chaos. Through a tiny rent in the fabric of reality, the golem's creator draws forth the same spirit stuff tapped by the gods and the primordials when they created the creatures of the world. This tiny spark of life has no memory, personality, or history. It is merely the impetus to move and obey. It sees and knows its creator, and nothing else matters.

> *"Live, my darling, my precious one. Live!"*
> —Drellin the Mad

Stone Golem
Large natural animate (construct)

Level 17 Elite Soldier
XP 3,200

HP 336; **Bloodied** 168	**Initiative** +8
AC 33, **Fortitude** 31, **Reflex** 26, **Will** 26	**Perception** +7
Speed 6 (cannot shift)	Darkvision
Immune disease, poison	
Saving Throws +2; **Action Points** 1	

STANDARD ACTIONS

⊕ **Slam** ✦ At-Will

Attack: Melee 2 (one creature); +22 vs. AC

Hit: 4d6 + 11 damage, and the golem can push the target 1 square.

⚓ **Double Attack** ✦ At-Will

Effect: The golem uses *slam* twice. Each attack knocks the target prone if it hits.

⚓ **Golem Rampage** ✦ Recharge ⚄ ⚅

Effect: The golem moves up to its speed + 2. During this movement, the golem can move through enemies' spaces, and when the golem first enters any creature's space, it uses *slam* against that creature.

TRIGGERED ACTIONS

↤ **Death Burst**

Trigger: The golem drops to 0 hit points.

Attack (No Action): Close burst 1 (creatures in the burst); +22 vs. AC

Hit: 2d12 + 10 damage.

Effect: The golem is destroyed. The area of the burst becomes difficult terrain until cleared.

Str 24 (+15)	**Dex** 7 (+6)	**Wis** 8 (+7)
Con 24 (+15)	**Int** 3 (+4)	**Cha** 3 (+4)
Alignment unaligned	**Languages** –	

Witless Wonders: A golem cannot think or act for itself. It can understand its creator's commands perfectly, but it has no grasp of language beyond that understanding. Thus, a golem cannot be reasoned with or confused. In a way, nothing exists for the golem but its creator's commands, and it takes their intent literally. This characteristic is the golem's greatest strength and its greatest weakness.

When its creator is on hand to command it, a golem performs flawlessly. However, if that creator leaves the golem with instructions or is incapacitated, the golem continues to follow its last orders to the best of its ability. A golem knows the intent of its creator's orders, but when it cannot fulfill such orders or does not know how to do so, it might react violently or simply stand and do nothing. A golem that has conflicting orders might alternate between them. A golem told to guard the door of a treasure vault against entry might break down the door itself if it detects intruders inside. A golem commanded to kill a foe might do so and then simply stop if it cannot hear its master's calls to return and does not have standing orders to return once its task is complete.

Some creators grant another person or any person with a special symbol the right to command a golem. Such practices allow for the possibility that the golem might be used against its creator's interests, if not against the creator directly, and those powerful enough to create a golem are usually loath to accept that risk.

Iron Golem	Level 20 Elite Soldier
Large natural animate (construct)	XP 5,600

HP 386; **Bloodied** 193	**Initiative** +14
AC 36, **Fortitude** 36, **Reflex** 30, **Will** 28	**Perception** +10
Speed 6 (cannot shift)	Darkvision
Immune disease, poison	
Saving Throws +2; **Action Points** 1	

TRAITS

☼ Noxious Fumes (poison) ✦ **Aura** 2
While the golem is bloodied, any creature that enters the aura or starts its turn there takes 5 poison damage.

Energizing Flames
The first time the golem takes fire damage each turn, it can shift up to 2 squares as a free action, even if it could not normally shift.

Interfering Bolts
When the golem takes lightning damage, it is slowed until the end of its next turn.

STANDARD ACTIONS

⊕ Iron Blade ✦ **At-Will**
Attack: Melee 2 (one creature); +25 vs. AC
Hit: 3d10 + 12 damage.
Effect: The golem marks the target (save ends).

⊣ Cleave ✦ **At-Will**
Effect: The golem uses *iron blade* twice, each time against a different target.

⟸ Breath Weapon (poison) ✦ **Recharge** 🝙 🝚
Attack: Close blast 3 (creatures in the blast); +23 vs. Fortitude
Hit: 4d8 + 9 poison damage, and ongoing 15 poison damage (save ends).

TRIGGERED ACTIONS

⊣ Dazing Fist ✦ **At-Will**
Trigger: A creature that is within 2 squares of the golem and marked by it moves.
Attack (Immediate Interrupt): Melee 2 (triggering creature); +23 vs. Fortitude
Hit: The target is dazed (save ends).

⟸ Toxic Death (poison) ✦ **At-Will**
Trigger: The golem is first bloodied or drops to 0 hit points.
Attack (No Action): Close burst 3 (each creature in the burst); +23 vs. Fortitude
Hit: 2d8 + 11 poison damage, and ongoing 10 poison damage (save ends).

Str 27 (+18)	**Dex** 15 (+12)	**Wis** 11 (+10)
Con 25 (+17)	**Int** 3 (+6)	**Cha** 3 (+6)
Alignment unaligned	**Languages** –	

"This apparatus will channel the fury of the storm above us into the iron body of the construct, opening a tiny portal to the Elemental Chaos and enabling the merest spark of life to give it animation."

—Archimandrius of Vor Rukoth

HAG

Black-hearted hags embody all that is ugly and frightful in nature. These hideous fey relish the opportunity to ruin lives and disrupt the natural order. Wicked doesn't even begin to describe them.

Ancient and cunning, hags are wrathful, greedy, deceptive, and cruel. Despite these characteristics, hags can be bargained with, if one has the courage to attempt doing so. Hags' schemes are patient, their webs of manipulation wide, and their lives long; they can afford to talk a little. Besides, the generosity of hags has felled far more heroes than their claws.

Strange Sisters: Hags come in a bewildering variety, each tied to nature or some ancient force. They share certain traits, such as having withered, hideous female forms. Hags also share the ability to disguise their true shapes magically. Most can adopt the appearance of an old woman of any humanoid race, and some can assume comely guises.

"Teeth! Teeth! I'll tie your teeth to my necklace with thread from your sinews!"
—Korrigan, green hag of the Mistmarsh

Tales tell of hags coming into being through various weird means: being birthed after a hag unites with an ensorcelled man; springing from cows that give venom instead of milk; hatching from snakes' eggs kissed by virgins; incubating in the coffins of the unconsecrated dead; a hag transforming a cursed baby into another hag; and being poured whole out of cauldrons of boiling blood.

Bog Hag
Medium fey humanoid (aquatic)

Level 10 Skirmisher
XP 500

HP 107; **Bloodied** 53
AC 24, **Fortitude** 23, **Reflex** 21, **Will** 19
Speed 8 (swamp walk), swim 8

Initiative +11
Perception +7
Low-light vision

TRAITS

✧ **Unwholesome Presence** ✦ **Aura** 3
When an enemy within the aura spends a healing surge to regain hit points, that enemy regains only half the normal hit points.

Aquatic
The hag can breathe underwater. In aquatic combat, it gains a +2 bonus to attack rolls against nonaquatic creatures.

Evasive Charge
The hag can take a single free action to shift up to 2 squares immediately after charging.

STANDARD ACTIONS

⊕ **Claw** ✦ **At-Will**
Attack: Melee 1 (one creature); +15 vs. AC
Hit: 2d8 + 9 damage.
Effect: The hag can shift up to 2 squares.

✦ **Rending Claws** ✦ **Recharge** when first bloodied
Effect: The hag uses *claw* twice against the same target. If both attacks hit, the target takes 5 extra damage.

MINOR ACTIONS

Skin Shift (polymorph) ✦ **At-Will**
Effect: The hag alters its physical form to appear as a young female elf, half-elf, eladrin, or human until it uses *change shape* again or until it drops to 0 hit points. To assume a specific individual's form, the hag must have seen that individual. Other creatures can make a DC 31 Insight check to discern that the form is a disguise.

Skills Intimidate +12, Nature +12, Stealth +14

Str 22 (+11)	**Dex** 18 (+9)	**Wis** 15 (+7)
Con 19 (+9)	**Int** 12 (+6)	**Cha** 14 (+7)
Alignment evil	**Languages** Common, Elven	

Regardless of their origins, hags see one another as sisters. And like sisters, they squabble. A rivalry can deteriorate into outright enmity. Such feuds between sisters might last for decades or even centuries, as the hags manipulate events against one another. Also like sisters, the hags might reconcile, especially if they share some new focus for their hatred.

Bizarre and Dangerous Lairs: Hags dwell in the most desolate locales: boot-sucking fens, mist-shrouded moors, howling mountain passes, forbidding tundra, damp caves, dark and thorny woods. In these lonesome places, hags twist Feywild magic to create eerie homes that suit their wicked sense of humor and unsettling aesthetics. A green hag's lair might be within a tree grown into the shape of an enormous headless body, and the hag might fly about in a titan's skull, which it leaves atop its house when within. A night hag could travel with a menagerie of monsters and slaves kept in cages, and all disguised by illusions to

Green Hag — Level 12 Controller

Medium fey humanoid (shapechanger) — XP 700

HP 124; **Bloodied** 62
AC 26, **Fortitude** 25, **Reflex** 24, **Will** 23
Speed 8 (forest walk, swamp walk), swim 8
Resist 10 poison

Initiative +10
Perception +14
Low-light vision

STANDARD ACTIONS

⊕ Hurl through the Earth (teleportation) ✦ At-Will
Attack: Melee 1 (one creature); +17 vs. AC
Hit: 2d6 + 9 damage.
Effect: The hag teleports the target up to 3 squares.

✳ Grasping Roots ✦ At-Will
Attack: Area burst 2 within 5 (creatures in the burst); +15 vs. Reflex
Hit: The target is restrained (save ends).
Miss: The target is slowed until the end of the hag's next turn.

✳ Rampant Growth (zone) ✦ Encounter
Attack: Area burst 2 within 5 centered on a creature restrained by *grasping roots* (creatures in the burst); +15 vs. Reflex
Hit: 2d8 + 8 damage.
Effect: The burst creates a zone that lasts until the end of the encounter. Squares in the zone are difficult terrain for any creature that doesn't have forest walk, and such a creature takes 5 damage for each square of movement in the zone.

✳ Stagnant Miasma (poison, zone) ✦ Recharge ⚄ ⚅
Attack: Area burst 2 within 5 (creatures in the burst); +15 vs. Fortitude
Hit: 2d10 + 11 poison damage.
Effect: The burst creates a zone of lightly obscured squares that lasts until the end of the hag's next turn. Any creature that ends its turn in the zone takes 10 poison damage.

MINOR ACTIONS

Change Shape (polymorph) ✦ At-Will
Effect: The hag alters its physical form to appear as a crone or a young woman of any Medium humanoid race until it uses *change shape* again or until it drops to 0 hit points. To assume a specific individual's form, the hag must have seen that individual. Other creatures can make a DC 33 Insight check to discern that the form is a disguise.

Skills Bluff +14, Stealth + 15

Str 21 (+11)	**Dex** 19 (+10)	**Wis** 16 (+9)
Con 20 (+11)	**Int** 15 (+8)	**Cha** 16 (+9)

Alignment evil   **Languages** Common, Elven

lure in hapless victims. Bog hags dwell in swamps and mires, from where they emerge to ambush unwary travelers.

Foul Covens: Hags often gather in covens of like-minded members numbering three to thirteen. A coven shares foul goals, and its members share information and magical knowledge. Together a coven's members can perform powerful rituals to scry upon distant places, control weather, command beasts, cause plagues, divine the future, and lay curses.

Night Hag
Medium fey humanoid (shapechanger)

Level 14 Lurker
XP 1,000

HP 109; **Bloodied** 54
AC 27, **Fortitude** 28, **Reflex** 26, **Will** 26
Speed 8

Initiative +15
Perception +10
Darkvision

TRAITS

✪ **Shroud of Night** ✦ **Aura** 10
Within the aura, bright light is dim light, and dim light is darkness.

STANDARD ACTIONS

⊕ **Claw** ✦ **At-Will**
Attack: Melee 1 (one creature); +19 vs. AC
Hit: 1d6 + 6 damage. If the hag has combat advantage against the target, the target is also stunned (save ends).

⸸ **Dream Haunting** (psychic) ✦ **At-Will**
Attack: Melee 1 (one stunned or unconscious creature); +18 vs. Will
Hit: 3d6 + 4 psychic damage, and the hag disappears into the target's mind. While in this state, the hag is removed from play and does nothing on subsequent turns but deal 3d6 + 4 psychic damage to the target (no attack roll required). When the target is no longer stunned or unconscious, or when the target dies, the hag reappears adjacent to the target and is insubstantial until the start of its next turn.

⬳ **Wave of Sleep** (charm, psychic) ✦ **Recharge** ⚅ ⚅
Attack: Close blast 5 (creatures in the blast); +17 vs. Will
Hit: 1d8 + 3 psychic damage, and the target is dazed (save ends).
First Failed Saving Throw: The target is unconscious instead of dazed (save ends).

MINOR ACTIONS

Change Shape (polymorph) ✦ **At-Will**
Effect: The hag alters its physical form to appear as a crone of any Medium humanoid race until it uses *change shape* again or until it drops to 0 hit points. To assume a specific individual's form, the hag must have seen that individual. Other creatures can make a DC 33 Insight check to discern that the form is a disguise.

Skills Arcana +14, Bluff +16, Intimidate +16, Stealth +16
Str 22 (+13)	**Dex** 18 (+11)	**Wis** 17 (+10)
Con 19 (+11)	**Int** 14 (+9)	**Cha** 18 (+11)

Alignment evil   **Languages** Common, Elven

Covens often seek to control the area around their meeting place, either through secret manipulation or open dominance. A single hag might bully and trick a glade of dryads or a tribe of ogres into following her commands, whereas covens can martial far more forces, with each hag bringing new followers into the alliance. The most powerful hag coven might command a kingdom, from either behind the throne or on it.

HALFLING

Halflings say they travel the world, flowing with life's ups and downs and offering friendship to all. Some non-halflings think the little folk are criminals on the run. The truth is a complication that halflings prefer to leave in their wake.

Wherever waters run, halflings roam. These outwardly amiable wanderers move their settlements all over the world, using waterways as their highways.

> "There's no need for a fight. Why don't we talk about this?"
> —Jarrett Farwhere

When a quick wit and a guileless grin fail them, a quicker blade or a sly hand carries them through.

Friendly but Dangerous: Smiles hide more threats than shadows, or so the halfling saying goes. Halflings instinctively present a friendly face in front of even the most intimidating behavior. Open bloodshed does provoke a more serious attitude from a halfling, but halflings prefer to talk their way out of trouble—or talk enemies into it.

Living by Their Own Laws: Halflings lack domains of their own, but they share a culture and a sense of fellowship all over the world. This culture includes reliance on their own justice. As wanderers who glide in and out of settled lands and alliances, halflings have developed their own code of conduct. Like any system of justice, it can be harsh, but it protects them and provides stability in their wandering way of life.

DAVID GRIFFITH

Halfling Thief — Level 2 Skirmisher
Small natural humanoid — XP 125

HP 34; **Bloodied** 17
AC 16, **Fortitude** 13, **Reflex** 16, **Will** 14
Speed 6

Initiative +6
Perception +1

TRAITS
Nimble Reaction
The halfling gains a +2 bonus to AC against opportunity attacks.

STANDARD ACTIONS
⊕ **Dagger** (weapon) ✦ At-Will
Attack: Melee 1 (one creature); +7 vs. AC
Hit: 2d4 + 5 damage, plus 1d6 if the halfling has combat advantage against the target.
Effect: The halfling can shift 1 square.

⊗ **Throwing Dagger** (weapon) ✦ At-Will
Attack: Ranged 5 (one creature); +7 vs. AC
Hit: 2d4 + 5 damage, plus 1d6 if the halfling has combat advantage against the target.

✠ **Mobile Melee Attack** ✦ At-Will
Effect: The halfling moves up to 4 squares, using *dagger* at any point during the move. This movement does not provoke opportunity attacks from the target of the attack.

Skills Acrobatics +9, Stealth +9, Thievery +9
| Str 12 (+2) | Dex 16 (+4) | Wis 11 (+1) |
| Con 10 (+1) | Int 10 (+1) | Cha 14 (+3) |

Alignment unaligned   **Languages** Common
Equipment leather armor, 6 daggers

Halfling Trickster — Level 3 Lurker
Small natural humanoid — XP 150

HP 35; **Bloodied** 17
AC 17, **Fortitude** 15, **Reflex** 17, **Will** 17
Speed 6

Initiative +9
Perception +6

TRAITS
Nimble Reaction
The halfling gains a +2 bonus to AC against opportunity attacks.

Bamboozle
When the halfling ends a turn in which it did not attack and it has cover or concealment from a creature, it is hidden from that creature until the end of its next turn.

STANDARD ACTIONS
⊕ **Short Sword** (weapon) ✦ At-Will
Attack: Melee 1 (one creature); +8 vs. AC
Hit: 1d6 + 4 damage, or 4d6 + 8 if the halfling was hidden from the target when it attacked.

MINOR ACTIONS
❋ **Smoke Pellet** ✦ At-Will
Effect: Area burst 1 within 10. Squares in the burst are lightly obscured until the end of the halfling's next turn.

Skills Acrobatics +12, Athletics +8, Bluff +10, Thievery +12
| Str 14 (+3) | Dex 19 (+5) | Wis 11 (+1) |
| Con 11 (+1) | Int 11 (+1) | Cha 18 (+5) |

Alignment unaligned   **Languages** Common
Equipment leather armor, short sword, 4 smoke pellets

HUMAN

The human race is the most populous in the world, and its members burn through their short lives alight with ambition, resilience, and fierce independence.

Human Goon	Level 2 Minion Soldier
Medium natural humanoid, human	XP 31

HP 1; a missed attack never damages a minion. **Initiative** +3
AC 15, **Fortitude** 13, **Reflex** 11, **Will** 11   **Perception** +2
Speed 6

TRAITS

Mob Rule
While at least two other human goons are within 5 squares of the goon, it gains a +2 power bonus to all defenses.

STANDARD ACTIONS

⊕ **Club** (weapon) ✦ **At-Will**
Attack: Melee 1 (one creature); +7 vs. AC
Hit: 5 damage.

Str 14 (+3)	**Dex** 11 (+1)	**Wis** 12 (+2)
Con 12 (+2)	**Int** 9 (+0)	**Cha** 13 (+2)

Alignment unaligned   **Languages** Common
Equipment club

Common Bandit	Level 2 Skirmisher
Medium natural humanoid, human	XP 125

HP 37; **Bloodied** 18   **Initiative** +6
AC 16, **Fortitude** 12, **Reflex** 14, **Will** 12   **Perception** +1
Speed 6

TRAITS

Combat Advantage
The bandit deals 1d6 extra damage against any creature granting combat advantage to it.

STANDARD ACTIONS

⊕ **Mace** (weapon) ✦ **At-Will**
Attack: Melee 1 (one creature); +7 vs. AC
Hit: 1d8 + 5 damage, and the bandit can shift 1 square.

⟐ **Dagger** (weapon) ✦ **At-Will**
Attack: Ranged 10 (one creature); +7 vs. AC
Hit: 1d4 + 5 damage, and the bandit can shift 1 square.

↯ **Dazing Strike** (weapon) ✦ **Recharge** when the attack misses
Attack: Melee 1 (one creature); +7 vs. AC
Hit: 1d8 + 5 damage, and the target is dazed until the end of the bandit's next turn.
Effect: The bandit can shift 1 square.

Skills Stealth +9, Streetwise +7, Thievery +9

Str 12 (+2)	**Dex** 17 (+4)	**Wis** 11 (+1)
Con 13 (+2)	**Int** 10 (+1)	**Cha** 12 (+2)

Alignment unaligned   **Languages** Common
Equipment leather armor, mace, 4 daggers

When compared to other humanoid races, humans sprint through existence. They leave blazing trails of emotion that warp and weft across the natural world.

Great Ambition: From the first days of life, aspiration colors a human's squalls and animates its features. Members of some races believe that humans never really leave an infant state. However, most acknowledge that humans pursue their goals with unmatched zeal and fervor. Although few humans reach great heights, those who do so can alter the world.

"You humans—in such a rush to get to the end of your hurried lives."
—Vyndra Sysvani of Mithrendain

Susceptible to Temptation: The flip side of humankind's great ambition is its susceptibility to corruption. Unparalleled passion regularly overshadows logic and mercy. A human might rise up as an epic hero worthy of bardic song, but he or she might also sink to the deepest lows, bathing in treachery and villainy to succeed.

Town Guard	Level 3 Soldier
Medium natural humanoid, human	XP 150

HP 47; **Bloodied** 23	**Initiative** +5
AC 19, **Fortitude** 16, **Reflex** 15, **Will** 14	**Perception** +6
Speed 5	

STANDARD ACTIONS

⊕ **Halberd** (weapon) ✦ At-Will
Attack: Melee 2 (one creature); +8 vs. AC
Hit: 1d10 + 5 damage, and the town guard marks the target until the end of the town guard's next turn.

⊛ **Crossbow** (weapon) ✦ At-Will
Attack: Ranged 20 (one creature); +8 vs. AC
Hit: 1d8 + 5 damage.

✦ **Powerful Strike** (weapon) ✦ **Recharge** ⚅ ⚅
Attack: Melee 2 (one creature); +8 vs. AC
Hit: 2d10 + 5 damage, and the target falls prone.

TRIGGERED ACTIONS

✦ **Interceding Strike** (weapon) ✦ At-Will
Trigger: An enemy marked by the town guard makes an attack that doesn't include it as a target.
Attack (Immediate Interrupt): Melee 2 (triggering enemy); +8 vs. AC
Hit: 1d10 + 5 damage.

Skills Streetwise +7

Str 16 (+4)	**Dex** 14 (+3)	**Wis** 11 (+1)
Con 15 (+3)	**Int** 10 (+1)	**Cha** 12 (+2)

Alignment unaligned   **Languages** Common
Equipment chainmail, halberd, crossbow, 20 bolts

Human Thug
Level 7 Minion Skirmisher

Medium natural humanoid

XP 75

HP 1; a missed attack never damages a minion.
AC 21, **Fortitude** 20, **Reflex** 17, **Will** 18
Speed 6

Initiative +5
Perception +4

TRAITS
Rush into Battle
Whenever the thug hits a creature with a charge attack, the target grants combat advantage until the end of the thug's next turn.

STANDARD ACTIONS
⊕ **Club** (weapon) ✦ **At-Will**
Attack: Melee 1 (one creature); +12 vs. AC
Hit: 7 damage.

Str 14 (+5)	Dex 11 (+3)	Wis 12 (+4)
Con 13 (+4)	Int 10 (+3)	Cha 13 (+4)

Alignment unaligned **Languages** Common
Equipment club

Human Transmuter
Level 7 Controller

Medium natural humanoid

XP 300

HP 77; **Bloodied** 38
AC 21, **Fortitude** 18, **Reflex** 19, **Will** 20
Speed 6

Initiative +3
Perception +11

STANDARD ACTIONS
⊕ **Staff** (weapon) ✦ **At-Will**
Attack: Melee 1 (one creature); +12 vs. AC
Hit: 2d6 + 6 damage.

⚜ **Capricious Earth** (charm, implement) ✦ **At-Will**
Attack: Area burst 2 within 5 (enemies in the burst); +10 vs. Will
Hit: 2d10 + 6 damage, and the transmuter slides the target up to 3 squares.
Miss: The transmuter can slide the target 1 square.

➷ **Beast Curse** (implement, polymorph) ✦ **Recharge** ⚄ ⚅
Attack: Ranged 5 (one hexed enemy); +10 vs. Fortitude
Hit: The transmuter alters the target's physical form to appear as a Tiny animal until the end of the transmuter's next turn. While in this form, the target cannot use powers or make attacks.

MOVE ACTIONS
Hex Jump (teleportation) ✦ **Encounter**
Effect: Close burst 5 (one hexed creature in the burst). The transmuter and the target teleport, swapping positions.

MINOR ACTIONS
⇐ **Hex** (charm, implement) ✦ **At-Will** (1/round)
Attack: Close burst 5 (one enemy in the burst); +10 vs. Will
Hit: The target is hexed until the end of the transmuter's next turn. While hexed, the target is slowed and takes a -2 penalty to attack rolls and damage rolls against the transmuter.

Skills Arcana +10, Nature +11

Str 10 (+3)	Dex 11 (+3)	Wis 17 (+6)
Con 13 (+4)	Int 15 (+5)	Cha 14 (+5)

Alignment unaligned **Languages** Common
Equipment staff, robes

(Left to right) town guard, human duelist, human transmuter

Human Duelist	Level 8 Soldier
Medium natural humanoid	XP 350

HP 85; **Bloodied** 42
AC 24, **Fortitude** 20, **Reflex** 22, **Will** 20
Speed 6

Initiative +11
Perception +7

TRAITS

Duelist's Poise

Whenever the duelist hits an enemy granting combat advantage to it, the enemy is immobilized until the end of the enemy's next turn.

STANDARD ACTIONS

⊕ **Longsword** (weapon) ✦ **At-Will**

Attack: Melee 1 (one creature); +13 vs. AC

Hit: 2d8 + 7 damage.

Effect: The duelist marks the target until the end of the swordsman's next turn.

TRIGGERED ACTIONS

⸸ **Advantageous Jab** (weapon) ✦ **At-Will**

Trigger: An enemy marked by the duelist makes an attack that doesn't include it as a target.

Attack (Immediate Interrupt): Melee 1 (triggering enemy); +13 vs. AC

Hit: 1d8 + 8 damage.

Effect: The target takes a -2 penalty to attack rolls until the end of this turn.

Skills Athletics +12

Str 16 (+7)	**Dex** 20 (+9)	**Wis** 17 (+7)
Con 13 (+5)	**Int** 10 (+4)	**Cha** 9 (+3)

Alignment unaligned | **Languages** Common
Equipment leather armor, longsword

HYDRA

Reptilian heads extend from a hydra's thick, serpentine body, poised to snap at any creature that comes within reach.

Hydras are legendary creatures that stand alongside giants and dragons in the world's lore. Most humanoids know hydras from chilling bedtime stories. The same cannot be said of adventurers, sailors, and peddlers, who witness these multiheaded predators stalking the hinterlands. These travelers know that the myths of hydras are rooted in reality.

Born of Primordial Blood: In the age before the Dawn War, the primordial Bryakus pulsed through the uncharted reaches of the Elemental Chaos, moving like a kraken through the deepest seas. Bryakus was so tall that stars danced

Hydra	Level 10 Solo Brute
Large natural beast (reptile, water)	XP 2,500

HP 432; **Bloodied** 216	**Initiative** +8
AC 24, **Fortitude** 23, **Reflex** 21, **Will** 21	**Perception** +13
Speed 5, swim 10	All-around vision, darkvision
Saving Throws +5; **Action Points** 2	

TRAITS

All-Around Vision
Enemies can't gain combat advantage by flanking the hydra.

Many Headed
While stunned or dominated, the hydra can take free actions.

Regenerating Heads
The hydra starts an encounter with four heads. When the hydra's hit points first go below 324, 216, and 108, one of its heads is destroyed. Whenever a head is destroyed, the hydra grows two heads at the start of its next turn unless it takes fire or acid damage before then.

Threatening Reach
The hydra can make opportunity attacks against enemies within 2 squares of it.

STANDARD ACTIONS

⊕ **Bite ✦ At-Will**
Attack: Melee 2 (one creature); +15 vs. AC
Hit: 3d10 damage.

✦ **Hydra Fury ✦ At-Will**
Effect: The hydra uses *bite* a number of times equal to the number of heads it currently has. If it has only two heads, it gains a +5 bonus to damage rolls with *bite*. If it has only one head, it gains a +15 bonus to damage rolls with *bite*.

TRIGGERED ACTIONS

✦ **Snapping Jaws ✦ At-Will**
Trigger: An enemy ends its turn within 2 squares of the hydra.
Effect (Free Action): The hydra uses *bite* twice against the triggering enemy.

Skills Stealth +13		
Str 21 (+10)	**Dex** 16 (+8)	**Wis** 16 (+8)
Con 20 (+10)	**Int** 2 (+1)	**Cha** 8 (+4)
Alignment unaligned	**Languages** —	

around his crown. His enormous hands bore hundreds of draconic heads, and his legs were tangles of viper coils capped with hissing, venomous maws. Bryakus, the Colossus of Chaos, the Father of Fear, awed even the gods.

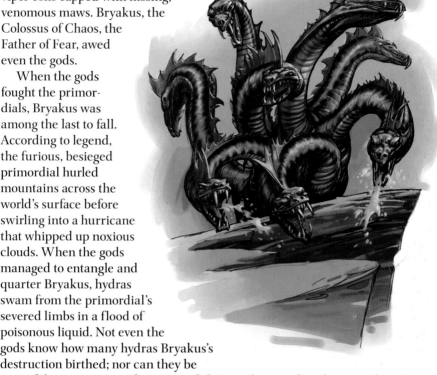

When the gods fought the primordials, Bryakus was among the last to fall. According to legend, the furious, besieged primordial hurled mountains across the world's surface before swirling into a hurricane that whipped up noxious clouds. When the gods managed to entangle and quarter Bryakus, hydras swam from the primordial's severed limbs in a flood of poisonous liquid. Not even the gods know how many hydras Bryakus's destruction birthed; nor can they be sure of the various manifestations of elemental power found among the creatures. As a result of Bryakus's death, hydras spread across the planes, thriving in virtually every environment.

Predatory Water Dwellers: Although hydras cannot breathe underwater, they are natural swimmers and prefer rivers, lakes, or oceans to land. A hydra can hold its breath for hours, and only a single head must surface for the hydra to breathe.

Hydras slither through swamps, lurk in lakes, and slink through rivers. Some find their way into city sewers or use underground waterways to emerge from village wells. Hydras also slide through Underdark tunnels, depleting the prey from one body of water before moving on to another. Huge venom-maw hydras swim through the depths of an ocean, rising to threaten ships.

When a hydra rests, only half its heads sleep. A hydra rarely requires shelter from the elements, so it usually doesn't claim a cave or a ruin. In frosty climes, a hydra might move into the depths of a cavern for warmth during the coldest seasons. A hydra's preferred lair is a wallow where it can submerge its body except for a couple of wakeful heads that keep watch above water or mud. Such

Flamekiss Hydra — Level 12 Solo Brute

Flamekiss Hydra
Large natural beast (reptile)

Level 12 Solo Brute
XP 3,500

HP 496; **Bloodied** 248
AC 25, **Fortitude** 26, **Reflex** 23, **Will** 22
Speed 5
Resist 10 fire
Saving Throws +5; **Action Points** 2

Initiative +9
Perception +15
All-around vision, darkvision

TRAITS

All-Around Vision
Enemies can't gain combat advantage by flanking the hydra.

Many Headed
While stunned or dominated, the hydra can take free actions.

Regenerating Heads
The hydra starts an encounter with four heads. When the hydra's hit points first go below 372, 248, and 124, one of its heads is destroyed. Whenever a head is destroyed, the hydra grows two heads at the start of its next turn unless it takes cold or acid damage before then.

Threatening Reach
The hydra can make opportunity attacks against enemies within 2 squares of it.

STANDARD ACTIONS

⊕ **Bite ✦ At-Will**
Attack: Melee 2 (one creature); +17 vs. AC
Hit: 3d12 damage.

⟵ **Flame Kiss (fire) ✦ Recharge** when the hydra loses a head
Attack: Close blast 3 (creatures in the blast); +13 vs. Reflex
Hit: 2d8 + 5 fire damage, and ongoing 10 fire damage (save ends). The hydra pushes the target up to 3 squares.

Hydra Fury ✦ At-Will
Effect: The hydra attacks a number of times equal to the number of heads it currently has, using either *bite* or *flame kiss* for each attack. If it has only two heads, it gains a +5 bonus to damage rolls with the attacks. If it has only one head, it gains a +15 bonus to damage rolls with the attack.

TRIGGERED ACTIONS

⊦ **Snapping Jaws ✦ At-Will**
Trigger: An enemy ends its turn within 2 squares of the hydra.
Attack (Free Action): The hydra uses *bite* twice against the triggering enemy.

Str 22 (+12)	Dex 17 (+9)	Wis 18 (+10)
Con 20 (+11)	Int 2 (+2)	Cha 8 (+5)

Alignment unaligned   **Languages** –

behavior makes a hydra adaptable to threats while relieving it of the vulnerability that usually comes with sleep.

Deadly Pets: A hydra is a terrifying creature and a cunning hunter, but it is still only a beast. Unless trained to do otherwise, it kills to eat. Despite having numerous heads, a hydra in the wild seems no more intelligent than a crocodile or a dog. Indeed, a hydra's own heads might fight over prey or choice bits of meat.

Despite their limited intellect, hydras removed from the wild have proved capable of learning and following commands. Each hydra presents a trainer with at least four students. When one of a hydra's heads learns a trick, the others instantly assimilate the knowledge. A trainer that survives the initial stages of training a hydra can usually teach the creature far more commands than a typical beast could follow.

Giants, minotaurs, and powerful spellcasters use hydras as guardians or war beasts. Occasionally, a formidable human, goblin, halfling, or elf leader manages to adopt a hydra. Given the creatures' proclivity for water, these pets can be found lurking in moats, swimming alongside warships, or dwelling in constructed pools near objects or locations in need of protecting.

Venom-Maw Hydra	Level 17 Solo Brute
Huge natural beast (reptile, water)	XP 8,000

HP 672; Bloodied 336	Initiative +13
AC 31, Fortitude 31, Reflex 29, Will 28	Perception +17
Speed 7, swim 10	All-around vision, darkvision
Resist 10 poison	
Saving Throws +5; Action Points 2	

TRAITS

All-Around Vision
Enemies can't gain combat advantage by flanking the hydra.

Many Headed
While stunned or dominated, the hydra can take free actions.

Regenerating Heads
The hydra starts an encounter with four heads. When the hydra's hit points first go below 504, 336, and 168, one of its heads is destroyed. Whenever a head is destroyed, the hydra grows two heads at the start of its next turn unless it takes fire or acid damage before then.

Threatening Reach
The hydra can make opportunity attacks against enemies within 3 squares of it.

STANDARD ACTIONS

⊕ **Bite** (poison) ✦ At-Will
Attack: Melee 3 (one creature); +22 vs. AC
Hit: 3d12 damage, and ongoing 10 poison damage, or ongoing 20 poison damage if the hydra is bloodied (save ends).

⤳ **Venomous Spit** (poison) ✦ At-Will
Attack: Ranged 10 (one creature); +20 vs. Reflex. This attack does not provoke opportunity attacks.
Hit: 2d12 + 5 poison damage, and the target falls prone.

Hydra Fury ✦ At-Will
Effect: The hydra attacks a number of times equal to the number of heads it currently has, using either *bite* or *venomous spit* for each attack. If it has only two heads, it gains a +5 bonus to damage rolls with the attacks. If it has only one head, it gains a +15 bonus to damage rolls with the attack.

TRIGGERED ACTIONS

↯ **Snapping Jaws** ✦ At-Will
Trigger: An enemy ends its turn within 2 squares of the hydra.
Effect (Free Action): The hydra uses *bite* twice against the triggering enemy.

Skills Stealth +18

Str 25 (+15)	Dex 20 (+13)	Wis 18 (+12)
Con 24 (+15)	Int 2 (+4)	Cha 8 (+7)

Alignment unaligned   **Languages** —

KOBOLD

The small stature and cowardly behavior of these reptilian savages disguises a devious and murderous cunning.

Kobold. Few can say the word with anything but disgust and disdain—few except for the proud and proliferate kobolds, of course. These primitive reptilian humanoids pose a threat to civilized people who allow the scaly monsters to encroach on their settlements. Although kobolds are cowardly and somewhat dim, many braver and smarter foes have fallen to their cunning after underestimating the diminutive savages.

Trap-Filled Warrens: Kobold tribes seek out the shelter of a warren. Like rats, they think nothing of tunneling through the ground to make a maze of crisscrossing passages and stacked chambers. A warren's complex structure gives the kobolds multiple routes for escape or ambush, and the passages provide ample room for traps and murder holes in case anything tries to root out the creatures. Nomadic kobolds litter their camps with snares, deadfalls, and trip wires. Once an area is trapped, they dig shallow pits in which to sleep, or else drag together hollow logs that work as makeshift warrens.

JIM NELSON

Kobold Tunneler

Level 1 Minion Skirmisher

Small natural humanoid (reptile)

XP 25

HP 1; a missed attack never damages a minion.	**Initiative** +5
AC 15, **Fortitude** 12, **Reflex** 14, **Will** 12	**Perception** +1
Speed 6	Darkvision

STANDARD ACTIONS

⊕ **Javelin** (weapon) ✦ At-Will

Attack: Melee 1 (one creature); +6 vs. AC

Hit: 4 damage.

⊗ **Javelin** (weapon) ✦ At-Will

Attack: Ranged 10 (one creature); +6 vs. AC

Hit: 4 damage.

MINOR ACTIONS

Shifty ✦ At-Will

Effect: The kobold shifts 1 square.

TRIGGERED ACTIONS

Narrow Escape ✦ Encounter

Trigger: A close or an area attack hits or misses the kobold.

Effect (Immediate Interrupt): The kobold shifts up to 3 squares.

Str 8 (-1)	**Dex** 16 (+3)	**Wis** 12 (+1)
Con 12 (+1)	**Int** 9 (-1)	**Cha** 10 (+0)

Alignment evil **Languages** Common, Draconic

Equipment leather armor, 3 javelins

Mines, abandoned or otherwise, are favorite kobold haunts. The sites offer only a small number of entrances but provide vast interior spaces. If a mine isn't depleted, kobolds might continue to dig ore in order to gain wealth or make weapons. When a mine isn't available, a tribe of kobolds might inhabit a cave, a ruin, or a city sewer. Any place that puts a roof over their heads and can accommodate new passages can become a stronghold.

Creature Keepers: Kobold tribes rarely live alone in warrens. Rather, they keep local beasts as barely tamed pets and allow larger creatures to lair in sections of the warren that the kobolds then avoid. Insects of all sizes, odd slimes and oozes, burrowing animals, and deadlier threats such as stirges and cave bears, can be found dwelling side by side with kobolds.

Devious Thieves and Cunning Killers: It is a mistake to think of kobolds as daft simpletons. In reality, their feeble appearance masks a devious and murderous mentality.

Kobolds prefer to live in the vicinity of a dragon's lair or near communities from which they can steal goods and consumables. Although they are vicious foes if confronted, kobolds work to avoid notice. They can steal from fields and storehouses for months before their presence is discovered. They rarely reveal their true numbers, and they don't set traps outside their strongholds until after the surrounding inhabitants realize the kobolds are in residence.

Communities that declare war on an established kobold tribe often face destruction. When kobolds know the jig is up, they go on the offensive, booby trapping buildings and ambushing residents in their homes. Overnight,

Kobold Slinger
Level 1 Artillery
Small natural humanoid (reptile)

XP 100

HP 24; **Bloodied** 12
AC 13, **Fortitude** 12, **Reflex** 14, **Will** 12
Speed 6

Initiative +3
Perception +1
Darkvision

STANDARD ACTIONS

⊕ **Dagger** (weapon) ✦ **At-Will**

Attack: Melee 1 (one creature); +8 vs. AC

Hit: 1d4 + 3 damage.

⊙ **Sling** (weapon) ✦ **At-Will**

Attack: Ranged 20 (one creature); +8 vs. AC

Hit: 1d6 + 5 damage.

⤳ **Special Shot** (weapon) ✦ **At-Will** (3/encounter)

Attack: Ranged 20 (one creature); +8 vs. AC

Hit: 1d6 + 5 damage plus one of the following effects (roll a d6):

⚀ ⚁ *Stinkpot:* The target takes a -2 penalty to attack rolls (save ends).

⚂ ⚃ *Firepot* (fire): The target takes ongoing 2 fire damage (save ends).

⚄ ⚅ *Gluepot:* The target is immobilized (save ends).

MINOR ACTION

Shifty ✦ **At-Will**

Effect: The kobold shifts 1 square.

Skills Stealth +8

| Str 9 (-1) | Dex 17 (+3) | Wis 12 (+1) |
| Con 12 (+1) | Int 9 (-1) | Cha 10 (+0) |

Alignment evil

Languages Common, Draconic

Equipment leather armor, dagger, sling, 20 sling bullets, 3 rounds of special shot

---

Kobold Quickblade
Level 1 Skirmisher
Small natural humanoid (reptile)

XP 100

HP 29; **Bloodied** 14
AC 15, **Fortitude** 12, **Reflex** 14, **Will** 12
Speed 6

Initiative +5
Perception +1
Darkvision

STANDARD ACTIONS

⊕ **Short Sword** (weapon) ✦ **At-Will**

Attack: Melee 1 (one creature); +6 vs. AC

Hit: 1d6 + 3 damage. The attack deals 2 extra damage per square the kobold has shifted since the start of its turn.

MOVE ACTIONS

Fleet Feet ✦ **At-Will**

Effect: The kobold shifts up to 3 squares.

MINOR ACTIONS

Shifty ✦ **At-Will**

Effect: The kobold shifts 1 square.

Skills Athletics +4, Stealth +8, Thievery +8

| Str 8 (-1) | Dex 17 (+3) | Wis 13 (+1) |
| Con 13 (+1) | Int 9 (-1) | Cha 10 (+0) |

Alignment evil

Languages Common, Draconic

Equipment leather armor, light shield, short sword

Kobold Dragonshield	Level 2 Soldier
Small natural humanoid (reptile)	XP 125

HP 36; **Bloodied** 18	**Initiative** +4
AC 18, **Fortitude** 14, **Reflex** 13, **Will** 13	**Perception** +2
Speed 5	Darkvision

STANDARD ACTIONS

⊕ **Short Sword** (weapon) ✦ At-Will

Attack: Melee 1 (one creature); +7 vs. AC

Hit: 1d6 + 6 damage.

Effect: The kobold marks the target until the end of the kobold's next turn.

⸽ **Dirty Tactics** (weapon) ✦ Encounter

Attack: Melee 1 (one creature); +5 vs. Reflex

Hit: 2d6 + 7 damage, and the target is immobilized until the end of the kobold's next turn.

Miss: Half damage, and the target is slowed until the end of the kobold's next turn.

MINOR ACTIONS

Shifty ✦ At-Will

Effect: The kobold shifts 1 square.

TRIGGERED ACTIONS

Dragonshield Tactics ✦ At-Will

Trigger: An enemy adjacent to the kobold shifts or an enemy moves to a square adjacent to the kobold.

Effect (Immediate Reaction): The kobold shifts 1 square.

Skills Athletics +8, Stealth +7, Thievery +7		
Str 14 (+3)	**Dex** 13 (+2)	**Wis** 12 (+2)
Con 12 (+2)	**Int** 9 (+0)	**Cha** 10 (+1)

Alignment evil	**Languages** Common, Draconic

Equipment scale armor, light shield, short sword

settlements can become battlegrounds. If a militia tries to take the fight to the kobold warren, the crafty fiends make themselves scarce, allowing the hapless invaders to stumble into the tribe's deadly traps and pets.

Dragon Worshipers: Dragons rarely take notice of the tiny humanoids crawling, wormlike, from holes in the ground, which is why kobolds can survive in the vicinity of the creatures. A tribe goes to any length to worship at a dragon's feet. The sight of one of the majestic creatures in flight sends a tribe into frenzied activity. Its members don cobbled-together dragon costumes and heap up offerings in hopes of the dragon returning. When a lucky kobold tribe attracts a dragon's attention with its odd displays, doing so can have fatal results. Numerous deaths do nothing to dampen a tribe's enthusiasm for a dragon. Kobolds consider it an honor to be consumed by a dragon.

Young dragons capable of tolerating fawning kobolds occasionally sponsor a tribe's presence in or around their lairs. The kobolds prove useful as servants, guardians, and early alerts to danger. Older dragons interested in employing minions flush out kobold infestations and turn to more powerful servants. Even in such events, a few cunning kobolds might survive to serve their angry gods in secret. These kobolds often come to resent a dragon's new servants, though, so they might seek to harm new minions or sabotage the creatures' efforts.

LICH

A dark spellcaster who covets immortality and spend his or her life in pursuit of nec-
romantic power might gain the ability to become a lich. A lich ties its life force to a
phylactery, ensuring that its body will coalesce in a hidden location even if some creature
were to slay it.

A lich views the world through a prism of endless opportunity, where time is no longer a relevant concern. It severs ties to its past life, shedding its mortal name to adopt a false title, such as the Forgotten King or the Bronze Lich. Self-centered and black-hearted, a lich abuses and maims with ease as it collects knowledge and gains influence.

The prospect of a lich rising to power isn't hypothetical. The god Vecna, the githyanki queen Vlaakith, and the demilich Acererak have won great power and infamy. A lich left unchecked conquers free lands, bends influential people to its will, and destroys anyone and anything that stands between it and its ambitions.

Complex Scheming: A lich seeks mortals to dominate, places to control, wealth to acquire, and magic to harness. Its thirst for power and knowledge is never quenched. As a mortal spellcaster, it worked feverishly, racing the sands of time to attain its goals. But with eternity in its pocket, a lich can afford to be patient. A lich's plans might ripen over generations as it taints a royal bloodline with magic, forms and fosters an evil organization, or reanimates legions of undead warriors. The complexity of a lich's scheme usually

UDON

Lich Necromancer   Level 14 Elite Controller

Medium natural humanoid (undead)   XP 2,000

HP 268; **Bloodied** 134   **Initiative** +8
AC 28, **Fortitude** 24, **Reflex** 28, **Will** 27   **Perception** +9
Speed 6   Darkvision
Immune disease, poison; **Resist** 10 necrotic
Saving Throws +2; **Action Points** 1

Traits

⚙ **Necromantic Aura** (necrotic) ✦ **Aura** 5

Any living creature that ends its turn in the aura takes 5 necrotic damage. Whenever the lich takes radiant damage, its aura is deactivated until the end of the lich's next turn.

Soul Phylactery

When the lich drops to 0 hit points, its body and possessions crumble into dust and it disappears, but it is not destroyed. It reappears (along with its possessions) in 1d10 days within 1 square of its phylactery, unless the phylactery is destroyed.

Standard Actions

⊕ **Vampiric Touch** (healing, necrotic) ✦ **At-Will**

Attack: Melee 1 (one creature); +17 vs. Fortitude
Hit: 2d8 + 7 necrotic damage, and the lich regains hit points equal to the damage dealt.

⌁ **Freezing Claw** (cold, necrotic) ✦ **At-Will**

Attack: Ranged 5 (one or two creatures); +17 vs. Reflex
Hit: 2d8 + 10 cold and necrotic damage, and the target is immobilized (save ends).
Miss: The target is slowed (save ends).

✷ **Enervating Tendrils** (necrotic) ✦ **Recharge** when first bloodied

Attack: Area burst 1 within 10 (enemies in the burst); +17 vs. Fortitude
Hit: 6d6 + 7 necrotic damage, and the target is weakened (save ends).
Miss: Half damage.

Move Actions

Shadow Walk (teleportation) ✦ **Encounter**

Effect: The lich teleports up to twice its speed.

Minor Actions

Lich's Control ✦ **Recharge** ⚄ ⚅

Effect: Close burst 10 (one enemy in the burst that is subject to an effect a save can end). The target takes a -5 penalty to its next saving throw.

Skills Arcana +18, History +18, Insight +14

Str 10 (+7)	**Dex** 12 (+8)	**Wis** 15 (+9)
Con 14 (+9)	**Int** 23 (+13)	**Cha** 20 (+12)

Alignment evil   **Languages** Abyssal, Common

---

stymies its pursuers. Scholars say that discovering a lich's motivation requires delving into the creature's former life to find clues about why it first became a dark necromancer.

Insane and Irredeemably Evil: To become a lich, a spellcaster must be devoted to evil and adept at performing unspeakable acts of violence. Few spellcasters have a shred of morality remaining after their transformations into liches. The process of attaining lichdom bends the mortal mind in unnatural and crippling ways. Many liches rise up insane, but even they enact cunning plans; they just do so for incomprehensible reasons.

Lich Remnant	Level 16 Minion Artillery
Medium natural humanoid (undead)	XP 350

MINION

HP 1; a missed attack never damages a minion.	Initiative +10
AC 30, Fortitude 25, Reflex 29, Will 28	Perception +11
Speed 6	Darkvision
Immune disease; Resist 20 necrotic, 20 poison	

Standard Actions

(+) **Shadow Touch** (necrotic) ✦ **At-Will**

Attack: Melee 1 (one creature); +19 vs. Fortitude

Hit: 8 necrotic damage.

(↗) **Shadow Ray** (necrotic) ✦ **At-Will**

Attack: Ranged 20 (one creature); +21 vs. Fortitude

Hit: 12 necrotic damage.

✳ **Orb of Obliteration** (fire, necrotic) ✦ **At-Will**

Attack: Area burst 1 within 20 (enemies in the burst); +21 vs. Reflex

Hit: 10 fire and necrotic damage.

Miss: Half damage.

Obliteration Empowerment ✦ **At-Will**

Effect: Ranged 5 (one lich remnant). The next time the target uses *orb of obliteration* before the end of its next turn, the size of the power's burst increases by 1, and the power deals 5 extra damage. *Obliteration empowerment* stacks with other uses of *obliteration empowerment*.

Str 9 (+7)	Dex 14 (+10)	Wis 17 (+11)
Con 20 (+13)	Int 28 (+17)	Cha 26 (+16)
Alignment evil	Languages Abyssal, Common	

Evil Sanctuaries: A spellcaster must travel far—even across the planes—to collect the scraps of lore and esoteric components needed to enact the ritual to transform into a lich. After the transformation, though, a lich typically returns to its home plane and moves back into its old tower or stronghold. A lich fears anything that might jeopardize its eternal life or acquisition of power. Thus, it surrounds its lair with deadly traps, arcane tests and riddles, and forbidding terrain. A lich might travel out into the world if its scheme depends on it, but it prefers to send magical messages while staying close to its citadel.

"With an eternal semblance of life to study and practice their magic, most liches are incredibly powerful—and insatiably restless."

—Mari Valmidren, cleric of Ioun

Few and Faithful Allies: A lich spends its time alone in its sanctuary. It dislikes being tied to allies, most of which have life spans too short to be of use. Malevolent creatures idolize liches, though, serving them willingly so they can bask in the undead creature's depths of depravity. A lich uses such hangers-on as field agents, usually because its preferred servants—undead and constructs—have a hard time blending in.

The Precious Phylactery: The act of becoming a lich encases a mortal's life force in a specially prepared item called a phylactery. The most common type is a metal box that contains strips of parchment with arcane writing. Any small item, such as a gemstone, a ring, or a statue, can be a phylactery. Destroying a lich's phylactery prevents the undead creature from rematerializing, which makes the item's concealment and safekeeping a top priority for a lich.

A lich, fearing being separated from its citadel of power, might keep its phylactery in a hidden room or nearby town. Another, focused on secrecy, might secure its phylactery on another plane. The most cautious liches place their phylacteries in changing or confusing locations. A phylactery might be hidden on a traveling ship with a band of devotees, or its appearance might be duplicated in a dozen copies that are distributed across world, ensuring that no one knows which version is the true phylactery.

Magic wards and physical barriers are a phylactery's final defense. Even if a mortal survives a lich's allies, that person must still overcome powerful magic to destroy a phylactery.

Lich Soulreaver	Level 22 Artillery (Leader)
Medium natural humanoid (undead)	XP 4,150

HP 156; **Bloodied** 78 | **Initiative** +16
AC 36, **Fortitude** 32, **Reflex** 36, **Will** 35 | **Perception** +14
Speed 6 | Darkvision
Immune disease, poison; **Resist** 20 necrotic

TRAITS

⟳ **Necromantic Aura** (necrotic) ✦ **Aura 5**
Any living creature that ends its turn in the aura takes 10 necrotic damage. Whenever the lich takes radiant damage, its aura is deactivated until the end of the lich's next turn.

Soul Phylactery
When the lich drops to 0 hit points, its body and possessions crumble into dust and it disappears, but it is not destroyed. It reappears (along with its possessions) in 1d10 days within 1 square of its phylactery, unless the phylactery is destroyed.

STANDARD ACTIONS

⊕ **Vampiric Touch** (healing, necrotic) ✦ **At-Will**
Attack: Melee 1 (one creature); +25 vs. Fortitude
Hit: 4d8 + 6 necrotic damage, and the lich regains hit points equal to the damage dealt.

⟐ **Dark Bolts** (lightning, necrotic) ✦ **At-Will**
Attack: Ranged 20 (one or two creatures); +27 vs. Reflex
Hit: 3d6 + 10 lightning and necrotic damage, and an ally adjacent to the target shifts up to 2 squares.

❋ **Black Flames** (fire, necrotic) ✦ **Recharge when first bloodied**
Attack: Area burst 2 within 10 (enemies in the burst); +27 vs. Reflex
Hit: 3d10 + 8 fire and necrotic damage, and the target takes ongoing 15 fire and necrotic damage and grants combat advantage (save ends both).
Miss: Half damage, and ongoing 10 fire and necrotic damage (save ends).

MOVE ACTIONS

Shadow Walk (teleportation) ✦ **Encounter**
Effect: The lich teleports up to twice its speed.

Skills Arcana +24, History +24, Insight +19

Str 14 (+13)	Dex 20 (+16)	Wis 17 (+14)
Con 18 (+15)	Int 27 (+19)	Cha 24 (+18)

Alignment evil | **Languages** Abyssal, Common, Elven

LIZARDFOLK

These primitive hunters stalk swamps and jungles, springing with ease from murky water and overgrown foliage. Lizardfolk tribes pair sacrificial rituals with uproarious feasts, cooking up beasts and trespassers alike.

"Fog rose up around us as evening settled in, carrying the stench of the swamp with it. Then the weeds and vines started coiling around our legs."
—Anders Partieren of Fallcrest

Lizardfolk live in forbidding grottos, dangerous tropical isles, abandoned jungle temples, and underground caverns that water-filled passageways protect. Lizardfolk can create hut villages, but they prefer to slaughter inhabitants of a jungle city or temple and take over the ready-made site.

Fiercely territorial, lizardfolk use camouflaged snares and scouts to guard the tribe's encampment. They rarely are caught unawares on their home turf. When unwelcome visitors approach the outskirts of lizardfolk territory, a hunting band is sent to ambush or harass the trespassers. If the interlopers appear too threatening as a group, the band tricks some into blundering into the lairs of crocodiles or other dangerous animals.

(**Left to right**) *greenscale bog mystic, blackscale crusher, greenscale raider, poisonscale needler*

STEVE PRESCOTT

Poisonscale Needler — Level 3 Minion Artillery

Medium natural humanoid (reptile), lizardfolk — XP 38

HP 1; a missed attack never damages a minion.
AC 17, **Fortitude** 13, **Reflex** 16, **Will** 14
Speed 6 (swamp walk)
Initiative +5
Perception +3

TRAITS

Sniper
A hidden needler that misses with a ranged attack remains hidden.

STANDARD ACTIONS

⊕ **Claw** (weapon) ✦ At-Will
Attack: Melee 1 (one creature); +8 vs. AC
Hit: 5 damage.

⊗ **Blowgun** (poison, weapon) ✦ At-Will
Attack: Ranged 10 (one creature); +10 vs. AC
Hit: 5 poison damage. On a critical hit, the target also falls unconscious (save ends).

Str 12 (+2)	**Dex** 18 (+5)	**Wis** 15 (+3)
Con 11 (+1)	**Int** 7 (-1)	**Cha** 9 (+0)

Alignment unaligned   **Languages** Draconic
Equipment blowgun, 10 poisoned blowgun needles

Poisonscale Brawler — Level 3 Brute

Medium natural humanoid (reptile), lizardfolk — XP 150

HP 55; **Bloodied** 27
AC 15, **Fortitude** 15, **Reflex** 13, **Will** 12
Speed 6 (swamp walk)
Initiative +3
Perception +1

STANDARD ACTIONS

⊕ **Club** (weapon) ✦ At-Will
Attack: Melee 1 (one creature); +8 vs. AC
Hit: 2d6 + 7 damage.

⊹ **Crushing Grasp** ✦ At-Will
Attack: Melee 1 (one creature grabbed by the brawler); +6 vs. Fortitude
Hit: 3d6 + 7 damage.
Miss: Half damage.

MINOR ACTIONS

⊹ **Feral Grab** ✦ At-Will (1/round)
Requirement: The brawler must not be grabbing a creature.
Attack: Melee 1 (one creature that isn't grabbed); +6 vs. Reflex
Hit: The brawler grabs the target (escape DC 13).

Skills Athletics +10, Stealth +8

Str 18 (+5)	**Dex** 15 (+3)	**Wis** 10 (+1)
Con 15 (+3)	**Int** 7 (-1)	**Cha** 8 (+0)

Alignment unaligned   **Languages** Draconic
Equipment club

Intruders aren't the only creatures in danger. Since lizardfolk are dominant hunters, a tribe quickly clears its territory of choice small prey. Once lizardfolk begin searching for new meat sources, they come into conflict with civilized tribes or cities. Unlike a brutal orc attack, a lizardfolk raid is brief and mysterious. A silent band breaks from nearby cover to swiftly capture a few succulent, small humanoids. Then the hunters disappear back into the wilderness. Rescuing captured victims involves tracking the lizardfolk through their native terrain, an often deadly proposition.

Masters of Traps and Tricks: Though far from being great thinkers, lizardfolk are clever predators in their home environment. Hunters carry nets and poison darts, and trappers set well-hidden snares and pitfalls. Weaker lizardfolk, especially the poisonscales, harvest toxic plants with which to brew a spectrum of poisons. Excepting some of the more brutish blackscales, all lizardfolk become masters of camouflage. They liberally apply mud and leaves from the swamp or jungle floor, and they move silently through thick underbrush and still water alike.

Lizardfolk share a predatory mindset and other echoes of their reptilian heritage. They grow docile on sunny days and bicker and spar when clouds obscure the sky.

Greenscale Raider	Level 3 Soldier
Medium natural humanoid (reptile), lizardfolk	XP 150

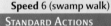

HP 45; **Bloodied** 22   **Initiative** +5
AC 19, **Fortitude** 17, **Reflex** 15, **Will** 13   **Perception** +1
Speed 6 (swamp walk)

STANDARD ACTIONS

⊕ **Club** (weapon) ✦ **At-Will**
Attack: Melee 1 (one creature); +8 vs. AC
Hit: 1d10 + 5 damage.
Effect: The raider marks the target until the end of the raider's next turn.

MINOR ACTIONS

⊕ **Tail Sweep** ✦ **At-Will**
Requirement: The raider must be bloodied.
Attack: Melee 1 (one creature); +6 vs. Reflex
Hit: The target falls prone.

TRIGGERED ACTIONS

↯ **Hunter's Response** ✦ **Recharge** ⚄ ⚅ ⚃
Trigger: An enemy adjacent to the raider shifts.
Attack (Immediate Interrupt): Melee 1 (triggering enemy); +8 vs. AC
Hit: 2d10 + 3 damage.
Miss: Half damage.

Skills Athletics +10, Stealth +8
| **Str** 18 (+5) | **Dex** 15 (+3) | **Wis** 10 (+1) |
| **Con** 13 (+2) | **Int** 8 (+0) | **Cha** 8 (+0) |

Alignment unaligned   **Languages** Draconic
Equipment turtle shell shield, club

Greenscale Trapper — Level 3 Controller

Medium natural humanoid (reptile), lizardfolk — XP 150

HP 46; **Bloodied** 23	**Initiative** +5
AC 17, **Fortitude** 14, **Reflex** 16, **Will** 14	**Perception** +3
Speed 6 (swamp walk)	

STANDARD ACTIONS

⊕ **Spear** (weapon) ✦ At-Will

Attack: Melee 1 (one creature); +8 vs. AC

Hit: 1d8 + 6 damage.

⟜ **Net Toss** (weapon) ✦ At-Will

Requirement: The trapper must be wielding a net.

Attack: Close blast 2 (enemies in the blast); +6 vs. Reflex

Hit: 1d4 + 3 damage, and the target is immobilized (save ends).

Miss: The trapper can slide the target 1 square to a square not in the blast.

MOVE ACTIONS

Net Drag ✦ At-Will

Effect: The trapper moves up to its speed, pulling creatures immobilized by its net an equal number of squares. This movement does not provoke opportunity attacks from creatures immobilized by the trapper's net.

MINOR ACTIONS

⨪ **Feral Kick** ✦ At-Will

Requirement: The trapper must be bloodied.

Attack: Melee 1 (one creature); +6 vs. Reflex

Hit: The trapper can slide the target 1 square.

Skills Athletics +7, Stealth +10

Str 13 (+2)	Dex 18 (+5)	Wis 14 (+3)
Con 14 (+3)	Int 8 (+0)	Cha 8 (+0)

Alignment unaligned — **Languages** Draconic

Equipment 3 nets, spear

Greenscale Raider — Level 4 Skirmisher

Medium natural humanoid (reptile), lizardfolk — XP 175

HP 54; **Bloodied** 27	**Initiative** +6
AC 18, **Fortitude** 17, **Reflex** 16, **Will** 15	**Perception** +8
Speed 6 (swamp walk)	

STANDARD ACTIONS

⊕ **Spear** (weapon) ✦ At-Will

Attack: Melee 1 (one creature); +9 vs. AC

Hit: 1d8 + 6 damage.

⨪ **Sidestep Attack** (weapon) ✦ At-Will

Effect: The hunter can shift 1 square and then use *spear*.

MINOR ACTIONS

⨪ **Feral Tail Lash** ✦ At-Will

Requirement: The hunter must be bloodied.

Attack: Melee 1 (one creature); +9 vs. AC

Hit: 1d6 damage, and the hunter can shift 1 square.

Skills Athletics +10, Stealth +9

Str 17 (+5)	Dex 15 (+4)	Wis 12 (+3)
Con 14 (+4)	Int 8 (+1)	Cha 8 (+1)

Alignment unaligned — **Languages** Draconic

Equipment light shield, spear

Greenscale Bog Mystic — Level 6 Controller (Leader)

Medium natural humanoid (reptile), lizardfolk — XP 250

HP 70; **Bloodied** 35
AC 20, **Fortitude** 17, **Reflex** 16, **Will** 19
Speed 6 (swamp walk)

Initiative +4
Perception +7

TRAITS

☼ Swamp Tangle ✦ Aura 5
Whenever an enemy in the aura is hit by an attack, squares in the aura are difficult terrain for that enemy until the end of its next turn.

STANDARD ACTIONS

⊕ Spear (weapon) ✦ At-Will
Attack: Melee 1 (one creature); +11 vs. AC
Hit: 2d8 + 5 damage.

✳ Bog Cloud (poison) ✦ Recharge ⚄ ⚅
Attack: Area burst 2 within 5 (creatures in the burst); +9 vs. Fortitude
Hit: 2d6 + 7 poison damage, and the target is dazed until the end of the mystic's next turn.
Miss: The target grants combat advantage until the end of the mystic's next turn.

✳ Swamp's Grasp (zone) ✦ Encounter
Attack: Area burst 2 within 5 (enemies in the burst); +9 vs. Reflex
Hit: 2d6 + 4 damage, and the target is immobilized (save ends).
Miss: Half damage, and the target is slowed (save ends).
Effect: The burst creates a zone of difficult terrain until the end of the encounter. The zone does not affect creatures that have swamp walk.

MINOR ACTIONS

⫟ Feral Tail Lash ✦ At-Will
Requirement: The mystic must be bloodied.
Attack: Melee 1 (one creature); +9 vs. Reflex
Hit: 1d6 damage, and the target is slowed until the end of the mystic's next turn.

Skills Athletics +10, Nature +12, Stealth +9

Str 15 (+5)	Dex 13 (+4)	Wis 19 (+7)
Con 14 (+5)	Int 10 (+3)	Cha 12 (+4)

Alignment evil — **Languages** Draconic
Equipment spear

Many Breeds, Each Deadly: The lizardfolk lineage splits into several breeds, each of which has a specific purpose within the tribe. Greenscales, the most common variety, hunt medium-sized game and build traps. Most mystics come from the ranks of the greenscales, as do lizardfolk adept at training wild beasts. The hulking blackscales provide the intimidation factor, lending brute strength to their more clever and deft kin. A tribe has only a few blackscales. Even though they aren't suited to leadership roles, their physical might is a boon to their kinsfolk. Poisonscales are the smallest of the lizardfolk. They are the tribe's stealthiest members and masters of crafting poison. When raiding, they hide in trees or shallow pools, attacking soundlessly. Poisonscales frequently serve as teachers for young greenscales, which are the same size as full-grown poisonscales.

Intimidation and Fanaticism: Might makes right in the patriarchal structure of a lizardfolk tribe. The strongest of mind and body becomes the lizard king. Mystics also wield great power among these easily awed creatures. Mysterious outsiders can win slavish devotion with a few well-timed tricks or overt uses of magic.

Powerful creatures, especially dragons, can be found ruling lizardfolk tribes. Even young dragons or wyrmlings can seem like terrifying gods to lizardfolk. Adventurers who defeat the lizard king might earn a horde of unwanted worshipers. Although most lizardfolk are unaligned, their leaders are typically evil. Even lizardfolk that serve good-intentioned masters behave brutishly and succumb to their baser instincts more often than not.

Great Feasts and Sacrifices: After capturing creatures, especially humanoids, lizardfolk throw huge feasts and riotous religious festivities. Their rites include dancing, chittering, and wrestling. Victims are either cooked and fed to the tribe or sacrificed to a god. Lizardfolk don't know much about true deities. Instead, they worship a motley combination of primal spirits and powerful mundane creatures.

Blackscale Crusher	Level 6 Brute
Large natural humanoid (reptile), lizardfolk	XP 250

HP 86; **Bloodied** 43	**Initiative** +6
AC 18, **Fortitude** 19, **Reflex** 16, **Will** 16	**Perception** +4
Speed 8 (swamp walk)	

STANDARD ACTIONS

⊕ **Greatclub** (weapon) ✦ At-Will
Attack: Melee 2 (one creature); +11 vs. AC
Hit: 2d10 + 6 damage, and the bruiser can push the target 1 square.

MINOR ACTIONS

⊕ **Feral Bite** ✦ At-Will
Requirement: The bruiser must be bloodied.
Attack: Melee 1 (one creature); +11 vs. AC
Hit: 1d6 + 4 damage.

TRIGGERED ACTIONS

↤ **Tail Swipe** ✦ Recharge when first bloodied
Trigger: The bruiser takes damage from an enemy.
Attack (Immediate Reaction): Close blast 2 (creatures in the blast); +9 vs. Reflex
Hit: 2d8 + 6 damage, and the target falls prone.

Str 22 (+9)	Dex 16 (+6)	Wis 12 (+4)
Con 16 (+6)	Int 5 (+0)	Cha 6 (+1)

Alignment unaligned   **Languages** Draconic
Equipment greatclub

LYCANTHROPE

Lycanthropes shift between human and animal forms, comfortably traveling both in society and in the wild.

Shapeshifters remain in human form around other creatures, revealing their bestial nature only when in the company of other lycanthropes or moments before a kill. The carnivorous creatures are born with a craving for human flesh. An instinct to survive and the awareness that discovery means death drives lycanthropes to lie, cheat, steal, and murder.

True lycanthropes are born only to shapeshifter mates, but legends tell a different story. According to these myths, a lycanthrope's bite or a mystic's curse can infect a mortal with lycanthropy.

Masters of Infiltration: Lycanthropes in human form blend easily into crowds. They use their talents of deception to infiltrate organizations for personal gain, possibly to grow wealthy or to win access to a specific victim. Some shapeshifters work for hire. Even a modest-sized group might have werecreature members.

When a lycanthrope gains access to its intended prey, the creature shifts into hybrid form to gloat before meting out the killing blow. A lycanthrope is typically patient, content to enjoy the intricacies of the chase. When it feels threatened, though, it tends to make rash decisions.

A lycanthrope's human form hints at its bestial nature. Wererats are short, wiry, and naturally fidgety; werewolves have prominent canine teeth and a fierce gleam in their eyes.

Three Forms for Three Worlds: Lycanthropes live in three distinct worlds: humanoid society, shapeshifter clans, and animal packs. In cities, they remain in human form, going to great lengths to avoid revealing their bestial forms. Only the most vicious lycanthropes—creatures that revel in debauchery, theft, and violence—spend more time than absolutely necessary in civilization. Among clan members, lycanthropes form cabals and remain in their hybrid forms. Shapeshifters that rarely part from clan society typically embrace a baser lifestyle as they age, combining the cruelest characteristics of humankind with the brutality of beasts. Sometimes, these cabals take over small villages and enslave the inhabitants.

"The moon rises full tonight, and I've heard wolves howling on the downs. Best lock your doors."

—Salvana Wrafton
of Winterhaven

Tied to the Moon: When the full moon rises, werecreatures stalk city streets and wild places alike. Their howls echo across the land, filling settlers with dread. Families make offerings to Sehanine, goddess of the moon, beseeching her to protect them from shapeshifters. Silver is associated with the moon, but it causes werecreatures pain and prevents their wounds from healing as quickly as normal. Hunting parties intent on slaying a lycanthrope are wise to use silver-coated weapons.

Rulers of the Underworld: The most urban of lycanthropes, wererats dwell in packs inside sewers or catacombs. More cunning and materialistic than their shapeshifter kin, wererats join criminal organizations or start their own. A wererat might be a pickpocket, a criminal mastermind, or a spy.

Living on the Fringe: Brutish and feral, werewolves dwell alone or in small wilderness clans. They frequently run with wolf packs, especially when the moon is full. They sometimes join bandit gangs or become mercenaries. Werewolves prefer to stick to the borderlands but occasionally work inside cities. Anyone who employs a werewolf must be prepared to satisfy the creature's thirst for human blood.

Scurrying Wererat — Level 3 Skirmisher

Medium natural humanoid (shapechanger), human   XP 150

HP 37; **Bloodied** 18 | **Initiative** +7
AC 17, **Fortitude** 16, **Reflex** 14, **Will** 13 | **Perception** +7
Speed 6, climb 4 (rat or hybrid form only) | Low-light vision

TRAITS

Regeneration
The wererat regains 5 hit points whenever it starts its turn and has at least 1 hit point. When the wererat takes damage from a silvered weapon, its regeneration does not function on its next turn.

STANDARD ACTIONS

⊕ **Dagger** (weapon) ✦ **At-Will**
Requirement: The wererat must be in human or hybrid form.
Attack: Melee 1 (one creature); +8 vs. AC
Hit: 1d6 + 6 damage, or 2d6 + 6 if the wererat has combat advantage against the target.

⊕ **Bite** (disease) ✦ **At-Will**
Requirement: The wererat must be in rat or hybrid form.
Attack: Melee 1 (one creature); +8 vs. AC
Hit: 1d4 + 4 damage. If the target is granting combat advantage to the wererat, it also takes ongoing 5 damage (save ends). At the end of the encounter, the target makes a saving throw. On a failure, the target contracts wererat filth fever (stage 1).

MOVE ACTIONS

Rat Scurry ✦ **At-Will**
Requirement: The wererat must be in rat form.
Effect: The wererat shifts up to its speed.

MINOR ACTIONS

Change Shape (polymorph) ✦ **At-Will**
Effect: The wererat alters its physical form to appear as a Tiny rat, or a Medium unique human or hybrid.

Skills Bluff +6, Stealth +10
Str 10 (+1) | **Dex** 18 (+5) | **Wis** 12 (+2)
Con 15 (+3) | **Int** 13 (+2) | **Cha** 11 (+1)
Alignment evil | **Languages** Common
Equipment dagger

Wererat Filth Fever — Level 3 Disease

Those infected by this disease waste away as they alternately suffer chills and hot flashes.

Stage 0: The target recovers from the disease.
Stage 1: While affected by stage 1, the target loses a healing surge.
Stage 2: While affected by stage 2, the target loses a healing surge. The target also takes a -2 penalty to AC, Fortitude, and Reflex.
Stage 3: While affected by stage 3, the target loses all healing surges and cannot regain hit points. The target also takes a -2 penalty to AC, Fortitude, and Reflex.
Check: At the end of each extended rest, the target makes an Endurance check if it is at stage 1 or 2.
8 or Lower: The stage of the disease increases by 1.
9-12: No change.
13 or Higher: The stage of the disease decreases by 1.

Frenzied Werewolf — Level 6 Brute

Medium natural humanoid (shapechanger), human   XP 250

HP 78; **Bloodied** 39   **Initiative** +6
AC 18, **Fortitude** 19, **Reflex** 18, **Will** 16   **Perception** +9
Speed 6 (8 in wolf form)   Low-light vision

Traits

Regeneration

The werewolf regains 5 hit points whenever it starts its turn and has at least 1 hit point. When the werewolf takes damage from a silvered weapon, its regeneration does not function on its next turn.

Standard Actions

⊕ **Claw** ✦ At-Will

Requirement: The werewolf must be in wolf or hybrid form.
Attack: Melee 1 (one creature); +11 vs. AC
Hit: 2d8 + 3 damage, or 2d8 + 8 against a bloodied target, and the target falls prone.

⊕ **Bite** (disease) ✦ At-Will

Requirement: The werewolf must be in wolf or hybrid form.
Attack: Melee 1 (one creature); +11 vs. AC
Hit: 1d10 + 7 damage. At the end of the encounter, the target makes a saving throw. On a failure, the target contracts werewolf moon frenzy (stage 1).

⊕ **Club** (weapon) ✦ At-Will

Requirement: The werewolf must be in human or hybrid form.
Attack: Melee 1 (one creature); +11 vs. AC
Hit: 2d8 + 4 damage, or 2d8 + 9 against a bloodied target.

↯ **Lycanthrope Fury** ✦ At-Will

Requirement: The werewolf must be in hybrid form.
Effect: The werewolf uses *claw* and *bite*. Then the werewolf takes 5 damage.

Minor Actions

Change Shape (polymorph) ✦ At-Will

Effect: The werewolf alters its physical form to appear as a Medium wolf, unique human, or hybrid.

Skills Bluff +8, Intimidate +8

Str 19 (+7)	**Dex** 17 (+6)	**Wis** 13 (+4)
Con 18 (+7)	**Int** 10 (+3)	**Cha** 11 (+3)

Alignment evil   **Languages** Common
Equipment club

Werewolf Moon Frenzy — Level 6 Disease

This disease starts with a fever, which soon becomes a violent and unpredictable rage.

Stage 0: The target recovers from the disease.
Stage 1: While affected by stage 1, the target takes a -2 penalty to Will.
Stage 2: While affected by stage 2, whenever the target becomes bloodied, it makes a melee basic attack as a free action against an ally adjacent to it.
Stage 3: While affected by stage 3, whenever the target is hit by an attack, it makes a melee basic attack as a free action against an ally adjacent to it.
Check: At the end of each extended rest, the target makes an Endurance check if it is at stage 1 or 2.
   10 or Lower: The stage of the disease increases by 1.
   11-14: No change.
   15 or Higher: The stage of the disease decreases by 1.

MANTICORE

Flying hunters with leonine bodies, manticores swoop from mountainside lairs to seize prey. They are vicious, dim-witted beasts that kill for pleasure.

Manticores hunt alone or in small prides and prefer earthbound prey. Travelers who venture near caves or rocky ledges where manticores lair risk death. The fearsome predators claim expansive hunting grounds, and a settlement could be annexed into a manticore's territory without warning. Some evil humanoids capitalize on manticores' predictable hunting behavior. Most people prefer to avoid the beasts, though, and they go to great lengths to stay clear of potential manticore habitats.

Voracious Monsters: Manticores eat all types of meat, but they most enjoy dwarf and human flesh. Poorly guarded caravans and inexperienced hunting parties make ideal targets. Although a manticore has vicious teeth, it prefers to attack with its tail and claws, leaving its fangs for tearing at the flesh of its kill. A passerby who comes across a massacre site might find iron spikes and serrated teeth, sure signs that at least one manticore was involved in the attack.

> *"They call a group of manticores a pride, just like lions. But there's nothing proud or noble about those beasts."*
>
> —Kelana Dhoram, mayor of Moonstair

Manticores regularly shed their three rows of teeth. Finding a tooth warns that one of the vicious creatures could be near, but it is also considered an ill omen. Rampant fear of the winged beasts infects borderland communities. In such a place, someone who finds a tooth might not reveal that information, for fear of facing life as a pariah if his or her compatriots learn of the discovery. And thus, what little warning the settlement might have had about an impending attack goes unheeded.

Brutish and Violent: Although they're smarter than most beasts, manticores operate mostly on instinct and their hateful emotions. Much like ogres, manticores have a reputation as brutish beasts that live in rural areas and end up under the command of smarter creatures. Manticores have barely enough intelligence to speak, but they don't often care to. With its short temper and limited ability to reason, a manticore takes offense at concepts and innuendos it doesn't understand. When a manticore wants to make a point, it uses claws, teeth, and spikes rather than words.

Steeds of Evil: Manticores fight alongside other evil creatures, often serving as mounts. Some humanoids, especially hobgoblins, steal and train manticore cubs. There's no guarantee that the winged beasts won't turn on their trainers, however. Bribery remains the safest method for making and keeping manticore allies. The creatures have a strong mercenary streak and accept food and treasure in exchange for service. It's not uncommon for a tribe of goblins or ogres to

pay tribute to a nearby manticore in hopes of securing the predator's aid in an attack. A manticore might turn up at the battle, but it fights for its own enjoyment. If it becomes tired or irritated, the manticore will fly away and leave its temporary allies to die.

Symbols of Danger: In heraldry and iconography, the manticore represents peril or viciousness. A sign at an abandoned mine might depict a manticore or a symbol of a manticore's tooth to warn that the area inside is unstable or dangerous. Groups of adventurers, mercenaries, or thugs sometimes choose a manticore as a symbol of their ruthlessness. Warriors who want to look especially tough hunt down manticores to gather trophies. They wear the beasts' pelts as capes, string manticore teeth on necklaces, or turn iron tail spikes into weapons and adornments.

Devils' Unlikely Allies: Devils make use of manticores, despite the beasts' unpredictable temperament. Devils claim that Alloces, the Butcher of Nessus, created the first manticores in experiments that weaved together the flesh of men, lions, and bats. Although manticores seem more sedate around devils, the fiends still have to pay or enslave manticores to ensure their service.

Manticore Striker — Level 10 Skirmisher
Large natural magical beast — XP 500

HP 106; **Bloodied** 53	**Initiative** +12
AC 24, **Fortitude** 23, **Reflex** 23, **Will** 20	**Perception** +13
Speed 6, fly 8	

STANDARD ACTIONS

⊕ Claw ✦ At-Will

Attack: Melee 1 (one creature); +15 vs. AC

Hit: 2d10 + 7 damage, or 2d10 + 10 with a charge attack.

Effect: After the attack, the manticore shifts up to 2 squares.

⤳ Tail Spike ✦ At-Will

Attack: Ranged 10 (one creature); +15 vs. AC

Hit: 2d8 + 4 damage.

Effect: After the attack, the manticore shifts up to 2 squares.

TRIGGERED ACTIONS

⤳ Spike Counterattack ✦ At-Will

Trigger: An enemy hits the manticore.

Effect (Immediate Reaction): The manticore uses *tail spike* against the triggering enemy. This attack does not provoke opportunity attacks.

Str 20 (+10)	**Dex** 20 (+10)	**Wis** 16 (+8)
Con 18 (+9)	**Int** 4 (+2)	**Cha** 11 (+5)

Alignment chaotic evil   **Languages** Common

Manticore Impaler — Level 11 Brute
Large natural magical beast — XP 600

HP 138; **Bloodied** 69	**Initiative** +11
AC 23, **Fortitude** 23, **Reflex** 23, **Will** 20	**Perception** +14
Speed 6, fly 8	

STANDARD ACTIONS

Hindered Takeoff

While the manticore is grabbing a creature, it can't fly higher than 6 squares above the ground.

STANDARD ACTIONS

⊕ Claw ✦ At-Will

Attack: Melee 1 (one creature); +14 vs. AC

Hit: 3d10 + 8 damage.

↯ Tail Lance ✦ At-Will

Attack: Melee 2 (one creature); +14 vs. AC

Hit: 2d8 + 6 damage, and the manticore grabs the target (escape DC 19) if it does not have a creature grabbed. Until the grab ends, the target takes ongoing 5 damage.

⤳ Tail Spike ✦ At-Will

Attack: Ranged 10 (one creature); +16 vs. AC

Hit: 2d8 + 6 damage.

MOVE ACTIONS

Prepare to Drop ✦ At-Will

Effect: The manticore flies up to half its speed and pulls a creature it has grabbed with it. This movement does not provoke opportunity attacks from the grabbed creature, and the manticore can pull the grabbed creature vertically.

Str 22 (+11)	**Dex** 22 (+11)	**Wis** 18 (+9)
Con 18 (+9)	**Int** 4 (+2)	**Cha** 10 (+5)

Alignment chaotic evil   **Languages** Common

Manticore Spike Hurler — Level 13 Artillery

Large natural magical beast — XP 800

HP 100; **Bloodied** 50
AC 27, **Fortitude** 25, **Reflex** 26, **Will** 23
Speed 6, fly 8
Initiative +12
Perception +14

STANDARD ACTIONS

⊕ **Claw ✦ At-Will**
Attack: Melee 1 (one creature); +18 vs. AC
Hit: 3d6 + 9 damage.

↗ **Tail Spike ✦ At-Will**
Attack: Ranged 10 (one creature); +20 vs. AC
Hit: 2d8 + 12 damage.

✳ **Spike Volley ✦ At-Will**
Attack: Area burst 1 within 10 (creatures in the burst); +20 vs. AC
Hit: 2d8 + 9 damage.

| Str 21 (+11) | Dex 22 (+12) | Wis 17 (+9) |
| Con 16 (+9) | Int 4 (+3) | Cha 12 (+7) |

Alignment chaotic evil — **Languages** Common

Manticore Sky Hunter — Level 13 Soldier (Leader)

Large natural magical beast — XP 800

HP 130; **Bloodied** 65
AC 29, **Fortitude** 26, **Reflex** 26, **Will** 23
Speed 6, fly 8
Initiative +14
Perception +14

TRAITS

☼ **Shielding Wings ✦ Aura 1**
Allies gain a +2 bonus to AC and Reflex while in the aura.

STANDARD ACTIONS

⊕ **Claw ✦ At-Will**
Attack: Melee 1 (one creature); +18 vs. AC
Hit: 2d10 + 10 damage, or 2d10 + 12 if the target is marked by the manticore.

↗ **Tail Spike ✦ At-Will**
Attack: Ranged 10 (one creature); +18 vs. AC
Hit: 2d8 + 6 damage.

MINOR ACTIONS

Threatening Roar (charm) **✦ At-Will**
Effect: Close burst 1 (enemies in the burst). The manticore marks each target until the end of the manticore's next turn.

TRIGGERED ACTIONS

↗ **Defender's Spike ✦ At-Will**
Trigger: An enemy within 5 squares of the manticore and marked by the manticore makes an attack that doesn't include it as a target.
Effect (Immediate Reaction): The manticore uses *tail spike* against the triggering enemy. This attack does not provoke opportunity attacks.

| Str 23 (+12) | Dex 22 (+12) | Wis 17 (+9) |
| Con 18 (+10) | Int 4 (+3) | Cha 10 (+6) |

Alignment chaotic evil — **Languages** Common

MEDUSA

Medusas are a people of such hideous aspect that their gazes render flesh to stone. Lithe females with snakes for hair and powerful males whose glances poison body and mind, they are deadly adversaries.

Fey creatures believe medusas are the cursed descendants of elves, betrayers who willingly bowed to Zehir and helped slaughter an entire city of eladrin. Human and dwarf sages think medusas are the progeny of yuan-ti and basilisk blood, created to be a slave race to the yuan-ti. Other scholars theorize that Zehir remade dragonborn or humans during the chaos following the Dawn War. No matter how the medusas were created, all races believe them to be unnatural creatures. Maybe some truth can be plucked from all three stories.

Deadly in Different Ways: Medusa males and females are inherently different beyond their gender. All medusas have scaled bodies, forked tongues, and snakelike eyes, and are resistant to poison. The similarities end there, however. Males are bald-headed, while females grow dozens of poisonous snakes from their scalps. Males' eyes project mind-infecting poison, while females' eyes turn creatures to stone. No female can turn another female to stone, but only special males are immune to their mates' petrifying glares.

The sexual dimorphism of the race would appear to put the genders on equal footing. Invariably, however, the females form a matriarchy within which males fill subservient roles as hunters, guardians, scouts, and mates. Only males that have immunity to petrification can hope to rise above females in medusa society.

Such males are singled out by females for special treatment from birth, and they have little sympathy for their brothers.

Domineering and Proud:
Medusas believe that their killing gaze is evidence that they are destined to rule over other humanoids. A medusa is sensitive to its mortality and the limited distance of its petrifying gaze, so it chooses its adversaries carefully. Small medusa clans move through the wilderness in search of weak settlements to rule. Individuals settle in cities to build up criminal guilds and eventually make a play for power. Medusas that gain control bully the populace, quelling dissent with statuary gardens, venomous snakes in surprising places, and the deaths of those who speak against them. Some medusas claim godhood and demand worship, while others tout themselves as oracles.

"It's easy to underestimate a male medusa, the one without the snakes on its head. Easy, but deadly. It won't turn you to stone, but it will tear your mind apart."
— Vadriar the Sage

Medusa Bodyguard	Level 12 Soldier
Medium natural humanoid	XP 700

HP 123; **Bloodied** 61 — **Initiative** +11
AC 28, **Fortitude** 25, **Reflex** 23, **Will** 24 — **Perception** +15
Speed 6
Resist 10 poison

STANDARD ACTIONS

⊕ **Bastard Sword** (poison, weapon) ✦ **At-Will**
Attack: Melee 1 (one creature); +17 vs. AC
Hit: 2d10 + 4 damage, and ongoing 5 poison damage (save ends).
Effect: The bodyguard marks the target until the end of the bodyguard's next turn.

⤜ **Longbow** (poison, weapon) ✦ **At-Will**
Attack: Ranged 30 (one creature); +17 vs. AC
Hit: 1d10 + 9 damage, and ongoing 5 poison damage (save ends).

TRIGGERED ACTIONS

⟲ **Mind-Venom Gaze** (charm, poison, psychic) ✦ **Recharge when the bodyguard hits with** *bastard sword*
Trigger: An enemy marked by the bodyguard makes an attack that does not include it as a target.
Attack (Immediate Interrupt): Close blast 5 (enemies in the blast); +15 vs. Will. The attack must include the triggering enemy as a target.
Hit: 2d6 + 3 poison and psychic damage, and if the target is the triggering enemy, the target is stunned until the end of its turn.

Skills Bluff +14, Stealth +14
| **Str** 22 (+12) | **Dex** 17 (+9) | **Wis** 19 (+10) |
| **Con** 19 (+10) | **Int** 12 (+7) | **Cha** 17 (+9) |

Alignment evil — **Languages** Common
Equipment bastard sword, longbow

Yuan-ti Allies: Like the yuan-ti, medusas worship Zehir, but the strange ties between the two races run deeper than religion. Medusas are deeply loyal to yuan-ti. A medusa's arrogance vanishes in the presence of even one of these serpentine tyrants. Yuan-ti say medusas owe their existence to them, but this eerie obeisance goes further than honoring ancestral ties. Even the snakes atop a medusa's head bow when a yuan-ti passes.

Medusa Venom Arrow	Level 12 Artillery
Medium natural humanoid, female	XP 700

HP 96; Bloodied 48	Initiative +12
AC 26, Fortitude 23, Reflex 25, Will 23	Perception +14
Speed 6	
Immune petrification; Resist 10 poison	

STANDARD ACTIONS

⊕ **Serpent Hair** (poison) ✦ **At-Will**

Attack: Melee 1 (one creature); +17 vs. AC

Hit: 2d6 + 6 poison damage, and the target takes a -2 penalty to saving throws until the end of the medusa's next turn.

⊗ **Shortbow** (poison, weapon) ✦ **At-Will**

Attack: Ranged 30 (one creature); +19 vs. AC

Hit: 1d10 + 7 damage, and the target takes ongoing 5 poison damage and is slowed (save ends both).

TRIGGERED ACTIONS

Petrifying Stare ✦ **At-Will**

Trigger: An enemy starts its turn within 2 squares of the medusa.

Effect (Opportunity Action): Close blast 2 (triggering enemy in the blast). The target is slowed (save ends).

First Failed Saving Throw: The target is immobilized instead of slowed (save ends).

Second Failed Saving Throw: The target is petrified until one of the following conditions is satisfied.

✦ The use of an appropriate power, such as *divine cleansing.*

✦ The willing kiss of the medusa that petrified the creature (a medusa might do this to gain information or to luxuriate in the victim's fear before returning it to stone).

✦ The medusa responsible for the petrification is killed and its blood is applied to the stony lips of the victim before a full day passes.

Skills Bluff +15, Stealth +17		
Str 14 (+8)	**Dex** 22 (+12)	**Wis** 17 (+9)
Con 18 (+10)	**Int** 12 (+7)	**Cha** 19 (+10)
Alignment evil	**Languages** Common	
Equipment shortbow		

Medusa Spirit Charmer	Level 13 Controller
Medium natural humanoid, female	XP 800

HP 130; **Bloodied** 65   **Initiative** +9
AC 27, **Fortitude** 25, **Reflex** 25, **Will** 27   **Perception** +14
Speed 6
Immune petrification; **Resist** 10 poison

STANDARD ACTIONS

⊕ **Serpent Hair** (poison) ✦ At-Will

Attack: Melee 1 (one creature); +18 vs. AC

Hit: 2d6 + 6 poison damage, and the target takes a -2 penalty to saving throws until the end of the medusa's next turn.

↤ **Spirit Charm** (charm, psychic) ✦ At-Will

Attack: Close blast 5 (enemies in the blast); +16 vs. Will

Hit: 1d6 + 6 psychic damage, and the target must end its next turn 2 squares closer to or adjacent to the medusa or else take 3d6 psychic damage.

❊ **Swords to Snakes** (fear, illusion) ✦ Encounter

Attack: Area burst 1 within 10 (enemies in the burst); +16 vs. Will

Hit: The target's weapons and implements appear to become snakes, and the target cannot use weapon or implement powers (save ends).

TRIGGERED ACTIONS

↤ **Stony Glare** ✦ At-Will

Trigger: An enemy ends its turn within 2 squares of the medusa.

Attack (Immediate Reaction): Close blast 2 (triggering enemy in the blast); +16 vs. Fortitude

Hit: The target is petrified (save ends).

Third Failed Saving Throw: The target is petrified until one of the following conditions is satisfied.

✦ The use of an appropriate power, such as *divine cleansing*.

✦ The willing kiss of the medusa that petrified the creature (a medusa might do this to gain information or to luxuriate in the victim's fear before returning it to stone).

✦ The medusa responsible for the petrification is killed and its blood is applied to the stony lips of the victim before a full day passes.

Skills Bluff +17, Stealth +14

Str 14 (+8)	**Dex** 16 (+9)	**Wis** 17 (+9)
Con 18 (+10)	**Int** 19 (+10)	**Cha** 22 (+12)

Alignment evil	**Languages** Common

"The snakes on its head that pass for hair—they're not just for show. Let one bite you, and you'll find it's that much harder to resist the medusa's gaze."

—Malaphar of the Golden Wyvern

MIND FLAYER

The ultimate megalomaniacs, mind flayers use their ability to enslave minds to play puppeteer to countless thralls while they feast on the brains of less useful creatures. Their goal is nothing short of world domination.

As ambitious as they are sinister, mind flayers hatch sprawling plots to achieve dominion. A single mind flayer might control an entire dungeon or settlement; a small cabal could set its sights on ruling a continent; a city of mind flayers aims to conquer and reshape the planes.

Mind flayers, or illithids as they call themselves, are the embodiment of mortals' worst fears. They dwell in darkness and order monsters on foul errands. They slaughter or enslave multitudes of peaceful creatures and exert total dominance over prisoners. Mind flayers have spent centuries on selective breeding and magical manipulation experiments in an attempt to create the perfect slave race. Their efforts birthed the githyanki race, which eventually escaped the mind flayers' control. Mind flayers can control countless thralls at once. No one knows how many worlds have crumbled under their deadly embrace, nor how many innocents have nourished the mind flayer hordes. Perhaps the most horrifying and repulsive attribute of the illithids is their physical form, a grisly mockery of the humanoid victims from which they were birthed. Mind flayers use other creatures to reproduce. They implant a juvenile illithid inside a victim's skull, where the tadpole-shaped offspring eats the creature's brain.

TODD LOCKWOOD

Mind Flayer Thrall Master   Level 14 Elite Controller (Leader)

Medium aberrant humanoid   XP 2,000

HP 260; **Bloodied** 130   **Initiative** +9
AC 28, **Fortitude** 23, **Reflex** 27, **Will** 26   **Perception** +10
Speed 7   Darkvision
Saving Throws +2; **Action Points** 1

STANDARD ACTIONS

⊕ Tentacles ✦ At-Will

Requirement: The mind flayer must not have a creature grabbed.

Attack: Melee 1 (one creature); +17 vs. Reflex. This attack automatically hits a dazed or stunned target.

Hit: 3d6 + 5 damage, and the mind flayer grabs the target (escape DC 21) if it does not have a creature grabbed.

⟂ Manipulate Brain ✦ At-Will

Attack: Melee 1 (one creature grabbed by the mind flayer); +17 vs. Fortitude

Hit: 4d6 + 10 damage, and the target is stunned until it is no longer grabbed by the mind flayer. If this attack reduces the target to 0 hit points or fewer, the mind flayer does one of the following.

Eat Brain (healing): The target dies, and the mind flayer regains 20 hit points.

Thrall Surgery (charm): Instead of dropping to 0 hit points or fewer, the target remains at 1 hit point. It is dominated until the mind flayer dies.

⟵ Mind Blast (psychic) **✦ Recharge ▣ ▦**

Attack: Close blast 5 (enemies in the blast); +17 vs. Will

Hit: 3d8 + 10 psychic damage, and the target is dazed (save ends). If the mind flayer scores a critical hit against the target, the target is dominated instead of dazed (save ends).

Miss: Half damage.

MINOR ACTIONS

Thrall Strike (charm) **✦ At-Will (1/round)**

Effect: Ranged sight (one ally or creature dominated by the mind flayer). The target makes a basic attack as a free action.

TRIGGERED ACTIONS

Teleport Thrall (teleportation) **✦ At-Will**

Trigger: An enemy targets the mind flayer with a melee attack.

Effect (Immediate Interrupt): Close burst 5 (one ally or creature in the burst dominated by the mind flayer). The mind flayer teleports up to 5 squares and teleports the target to the square it vacated. The triggering attack targets the target instead of the mind flayer.

Skills Arcana +18, Insight +15

Str 14 (+9)	**Dex** 15 (+9)	**Wis** 17 (+10)
Con 10 (+7)	**Int** 23 (+13)	**Cha** 20 (+12)

Alignment evil	**Languages** Deep Speech, telepathy 20

The progeny's Far Realm essence irrevocably alters the creature's form, turning it into an adult illithid with features that hint at its former occupant. Some mind flayer cabals search out specific vessels for their young, believing that a powerful host body makes for a strong illithid.

Solitary Masterminds: With far-reaching plans and a vast pool of thralls, a mind flayer dips its tentacles into regional affairs without getting involved in them. The fiend prefers to remain unnoticed, notching milestone after milestone until its overarching goal is realized. A mind flayer isn't solitary in the sense that it lives alone. Rather, it abides only the company of mindless thralls and illithids

Mind Flayer Unseen
Medium aberrant humanoid

Level 18 Lurker
XP 2,000

HP 126; **Bloodied** 63
AC 32, **Fortitude** 28, **Reflex** 31, **Will** 30
Speed 7

Initiative +20
Perception +18
Darkvision

TRAITS

Unseen Focus (illusion)
  The mind flayer is invisible while it has a creature grabbed.

STANDARD ACTIONS

⊕ **Tentacles ✦ At-Will**
  Requirement: The mind flayer must not have a creature grabbed.
  Attack: Melee 1 (one creature); +21 vs. Reflex. This attack automatically hits a dazed or stunned target.
  Hit: 1d6 + 6 damage, and the mind flayer grabs the target (escape DC 23) if it does not have a creature grabbed.

⚕ **Extract Brain** (healing) **✦ At-Will**
  Attack: Melee 1 (one creature grabbed by the mind flayer); +21 vs. Fortitude
  Hit: 6d6 + 20 damage, and the target is dazed until it is no longer grabbed. If the attack reduces the target to 0 hit points or fewer, the target dies and the mind flayer regains 15 hit points.

↤ **Mind-Clouding Blast** (illusion, psychic) **✦ Encounter**
  Attack: Close blast 5 (enemies in the blast); +21 vs. Will
  Hit: 3d8 + 7 psychic damage, and the target is dazed (save ends).
  Miss: Half damage.

MOVE ACTIONS

Mental Cloak (illusion, teleportation) **✦ Recharge** when an attack hits the mind flayer
  Effect: The mind flayer teleports up to its speed, and it becomes invisible until the end of its next turn.

Skills Arcana +20, Insight +18, Stealth +21

Str 18 (+13)	**Dex** 25 (+16)	**Wis** 18 (+13)
Con 12 (+10)	**Int** 23 (+15)	**Cha** 22 (+15)

Alignment evil	**Languages** Deep Speech, telepathy 20

that have goals identical to its own. Illithids believe all creatures are their inferiors. To an illithid, other creatures exist for one of three purposes: host vessel, food, or slave. When a mind flayer aligns with another creature, it has already plotted how and when it will betray its new ally.

Canny But Not Cowardly: An illithid is intent on keeping its location and involvement secret until it can claim victory. Its thralls serve as decoys and a buffer against attack. When a mind flayer's sanctum is breached or when its plans are at risk of failing, the fiend doesn't hesitate to enter combat or make its presence known.

Only the most arrogant illithid operates without an escape plan. A mind flayer rarely risks its life, for it believes that nothing else is more valuable. In fact, numerous mind flayers become liches or search for other ways to extend their life spans.

Masters in the Underdark: Mind flayers are most comfortable in the Underdark's black chasms. They enslave subterranean races and send their thralls into the harsh topside light to collect victims. Only a few illithid cities exist, in great caverns where even drow and other formidable Underdark races fear to tread.

Mind flayers of a great city follow the commands of an elder brain—a living, pulsating conglomeration of the knowledge and mental strength sucked from dozens or even hundreds of mind flayers that died to create their king. The elder brain speaks telepathically, giving orders from its briny pool in a well-guarded section of the city and orchestrating a vast conspiracy of its own design.

Goal Oriented: At its basic level, a mind flayer needs brains for sustenance, and it prefers to use thralls to collect would-be victims. When first building its power base, a mind flayer might live hand to mouth for a while. As an illithid's legions reach a healthy size, it launches into the heart of its plans. It might collect arcane writings and items of power to increase its knowledge; it could meddle in the politics of the surface world; it might even be intent on creating portals to summon more of its kin from the Far Realm.

The ultimate crown every mind flayer covets is rulership over the planes, which would be reshaped in the Far Realm's image. Given a chance, illithids would extinguish the sun, blister the world, warp flesh into aberrant forms, and rewrite every natural race's history with mad gibbering.

Concordant Mind Flayer	Level 19 Controller (Leader)
Medium aberrant humanoid	XP 2,400

HP 174; **Bloodied** 87	**Initiative** +12
AC 33, **Fortitude** 29, **Reflex** 32, **Will** 33	**Perception** +15
Speed 7	Darkvision

STANDARD ACTIONS

⊕ **Tentacles** ✦ **At-Will**

Requirement: The mind flayer must not have a creature grabbed.

Attack: Melee 1 (one creature); +22 vs. Reflex. This attack automatically hits a dazed or stunned target.

Hit: 3d6 + 8 damage, and the mind flayer grabs the target (escape DC 24) if it does not have a creature grabbed.

⨁ **Enthrall Brain** (charm) ✦ **At-Will**

Attack: Melee 1 (one creature grabbed by the mind flayer); +22 vs. Fortitude

Hit: 5d6 + 10 damage, and the target is dazed until it is no longer grabbed. If the attack reduces the target to 0 hit points or fewer, the target instead has 1 hit point, and it is dominated until the mind flayer dies.

↞ **Mind Blast** (psychic) ✦ **Encounter**

Attack: Close blast 5 (enemies in the blast); +22 vs. Will

Hit: 3d8 + 10 psychic damage, and the target is dazed (save ends). If the mind flayer scores a critical hit against the target, the target is dominated instead of dazed (save ends).

TRIGGERED ACTIONS

Shared Pain (psychic) ✦ **At-Will**

Trigger: An ally within 5 squares of the mind flayer takes damage from an attack.

Effect (Immediate Reaction): Close burst 5 (one creature dominated by the mind flayer other than the triggering ally in the burst). The target takes 20 psychic damage, which ignores any of the target's resistances.

Skills Arcana +21, Insight +20		
Str 18 (+13)	**Dex** 17 (+12)	**Wis** 22 (+15)
Con 14 (+11)	**Int** 24 (+16)	**Cha** 26 (+17)
Alignment evil	**Languages** Deep Speech, telepathy 20	

MINOTAUR

Minotaurs present the world's other races with a dilemma. On the one side, minotaur cities and clans can be mighty allies and determined partners in civilizing the world. On the other, their baffling culture and demon-worshiping ways threaten to bring anyone they meet to ruin.

An old adage says, "No road in a minotaur kingdom runs straight for long." It refers to the queer civil engineering that minotaurs employ as well as their way of thinking. The bull-headed brutes' impressive strength and baffling culture is enough to make most people avoid the creatures.

Minds Like Mazes: Minotaurs approach life as if it were a labyrinth. Taking an action is stepping onto a path. Roads can lead away from the past, circumnavigate critical destinations, hit dead ends, or open new passageways. This moment-by-moment drama isn't only a philosophy; it's an internal decision-making mechanism inherent to minotaurs.

The minotaurs' diplomatic and commercial partners struggle to unravel the convoluted negotiation style that fuels the creatures' politics and customs. They debate, bargain, argue, distract, equivocate, and generally appear to procrastinate for a long time. Then suddenly a decision is made, and they roar into action with single-minded vigor. The swiftly shifting social cues of aggression and compliance leave outsiders blundering along completely unaware of the debate's

Minotaur Soldier	Level 8 Soldier
Medium natural humanoid	XP 350

HP 89; **Bloodied** 44	**Initiative** +8
AC 24, **Fortitude** 22, **Reflex** 19, **Will** 19	**Perception** +11
Speed 6	

STANDARD ACTIONS

⊕ **Battleaxe** (weapon) ✦ **At-Will**
Attack: Melee 1 (one creature); +13 vs. AC
Hit: 1d10 + 8 damage, and the minotaur uses *shield bash* against the same target.

MINOR ACTIONS

⊹ **Shield Bash** ✦ **At-Will** (1/round)
Requirement: The minotaur must be using a shield.
Attack: Melee 1 (one creature); +11 vs. Fortitude
Hit: 1d6 damage, and the target falls prone.

TRIGGERED ACTIONS

⊹ **Goring Toss** ✦ **At-Will**
Trigger: An enemy adjacent to the minotaur shifts.
Attack (Immediate Interrupt): Melee 1 (triggering enemy); +11 vs. Reflex
Hit: 1d6 + 5 damage, the target is immobilized until the end of its turn, and the minotaur slides the target up to 2 squares to a square adjacent to the minotaur.

Str 20 (+9)	**Dex** 14 (+6)	**Wis** 14 (+6)
Con 17 (+7)	**Int** 10 (+4)	**Cha** 13 (+5)

Alignment unaligned   **Languages** Common
Equipment heavy shield, battleaxe

Minotaur Charger
Medium natural humanoid

Level 9 Skirmisher
XP 400

HP 94; **Bloodied** 47	**Initiative** +9
AC 23, **Fortitude** 23, **Reflex** 21, **Will** 20	**Perception** +10
Speed 6	

TRAITS
Deft Charge
While the minotaur is charging, its movement does not provoke opportunity attacks.

STANDARD ACTIONS
⊕ **Falchion** (weapon) ✦ **At-Will**
Attack: Melee 1 (one creature); +14 vs. AC
Hit: 4d4 + 7 damage.

⤳ **Handaxe** (weapon) ✦ **At-Will**
Attack: Ranged 10 (one creature); +14 vs. AC
Hit: 2d6 + 7 damage.

TRIGGERED ACTIONS
⫟ **Goring Rush** ✦ **At-Will**
Trigger: An enemy adjacent to the minotaur deals damage to the minotaur.
Attack (Immediate Reaction): Melee 1 (triggering enemy); +12 vs. Fortitude
Hit: 1d6 + 5 damage, and the minotaur can push the target 1 square and shift 1 square to the square the target occupied. The minotaur can push the target and shift four more times in this way.

Str 20 (+9)	**Dex** 17 (+7)	**Wis** 13 (+5)
Con 14 (+6)	**Int** 10 (+4)	**Cha** 14 (+6)

Alignment unaligned	**Languages** Common
Equipment falchion, 4 handaxes	

---

nuances. For a minotaur, though, a decision's minutia has far-reaching consequences. A minotaur believes that each time it agrees to a contract or a condition, it actively declines taking the opposing path.

"I've known some minotaurs to be honorable, brave, and stalwart allies. But even some of them gave in to the beast within during the time I lived among them. Baphomet's touch is like a curse that dooms the entire race to savagery, much as some of them try to stave it off."

—Deric Widewanderer

Labyrinthine Lands: Minotaurs prefer landscapes that mimic their worldview. They feel at home among islands in a web of rivers, interlacing caverns, jumbled valleys, and other natural features that might at first appear chaotic. In such locales, minotaurs and their slaves construct their infamous cities. Roads on open plains twist; halls bend when they could go straight; dead ends, which confound outsiders, form the foundation of the race's architectural style.

Minotaur Magus — Level 9 Controller (Leader)
Medium natural humanoid — XP 400

HP 96; **Bloodied** 48 | **Initiative** +5
AC 23, **Fortitude** 21, **Reflex** 20, **Will** 23 | **Perception** +12
Speed 6

Traits

☼ Unleash the Beast Within ✦ Aura 3
Any ally that starts its turn in the aura gains a +2 power bonus to attack rolls and damage rolls on attacks made as part of charges until the end of that ally's turn.

Standard Actions

⊕ Glaive ✦ At-Will
Attack: Melee 2 (one creature); +14 vs. AC
Hit: 2d4 + 10 damage, and the magus slides the target up to 2 squares.
Miss: The magus can slide the target 1 square.

↷ Baphomet's Rage (charm, psychic) **✦ At-Will**
Attack: Ranged 10 (one creature); +12 vs. Will
Hit: 1d6 + 4 psychic damage, and the target uses a free action to charge a creature of the magus's choosing.

⤳ Crimson Bolt (fire, lightning) **✦ Recharge** ⚄ ⚅
Attack: Ranged 20 (one creature); +12 vs. Reflex
Hit: 2d10 + 5 lightning damage, and the target takes ongoing 5 fire damage and cannot shift (save ends both).

Triggered Actions

↯ Goring Fling ✦ At-Will
Trigger: An enemy adjacent to the magus deals damage to the magus.
Attack (Immediate Reaction): Melee 1 (triggering enemy); +12 vs. Fortitude
Hit: 1d6 + 4 damage, and the magus pushes the target up to 3 squares.

Skills Bluff +14, Insight +12
Str 18 (+8)	**Dex** 12 (+5)	**Wis** 16 (+7)
Con 16 (+7)	**Int** 15 (+6)	**Cha** 20 (+9)

Alignment chaotic evil — **Languages** Abyssal, Common

The famous minotaur settlement known as the Labyrinth City of Leng is a haunting testament to the power of the minotaurs' construction when paired with the creatures' unique mindset. Hidden in a serpentine volcanic landscape of mazelike canyons, the massive settlement withstood centuries of war before collapsing into ruins at the minotaurs' own hands. Now demons, maddened minotaurs, and ghosts guard the nation's treasures and buried secrets.

Demon Worshipers: Baphomet, known as the Horned King, Demon Prince of Beasts, and the Minotaur Lord, plays a crucial role in minotaur society. His creed—"Unleash the beast within"—frees his followers from the moral and mental complexities of their decisions and teaches them to live by instinct. His cults honor savagery, wrath, and brute strength. In the Temples of Ire, minotaur cabalists spill blood in Baphomet's name and engage in cannibalism. Even some humans, elves, and orcs pay secret homage to him.

In about half the minotaur cities, the cult of Baphomet openly seeks converts and serves an important role in the settlements' armies and defenses. Minotaurs that are infused with demonic blood are driven mad with savagery and grow to stupendous strength and size.

Demonic Savage Minotaur
Level 11 Brute

Large natural humanoid

XP 600

HP 140; **Bloodied** 70	**Initiative** +8
AC 23, **Fortitude** 25, **Reflex** 22, **Will** 20	**Perception** +7
Speed 8	

STANDARD ACTIONS

⊕ Claws ✦ At-Will

Attack: Melee 2 (one or two creatures); +16 vs. AC. If the minotaur targets only one creature, it can make this attack twice against that creature.

Hit: 2d6 + 5 damage, and the minotaur grabs the target (escape DC 19) if it has fewer than two creatures grabbed.

⨑ Impale ✦ At-Will

Attack: Melee 1 (one creature grabbed by the minotaur); +14 vs. Fortitude

Hit: 5d8 + 13 damage. The target falls prone and is no longer grabbed by the minotaur.

TRIGGERED ACTIONS

⨑ Goring Assault ✦ At-Will

Trigger: An enemy within 10 squares of the minotaur hits it with a ranged or area attack.

Effect (Immediate Reaction): The minotaur charges the triggering enemy.

Str 22 (+11)	**Dex** 16 (+8)	**Wis** 15 (+7)
Con 20 (+10)	**Int** 5 (+2)	**Cha** 7 (+3)
Alignment chaotic evil	**Languages** Abyssal, Common	

The cult keeps these bestial monsters in check and unleashes them in times of war or during wild festivals and bloody contests. In other minotaur communities, the cult must work behind a respectable facade. So as the magi summon demons in the dark, the diabolical organization works to win accolades as a noble fraternity or an honorable guild.

MUMMY

A mummy embodies the wrath of the dead. It rises from its stillness to avenge a transgression.

The slow and shuffling gait of a mummy can paralyze a creature with fear. In its shambling steps, a foe sees not just the present danger but also the inevitability of death. The inexorable approach of a mummy replaces confidence with dread and hope with doom.

"Such a fate! To rule a vast empire, die honored and revered, enjoy a lavish royal funeral . . . and then spend a thousand years waiting for some fool to come try to plunder your tomb. No wonder he seemed a little crazed."

—Uldane of Winterhaven

Retribution Fueled: Whether created in the dry desert heat, the sucking moisture of a desolate bog, or the frozen heights of a lofty mountain, a mummy exists for vengeance. A number of sins can awaken a mummy, from disturbing its tomb, despoiling a place sacred to it in life, or the theft of a prized object. Some mummies seek to avenge less material offenses, such as a loved one marrying someone the mummy loathes or an unwelcome alliance of the mummy's enemies

Shambling Mummy	Level 8 Brute
Medium natural humanoid (undead)	XP 350

HP 104; **Bloodied** 52	**Initiative** +3
AC 20, **Fortitude** 22, **Reflex** 17, **Will** 21	**Perception** +5
Speed 4	Darkvision
Immune disease; **Resist** 10 necrotic, 10 poison	

TRAITS

Flammable Corpus
 Whenever the mummy takes fire damage, it also takes ongoing 5 fire damage (save ends).

STANDARD ACTIONS

⊕ **Rotting Grasp** (necrotic) ✦ At-Will
 Attack: Melee 1 (one creature); +11 vs. Fortitude
 Hit: 2d8 + 8 necrotic damage, and the target can't regain hit points until the end of the mummy's next turn.

MINOR ACTIONS

Warding Curse (necrotic) ✦ At-Will
 Effect: Ranged 10 (one creature). The target takes 5 necrotic damage whenever it attacks until the mummy uses this power again or until the end of the encounter.

Str 19 (+8)	Dex 8 (+3)	Wis 12 (+5)
Con 14 (+6)	Int 6 (+2)	Cha 17 (+7)
Alignment unaligned	**Languages** Common	

Moldering Mummy — Level 10 Minion Brute
Medium natural humanoid (undead) — XP 125

HP 1; a missed attack never damages a minion.
AC 22, **Fortitude** 24, **Reflex** 19, **Will** 23
Speed 4
Immune disease; **Resist** 10 necrotic, 10 poison

Initiative +4
Perception +6
Darkvision

STANDARD ACTIONS

⊕ Clutch of the Dead ✦ At-Will

Attack: Melee 1 (one creature); +13 vs. Fortitude

Hit: 11 damage, and the mummy grabs the target (escape DC 18) if it does not have a creature grabbed.

TRIGGERED ACTIONS

⌁ Final Curse

Trigger: An enemy's attack that does not deal fire damage reduces the mummy to 0 hit points.

Attack (No Action): Ranged 10 (triggering enemy); +13 vs. Will

Hit: The target regains half the normal number of hit points from the next healing surge it spends.

Str 19 (+9)	Dex 8 (+4)	Wis 12 (+6)
Con 14 (+7)	Int 6 (+3)	Cha 16 (+8)

Alignment unaligned   **Languages** —

Mummy Tomb Guardian — Level 11 Soldier
Medium natural animate (undead) — XP 600

HP 111; **Bloodied** 55
AC 27, **Fortitude** 24, **Reflex** 21, **Will** 23
Speed 5
Immune disease; **Resist** 10 necrotic, 10 poison; **Vulnerable** 5 radiant

Initiative +6
Perception +6
Darkvision

TRAITS

Flammable Corpus

When the mummy takes fire damage, it also takes ongoing 5 fire damage (save ends).

STANDARD ACTIONS

⊕ Khopesh (weapon) **✦ At-Will**

Attack: Melee 1 (one creature); +16 vs. AC

Hit: 2d8 + 10 damage, and the target cannot shift (save ends).

MINOR ACTIONS

Curse of No Escape ✦ At-Will

Effect: Ranged 10 (one creature). The target is slowed until the mummy curses a different creature or the mummy is destroyed.

TRIGGERED ACTIONS

Overwhelming Fear (fear) **✦ Encounter**

Trigger: An enemy within 10 squares gains line of sight to any tomb guardian for the first time this encounter.

Attack (No Action): Ranged 10 (triggering enemy); +14 vs. Will

Hit: The target is stunned until the end of the tomb guardian's next turn.

Str 22 (+11)	Dex 8 (+4)	Wis 12 (+6)
Con 15 (+7)	Int 6 (+3)	Cha 19 (+9)

Alignment unaligned   **Languages** Common

in life. Sometimes, a dead master's servants awaken it to continue its life's frustrated ambitions. Great kings and queens of malign power have returned as mummies to extend their reigns in undeath.

Created to Destroy: Albeit rare, some mummies arise spontaneously from dry corpses when a particularly provocative transgression touches their souls in the afterlife. Most mummies, however, possess the power to act after death because someone wanted them to have it. The long rituals of burial that

Royal Mummy	Level 12 Elite Controller (Leader)
Medium natural humanoid (undead)	XP 1,400

HP 236; Bloodied 118	Initiative +5
AC 26, Fortitude 24, Reflex 22, Will 26	Perception +9
Speed 4	Darkvision
Immune disease; Resist 10 necrotic, 10 poison	
Saving Throws +2; Action Points 1	

TRAITS

✷ **Regal Presence** ✦ **Aura 5**
Whenever an ally starts its turn in the aura, the mummy slides that ally up to 2 squares as a free action.

✷ **Curse of Fear** (fear) ✦ **Aura 5**
Enemies take a -2 penalty to all defenses against the mummy's attacks while in the aura.

Flammable Corpus
Whenever the mummy takes fire damage, it also takes ongoing 5 fire damage (save ends).

STANDARD ACTIONS

⊕ **Scepter** (weapon) ✦ **At-Will**
Attack: Melee 1 (one creature); +17 vs. AC
Hit: 2d8 + 9 damage.

⊛ **Plague Chant** (necrotic) ✦ **At-Will**
Attack: Ranged 10 (one creature); +15 vs. Fortitude
Hit: 2d6 + 6 necrotic damage, and ongoing 5 necrotic damage (save ends). Each time the target takes this ongoing damage, each ally adjacent to it takes 5 necrotic damage.

⊀ **Grip of Despair** (fear, psychic) ✦ **At-Will**
Attack: Ranged 10 (one creature); +15 vs. Will
Hit: 1d12 + 9 psychic damage, and the target is immobilized and takes a -2 penalty to attack rolls until the end of the mummy's next turn.

⊀ **Sow Fear and Pestilence** ✦ **At-Will**
Effect: The mummy uses *plague chant* and *grip of despair*.

⬸ **Grave Terror** (fear, psychic) ✦ **Encounter**
Attack: Close burst 3 (enemies in the burst); +15 vs. Will
Hit: 2d10 + 13 psychic damage, and the mummy pushes the target up to 4 squares.
Miss: Half damage, and the mummy pushes the target up to 2 squares.

MINOR ACTIONS

Enfeebling Curse ✦ **At-Will** (1/round)
Effect: Ranged 10 (one creature). Whenever the target spends a healing surge, it becomes weakened until the end of its next turn. This effect lasts until the mummy uses this power again or until the target takes an extended rest.

Skills Insight +14, Religion +13		
Str 20 (+11)	Dex 8 (+5)	Wis 16 (+9)
Con 14 (+8)	Int 14 (+8)	Cha 22 (+12)
Alignment unaligned	Languages Common	

accompany a mummy's entomb-
ment help protect its body from rot.
Soft organs are removed and placed
in special jars, and the corpse is
treated with preserving oils,
herbs, and wrappings. Less
common means of preser-
vation include freezing a
body, baking it in dry heat, or
using magic.

A mummy's creator usually
seeks to use the creature to crush
the life out of a victim, yet a
mummy is not an easy weapon to
wield. It cannot be forced to behave
in a certain way. Once awakened, a
mummy behaves according to the
will of the amoral animus that gives
movement to the creature's form.
The animus causes a body to do
in undeath what its living essence
might not have consented to in
life. It is wrath incarnate, so even
a minor wrong might be met with
the deadly force of the mummy's
strength and the unwholesome
energy of its curse. The trick to
shaping a mummy's rampage
is imbuing the corpse through
ritual with the proper reason
to rise. This reason draws from the
passionate beliefs and prejudices of the
body's original owner. Once a person creates a mummy, he or she need only stay
out of the way and let the mummy do its job.

Ending a Mummy's Curse: Each mummy awakens with the power to
curse its enemies. Thus, when it dies a second death, it can still have its revenge.
Rituals can remove these debilitating hexes, and the surest way to put an end to a
mummy's affliction is to undo the transgression that caused the corpse to rise.

Redressing the wrong can remove the curse and sometimes cause the
mummy to return to rest. A sacred idol might be replaced in its niche, a stolen
treasure could be returned to its tomb, or a temple might be cleansed of the
evidence of unwelcome blood. More ephemeral or permanent offenses, such
as revealing a secret the mummy wished kept or killing someone the mummy
loved, cannot be so easily remedied. In such cases, a mummy might slaughter
everyone responsible and still not find its anger sated.

OGRE

Ogres are brutish, stupid, and grand in number. They kill for food and pleasure, often combining those pursuits.

Big, dumb, brutal, savage. Even though these words accurately describe ogres, none succeeds in capturing the extent to which the massive humanoids embody these traits. An ogre smashes a creature's head for laughs and then eats its victim raw after it forgets how to make fire. If enough parts remain after the brute has gorged itself, the ogre might make a loincloth from its quarry's skin and a necklace from any leftover bones. By the time it's finished, the ogre is probably hungry again.

Legendary Stupidity: Few ogres can count to ten, even with their fingers in front of them. Most can barely speak a rudimentary form of Giant and know only a handful of Common words, with "smash," "gimme," and "food" being the most prevalent. Ogres are easy to fool or confuse, though they smash things they don't understand. Silver-tongued tricksters who test their talents on these savages typically end up eating their eloquent words along with an ogre's club.

Ogre	Level 6 Brute
Large natural humanoid (giant)	XP 250
HP 90; **Bloodied** 45	**Initiative** +5
AC 18, **Fortitude** 20, **Reflex** 17, **Will** 16	**Perception** +3
Speed 8	

STANDARD ACTIONS

⊕ **Greatclub** (weapon) ✦ **At-Will**
Attack: Melee 2 (one creature); +11 vs. AC
Hit: 2d10 + 6 damage.

↗ **Rock** (weapon) ✦ **At-Will**
Attack: Ranged 10 (one creature); +11 vs. AC
Hit: 2d6 + 5 damage.

⤓ **Grand Slam** (weapon) ✦ **Encounter**
Attack: Melee 2 (one creature); +11 vs. AC
Hit: 4d10 + 4 damage, and the ogre pushes the target up to 2 squares and knocks it prone.
Miss: Half damage, and the target falls prone.

Str 21 (+8)	Dex 14 (+5)	Wis 11 (+3)
Con 20 (+8)	Int 4 (+0)	Cha 6 (+1)

Alignment chaotic evil	**Languages** Giant
Equipment greatclub, 4 rocks	

Primitive Wanderers: Ogres live in small, nomadic groups. Various bands trade or capture members when they meet, depending on how the encounter goes. Being only slightly more cultured than a pride of lions, ogres lack a true sense of tribalism. They switch groups easily, especially if the welcoming band is momentarily flush with food and weapons.

Ogres aren't great crafters. They use pelts for clothing and uproot trees and boulders as crude tools and weapons. They prefer stone-tipped javelins for hunting and stone axes for fighting.

(Left to right) ogre hunter, ogre mercenary, ogre

Ogres don't erect shelters. They sleep in caves, animal dens, or under overhangs or trees. When they find other forms of shelter, such as a cabin in the woods, ogres kill the inhabitants and lair there. An ogre with a lair is a lazy lout. When bored or hungry, it heads out to find something to kill, attacking virtually anything that crosses its path. Once an ogre has depleted an area of quarry, it moves on. Ogres often lair near the rural swaths of civilized lands, where they take advantage of poorly protected livestock, undefended larders, and unwary farmers.

Bloodthirsty and Casually Cruel: Calling someone an ogre is a grave insult, and not just because of the race's well-known witlessness. Cruelty is an ogre's dominant trait. Amoral and brutal, these fiends refrain from slaughtering one another out of a sense of familiarity and a kind of camaraderie. If an ogre doesn't kill its quarry straightaway, it saves the hapless creature as a treat for later. Lacking focus, however, the brute might forget about its captive and allow it to starve or freeze to death.

Lazy, Surly, and Easily Cowed: As terrible as ogres are, far worse creatures exist in the world. Such creatures often round up ogres as slaves or willing servants. Even weaker creatures can frighten an ogre into submission if their numbers are great enough. Since power rules ogres' lives, they understand strength and readily bow to domineering opponents. Large orc tribes, giants, hags, dragons, gnolls, and others employ ogres as warriors and workers. Some especially bright ogres learn to work for pay and equipment, becoming mercenaries for bosses who can tolerate their crude and bloodthirsty behavior.

SAM WOOD

Ogre Hunter — Level 7 Skirmisher
Large natural humanoid (giant) — XP 300

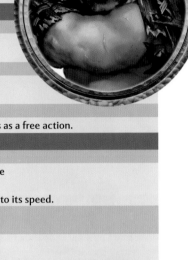

HP 84; Bloodied 42	Initiative +8
AC 21, Fortitude 20, Reflex 18, Will 17	Perception +5
Speed 8	

STANDARD ACTIONS

⊕ **Club** (weapon) ✦ At-Will

Attack: Melee 2 (one creature); +12 vs. AC

Hit: 2d8 + 6 damage.

↗ **Javelin** (weapon) ✦ At-Will

Attack: Ranged 20 (one creature); +12 vs. AC

Hit: 1d8 + 9 damage.

↗ ✦ **Hurling Charge** ✦ Recharge ⚄ ⚅ ⚅

Effect: The ogre uses *javelin*. If its attack hits, the ogre charges as a free action.

MOVE ACTIONS

↩ **Clear the Ground** ✦ At-Will

Attack: Close burst 2 (creatures in the burst); +10 vs. Fortitude

Hit: The ogre pushes the target up to 2 squares.

Effect: If the attack hits any of the targets, the ogre moves up to its speed.

Str 21 (+8)	Dex 16 (+6)	Wis 15 (+5)
Con 20 (+8)	Int 4 (+0)	Cha 7 (+1)

Alignment chaotic evil **Languages** Giant

Equipment club, 6 javelins

Ogre Mercenary — Level 8 Soldier
Large natural humanoid (giant) — XP 350

HP 93; Bloodied 46	Initiative +8
AC 24, Fortitude 22, Reflex 19, Will 19	Perception +6
Speed 8	

STANDARD ACTIONS

⊕ **Morningstar** (weapon) ✦ At-Will

Attack: Melee 2 (one creature); +13 vs. AC

Hit: 2d8 + 7 damage.

Effect: The ogre marks the target until the end of the ogre's next turn.

↗ **Handaxe** (weapon) ✦ At-Will

Attack: Ranged 10 (one creature); +13 vs. AC

Hit: 1d8 + 7 damage.

↩ **Brutal Sweep** (weapon) ✦ At-Will

Attack: Close blast 2 (creatures in the blast); +13 vs. AC

Hit: 1d8 + 7 damage, and the target falls prone.

Str 22 (+10)	Dex 15 (+6)	Wis 15 (+6)
Con 21 (+9)	Int 7 (+2)	Cha 8 (+3)

Alignment chaotic evil **Languages** Giant

Equipment 2 handaxes, morningstar

Ogre Juggernaut — Level 10 Brute
Large natural humanoid (giant) — XP 500

HP 131; **Bloodied** 65
AC 22, **Fortitude** 24, **Reflex** 20, **Will** 20
Speed 8

Initiative +7
Perception +7

STANDARD ACTIONS

⊕ **Greatclub** (weapon) ✦ **At-Will**
Attack: Melee 2 (one creature); +15 vs. AC
Hit: 4d8 + 5 damage.

⟐ **Rock** ✦ **At-Will**
Attack: Ranged 5 (one creature); +15 vs. AC
Hit: 3d6 + 7 damage.

↟ **Juggernaut Push** ✦ **Recharge** ⚄ ⚅
Attack: Melee 1 (one creature); +13 vs. Fortitude
Hit: The ogre pushes the target 1 square and knocks it prone. The ogre then shifts 1 square to the square the target vacated. The ogre can push the target an additional number of squares equal to the ogre's speed, shifting an equal number of squares and remaining adjacent to it. The target takes 1d8 damage for each additional square the ogre pushes it.

Str 24 (+12)	Dex 15 (+7)	Wis 15 (+7)
Con 21 (+10)	Int 4 (+2)	Cha 6 (+3)

Alignment chaotic evil   **Languages** Giant
Equipment greatclub, 4 rocks

Arena-Trained Ogre — Level 14 Brute
Large natural humanoid — XP 1,000

HP 173; **Bloodied** 86
AC 26, **Fortitude** 27, **Reflex** 25, **Will** 24
Speed 8

Initiative +9
Perception +10

STANDARD ACTIONS

⊕ **Greataxe** (weapon) ✦ **At-Will**
Attack: Melee 2 (one creature); +19 vs. AC
Hit: 3d12 + 8 damage.

↟ **Vorpal Sweep** (weapon) ✦ **Recharge** ⚅
Attack: Close burst 2 (enemies in the burst); +19 vs. AC
Hit: 2d12 + 5 damage, and ongoing 10 damage (save ends).

Skills Intimidate +10

Str 23 (+13)	Dex 19 (+11)	Wis 17 (+10)
Con 23 (+13)	Int 8 (+6)	Cha 6 (+5)

Alignment chaotic evil   **Languages** Common, Giant
Equipment hide armor, greataxe

"Brutally strong, absolutely fearless, and dumb as rocks. That's what makes ogres so useful . . . and so dangerous."

—Rothar of the Seven-Pillared Hall

OOZE

Among the more peculiar creatures in the world, formless oozes squeeze through dank underground passages, mindlessly feeding on creatures and objects that dissolve in their acidic bodies.

Similar to a goopy melding of vermin and natural hazard, oozes are a nuisance and a danger. Ordinary folks know the creepy creatures exist and follow a simple rule: If you see an ooze, go the other way. Survivors swear by the maxim. Of course, oozes aren't always easy to spot, because the sludgy predators tend to cling to ceilings and seep from unlikely crevices.

Ochre Jelly	Level 3 Elite Brute
Large natural beast (blind, ooze)	XP 300

HP 102; **Bloodied** 51	**Initiative** +0
AC 15, **Fortitude** 16, **Reflex** 14, **Will** 14	**Perception** +2
Speed 4, climb 4	Blindsight
Immune blinded, gaze effects; **Resist** 5 acid	
Saving Throws +2; **Action Points** 1	

TRAITS

Ooze
  While squeezing, the ooze moves at full speed rather than half speed, it doesn't take the -5 penalty to attack rolls, and it doesn't grant combat advantage for squeezing.

STANDARD ACTIONS

⊕ **Slam** (acid) ✦ **At-Will**
  Attack: Melee 1 (one creature); +8 vs. AC
  Hit: 2d6 + 1 damage, and ongoing 5 acid damage (save ends).

MOVE ACTIONS

Flowing Form ✦ **At-Will**
  Effect: The ochre jelly shifts up to 4 squares.

TRIGGERED ACTIONS

Split ✦ **Encounter**
  Trigger: The ochre jelly becomes bloodied.
  Effect (No Action): The jelly splits into two creatures, each with hit points equal to one-half its current hit points. Effects on the original ochre jelly do not apply to the second one.

Str 13 (+2)	Dex 8 (+0)	Wis 12 (+2)
Con 11 (+1)	Int 1 (-4)	Cha 1 (-4)
Alignment unaligned	**Languages** —	

Lurk in the Dark: Oozes dwell in tunnels, caverns, and sewers. They slink along the ground, drip from walls and ceilings, spread across the bottoms of underground pools, and squeeze through narrow tunnels. The dark and damp keep the creatures comfortable, and they shun areas with light or extreme temperatures. Other underground creatures easily avoid oozes. Bats or stirges even live in rooms surrounding an ooze's lair. More intelligent cave-dwellers, such as ropers, wait for creatures to wander into an ooze's domain and capitalize on the situation to snag an easy meal.

Green Slime
Medium natural beast (blind, ooze)

Level 4 Lurker
XP 175

HP 47; **Bloodied** 23
AC 18, **Fortitude** 17, **Reflex** 17, **Will** 14
Speed 4, climb 4
Immune blinded, gaze effects; **Resist** 5 acid; **Vulnerable** 5 fire, 5 radiant

Initiative +9
Perception +2
Blindsight 10

Traits

Ooze
While squeezing, the ooze moves at full speed rather than half speed, it doesn't take the -5 penalty to attack rolls, and it doesn't grant combat advantage for squeezing.

Standard Actions

ⓐ **Slam** (acid) ✦ **At-Will**
Attack: Melee 1 (one creature); +7 vs. Reflex
Hit: 5 acid damage, and ongoing 5 acid damage (save ends).

✦ **Engulf** (acid) ✦ **At-Will**
Attack: Melee 1 (one creature); +7 vs. Reflex
Hit: 1d6 + 3 acid damage, and the slime grabs the target (escape DC 18). Until the grab ends, the target takes ongoing 10 acid damage. Attacks that hit the slime deal half damage to the slime and half damage to a single creature grabbed by the slime.

Skills Stealth +10

Str 11 (+2)	**Dex** 16 (+5)	**Wis** 11 (+2)
Con 17 (+5)	**Int** 1 (-3)	**Cha** 1 (-3)

Alignment unaligned   **Languages** –

Everything Is Food: Oozes don't really think. Even insects have a better sense of tactics and self-preservation. Consequently, the creatures are direct and predictable. An ooze finds something, attacks it, and eats it. Every variety of ooze secretes digestive acids that dissolve materials. Most can consume flesh and wood (albeit slowly), but a few are capable of eating through metal and stone.

Oozes are drawn to movement and warmth, which means they frequently eat creatures. They also consume the grime that coats dungeons, so an immaculate passage is a likely sign that an ooze lairs nearby. When an ooze is sated, it falls into a torpor and remains motionless on the ground. Since not all oozes digest all

WARREN MAHY

substances, some have coins, metal gear, bones, or debris suspended inside their bodies. A slain ooze can be a windfall for its killers.

Death Is Slow: An ooze dissolves its prey slowly. Some varieties, such as the gelatinous cube, anesthetize their meals first, a process that numbs victims and muddies their senses. Most oozes don't, though, and their meals die in agony as the creature's acid digests bits of flesh at a time. The upside of these torturous, digestive deaths is that a morsel's comrades might rescue him before he's fully consumed.

Easy to Trick: Though oozes aren't capable of aligning with creatures, they sometimes end up fighting for or alongside others after being lured to a particular cellar or cave. Clever monsters might keep oozes around to defend passageways or dispose of refuse. Likewise, an ooze could be enticed into a pit, where its captors feed it only enough to keep it from coming after them. Crafty creatures place torches and flaming braziers in prime spots to dissuade an ooze from leaving a particular tunnel or room.

Unknown Origins: Some oozes are found in nature, but nobody knows where they originate from. Phenomena and magical experimentation have been known to create such creatures. Similarly, failed attempts at performing a powerful ritual could cause an ooze to spontaneously appear. The creatures are simple to summon as well. So even inexperienced spellcasters can bring these creatures—uncontrolled—into battle at a moment's notice.

Gelatinous Cube	Level 5 Elite Brute
Large natural beast (blind, ooze)	XP 400

HP 156; Bloodied 78	Initiative +4
AC 17, Fortitude 18, Reflex 16, Will 15	Perception +3
Speed 3, climb 3	Blind, blindsight 5
Immune blinded, gaze effects; Resist 5 acid	
Saving Throws +2; Action Points 1	

TRAITS

Ooze
While squeezing, the ooze moves at full speed rather than half speed, it doesn't take the -5 penalty to attack rolls, and it doesn't grant combat advantage for squeezing.

Translucent
The cube is invisible until seen (Perception DC 25) or until it attacks. A creature that fails to notice the cube might walk into it, automatically being hit with *engulf*.

STANDARD ACTIONS

⊕ **Slam** (acid) ✦ **At-Will**
Attack: Melee 1 (one creature); +8 vs. Fortitude
Hit: 2d6 + 9 acid damage, and the target is immobilized (save ends).

✦ **Engulf** (acid) ✦ **At-Will**
Requirement: The cube must have no more than two creatures grabbed.
Attack: Melee 1 (one or two creatures); +8 vs. Reflex
Hit: The cube grabs the target (escape DC 15) and pulls the target into its space. Until the grab ends, the target takes ongoing 10 acid damage and is dazed. When the cube moves, it pulls with it any creature grabbed by it, and the creature remains grabbed and within the cube's space. This movement does not provoke an opportunity attack from the grabbed creature.

Str 14 (+4)	Dex 14 (+4)	Wis 13 (+3)
Con 18 (+6)	Int 1 (-3)	Cha 1 (-3)
Alignment unaligned	Languages —	

Black Pudding — Level 8 Elite Brute

Black Pudding | **Level 8 Elite Brute**
Large natural beast (blind, ooze) | XP 700

HP 218; **Bloodied** 109 | **Initiative** +6
AC 20, **Fortitude** 22, **Reflex** 20, **Will** 18 | **Perception** +4
Speed 4, climb 3 | Blind, tremorsense 10
Immune blinded, gaze effects; **Resist** 15 acid
Saving Throws +2; **Action Points** 1

TRAITS

Ooze
While squeezing, the pudding moves at full speed rather than half speed, it doesn't take the -5 penalty to attack rolls, and it doesn't grant combat advantage for squeezing.

STANDARD ACTIONS

⊕ **Slam** (acid) ✦ **At-Will**
Attack: Melee 1 (one creature); +11 vs. Fortitude
Hit: 4d6 + 6 acid damage.
Effect: Before or after the attack, the pudding shifts up to its speed.

↫ **Engulf** (acid) ✦ **At-Will**
Attack: Close blast 3 (creatures in the blast); +11 vs. Fortitude
Hit: 4d6 + 6 acid damage, and the pudding grabs the target (escape DC 16).

┼ **Melt** (acid) ✦ **At-Will**
Effect: Melee 1 (one creature grabbed by the pudding). The target takes 2d6 + 15 acid damage and loses a healing surge. It takes 10 extra acid damage if it has no healing surges.

TRIGGERED ACTIONS

Split ✦ **At-Will**
Trigger: An enemy hits the pudding with a weapon attack.
Effect (No Action): A black pudding spawn appears in the unoccupied square closest to the pudding.

Str 15 (+6)	**Dex** 14 (+6)	**Wis** 11 (+4)
Con 19 (+8)	**Int** 1 (-1)	**Cha** 1 (-1)

Alignment unaligned | **Languages** –

Black Pudding Spawn — Level 8 Minion Brute

Black Pudding Spawn | **Level 8 Minion Brute**
Medium natural beast (blind, ooze) | XP 88

HP 1; a missed attack never damages a minion. | **Initiative** +6
AC 20, **Fortitude** 22, **Reflex** 20, **Will** 18 | **Perception** +4
Speed 4, climb 3 | Blind, tremorsense 10
Immune blinded, gaze effects; **Resist** 15 acid

TRAITS

Ooze
While squeezing, the pudding moves at full speed rather than half speed, it doesn't take the -5 penalty to attack rolls, and it doesn't grant combat advantage for squeezing.

STANDARD ACTIONS

⊕ **Slam** (acid) ✦ **At-Will**
Attack: Melee 1 (one creature); +12 vs. Fortitude
Hit: 10 acid damage, and the pudding shifts up to its speed.

Str 15 (+6)	**Dex** 14 (+6)	**Wis** 11 (+4)
Con 19 (+8)	**Int** 1 (-1)	**Cha** 1 (-1)

Alignment unaligned | **Languages** –

MINION

ORC

Orcs put their faith in two things: their bloodthirsty, one-eyed god and the blind savagery of destruction.

Hate beats in their hearts, and rage runs through their veins. What thoughts emerge from the ignorant darkness of their minds are bent on ruination and death. They are orcs, and in their wakes, ash and bone remain.

Faith in Destruction: Orcs worship Gruumsh, and theirs is a primal religion of brutality and bloodletting. Orcs hear their god's voice in the storm's howl, recognize his wrath in the earth's quaking, and see his face in an avalanche's wreckage. Orcs slaughter the weak to earn Gruumsh's favor, and they pluck out one of their own eyes to prove their faith in him.

Tribes Like Plagues: Orc tribes scourge the land, devouring or driving off beasts and plundering villages. As each region is consumed, the monsters move on. A tribe divides into roving bands that search abroad for the choicest new hunting grounds, leaving a small contingency behind to receive returning parties. As the orcs filter in, they bring trophies and news of targets ripe for attack. Once the tribe is whole, the savages set out, desecrating the land and its creatures as they cut a path to their new territory. On rare occasion, a tribe's leader chooses to hold onto a particularly defensible lair for decades, and its orcs must range far into the countryside to sate their appetites.

(Left to right) orc storm shaman, orc archer, orc reaver

Battletested Orc	Level 3 Soldier
Medium natural humanoid	XP 150

HP 50; **Bloodied** 25   **Initiative** +5
AC 19, **Fortitude** 17, **Reflex** 15, **Will** 13   **Perception** +1
Speed 6 (8 when charging)   Low-light vision

STANDARD ACTIONS

⊕ **Battleaxe** (weapon) ✦ At-Will
Attack: Melee 1 (one creature); +8 vs. AC
Hit: 1d10 + 5 damage, or 1d10 + 10 with a charge attack.

⤙ **Handaxe** (weapon) ✦ At-Will
Attack: Ranged 10 (one creature); +8 vs. AC
Hit: 1d6 + 5 damage.

⤚ **Hacking Frenzy** (weapon) ✦ Recharge ⚄ ⚅
Attack: Close burst 1 (enemies in the burst); +6 vs. AC
Hit: 1d10 + 5 damage, and the orc marks the target until the end of the orc's next turn.
Effect: The orc grants combat advantage until the start of its next turn.

TRIGGERED ACTIONS

Savage Demise
Trigger: The orc drops to 0 hit points.
Effect (Free Action): The orc takes a standard action.

Str 18 (+5)	Dex 14 (+3)	Wis 10 (+1)
Con 18 (+5)	Int 8 (+0)	Cha 9 (+0)

Alignment chaotic evil   **Languages** Common, Giant
Equipment scale armor, heavy shield, battleaxe, 4 handaxes

Scavengers, Not Builders: Orcs on the move grudgingly camp in the open, but their instinct is to fortify for long residence. Ruins, cavern complexes, and defeated foes' villages are easily converted into strongholds. Orcs build only for defensive purposes, such as erecting log-and-earth walls to encircle huts. If orcs choose to live in their victim's homes, they close the gaps they exploited in the settlement's defenses. Orcs don't set traps around their lairs unless the makings for the trap existed prior to the tribe's arrival. Instead, the brutes build spiked walls and dig pits to ensnare invaders and buy sentries time to alert the tribe.

Although capable of ironworking and some subtler arts, orcs prefer the strong-arm method of procurement. After savaging a colony, they pick it and its dead clean of usable items and cart the booty back to their base. The skeletal remains of the settlement are then set alight.

Orcs often range through the hills and mountains that dwarves prefer. The countless battles between the two races have awarded orcs control over a handful of dwarven holds and mines. Yet even when controlling a prime location, orcs fail to do anything with it. The real pleasure had been in wresting control of the site from the dwarves. One unusually industrious orc sent slaves into a mine for a season, but the weaklings had the temerity to keep dying.

Bloodthirsty Cannibals: No one can negotiate with orcs unless perched in a position of overwhelming strength. Orcs see weakness outside their tribe as an exploitable source of food and treasure. Even weaker orc tribes are prey for stronger ones. Powerful creatures can direct an orc tribe's ferocity through intimidation, but none can hope for fine control or discipline.

Orc Savage — Level 4 Minion Brute

Medium natural humanoid — XP 44

HP 1; a missed attack never damages a minion. — **Initiative** +3
AC 16, **Fortitude** 16, **Reflex** 14, **Will** 12 — **Perception** +1
Speed 6 — Low-light vision

Standard Actions

Handaxe (weapon) ✦ **At-Will**
Attack: Melee 1 (one creature); +9 vs. AC
Hit: 8 damage, or 12 with a charge attack.

Handaxe (weapon) ✦ **At-Will**
Attack: Ranged 5 (one creature); +9 vs. AC
Hit: 6 damage.

Triggered Actions

Savage Demise
Trigger: The orc drops to 0 hit points.
Effect (Free Action): The orc takes a standard action.

Str 16 (+5)	**Dex** 13 (+3)	**Wis** 9 (+1)
Con 13 (+3)	**Int** 8 (+1)	**Cha** 8 (+1)

Alignment chaotic evil — **Languages** Common, Giant
Equipment hide armor, 4 handaxes

Orc Archer — Level 4 Artillery

Medium natural humanoid — XP 175

HP 42; **Bloodied** 21 — **Initiative** +6
AC 16, **Fortitude** 16, **Reflex** 18, **Will** 14 — **Perception** +2
Speed 6 — Low-light vision

Standard Actions

Handaxe (weapon) ✦ **At-Will**
Attack: Melee 1 (one creature); +9 vs. AC
Hit: 1d6 + 6 damage.

Longbow (weapon) ✦ **At-Will**
Attack: Ranged 30 (one creature); +11 vs. AC
Hit: 1d10 + 6 damage, and the orc can push the target 1 square.

Clustered Volley (weapon) ✦ **At-Will**
Attack: Area burst 1 within 20 (creatures in the burst); +9 vs. AC
Hit: 1d10 + 6 damage.

Triggered Actions

Savage Demise
Trigger: The orc drops to 0 hit points.
Effect (Free Action): The orc takes a standard action.

Str 15 (+4)	**Dex** 18 (+6)	**Wis** 10 (+2)
Con 12 (+3)	**Int** 8 (+1)	**Cha** 9 (+1)

Alignment chaotic evil — **Languages** Common, Giant
Equipment leather armor, handaxe, longbow, 30 arrows

Orc Reaver

Level 5 Skirmisher

Medium natural humanoid

XP 200

HP 63; **Bloodied** 31	**Initiative** +7
AC 19, **Fortitude** 18, **Reflex** 18, **Will** 16	**Perception** +3
Speed 6 (8 when charging)	Low-light vision

Traits

Charging Mobility

While charging, the orc gains a +4 bonus to all defenses.

Standard Actions

⊕ **Battleaxe** (weapon) ✦ At-Will

Attack: Melee 1 (one creature); +10 vs. AC

Hit: 1d10 + 8 damage.

Effect: After the attack, the orc can shift 1 square.

⚔ **Javelin** (weapon) ✦ At-Will

Attack: Ranged 20 (one creature); +10 vs. AC

Hit: 2d6 + 6 damage, and the orc can push the target 1 square.

Triggered Actions

⚔ **Blood-Crazed Charge** ✦ Encounter

Trigger: The orc hits an enemy.

Effect (Free Action): The orc charges an enemy.

Savage Demise

Trigger: The orc drops to 0 hit points.

Effect (Free Action): The orc takes a standard action.

Str 18 (+6)	**Dex** 17 (+5)	**Wis** 13 (+3)
Con 15 (+4)	**Int** 8 (+1)	**Cha** 8 (+1)

Alignment chaotic evil   **Languages** Common, Giant

Equipment hide armor, battleaxe, 4 javelins

Orcs have no qualms about eating any flesh, including that of other orcs. Cannibalism within a tribe remains taboo except in special savage rites of passage, such as when an orc eats its own eyeball in a religious ceremony or an incoming chief feasts on his predecessor to symbolize virility. Orcs are especially fond of how fattened animals taste. When the savages slaughter a farm's residents, they might eat the victims right away and save the animals for later meals. Orcs have no patience for animal husbandry, though, and such creatures are soon stewing in their own juices.

"Don't try to tell me there's a soul that can be redeemed inside that monster. An orc's little better than a demon."

—Caiphas, paladin of Pelor

Orc Rampager — Level 6 Brute
Medium natural humanoid — XP 250

HP 90; Bloodied 45	Initiative +5
AC 18, Fortitude 20, Reflex 18, Will 16	Perception +3
Speed 6	Low-light vision

Traits

Berserk Flailing
While the orc is bloodied and can take opportunity actions, any enemy that starts its turn adjacent to the orc takes 5 damage.

Standard Actions

⊕ **Heavy Flail** (weapon) ✦ At-Will
Attack: Melee 1 (one creature); +11 vs. AC
Hit: 2d6 + 6 damage.

⸭ **Rampage** ✦ At-Will
Effect: The orc shifts up to 3 squares and can use *heavy flail* against three enemies during the shift.

⤳ **Handaxe** (weapon) ✦ At-Will
Attack: Ranged 10 (one creature); +11 vs. AC
Hit: 2d6 + 6 damage, and the orc can push the target 1 square.

Triggered Actions

Savage Demise
Trigger: The orc drops to 0 hit points.
Effect (Free Action): The orc takes a standard action.

Str 21 (+8)	Dex 14 (+5)	Wis 10 (+3)
Con 20 (+8)	Int 8 (+2)	Cha 8 (+2)

Alignment chaotic evil   **Languages** Common, Giant
Equipment leather armor, 4 handaxes, heavy flail

Orc Pummeler — Level 6 Controller
Medium natural humanoid — XP 250

HP 76; Bloodied 38	Initiative +5
AC 20, Fortitude 20, Reflex 17, Will 16	Perception +3
Speed 6	Low-light vision

Standard Actions

⊕ **Stone Maul** (weapon) ✦ At-Will
Attack: Melee 1 (one creature); +11 vs. AC
Hit: 2d6 + 7 damage, and the target falls prone.

⤝ **Earthshaking Slam** ✦ Encounter
Attack: Close burst 2 (creatures in the burst); +9 vs. Fortitude
Hit: 3d6 + 5 damage, and the target is dazed until the end of the orc's next turn.
Effect: The orc pushes each target up to 2 squares.

Triggered Actions

⸭ **Intercepting Swat** ✦ Recharge ⚄ ⚅ ⚅
Trigger: An enemy makes an opportunity attack against the orc.
Effect (Free Action): The orc uses *stone maul* against the triggering enemy.

Savage Demise
Trigger: The orc drops to 0 hit points.
Effect (Free Action): The orc takes a standard action.

Str 21 (+8)	Dex 14 (+5)	Wis 10 (+3)
Con 20 (+8)	Int 8 (+2)	Cha 8 (+2)

Alignment chaotic evil   **Languages** Common, Giant
Equipment scale armor, stone maul

Orc Storm Shaman
Medium natural humanoid

Level 6 Artillery
XP 250

HP 54; **Bloodied** 27	**Initiative** +7
AC 20, **Fortitude** 16, **Reflex** 19, **Will** 18	**Perception** +6
Speed 6	Low-light vision

STANDARD ACTIONS

⊕ **Scimitar** (weapon) ✦ **At-Will**
Attack: Melee 1 (one creature); +11 vs. AC
Hit: 1d8 + 8 damage.

⊙ **Lightning Strike** (lightning) ✦ **At-Will**
Attack: Ranged 30 (one creature); +11 vs. Reflex
Hit: 1d10 + 8 lightning damage, and one enemy within 5 squares of the target takes 5 lightning damage.

✸ **Vengeful Whirlwind** (lightning, thunder, zone) ✦ **Recharge** when first bloodied
Attack: Area burst 1 within 10 (enemies in burst); +11 vs. Fortitude
Hit: 2d10 + 4 lightning and thunder damage, and the target falls prone. Then the shaman slides the target up to 2 squares.
Miss: Half damage, and the shaman can slide the target 1 square.
Effect: The burst creates a zone that lasts until the end of the orc's next turn. Any enemy that ends its turn in the zone takes 10 thunder and lightning damage.

TRIGGERED ACTIONS

Wind Walk ✦ **Encounter**
Trigger: The shaman is first bloodied.
Effect (Free Action): Until the end of the encounter, the shaman gains a fly speed of 8 but must land or fall at the end of each move.

Savage Demise
Trigger: The orc drops to 0 hit points.
Effect (Free Action): The orc takes a standard action.

Str 16 (+6)	**Dex** 19 (+7)	**Wis** 16 (+6)
Con 12 (+4)	**Int** 8 (+2)	**Cha** 9 (+2)

Alignment chaotic evil   **Languages** Common, Giant
Equipment hide armor, scimitar

"Whether it calls on some violent primal spirit, on a savage primordial of wind and thunder, or on a demon prince of storms, an orc storm shaman is a force to be reckoned with."

—Oak Warden Sharasta

OTYUGH

An otyugh's unsavory scent sets creatures to retching, an advantage the detritus-dwelling beast exploits.

These noisome monsters live in filth, subsisting on dung, rot, and carrion as they await fresh meat.

Rank Homes: Otyughs snuggle into squishy nests of decaying matter, which provide excellent camouflage for their mottled flanks. Heaps of moldering plants, piles of maggot-ridden bodies, pools of unidentifiable slime, and pits brimming with excrement are favored nesting sites. An otyugh can survive for some time on the gruesome gruel a well-steeped domicile provides.

Otyughs wallow in stagnant swamps, scum-filled ponds, and damp forest dells. The smell of civilization can attract the creatures as well. Fresh mass graves, city sewers, village middens, and manure-filled animal pens are sure to host one or more otyughs. The solitary creatures prefer to live far from others of their kind, but they don't become territorial unless suitable nesting sites are scarce or fresh prey wanders past.

Ambush Hunters: An otyugh is a natural ambusher. Its massive bulk and ungainly, three-legged form rule out speed-based attacks, but the rest of its body reeks of predatory ability.

The beast sinks into its wallow. Its center tentacle, which is outfitted with two eyes and nostrils, barely breaches the pit's surface as it watches a creature approach. Then it silently draws back and awaits the perfect moment to strike. With a great splash, an otyugh's other two tentacles, well muscled and equipped with claws, whip out to smash into startled prey. Even the creature's scent aids it in battle, as disoriented and sickened foes stumble around trying to settle their bellies long enough to unsheathe their weapons.

Strong but Needy Guardians: With plentiful sustenance, otyughs are content to grow fat in their wallows. Not even the desire to mate stirs one from its putrid stew. This sedentary nature and their hunger for refuse make otyughs valuable guard beasts and disposal units for unwanted guests. They are ideal pets for keeping interlopers from poorly guarded sewers, middens, dungeons, cesspools, oubliettes, and moats. However, some would-be masters underestimate how plentiful a supply of waste, carrion, and victims is needed to keep an otyugh from wandering off. And the creatures do not tame well, especially when peckish. Thus, more than one "trained" otyugh has eaten its master when its wallow has turned bland or tasteless.

Otyugh	Level 7 Soldier
Large natural beast	XP 300

HP 82; **Bloodied** 41	**Initiative** +5
AC 23, **Fortitude** 22, **Reflex** 16, **Will** 19	**Perception** +11
Speed 5, swim 5	Darkvision

TRAITS

⚙ **Otyugh Stench ✦ Aura 1**
Living enemies take a -2 penalty to attack rolls while in the aura.

STANDARD ACTIONS

⊕ **Tentacle ✦ At-Will**
Attack: Melee 3 (one creature); +12 vs. AC
Hit: 2d8 + 6 damage, and the otyugh pulls the target up to 2 squares and grabs it (escape DC 16).

† **Diseased Bite (disease) ✦ At-Will**
Attack: Melee 1 (one creature); +12 vs. AC
Hit: 1d10 + 8 damage, or 1d10 + 12 against a creature grabbed by the otyugh. In addition, at the end of the encounter, the target makes a saving throw. On a failure, the target contracts lesser otyugh filth fever (stage 1).

Skills Stealth +13			
Str 22 (+9)	**Dex** 11 (+3)		**Wis** 16 (+6)
Con 18 (+7)	**Int** 1 (-2)		**Cha** 5 (+0)
Alignment unaligned		**Languages** –	

Lesser Otyugh Filth Fever	
	Level 7 Disease

Those infected by this disease waste away as they alternately suffer chills and hot flashes.

Stage 0: The target recovers from the disease.
Stage 1: While affected by stage 1, the target loses a healing surge.
Stage 2: While affected by stage 2, the target loses a healing surge and takes a -2 penalty to AC, Fortitude, and Reflex.
Stage 3: While affected by stage 3, the target loses all healing surges and cannot regain hit points. The target also takes a -2 penalty to AC, Fortitude, and Reflex.
Check: At the end of each extended rest, the target makes an Endurance check if it is at stage 1 or 2.
  10 or Lower: The stage of the disease increases by 1.
  11-15: No change.
  16 or Higher: The stage of the disease decreases by 1.

Charnel Otyugh
Large natural beast

Level 10 Elite Soldier
XP 1,000

HP 212; **Bloodied** 106
AC 26, **Fortitude** 27, **Reflex** 21, **Will** 24
Speed 5, swim 5
Resist 5 necrotic
Saving Throws +2; **Action Points** 1

Initiative +7
Perception +13
Darkvision

TRAITS

✧ **Otyugh Stench ✦ Aura** 1
  Living enemies take a -2 penalty to attack rolls while in the aura.

STANDARD ACTIONS

⊕ **Charnel Lash** (necrotic) ✦ **At-Will**
  Attack: Melee 3 (one creature); +15 vs. AC
  Hit: 1d8 + 8 damage, and ongoing 5 necrotic damage (save ends). The otyugh pulls the target up to 2 squares and grabs it (escape DC 18).

⊢ **Rotting Bite** (disease, necrotic) ✦ **At-Will**
  Attack: Melee 1 (one creature); +15 vs. AC
  Hit: 2d12 + 6 necrotic damage, and ongoing 5 necrotic damage (save ends). In addition, at the end of the encounter, the target makes a saving throw. On a failure, the target contracts greater otyugh filth fever (stage 1).

↩ **Charnel Frenzy** (necrotic) ✦ **Recharge** ⚄ ⚅
  Attack: Close burst 3 (enemies in the burst); +15 vs. AC
  Hit: 1d8 + 8 damage, and ongoing 5 necrotic damage (save ends).

MINOR ACTIONS

⊢ **Life Leech** (healing, necrotic) ✦ **At-Will** (1/round)
  Attack: Melee 3 (one creature grabbed by the otyugh); +13 vs. Fortitude
  Hit: 10 necrotic damage, and the otyugh regains 5 hit points.

Skills Stealth +10

Str 22 (+11)	**Dex** 11 (+5)	**Wis** 16 (+8)
Con 18 (+9)	**Int** 6 (+3)	**Cha** 5 (+2)

Alignment evil   **Languages** –

Strange Mutations: Soaked in disease and decay, an otyugh gradually evolves in appearance to complement its environment. An otyugh living in offal turns a multihued brown, and its skin grows mottled. The skin of a creature dwelling in a pond scum-covered pool gains a bright green sheen and blisters that mimic the pool's slime bubbles.

An otyugh's propensity for mutating makes it particularly susceptible to Far Realm influences. If it eats an aberrant creature's flesh, the pit dweller rapidly morphs into a much larger, more intelligent, and deadlier neo-otyugh. It also gains psychic and telepathic abilities. Neo-otyughs form dangerous partnerships with allies, bargaining their services for payments in food they consider delicacies.

Neo-Otyugh
Level 11 Elite Controller

Huge aberrant magical beast — XP 1,200

HP 232; **Bloodied** 116 — **Initiative** +6
AC 25, **Fortitude** 26, **Reflex** 20, **Will** 23 — **Perception** +14
Speed 7, swim 7 — Darkvision
Saving Throws +2; **Action Points** 1

TRAITS

☼ **Otyugh Stench ✦ Aura 2**
Living enemies take a -2 penalty to attack rolls while in the aura.

Threatening Reach
The neo-otyugh can make opportunity attacks against enemies within 4 squares of it.

STANDARD ACTIONS

⊕ **Tentacle ✦ At-Will**
Attack: Melee 4 (one creature); +16 vs. AC
Hit: 3d6 + 9 damage, and the neo-otyugh pulls the target up to 3 squares and grabs the target (escape DC 19).

⦗ **Massive Maw of Decay** (disease, necrotic) ✦ **At-Will**
Attack: Close blast 2 (creatures in the blast); +16 vs. AC
Hit: 2d6 + 7 damage, or 2d6 + 10 against a creature grabbed by the neo-otyugh, and ongoing 5 necrotic damage (save ends). In addition, at the end of the encounter, the target makes a saving throw. On a failure, the target contracts greater otyugh filth fever (stage 1).

MINOR ACTIONS

⤳ **Disgusting Lure** (charm, psychic) ✦ **At-Will**
Attack: Ranged 20 (one creature); +14 vs. Will
Hit: 2d8 psychic damage, and if the target does not end its next turn adjacent to the neo-otyugh, the target takes 15 psychic damage.

TRIGGERED ACTIONS

⥊ **Body Shield ✦ At-Will**
Trigger: An enemy hits the neo-otyugh while the neo-otyugh has a creature grabbed.
Attack (Immediate Interrupt): Melee 1 (one creature grabbed by the neo-otyugh); +14 vs. Fortitude
Hit: The triggering enemy's attack hits the grabbed creature instead of the neo-otyugh.

Skills Stealth +16
Str 23 (+11) — **Dex** 13 (+6) — **Wis** 18 (+9)
Con 20 (+10) — **Int** 7 (+3) — **Cha** 15 (+7)
Alignment evil — **Languages** telepathy 10

Greater Otyugh Filth Fever
Level 11 Disease

Those infected by this disease waste away as they alternately suffer chills and hot flashes.

Stage 0: The target recovers from the disease.
Stage 1: While affected by stage 1, the target loses a healing surge.
Stage 2: While affected by stage 2, the target loses a healing surge and takes a -2 penalty to AC, Fortitude, and Reflex.
Stage 3: While affected by stage 3, the target loses all healing surges and cannot regain hit points. The target also takes a -2 penalty to AC, Fortitude, and Reflex.
Check: At the end of each extended rest, the target makes an Endurance check if it is at stage 1 or 2.
12 or Lower: The stage of the disease increases by 1.
13-18: No change.
19 or Higher: The stage of the disease decreases by 1.

Place a Large creature token inside this ring to create a Huge creature token.

OWLBEAR

Owlbears are terrifying, nocturnal predators that inhabit the forests of the world and the Feywild, where they hunt to satisfy their voracious appetites. Their haunting cries echo through valleys and across plains, warning to travelers that they are on the prowl.

An owlbear's innocuous name belies its deadly ferocity. These hunters possess more cunning than an owl and more ferocity than a bear, and they have a ravenous appetite far exceeding either animal.

Young Owlbear	Level 8 Brute
Large fey beast	XP 350

HP 106; **Bloodied** 53   **Initiative** +6
AC 20, **Fortitude** 21, **Reflex** 19, **Will** 20   **Perception** +12
Speed 7   Darkvision

STANDARD ACTIONS

⊕ **Claw** ✦ **At-Will**
  Attack: Melee 2 (one creature); +13 vs. AC
  Hit: 2d6 + 3 damage.

↓ **Double Attack** ✦ **At-Will**
  Effect: The owlbear uses *claw* twice. If both attacks hit the same creature, the owlbear grabs it (escape DC 16) if the owlbear has fewer than two creatures grabbed.

↓ **Beak Snap** ✦ **At-Will**
  Effect: Melee 1 (one creature grabbed by the owlbear). The target takes 2d8 + 11 damage.

⇐ **Dazing Hoot** ✦ **Recharge** when first bloodied
  Attack: Close blast 3 (creatures in the blast); +11 vs. Fortitude
  Hit: The target is dazed (save ends).

Str 19 (+8)	**Dex** 14 (+6)	**Wis** 16 (+7)
Con 16 (+7)	**Int** 2 (+0)	**Cha** 10 (+4)

Alignment unaligned   **Languages** —

Owlbear	Level 8 Elite Brute
Large fey beast	XP 700

HP 212; **Bloodied** 106	**Initiative** +6
AC 20, **Fortitude** 22, **Reflex** 18, **Will** 20	**Perception** +12
Speed 7	Darkvision
Saving Throws +2; **Action Points** 1	

STANDARD ACTIONS

⊕ **Claw ✦ At-Will**
Attack: Melee 2 (one creature); +12 vs. AC
Hit: 4d6 + 6 damage.

⨋ **Double Attack ✦ At-Will**
Effect: The owlbear uses *claw* twice. If both attacks hit the same creature, the owlbear grabs it (escape DC 16) if the owlbear has fewer than two creatures grabbed.

⨋ **Beak Snap ✦ At-Will**
Effect: Melee 1 (one creature grabbed by the owlbear). The target takes 4d8 + 22 damage.

TRIGGERED ACTIONS

↩ **Stunning Screech ✦ Encounter**
Trigger: The owlbear is first bloodied.
Attack (Free Action): Close blast 3 (creatures in the blast); +11 vs. Fortitude
Hit: The target is stunned (save ends).

Str 20 (+9)	Dex 14 (+6)	Wis 16 (+7)
Con 16 (+7)	Int 2 (+0)	Cha 10 (+4)

Alignment unaligned	**Languages** —	

An owlbear has a powerful body and bristly fur similar to that of a bear, but they also possess feathers, a wicked beak, and sharp talons. Despite its exotic appearance, an owlbear is not a magical beast, the creation of some mad wizard who sought to combine the bear and owl. Whatever its origin might be, the owlbear is a species unto itself, occurring with the same regularity that one might encounter other predatory beasts.

Consummate Predators: Gifted with the vision of an owl, an owlbear emerges from its den around sunset and hunts into the darkest hours of night. The creature's den, usually a cave, a ruin, or a hollow tree, is littered with shattered bones and offal, the ghastly remains of the creature's prey. When prey is plentiful, an owlbear drags its kills back to its lair, where it adorns nearby trees or rocks with the corpses. This flesh attracts scavengers, giving the owlbear more opportunities to catch prey. The scent of blood and rotting meat is thick near an owlbear's lair. Aside from the baleful hoot of the creatures, the smell is usually the only other warning that an owlbear is near.

Owlbears hunt alone or in mated pairs. If quarry is plentiful, a family of owlbears might remain together for longer than is required to rear cubs. Otherwise, the irascible creatures typically go their own ways as soon as their young are ready to hunt. Few things can dissuade a hungry owlbear from attacking. An owlbear is a stubborn predator that fights without a sense of self-preservation Even when it is about to die, an owlbear still keeps its victim clenched tightly in its claws, snapping at the foe with its bone-crushing beak.

Trained Owlbear	Level 9 Soldier
Large fey beast	XP 400

HP 96; Bloodied 48	Initiative +8
AC 24, Fortitude 23, Reflex 22, Will 20	Perception +7
Speed 7	Darkvision

STANDARD ACTIONS

⊕ **Claw ✦ At-Will**

Attack: Melee 2 (one creature); +14 vs. AC

Hit: 2d8 + 8 damage.

↩ **Thunderous Shriek** (thunder) **✦ Recharge** ⚄ ⚅

Attack: Close burst 2 (creatures in the burst); +12 vs. Fortitude

Hit: 4d6 + 5 thunder damage, and the target is knocked prone.

TRIGGERED ACTIONS

↯ **Guardian Claw ✦ At-Will**

Trigger: An enemy adjacent to the trained owlbear makes an attack that does not include it

Attack (Opportunity Action): Melee 1 (triggering enemy); +14 vs. AC

Hit: 2d8 + 8 damage.

Miss: 5 damage.

Str 19 (+8)	Dex 14 (+6)	Wis 16 (+7)
Con 16 (+7)	Int 2 (+0)	Cha 10 (+4)
Alignment unaligned	**Languages** -	

Supernatural Powers: Despite resembling fairly mundane animals, an owlbear possesses some extraordinary powers based on the environment in which it lives. All owlbears possess a magical call, and each species' call has a different effect. During the night, an owlbear hoots or screeches to declare territory, search for mates, or to flush prey terrain that is hazardous or has no escape route.

Savage Pets: An owlbear's carnivorous and violent nature doesn't rule out the ability to train them. Owlbears are difficult to tame, but with enough time and food, a person can train an owlbear to recognize him or her as a master. Owlbears are used as guard beasts and mounts, though even a trained owlbear can still be dangerous.

An elf community sometimes encourages owlbears to den beneath their treetop village, using the beasts as a natural defense during the night. Hobgoblins favor owlbears as war beasts when they manage to control them. A starved owlbear might show up in a gladiatorial arenas, where it eviscerates foes with ruthless efficiency. Large humanoids, such as hill or frost giants, sometimes keep owlbears as pets and playmates.

Wind-Claw Owlbear — Level 11 Elite Controller
Large fey beast (air)   XP 1,200

HP 228; Bloodied 114	Initiative +8
AC 25, Fortitude 25, Reflex 21, Will 23	Perception +14
Speed 7	Darkvision
Saving Throws +2; Action Points 1	

TRAITS

☼ **Keening Gale ✦ Aura 2**
Any enemy that ends its turn in the aura takes 5 damage, and the owlbear slides it up to 2 squares as a free action.

STANDARD ACTIONS

⊕ **Wind Claw ✦ At-Will**
Attack: Melee 2 (one creature); +16 vs. AC
Hit: 3d6 + 8 damage, and the owlbear slides the target up to 2 squares and knocks it prone.
Miss: The owlbear can slide the target 1 square.

⊢ **Disembowel ✦ At-Will**
Effect: The owlbear uses *wind claw* twice against one creature. If both attacks hit, that creature is stunned until the end of the owlbear's next turn.

⊢ **Beak Snap ✦ At-Will**
Effect: Melee 1 (one creature grabbed by the owlbear). The target takes 4d10 + 16 damage.

TRIGGERED ACTIONS

⟵ **Wind Howl ✦ Encounter**
Trigger: The owlbear is first bloodied.
Attack (Immediate Reaction): Close blast 5 (creatures in the blast); +14 vs. Fortitude
Hit: The owlbear pushes the target up to 3 squares and knocks it prone.
Miss: The owlbear can push the target 1 square.

Str 22 (+11)	Dex 16 (+8)	Wis 18 (+9)
Con 18 (+9)	Int 2 (+1)	Cha 10 (+5)

Alignment unaligned	**Languages** –

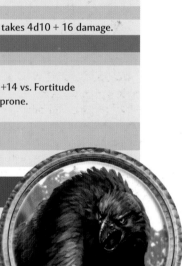

Winterclaw Owlbear — Level 14 Elite Soldier
Huge fey beast (cold)   XP 2,000

HP 280; Bloodied 140	Initiative +11
AC 28, Fortitude 28, Reflex 23, Will 24	Perception +15
Speed 7 (ice walk)	Darkvision
Saving Throws +2; Action Points 1	

STANDARD ACTIONS

⊕ **Winterclaw (cold) ✦ At-Will**
Attack: Melee 3 (one creature); +19 vs. AC
Hit: 2d8 + 14 cold damage.
Effect: The target is slowed until the end of the owlbear's next turn.

⊢ **Double Attack ✦ At-Will**
Effect: The owlbear uses *winterclaw* twice. If both attacks hit the same creature, that creature is immobilized (save ends).
Aftereffect: The target is slowed (save ends).

⟵ **Frost Wail (cold) ✦ Recharge when first bloodied**
Attack: Close blast 5 (creatures in the blast); +17 vs. Fortitude
Hit: 1d10 + 5 cold damage, and the target is immobilized (save ends).

Str 24 (+14)	Dex 14 (+9)	Wis 16 (+10)
Con 20 (+12)	Int 2 (+3)	Cha 12 (+8)

Alignment unaligned	**Languages** –

PURPLE WORM

Massive burrowing creatures, purple worms are feared for their ability to swallow enemies whole. They are capable of burrowing through solid rock and leave huge tunnels in their wake.

Purple worms are unintelligent beasts attracted to loud noises. They have no regard for other creatures, often interrupting battles, tearing through cities, or disrupting mining operations. Most purple worms are found in the Underdark or in rocky regions near mountains.

Ravenous Hunger: A purple worm is a voracious beast that is large enough to swallow a giant whole. Because a purple worm usually goes several days without eating, it tends to gorge when it finds food. A purple worm's emergence is difficult to predict, and the creature is prone to showing up at the worst possible times. Many underground civilizations, such as those of the drow, the duergar, and the mind flayers, maintain special wards around their fortresses and cities to deter the great beasts.

> *"Purple worms are among the largest beasts found in the world, enormous brutes driven by nothing but hunger and the instinctive drive to tunnel, to consume, to destroy."*
>
> —Zardkeran of Forgehome

A purple worm is widely regarded as a living natural disaster. The creatures are engines of chaos and destruction. Many Underdark races will sabotage their enemies' wards against the worms, leaving a settlement vulnerable to attack. A worm cares nothing for whom it helps or hinders. A purple worm is motivated only by hunger, so the only predictable characteristic of its attacks is that it favors larger groups over smaller ones. Dwarves have learned to take advantage of this behavior, luring the worm out with a large group only to slay it with artillery and massive siege weapons.

Weapons and Tools: A few people have discovered ways to turn purple worms into weapons. Stories tell of powerful spellcasters who specialized in charm and enchantment and were able to magically seize control of the creatures. The tales recount how these spellcasters could direct the worms at their enemies, wiping out entire cities or armies with a single worm.

Rumors also circulate that some drow priestesses hold worms under their sway and use them for defense in remote areas where reinforcements aren't available. Dwarves are known to use purple worms for mining and tunnel-building, yet despite centuries of effort, the beasts have never been tamed or domesticated. All attempts to control the beasts eventually end in disaster.

Boons of the Worm: When a purple worm burrows through the ground, it consumes earth and rock, breaking down the substances and quickly excreting

them. Hard substances, such as valuable metals and gems, remain within their bodies for weeks or months. A brave or foolhardy treasure hunter might attempt to hunt down a purple worm in hopes of claiming the treasures within its gizzard. A worm's body also has a boon to offer: Drow and assassins value the poison that a purple worm carries in its stinger.

A burrowing purple worm creates new corridors and highways throughout the Underdark. And, because a purple worm rarely returns to one of its tunnels, such passageways are usually safe from the beasts, as long as an interloper remains quiet. Areas that are rich in prey become interlaced with complex tunnel systems as a result of several worms hunting the area. It's not long after a purple worm forges a tunnel that smaller Underdark denizens begin to move into the tunnel to do their own hunting.

Adult Purple Worm · Level 14 Solo Brute

Huge natural beast (blind) XP 5,000

HP 560; **Bloodied** 280
AC 28, **Fortitude** 28, **Reflex** 26, **Will** 24
Speed 6, burrow 6 (tunneling)

Initiative +12
Perception +11
Blindsight 10,
tremorsense 10

Immune blinded, gaze effects
Saving Throws +5; **Action Points** 2

TRAITS

Ponderous

The purple worm can take immediate actions while stunned, dazed, or dominated.

Blooded Frenzy

While bloodied, the purple worm takes an extra minor action during its turn.

STANDARD ACTIONS

⊕ **Bite** ✦ **At-Will**

Attack: Melee 3 (one creature); +19 vs. AC
Hit: 4d8 + 8 damage.

↯ **Devour Whole** (acid) ✦ **At-Will**

Attack: Melee 3 (one creature); +17 vs. Fortitude
Hit: 3d10 + 7 damage, and the target is swallowed (escape DC 21). While swallowed, the target does not occupy a square and has neither line of sight nor line of effect to anything except the worm and other creatures swallowed by the worm; in addition, nothing has line of sight or line of effect to the target except other creatures swallowed by the worm. If the target attacks the worm using a close or an area attack, that attack targets all other creatures swallowed by the worm. While swallowed, the target takes 30 acid damage at the end of its turn. When the effect ends or the worm drops to 0 hit points, the target appears in an unoccupied square of its choice adjacent to the worm.

MINOR ACTIONS

↯ **Fling** ✦ **At-Will**

Attack: Melee 3 (one creature); +17 vs. Fortitude
Hit: 3d10 + 8 damage, and the purple worm slides the target up to 4 squares.

↯ **Poison Stinger** (poison) ✦ **At-Will**

Attack: Melee 3 (one creature); +19 vs. AC
Hit: 2d8 damage, and ongoing 15 poison damage (save ends).

Regurgitate ✦ **At-Will**

Effect: One creature swallowed by the purple worm appears in a square of the worm's choice within 4 squares of it. That creature is no longer swallowed and takes 3d10 + 8 damage.

TRIGGERED ACTIONS

↯ **Thrash** ✦ **At-Will**

Trigger: An attack hits the purple worm.
Attack (Immediate Reaction): Melee 3 (one or two creatures); +17 vs. Reflex
Hit: 3d12 + 5 damage, and the purple worm pushes the target up to 6 squares.

Str 25 (+14)	**Dex** 20 (+12)	**Wis** 19 (+11)
Con 20 (+12)	**Int** 2 (+3)	**Cha** 4 (+4)

Alignment unaligned **Languages** —

Purple Worm Tunneler   Level 19 Solo Skirmisher

Huge natural beast (blind)   XP 12,000

HP 728; **Bloodied** 364	**Initiative** +17
AC 33, **Fortitude** 33, **Reflex** 31, **Will** 29	**Perception** +14
Speed 8, burrow 8 (tunneling)	Blindsight 10,
Immune blinded, gaze effects	tremorsense 10
Saving Throws +5; **Action Points** 2	

TRAITS

Ponderous

The purple worm can take immediate actions while stunned, dazed, or dominated.

Blooded Frenzy

While bloodied, the purple worm takes an extra minor action during its turn.

STANDARD ACTIONS

⊕ **Bite ✦ At-Will**

Attack: Melee 3 (one creature); +24 vs. AC

Hit: 4d8 + 9 damage, and the purple worm shifts up to half its speed.

↓ **Devour Whole** (acid) **✦ At-Will**

Attack: Melee 3 (one creature); +22 vs. Fortitude

Hit: 3d10 + 8 damage, and the target is swallowed (escape DC 24). While swallowed, the target does not occupy a square and has neither line of sight nor line of effect to anything except the worm and other creatures swallowed by the worm; in addition, nothing has line of sight or line of effect to the target except other creatures swallowed by the worm. If the target attacks the worm using a close or an area attack, that attack targets all other creatures swallowed by the worm. While swallowed, the target takes 30 acid damage at the end of its turn. When the effect ends or the worm drops to 0 hit points, the target appears in an unoccupied square of its choice adjacent to the worm.

MOVE ACTIONS

↓ **Barrel Through ✦ At-Will**

Effect: The purple worm shifts up to its speed. Each time the purple worm enters a square adjacent to any enemy for the first time during the move, it makes the following attack against that enemy.

Attack: Melee 1; +22 vs. Reflex

Hit: 2d8 + 4 damage, and the purple worm pushes the target up to 2 squares.

MINOR ACTIONS

↓ **Stinger Impalement** (poison) **✦ At-Will**

Attack: Melee 3 (one creature); +24 vs. AC

Hit: 2d8 + 8 damage, and the purple worm slides the target up to 4 squares. The target takes ongoing 10 poison damage (save ends).

TRIGGERED ACTIONS

↓ **Thrash ✦ At-Will**

Trigger: An attack hits the purple worm.

Attack (Immediate Reaction): Melee 3 (one or two creatures); +22 vs. Reflex

Hit: 2d12 + 11 damage, and the purple worm pushes the target up to 6 squares.

Str 25 (+16)	**Dex** 23 (+15)	**Wis** 21 (+14)
Con 22 (+15)	**Int** 2 (+5)	**Cha** 4 (+6)
Alignment unaligned	**Languages** —	

RAKSHASA

Cunning masters of illusion, rakshasas are cruel, intelligent humanoids that resemble tigers. Rakshasas enjoy luxury and seldom appear without a veil of illusion to disguise their feline forms.

Rakshasas have mastered the power of illusion, and they use that power to conceal their catlike forms while living among other races. A rakshasa is one of the most intelligent and cunning humanoids that one will ever encounter, though a person is rarely aware that he or she is dealing with a rakshasa. Avaricious and self-serving, a rakshasa is capable of unspeakable evil in the pursuit of whatever it covets, be that wealth, power, influence, or hedonistic pleasure. To attain its goals, a rakshasa will ruin, injure, or kill anyone in its path.

Masters of Misdirection: A rakshasa conceals its true form and adopts whatever guise serves it best. Typically, it masquerades as a noble or a wealthy merchant, using money and clever lies to manipulate other creatures into doing its bidding. Rakshasas serve as villains and masterminds; they rarely face enemies unless they want to and unless backup plans are ready should an encounter go awry. Rakshasas prefer misdirection over combat, and they use their powers of illusion to turn potential adversaries against each other. When a rakshasa can't avoid battle, it becomes a fierce and ruthless foe. A rakshasa uses illusion to distract and deflect enemies, wearing them down and then striking when its foes are weakest.

PETE VENTERS

"I can see your nightmares and present them to your eyes. I can also show you your heart's deepest desires, or rip your throat out with my claws. And you think to toy with me?"

—Ashatra, rakshasa mage

Rakshasa Warrior	Level 15 Soldier
Medium natural humanoid	XP 1,200

HP 142; **Bloodied** 71   **Initiative** +13
AC 31, **Fortitude** 29, **Reflex** 27, **Will** 26   **Perception** +16
Speed 6   Low-light vision

STANDARD ACTIONS

⊕ **Longsword** (weapon) ✦ At-Will

Attack: Melee 1 (one creature); +20 vs. AC. The rakshasa makes two attack rolls and uses either result.

Hit: 2d8 + 7 damage, and the rakshasa marks the target until the end of the rakshasa's next turn.

⊕ **Claw** ✦ At-Will

Attack: Melee 1 (one creature); +20 vs. AC

Hit: 2d6 + 6 damage, and ongoing 10 damage (save ends).

MINOR ACTIONS

Deceptive Veil (illusion) ✦ At-Will

Effect: The rakshasa disguises itself to appear as a Medium humanoid until it uses *deceptive veil* again or until it drops to 0 hit points. Other creatures can make a DC 35 Insight check to discern that the form is an illusion.

Illusory Ambush (illusion) ✦ Encounter

Effect: The rakshasa becomes invisible, and an illusion of it appears in its square. The transition is indiscernible to observers, and the illusion lasts until the start of the rakshasa's next turn or until a creature attacks the illusion. After the illusion appears, the rakshasa shifts up to its speed.

TRIGGERED ACTIONS

↯ **Tiger Pounce** (teleportation) ✦ At-Will

Trigger: An enemy marked by and within 5 squares of the rakshasa shifts or makes an attack that does not include it as a target.

Effect (Immediate Reaction): The rakshasa teleports up to its speed and uses *claw* against the triggering enemy. If *claw* hits, the target also falls prone.

Str 20 (+12)	**Dex** 18 (+11)	**Wis** 18 (+11)
Con 14 (+9)	**Int** 12 (+8)	**Cha** 14 (+9)

Alignment evil   **Languages** Common
Equipment scale armor, heavy shield, longsword

Rakshasa Archer

Level 15 Artillery

Medium natural humanoid

XP 1,200

HP 110; **Bloodied** 55
AC 28, **Fortitude** 24, **Reflex** 26, **Will** 25
Speed 6

Initiative +12
Perception +16
Low-light vision

STANDARD ACTIONS

⊕ **Claw** ✦ **At-Will**

Attack: Melee 1 (one creature); +20 vs. AC

Hit: 2d6 + 6 damage, and ongoing 5 damage (save ends).

⊙ **Longbow** (weapon) ✦ **At-Will**

Attack: Ranged 20 (one creature); +22 vs. AC. The rakshasa makes two attack rolls and uses either result.

Hit: 1d10 + 9 damage.

⟐ **Double Attack** ✦ **At-Will**

Effect: The rakshasa uses *longbow* twice, making each attack against a different target.

⟐ **Ghost Arrow** (necrotic, weapon) ✦ **Recharge** ⚄ ⚅

Attack: Ranged 20 (one creature); +20 vs. Reflex

Hit: 3d10 + 18 necrotic damage, and the target cannot spend healing surges (save ends).

MINOR ACTIONS

Deceptive Veil (illusion) ✦ **At-Will**

Effect: The rakshasa disguises itself to appear as a Medium humanoid until it uses *deceptive veil* again or until it drops to 0 hit points. Other creatures can make a DC 35 Insight check to discern that the form is an illusion.

TRIGGERED ACTIONS

Illusory Escape (illusion) ✦ **Recharge** when first bloodied

Trigger: An enemy makes a ranged attack against the rakshasa.

Effect (Immediate Reaction): The rakshasa becomes invisible, and an illusion of it appears in its square. The transition is indiscernible to observers, and the illusion lasts until the start of the rakshasa's next turn or until a creature attacks the illusion. After the illusion appears, the rakshasa shifts up to its speed.

Str 17 (+10)	**Dex** 20 (+12)	**Wis** 18 (+11)
Con 14 (+9)	**Int** 12 (+8)	**Cha** 14 (+9)

Alignment evil   **Languages** Common
Equipment longbow, 20 arrows

A Life of Luxury: Most rakshasas love luxury and vice. For this reason, they often impersonate nobles, royalty, and other wealthy individuals. One of a rakshasa's favorite tactics is to infiltrate a noble house under the guise of a servant or a distant relative. Under this facade, the rakshasa studies the noble in charge of the house before eventually killing and replacing him or her. A rakshasa's self-indulgence is perhaps its one true weakness. A rakshasa will often blindly endanger itself in the pursuit of new pleasures.

Once a rakshasa has acquired a position of wealth and influence, it ruthlessly maintains that position. It disposes of anyone who threatens to reveal its identity, even if it must leave a trail of bodies in its wake. This fierce defense of one's status and wealth makes larger groups of rakshasas unable to work closely together. A single community rarely has enough wealth to satiate the desires of more than a few rakshasas. When rakshasas work together, the size of a group rarely exceeds three, for larger numbers inevitably lead to violent infighting.

Reincarnation: Upon its death, a rakshasa is immediately reincarnated, retaining all the memories and knowledge of its former lives. This trait is perhaps the main source of a rakshasa's cunning. A rakshasa has lifetimes to learn from its mistakes, and each rakshasa has the cumulative wisdom of a thousand lifetimes, giving it first-hand knowledge of history and the experience from tens of thousands of schemes. During its various incarnations, a rakshasa might learn many languages and skills that it can put to use against its adversaries.

Death is no barrier against a rakshasa taking revenge upon those that wrong it. When a person slays a rakshasa, it's usually a matter of time before the creature shows up to exact its vengeance. Rakshasas are also linked to a race of immortal beings called devas. Sages believe that rakshasas originate from evil devas who reincarnated in a new form that marked their vice and wickedness. Over time, the number of rakshasas has grown as more and more devas have succumbed to temptation. Few rakshasas ever seek the redemption necessary to reincarnate as a deva once more.

Rakshasa Mage	Level 16 Controller
Medium natural humanoid	XP 1,400

HP 153; **Bloodied** 76	**Initiative** +10
AC 30, **Fortitude** 26, **Reflex** 29, **Will** 28	**Perception** +11
Speed 6	Low-light vision

STANDARD ACTIONS

⊕ **Claw** (teleportation) ✦ **At-Will**
Attack: Melee 1 (one creature); +21 vs. AC
Hit: 3d6 + 10 damage, and the rakshasa teleports the target up to 3 squares.
Miss: The rakshasa can teleport the target 1 square.

✵ **Misleading Visions** (illusion, psychic) ✦ **At-Will**
Attack: Area burst 1 within 5 (enemies in the burst); +19 vs. Will
Hit: 2d10 + 11 psychic damage, and the rakshasa slides the target up to 4 squares.
Miss: The rakshasa can slide the target 1 square.

✵ **Visions of Terror** (fear, illusion, psychic) ✦ **Recharge** ⚄ ⚅
Attack: Area burst 1 within 5 (enemies in the burst); +19 vs. Will
Hit: 3d10 + 13 psychic damage, and the target is immobilized (save ends).
Miss: Half damage, and the target is slowed until the end of the rakshasa's next turn.

MINOR ACTIONS

Deceptive Veil (illusion) ✦ **At-Will**
Effect: The rakshasa disguises itself to appear as a Medium humanoid until it uses *deceptive veil* again or until it drops to 0 hit points. Other creatures can make a DC 36 Insight check to discern that the form is an illusion.

Persistent Image (illusion) ✦ **At-Will**
Effect: The rakshasa creates an illusion of a Medium or smaller object or creature in an unoccupied square within 10 squares of it. The illusion can be animate, but it does not produce noise. The illusion lasts until the end of the rakshasa's next turn. A creature that succeeds on a DC 22 Insight check can see through the illusion.
Sustain Minor: The illusion persists until the end of the rakshasa's next turn, and the rakshasa can move the illusion up to 6 squares.

Str 12 (+9)	Dex 14 (+10)	Wis 16 (+11)
Con 17 (+11)	Int 24 (+15)	Cha 21 (+13)
Alignment evil	**Languages** Common	

ROPER

Ravenous ropers jut up from the ground or hang from cavern ceilings. They look like stalagmites or stalactites until prey draws near, at which point they lash out with tentacles and pull quarry toward their toothy maws.

Ropers are methodical hunters that inhabit caves and passageways that are frequented by smaller creatures. A roper creeps into position and hides itself amid the rock. A roper's lair is safe only to creatures that have reached an understanding with the resident roper. A roper might have specific tastes, preferring to eat elves or humans over beasts or less civilized humanoids. When a roper kills a creature that has valuables, it devours the treasure, which it keeps inside its gizzard to help with digestion.

Impaling Roper

Large elemental magical beast (earth)

Level 10 Lurker

XP 500

HP 84; **Bloodied** 42   **Initiative** +13
AC 24, **Fortitude** 23, **Reflex** 22, **Will** 19   **Perception** +9
Speed 2, climb 2 (spider climb)   Darkvision

STANDARD ACTIONS

⊕ **Tentacle ✦ At-Will**

Attack: Melee 10 (one creature); +13 vs. Reflex

Hit: 1d8 + 5 damage.

Effect: The roper grabs the target (escape DC 26). Until the end of the roper's next turn, the roper gains resist 20 to all damage from any of the target's attacks. While the target is grabbed, any creature can attack the tentacle in the target's square. The tentacle uses the roper's defenses. An attack against a tentacle does not deal damage or otherwise affect the roper, but on a hit, the grab ends.

†**Impale ✦ At-Will**

Attack: Melee 10 (one creature grabbed by the roper); +13 vs. Reflex

Effect: The roper pulls the target up to 10 squares to a square adjacent to it.

Hit: 4d10 + 5 damage, and the grab ends.

Miss: Half damage, and the grab ends.

Skills Stealth +14

Str 21 (+10)	**Dex** 18 (+9)	**Wis** 18 (+9)
Con 18 (+9)	**Int** 11 (+5)	**Cha** 6 (+3)

Alignment evil   **Languages** Primordial

Deal Makers: Ropers might look like brainless beasts, but they're fairly intelligent and frequently make agreements with other creatures that live near them. These arrangements are usually truces between ropers and other underground denizens. For example, rather than fight a roper and lose numbers to it, a drow patrol might agree to bring a roper a prisoner or treasure as payment for passage. Canny Underdark creatures use the presence of ropers to thin the numbers in a group of intruders. A creature might lure a party into a cavern of ropers and then attack anyone a roper doesn't grab. Ropers have long life spans, so a deal with a roper might extend for several generations—as long as each side continues to honor the agreement. A humanoid community might be required to pay a seasonal or yearly tribute to appease a roper.

Slow to Act, Quick to Kill: Since ropers live in a dormant state most of the time, they don't share the voracious appetite that leads many dungeon monsters to attack anything they see. A roper waits until the time is right—until the perfect victim wanders by. It might wait for large traveling parties to pass, looking for a smaller group or a lone traveler. Once it does strike, the roper drags enemies toward its maw to devour them quickly. When facing a group, it hopes that seeing the grisly fate of the first victim will cause the others to retreat.

Living Treasure Troves: Adventurers and treasure hunters seek out ropers because of the wealth of gems and magic trinkets stored within the creatures' gizzards. Tales of roper treasure troves usually neglect to mention that a roper acquires such valuables over many generations of slaying travelers and adventurers. Thus, it's common for a townsperson or explorer to underestimate the power of a roper when he or she sets out to kill one. A roper sometimes regurgitates a few gems onto the floor near its hiding spot. It waits patiently, sometimes for

Cave Roper — Level 12 Elite Controller

Large elemental magical beast (earth) — XP 1,400

HP 252; **Bloodied** 126
AC 26, **Fortitude** 26, **Reflex** 21, **Will** 23
Speed 2, climb 2 (spider climb)
Saving Throws +2; **Action Points** 1

Initiative +7
Perception +9
Darkvision

TRAITS

Tentacle Release

Before a creature makes an attack roll against the roper, it can choose to target one of the roper's tentacles. The tentacles use the same defenses as the roper. If the attack hits, it does not deal damage or otherwise affect the roper, but one of the roper's grabs end (of the attacker's choice).

Stony Body

The roper can retract its tentacles and closes its eye and mouth to resembles a natural rock formation. While the roper is on a horizontal rock surface, a creature must succeed at a DC 28 Perception check to see through the roper's disguise.

STANDARD ACTIONS

⊕ **Tentacle** ✦ At-Will

Requirement: The roper must have fewer than two creatures grabbed.
Attack: Melee 10 (one creature); +15 vs. Reflex
Hit: 2d8 + 9 damage, and the roper grabs the target (escape DC 20). Until the grab ends, the target is weakened.

✦ **Double Attack** ✦ At-Will

Effect: The roper uses *tentacle* twice.

✦ **Bite** ✦ At-Will

Attack: Melee 1 (one creature grabbed by the roper); +17 vs. AC
Hit: 4d12 + 12 damage.
Miss: Half damage.

MINOR ACTIONS

✦ **Reel** ✦ At-Will (1/round)

Attack: Melee 10 (each creature grabbed by the roper); +17 vs. Fortitude
Hit: The roper pulls the target up to 5 squares.

Skills Stealth +12

Str 19 (+10)	**Dex** 12 (+7)	**Wis** 16 (+9)
Con 22 (+12)	**Int** 11 (+6)	**Cha** 9 (+5)

Alignment evil — **Languages** Primordial

---

weeks, until a foolhardy humanoid comes along, notices the gems, and bends over to recover the treasures.

Born in the Elemental Chaos: Although ropers are found throughout the caves and tunnels of the world, they hail from the Elemental Chaos. There, they cluster into huge colonies. Creatures inhabiting the Elemental Chaos are wary of a migrating earthmote called the Spired Hell, where hundreds of ropers live. When this earthmote crashes into another piece of land, ropers spread out across the new landscape. After stripping the area of living creatures, they return to the Spired Hell and hibernate until they crash into a new destination.

They Share Memories: A roper reproduces asexually and passes on all its memories to its offspring. As a result, a roper that has lived in one cave for its entire life can remember distant lands, and even other planes. If a roper is bribed

Crag Roper — Level 15 Elite Soldier

Large elemental magical beast (earth) — XP 2,400

HP 304; **Bloodied** 152	**Initiative** +10
AC 31, **Fortitude** 29, **Reflex** 24, **Will** 26	**Perception** +11
Speed 2, climb 2 (spider climb)	Darkvision
Saving Throws +2; **Action Points** 1	

Traits

☼ Lashing Tentacles ✦ Aura 5

Any enemy that enters the aura or starts its turn there is marked by the roper until it is no longer in the aura. Enemies marked by the roper cannot be marked by other creatures while the enemies are in the aura.

Stony Body

The roper can retract its tentacles and close its eye and mouth to resemble a natural rock formation. While the roper is on a horizontal rock surface, a creature must succeed on a DC 30 Perception check to see through the roper's disguise.

Standard Actions

⊕ Tentacle ✦ At-Will

Attack: Melee 10 (one creature); +18 vs. Reflex

Hit: 3d8 + 11 damage, and the roper pulls the target up to 5 squares.

† Double Attack ✦ At-Will

Effect: The roper uses *tentacle* twice.

† Bite ✦ At-Will

Attack: Melee 1 (one creature grabbed by the roper); +20 vs. AC

Hit: 4d12 + 18 damage.

Miss: Half damage.

Minor Actions

† Reel ✦ At-Will (1/round)

Attack: Melee 10 (each creature grabbed by the roper); +20 vs. Fortitude

Hit: The roper pulls the target up to 5 squares.

Triggered Actions

† Tentacle Retaliation ✦ At-Will

Trigger: An enemy marked by the roper makes an attack that doesn't include it as a target.

Effect (Immediate Reaction): The roper uses *tentacle* against the triggering enemy.

Skills Stealth +13		
Str 22 (+13)	**Dex** 12 (+8)	**Wis** 18 (+11)
Con 24 (+14)	**Int** 14 (+9)	**Cha** 9 (+6)
Alignment evil	**Languages** Primordial	

with treasure or a delectable living creature, it might reveal information or secrets from its ancient memories. A story that every roper knows (yet few will share) tells of the ropers' creation. The tale claims that the first ropers sloughed off from the rocky flesh of the primordial Vezzuvu, the Burning Mountain. At first, the ropers were fast and hot, like lava, but eventually they cooled and became the creatures they are today. Ropers believe that one day Vezzuvu will return and reignite them and call upon them to serve as his forces against the gods.

"It looks like a cursed stalagmite! It has no right to be this terrifying!"

—Last words of Agroth of the Winterbole

RUST MONSTER

Rust monsters are the bane of underground societies and subterranean adventurers. Their appetite for metals leads them to attack travelers and destroy magic items.

The ecology and habits of a rust monster have made the creatures a pestilence upon civilizations that rely upon metal. A rust monster's saliva and the substance it excretes from its carapace are highly corrosive and can break down metals quickly through rapid oxidation. These liquids are harmless to flesh but cause metal to corrode upon contact. The chemical is so powerful that some races work to harvest it for the removal of degraded metal in dilapidated structures. The difficulty in harvesting a rust monster's excretions makes a single vial of the substance rare and valuable.

Metal Eaters: A rust monster's diet consists primarily of metal. Refined metals, especially iron, steel, gold, silver, and platinum, are its favorite source of nutrients. For this reason, a rust monster will attack travelers and adventurers laden with armor, weapons, and magic items. In the absence of refined metal, a rust monster consumes raw ore, leading it to inhabit mines and old ore refineries.

A rust monster is an unintelligent beast that acts on instinct alone; it pursues a source of metal if it has even a small chance of acquiring food and escaping alive. The availability of food has an effect on the number of offspring that a pair of rust monsters can produce. In areas where metal is abundant, rust monsters can produce swarms of young, while in areas where food is sparse, they might have only a few offspring. A rust monster infestation can quickly become unmanageable, potentially wiping out a settlement. For this reason, people act quickly to eliminate rust monster nests.

Scourge of Civilization: Rust monsters typically dwell underground and gravitate toward mines, so dwarves, duergar, and other subterranean cultures consider them a pestilence on civilization. A rust monster might feed on mining equipment, metal support beams, or mine cart rails, disrupting operations and potentially causing the death of those working there. A group of rust monsters might devour the support beams for a dam holding back an underground lake. In the worst case, a locustlike swarm of rust monsters could wash over a subterranean city and, in a matter of hours, leave nothing behind but rubble and death.

Although a single rust monster is a minimal threat, once they grow numerous, only magic is likely to halt their advance. Some civilizations develop complex warding rituals to keep rust monsters away, but these magical defenses are expensive to perform, and rust monsters have a knack for finding ways through the wards. Some dwarven settlements have warning systems that allow clerics and spellcasters time to perform a defensive ritual before rust monsters overwhelm a town's defenses. When the early warning systems are disrupted, though, it can mean disaster for a settlement that relies only on magic wards.

Rust Monster	Level 6 Skirmisher
Medium natural beast	XP 250
HP 66; Bloodied 33	Initiative +10
AC 20, Fortitude 16, Reflex 21, Will 17	Perception +5
Speed 8	Low-light vision

TRAITS

Rusting Defense
Whenever an attack using a metal weapon hits the rust monster, the weapon used in the attack is rusting until the end of the encounter. While the weapon is rusting, attacks with the weapon take a -1 penalty to attack rolls. If the weapon used to attack the rust monster is already rusting, the penalty to attack rolls worsens by 1 (to a maximum penalty of -5).

STANDARD ACTIONS

⊕ **Bite ✦ At-Will**
Attack: Melee 1 (one creature); +11 vs. AC
Hit: 2d8 + 5 damage. If the target is wearing heavy armor, the armor is rusting until the end of the encounter. While the armor is rusting, the target takes a -1 penalty to AC. If the target is wearing armor that is already rusting, increase the penalty to AC by 1 (to a maximum penalty of -5).
Effect: The rust monster shifts 1 square.

✦ **Devour Metal ✦ Recharge** if the power misses
Attack: Melee 1 (one creature wearing or wielding a rusting item); +9 vs. Reflex
Hit: The rusting item is destroyed. If the item was magical, *residuum* worth the item's market value can be retrieved from the rust monster after the creature is slain.

Str 8 (+2)	Dex 20 (+8)	Wis 15 (+5)
Con 10 (+3)	Int 2 (-1)	Cha 12 (+4)
Alignment unaligned	**Languages** —	

Residuum Sources: Although most humanoids regard rust monsters as a plague, the creatures do offer a boon to anyone who manages to slay them. A rust monster often consumes magic items, and as it devours the metals of an object, its body stores deposits of *residuum* created by the decomposition of the item. *Residuum*, the valuable substance used in magic item creation, is prized by merchants and smiths, who hire specialized hunting parties to collect the material. Devious malcontents sometimes surreptitiously unleash rust monsters in armories or magic vaults and then offer to exterminate the creatures in exchange for the *residuum* stored in the monsters' bellies.

Gluttonous Rust Monster	Level 8 Brute
Medium natural beast	XP 350
HP 110; **Bloodied** 55	**Initiative** +7
AC 20, **Fortitude** 21, **Reflex** 19, **Will** 17	**Perception** +5
Speed 6	Low-light vision

TRAITS

Rusting Defense
Whenever an attack using a metal weapon hits the rust monster, the weapon used in the attack is rusting until the end of the encounter. While the weapon is rusting, attacks with the weapon take a -1 penalty to attack rolls. If the weapon used to attack the rust monster is already rusting, the penalty to attack rolls worsens by 1 (to a maximum penalty of -5).

STANDARD ACTIONS

⊕ **Bite ✦ At-Will**
Attack: Melee 1 (one creature); +13 vs. AC
Hit: 3d10 + 3 damage. If the target is wearing heavy armor, the armor is rusting until the end of the encounter. While the armor is rusting, the target takes a -1 penalty to AC. If the target is wearing armor that is already rusting, increase the penalty to AC by 1 (to a maximum penalty of -5).

⚔ **Devour Metal ✦ Recharge if the power misses**
Attack: Melee 1 (one creature wearing or wielding a rusting item); +11 vs. Reflex
Hit: The rusting item is destroyed. If the item was magic, *residuum* worth the item's market value can be retrieved from the rust monster after the creature is slain.

⚔ **Gluttonous Bite ✦ Encounter**
Attack: Melee 1 (one creature); +13 vs. AC
Hit: 4d10 + 8 damage. If the target is wearing heavy armor, the armor is rusting until the end of the encounter. While the armor is rusting, the target takes a -1 penalty to AC. If the target is wearing armor that is already rusting, the penalty to AC worsens by 1 (to a maximum penalty of -5). In addition, any weapon the target is wielding is rusting until the end of the encounter. While the weapon is rusting, attacks with the weapon take a -1 penalty to attack rolls. If the weapon is already rusting, the penalty to attack rolls worsens by 1 (to a maximum penalty of -5).
Miss: Half damage.

Str 16 (+7)	Dex 16 (+7)	Wis 12 (+5)
Con 20 (+9)	Int 2 (+0)	Cha 11 (+4)

Alignment unaligned	**Languages** –

Young Rust Monster Swarm
Medium natural beast (swarm)

Level 9 Soldier
XP 400

SWARM

HP 92; **Bloodied** 46
AC 25, **Fortitude** 19 **Reflex** 24, **Will** 19
Speed 6
Resist half damage from melee and ranged attacks;
Vulnerable 10 to close and area attacks

Initiative +12
Perception +5
Low-light vision

TRAITS

☼ Swarm Attack ✦ Aura 1

Any enemy that ends its turn in the aura takes 5 damage. If the enemy has a rusting item, it is also slowed until the end of its turn.

Rusting Defense

Whenever an attack using a metal weapon hits the rust monster, the weapon used in the attack is rusting until the end of the encounter. While the weapon is rusting, attacks with the weapon take a -1 penalty to attack rolls. If the weapon used to attack the rust monster is already rusting, the penalty to attack rolls worsens by 1 (to a maximum penalty of -5).

Swarm

The swarm can occupy the same space as another creature, and an enemy can enter its space, which is difficult terrain. The swarm cannot be pulled, pushed, or slid by melee or ranged attacks. It can squeeze through any opening that is large enough for at least one of the creatures it comprises.

STANDARD ACTIONS

✦ Swarm of Teeth ✦ At-Will

Attack: Melee 1 (one creature); +12 vs. Reflex

Hit: 3d8 + 4 damage. If the target is wearing heavy armor, the armor is rusting until the end of the encounter. While the armor is rusting, the target takes a -1 penalty to AC. If the target is wearing armor that is already rusting, the penalty to AC worsens by 1 (to a maximum penalty of -5).

Str 8 (+3)	**Dex** 22 (+10)	**Wis** 13 (+5)
Con 12 (+5)	**Int** 2 (+0)	**Cha** 12 (+5)
Alignment unaligned	**Languages** —	

"The problem with fighting a rust monster is that every time you think you have an opening and swing your sword, it raises its feelers eagerly, like you're handing it a snack."

—Tennaris of Silver Spire

SKELETON

Necromancy grants violent motion to these fleshless bones, letting them defy death and deliver it to others.

It is said that the history of a life is written in bone. The fall from a tree in youth, the kick of a horse in middle age, a trip upon the stairs in the late years of life—all make their marks upon bone. These scars are whispers of the past that echo quietly after death. Few parts of a person's life speak when all that remains is a barren skeleton. No memory or dream lingers in the empty shell of a skull. No hint of the joy or sorrow can be seen upon the grimacing teeth. For a few skeletons, though, death doesn't mean decay and ruin. These wordless forms might not speak, but their actions bear a clear message: They come to deliver death.

Symbol of Death: Even inanimate skeletons have the power to inspire fear. Bones are important pieces of life. They are an unseen part of the body that supports and sustains life. When bones appear, they are associated with death.

An animate skeleton provokes greater fear than ordinary bones can. These undead are twisted mockeries that lack everything that makes life worthwhile—sentience, emotion, pleasure. The walking dead know only how to obey.

Decrepit Skeleton — Level 1 Minion Skirmisher
Medium natural animate (undead)   XP 25

HP 1; a missed attack never damages a minion. **Initiative** +5
AC 16, **Fortitude** 13, **Reflex** 14, **Will** 13 **Perception** +2
Speed 6   Darkvision
Immune disease, poison; **Resist** 10 necrotic; **Vulnerable** 5 radiant

STANDARD ACTIONS

⊕ **Longsword** (weapon) ✦ At-Will
Effect: The skeleton can shift 1 square before the attack.
Attack: Melee 1 (one creature); +6 vs. AC
Hit: 4 damage.

⊙ **Shortbow** (weapon) ✦ At-Will
Effect: The skeleton can shift 1 square before the attack.
Attack: Ranged 20 (one creature); +6 vs. AC
Hit: 3 damage.

Str 15 (+2)	Dex 17 (+3)	Wis 14 (+2)
Con 13 (+1)	Int 3 (-4)	Cha 3 (-4)

Alignment unaligned   **Languages** –
Equipment longsword, shortbow, 20 arrows

Blazing Skeleton — Level 5 Artillery
Medium natural animate (undead)   XP 200

HP 53; **Bloodied** 26   **Initiative** +6
AC 19, **Fortitude** 15, **Reflex** 18, **Will** 16 **Perception** +4
Speed 6   Darkvision
Immune disease, poison; **Resist** 10 fire, 10 necrotic;
Vulnerable 5 radiant

TRAITS

✧ **Fiery Aura** (fire) ✦ Aura 1
Any creature that ends its turn in the aura takes 5 fire damage.

STANDARD ACTIONS

⊕ **Blazing Claw** (fire) ✦ At-Will
Attack: Melee 1 (one creature); +10 vs. AC
Hit: 1d6 + 3 damage, and ongoing 5 fire damage (save ends).

⊙ **Flame Orb** (fire) ✦ At-Will
Attack: Ranged 10 (one creature); +10 vs. Reflex
Hit: 2d4 + 4 damage, and ongoing 5 fire damage (save ends).

Str 13 (+3)	Dex 18 (+6)	Wis 15 (+4)
Con 17 (+5)	Int 4 (-1)	Cha 6 (+0)

Alignment unaligned   **Languages** –

"Nothing holds them together but magic, a necromantic binding that knits bone with scraps of soul and the merest hint of will."

—Kalarel, scion of Orcus

Mindless Horrors: A skeleton has no desires, passions, or goals. It knows neither good or evil. A skeleton's creation is considered a vile act, though, for it requires disturbing a creature's bones in the most profane way. A skeleton raised into undeath moves through the power of a soul's discarded animus; it is a primal force that binds the soul and body to make life possible. Without an animus, a skeleton cannot exist.

A skeleton might bear scars from its former life—a broken rib, a cracked femur, a missing hand. Some skeletons don the artifacts with which they were laid to rest out of an echo of memory or a vestige of habit. To an onlooker, these relics might be striking or horrifying. To a skeleton, though, the objects are meaningless like everything else in the world.

Driven by Another's Will: A skeleton does not want anything; a person or force is always responsible for a skeleton's actions. Many powers can cause a skeleton to rise from the grave: holy power, necrotic energy, a dark ritual, a necromantic spell or hex, a curse from the lips of a dying person. A skeleton that is animated and given little direction might wait in torpor for centuries, collecting moss or gradually growing brittle. A skeleton set to turn the winch of a bridge might crank it long after the bridge has fallen into disrepair. A skeleton commanded to slay all it encounters might wander a forest for decades. A group of skeletons set to guard a dwarven tomb might lack the wherewithal to distinguish between a dwarven descendant seeking an ancestral weapon and thieves seeking plunder. When a creature comes along to disturb a skeleton, the undead acts according to the exact instructions of its master or animate force, sometimes even blindly contradicting the true intent of the orders.

Deadly Servants: Skeletons are usually found in the service of one who requires faultless followers or remorseless killers. A spellcaster might employ skeletons for manual labor and menial tasks, but more often than not, they are used in battle or as guardians. Many continue to follow their final orders even after a master dies, though some skeletons have also been known to go berserk, behave erratically, or collapse into piles of bones after a master's death.

Skeletons do not always serve spellcasters; they might have various functions in a society. A noble family might ride through a city in a carriage drawn by skeletal horses, reveling in the fright of onlookers. A pirate captain could employ a skeleton crew so that none of the booty need be shared. Or, a group of assassins might command skeletons to kill a person publicly while the group's members remain safely in the shadows.

Skeletal Legionary   Level 7 Minion Soldier

Medium natural animate (undead)   XP 75

HP 1; a missed attack never damages a minion.   **Initiative** +9
AC 23, **Fortitude** 20, **Reflex** 20, **Will** 18   **Perception** +5
Speed 5   Darkvision
Immune disease, poison; **Resist** 10 necrotic

STANDARD ACTIONS

⊕ **Longsword** (weapon) ✦ **At-Will**
Attack: Melee 1 (one creature); +12 vs. AC
Hit: 7 damage.
Effect: The legionary marks the target until the end of the legionary's next turn.

⊙ **Javelin** (weapon) ✦ **At-Will**
Attack: Ranged 20 (one creature); +12 vs. AC
Hit: 7 damage.
Effect: The legionary marks the target until the end of the legionary's next turn.

Str 18 (+7)	**Dex** 19 (+7)	**Wis** 14 (+5)
Con 16 (+6)	**Int** 3 (-1)	**Cha** 3 (-1)

Alignment unaligned   **Languages** —
Equipment scale armor, heavy shield, longsword, 3 javelins

Skeletal Tomb Guardian   Level 10 Brute

Medium natural animate (undead)   XP 500

HP 126; **Bloodied** 63   **Initiative** +10
AC 23, **Fortitude** 22, **Reflex** 23, **Will** 20   **Perception** +12
Speed 8   Darkvision
Immune disease, poison; **Resist** 10 necrotic; **Vulnerable** 5 radiant

STANDARD ACTIONS

⊕ **Twin Scimitars** (weapon) ✦ **At-Will**
Attack: Melee 1 (one creature); +15 vs. AC. The guardian makes the attack twice against the same target.
Hit: 1d8 + 2 damage, or 1d8 + 10 if the guardian scores a critical hit.

↯ **Cascade of Steel** ✦ **At-Will**
Effect: The guardian uses *twin scimitars* twice.

TRIGGERED ACTIONS

↯ **Sudden Strike** ✦ **At-Will**
Trigger: An enemy adjacent to the guardian shifts.
Effect (Immediate Interrupt): The guardian uses *twin scimitars* against the triggering enemy.

Str 18 (+9)	**Dex** 20 (+10)	**Wis** 14 (+7)
Con 16 (+8)	**Int** 3 (+1)	**Cha** 3 (+1)

Alignment unaligned   **Languages** —
Equipment 4 scimitars

STIGE

Size is no concern for stirges. Swarms of these flying menaces can drain a large creature of blood in minutes. In their wake, stirges leave withered bags of skin and bones—food for any scavengers that dare to approach.

Few can forget the dreadful drone of stirge wings; the distinct sound of their dual wings flapping in time joins a cacophony of other stirge wings, creating a buzz that drowns out all other noises. With elements of lizard, bat, crab, and mosquito, a stirge might be comical if not for its feeding habits. A stirge hovers on four membranous wings, which support the creature as it searches for warm-blooded quarry. When a stirge spots prey, it flies up close and clamps onto the creature with four clawed limbs. The stirge then plunges its pointed proboscis into the victim's body, draining the victim of blood. When the creature has had its fill, it lifts its bloated body aloft and seeks a safe place to digest.

Hunters in Darkness: Like bats, stirges dwell in darkness. Caves, dungeons, hollow trees, cellars, sewers, and crypts make excellent places for stirges to sleep. Possessed of preternatural sight, stirges hunt in the darkest hours and the blackest places. On the surface of the world, a stirge swarm is a nocturnal threat, but in the confines of caves, there is no escape.

Widespread Threat: Stirges prefer to feast on creatures of halfling to horse size, so they live wherever people or herd animals dwell. They are a constant threat to humanoids, and each race has a strategy for dealing with the pests. The creatures sometimes hide in ships or caravans like rats, so merchants have developed repellents that are unpleasant to the creatures. Swarms of stirges menace halfling boat villages as they pass through swamps and down rivers, so halflings erect great nets and wicker lattices to protect them. Stirges also dwell in the sewers of human cities. They boil up at night, requiring residents to secure their doors and shutters as if as a hurricane were coming through. Elves resort

LARS GRANT-WEST

Stirge — Level 1 Lurker
Small natural beast — XP 100

HP 22; **Bloodied** 11 — **Initiative** +7
AC 15, **Fortitude** 12, **Reflex** 15, **Will** 12 — **Perception** +0
Speed 2, fly 6 — Darkvision

TRAITS
Nimble Bloodsucker
While the stirge has a creature grabbed, the stirge gains a +5 bonus to AC and Reflex.

STANDARD ACTIONS
⊕ Bite ✦ At-Will
Requirement: The stirge must not be grabbing a creature.
Attack: Melee 1 (one creature); +6 vs. AC.
Hit: 1d4 + 5 damage, and the stirge grabs the target (escape DC 12). Until the grab ends, the target takes ongoing 5 damage.

Skills Stealth +8
| Str 8 (-1) | Dex 16 (+3) | Wis 10 (+0) |
| Con 10 (+0) | Int 1 (-5) | Cha 4 (-3) |

Alignment unaligned — **Languages** —

"I always laugh when I hear some rube complaining about the biting insects of the Witchlight Fens. You think those bloodsuckers are bad?"

—Shara of Winterhaven

Stirge Suckerling — Level 5 Minion Lurker
Small natural beast — XP 50

HP 1; a missed attack never damages a minion. — **Initiative** +9
AC 19, **Fortitude** 16, **Reflex** 18, **Will** 15 — **Perception** +7
Speed 2, fly 6 — Darkvision

TRAITS
Nimble Bloodsucker
While the stirge has a creature grabbed, the stirge gains a +2 bonus to AC and Reflex.

STANDARD ACTIONS
⊕ Bite ✦ At-Will
Attack: Melee 1 (one creature); +10 vs. AC. While the stirge has a creature grabbed, it can use bite only against that creature, and it hits automatically.
Hit: 5 damage, and the stirge grabs the target (escape DC 15). Until the target is no longer grabbed by any suckerlings, it takes damage at the start of its turn equal to the number of stirge suckerlings grabbing it. The target takes this damage only once each turn, regardless of how many suckerlings are grabbing it.

Skills Stealth +10
| Str 7 (+0) | Dex 16 (+5) | Wis 10 (+2) |
| Con 12 (+3) | Int 1 (-3) | Cha 4 (-1) |

Alignment unaligned — **Languages** —

to setting fire to trees in which stirges nest. Dwarves, on the other hand, send out heavily armored extermination teams who cut the stirges to bits after luring them into a trap.

Other Stirge Threats: A stirge makes little distinction between horse or human, bear or basilisk. Blood draws it like a moth to flame. A stirge is dangerous for more than its lethal ability to drain blood, though. A survivor of a stirge attack might contract a strange illness as a result of the diseased blood the stirge transmits from another creature it has feasted upon.

Despite the dangers of stirges, some creatures value them for the very qualities that make others fear them. Kobolds capture stirges to use them in clever traps where cages containing stirges are dropped on foes. Practitioners of dark magic capture stirges and train them to retrieve blood for foul rituals. Necromancers trap stirges in the cavernous bodies of giant undead. When the undead opens its maw, famished stirges come pouring out to attack the nearest warm-blooded creature.

Death Husk Stirge	Level 6 Skirmisher
Small natural animate (undead)	XP 250

HP 71; **Bloodied** 35	**Initiative** +9
AC 20, **Fortitude** 16, **Reflex** 20, **Will** 18	**Perception** +6
Speed 2, fly 6	Darkvision
Immune poison; **Resist** 10 necrotic	

TRAITS

Necromantic Flyer
A death husk stirge that takes radiant damage cannot fly until the end of its next turn; if in the air, it falls.

STANDARD ACTIONS

⊕ **Bite** ✦ **At-Will**
Attack: Melee 1 (one creature); +11 vs. AC
Hit: 2d6 + 7 damage, and the death husk stirge recharges *rotted blood.*

↙ **Rotted Blood** (necrotic) ✦ **Encounter**
Attack: Close blast 3 (living creatures in the blast); +9 vs. Fortitude
Hit: 1d6 + 7 necrotic damage, and the target is blinded until the end of the stirge's next turn.
Effect: Undead in the blast can shift 2 squares as a free action.

MOVE ACTIONS

Nimble Wing ✦ **At-Will**
Effect: The death husk stirge flies 4 squares. This movement does not provoke opportunity attacks.

TRIGGERED ACTIONS

↙ **Necrotic Miasma** (necrotic) ✦ **At-Will**
Trigger: The death husk stirge drops to 0 hit points.
Attack (No Action): Close burst 2 (living creatures in the burst); +9 vs. Fortitude
Hit: 5 necrotic damage, and the target is weakened until the end of its next turn.

Str 6 (+1)	**Dex** 19 (+7)	**Wis** 16 (+6)
Con 15 (+5)	**Int** 4 (+0)	**Cha** 7 (+1)
Alignment evil	**Languages** -	

Dire Stirge
Small natural beast

Level 7 Lurker
XP 300

HP 60; **Bloodied** 30
AC 21, **Fortitude** 18, **Reflex** 20, **Will** 17
Speed 2, fly 6

Initiative +10
Perception +3
Darkvision

TRAITS

Nimble Bloodsucker

While the stirge has a creature grabbed, the stirge gains a +2 bonus to AC and Reflex.

STANDARD ACTIONS

⊕ **Bite** ✦ **At-Will**

Attack: Melee 1 (one creature); +12 vs. AC. While the stirge has a creature grabbed, it can use *bite* only against that creature, and it hits automatically.

Hit: 1d6 damage, and the stirge grabs the target (escape DC 16). Until the grab ends, the target takes ongoing 10 damage.

Skills Stealth +11

Str 10 (+3)	**Dex** 16 (+6)	**Wis** 10 (+3)
Con 12 (+4)	**Int** 1 (−2)	**Cha** 4 (+0)

Alignment unaligned   **Languages** —

Stirge Suckerling Swarm
Medium natural beast (swarm)

Level 10 Brute
XP 500

SWARM

HP 128; **Bloodied** 64
AC 22, **Fortitude** 22, **Reflex** 22, **Will** 20
Speed 2, fly 6
Resist half damage from melee and ranged attacks;
Vulnerable 5 to close and area attacks

Initiative +9
Perception +7
Darkvision

TRAITS

✧ **Blood Frenzy** ✦ **Aura** 1

Any enemy that starts its turn in the aura takes ongoing 5 damage (save ends). If that enemy is already taking untyped ongoing damage, that damage increases by 5.

Swarm

The swarm can occupy the same space as another creature, and an enemy can enter its space, which is difficult terrain. The swarm cannot be pulled, pushed, or slid by melee or ranged attacks. It can squeeze through any opening that is large enough for at least one of the creatures it comprises.

STANDARD ACTIONS

⊕ **Swarm of Suckerlings** ✦ **At-Will**

Attack: Melee 1 (one creature); +15 vs. AC
Hit: 3d6 + 1 damage, and ongoing 5 damage (save ends).

TRIGGERED ACTIONS

Hungry Flight ✦ **At-Will**

Trigger: An enemy moves away from the swarm.
Effect (Immediate Reaction): The swarm flies up to its fly speed to the triggering enemy's square or a square adjacent to that enemy. This movement does not provoke opportunity attacks.

Skills Stealth +14

Str 10 (+5)	**Dex** 19 (+9)	**Wis** 14 (+7)
Con 18 (+9)	**Int** 1 (+0)	**Cha** 4 (+2)

Alignment unaligned   **Languages** —

TIEFLING

Hellish power courses through the veins of tieflings—power they can use for great good, or for terrible evil.

Tieflings have a dark reputation as a result of their sinister past and uncertain future. They now live every day with the sins of their ancestors written across their faces.

A Hellish History: Long ago, the human empire of Bael Turath stood on the brink of chaos. To preserve the empire, its ruling class signed blood pacts with devils. Their compacts transformed the empire and the humans' bodies. Eventually, both infernal forces and the tieflings of Bael Turath would break their bargain, and the result would leave the empire in ruins.

Making Bad Choices: Despite their appearance, tieflings have as much freedom to set the course of their lives as humans do. Nonetheless, tieflings are still a target of prejudice and suspicion. Many tieflings eventually grow tired of fighting their reputation and choose to embrace it.

Tiefling Fury	Level 5 Soldier
Medium natural humanoid	XP 200

HP 63; **Bloodied** 31	**Initiative** +4
AC 21, **Fortitude** 18, **Reflex** 17, **Will** 18	**Perception** +2
Speed 6	Low-light vision
Resist 10 fire	

STANDARD ACTIONS

⊕ **Longsword** (weapon) ✦ At-Will
Attack: Melee 1 (one creature); +10 vs. AC
Hit: 1d8 + 8 damage.
Effect: The tiefling marks the target until the end of the target's next turn.

TRIGGERED ACTIONS

↯ **Tail Trip** ✦ At-Will
Trigger: An enemy marked by the tiefling shifts.
Attack (Immediate Interrupt): Melee 1 (triggering enemy); +10 vs. Reflex
Hit: The target falls prone, and the tiefling uses *longsword* against it.

Defiant Curse ✦ At-Will
Trigger: An enemy hits the tiefling.
Effect (Free Action): Close burst 10 (triggering enemy in the burst). The tiefling marks the target until the end of the target's next turn.

Skills Bluff +10, Stealth +7

Str 16 (+5)	**Dex** 11 (+2)	**Wis** 10 (+2)
Con 15 (+4)	**Int** 14 (+4)	**Cha** 16 (+5)

Alignment unaligned	**Languages** Common

Equipment leather armor, longsword

Tiefling Occultist

Level 8 Controller

Medium natural humanoid

XP 350

HP 87; **Bloodied** 43 | **Initiative** +4
AC 22, **Fortitude** 18, **Reflex** 20, **Will** 22 | **Perception** +5
Speed 6 | Low-light vision
Resist 10 fire

STANDARD ACTIONS

⊕ **Hell Rod** (fire, implement) ✦ **At-Will**
Attack: Melee 1 (one creature); +11 vs. Reflex
Hit: 2d6 + 6 fire damage, and ongoing 5 fire damage (save ends)

❋ **Soul Fire** (fear, fire, implement, psychic) ✦ **At-Will**
Attack: Area burst 1 within 10 (enemies in the burst); +11 vs. Reflex
Hit: Ongoing 10 fire damage (save ends). In addition, the first time the target willingly moves closer to the tiefling before the end of its next turn, the target takes 10 psychic damage.
Miss: Ongoing 5 fire damage (save ends).

MOVE ACTIONS

⤴ **Baleful Teleport** (teleportation) ✦ **Recharge** ⚄ ⚅
Effect: Before the attack, the tiefling teleports up to 10 squares.
Attack: Ranged 10 (one creature); +11 vs. Will
Hit: The tiefling teleports the target 10 squares to the square it just left.

TRIGGERED ACTIONS

⬳ **Fiery Transposition** (fire, teleportation) ✦ **Encounter**
Trigger: An enemy hits the tiefling.
Effect (Immediate Interrupt): Close burst 3 (creatures in the burst). Each target takes 5 fire damage, and then the tiefling and the triggering enemy teleport, swapping positions.

Skills Bluff +14, Stealth +9
Str 10 (+4) | **Dex** 11 (+4) | **Wis** 13 (+5)
Con 15 (+6) | **Int** 17 (+7) | **Cha** 20 (+9)
Alignment unaligned | **Languages** Common
Equipment leather armor, rod

(Left to right) tiefling occultist, tiefling fury

TREANT

A few great trees of the forest harbor the hearts of mighty fey. These titanic treants violently protect the wild, giving little regard to the consequences for civilized races.

Some parts of the forest seem more alive. The flowers grow bright even in deep shadows. The insects drone louder. Wind sways the high branches, causing the constant rustle of leaves. In these parts of the forest dwell the treants, living trees that are always alert for the enemies of nature.

Wild at Heart: A treant meditates through the cycle of seasons, often remaining dormant for decades or centuries before awakening when nature has need. During these periods of dormancy, a treant's roots entwine with a network of plants, and its branches serve as homes for animals. While a treant sleeps, it dreams of the world around it, remaining cognizant of the happiness or sorrow of the living things in the forest.

The thoughts of a treant flow as swiftly as those of humanoids, and its emotions run just as deep. A treant is passionate about the forest but cares little for the lives of any who live beyond the forest. The death of a humanoid is to a treant as the death of a tree is to a person. A whole city might erupt in flames, but the treant spares thought only for the danger to the wilderness surrounding the city.

LARS GRANT-WEST

Bramblewood Treant
Level 10 Soldier

Large fey magical beast (plant)

XP 500

HP 108; **Bloodied** 54
AC 26, **Fortitude** 23, **Reflex** 20, **Will** 24
Speed 8 (forest walk)

Initiative +9
Perception +11
Low-light vision

TRAITS

⚙ Bramble Branches ✦ Aura 2

Enemies treat squares within the aura as difficult terrain.

Wooden Body

Whenever the treant takes fire damage, it also takes ongoing 5 fire damage (save ends).

STANDARD ACTIONS

⊕ Slam ✦ At-Will

Attack: Melee 2 (one creature); +15 vs. AC

Hit: 1d12 + 12 damage.

Effect: The treant marks the target until the end of the treant's next turn.

⤳ Throw Stone ✦ At-Will

Attack: Ranged 20 (one creature); +15 vs. AC

Hit: 2d6 + 7 damage.

TRIGGERED ACTIONS

⤵ Entangling Branch ✦ At-Will

Trigger: An enemy within 2 squares of the treant moves.

Attack (Immediate Interrupt): Melee 2 (triggering enemy); +13 vs. Reflex

Hit: The treant grabs the target (escape DC 18).

Str 21 (+10)	**Dex** 14 (+7)	**Wis** 22 (+11)
Con 20 (+10)	**Int** 14 (+7)	**Cha** 12 (+6)

Alignment unaligned | **Languages** Elven

Civilization's Enemies: A treant sees the wilderness much like humans view their villages and towns; while people struggle to expand the light of civilization, a treant works to halt its growth and sometimes even to expunge it. A treant prefers nature in its purest and most untamed form, and many oppose even natural changes to its state such as fire, storm, or flood.

Their staunch opposition to civilization puts treants at odds with many societies. Unfortunately for their foes, treants are like nature's siege engines. A single crushing blow from one of these titans of the forest can crumple a person's body. Treants recognize their strength, and they expect little opposition once they have turned their thoughts toward destruction. Only terrible fire or a great number of foes can give pause to a group of treants.

Ally to Many, Friend to None: As a fey and a defender of the wild, a treant might ally with elves, eladrin, dryads, and other nature-loving fey. The connection between treants and elves or eladrin is related more to their mutually long lives than to any sympathy between them. Although some elves and eladrin have formed strong bonds with treants through decades of diplomacy, most regard treants warily, knowing that the tree creatures regard their civilizations in the same way they do other humanoid settlements.

A treant allies with any creature that respects its values and opposes its enemies. A treant might guard the lair of an orc tribe, so long as that tribe focuses its destruction outside the wilderness. Dryads and other plant creatures are treants' most frequent allies. A dryad and a treant share the same disposition and feelings about the forest, and their close proximity often leads the creatures to develop a symbiotic relationship. A follower of Melora can also find common cause with treants, so the tree creatures are sometimes found acting as oracles or leaders for Melora's druids or guarding locations sacred to the goddess.

A treant's allies should be careful to avoid doing anything a treant might perceive as betrayal. Like dryads, a treant is swift to anger and difficult to placate. It holds grudges long after the grandchildren of the offender have come and gone. A human who wrongs a treant might doom generations of unrelated humans to death in that treant's forest. A treant's bark might grow to conceal its scars, but the wood beneath the bark never forgets.

Treant	Level 16 Elite Controller
Huge fey magical beast (plant)	XP 2,800

HP 316; **Bloodied** 158	**Initiative** +9
AC 30, **Fortitude** 30, **Reflex** 26, **Will** 30	**Perception** +15
Speed 8 (forest walk)	Low-light vision
Saving Throws +2; **Action Points** 1	

TRAITS

⟳ **Grasping Roots ✦ Aura** 3
Squares in the aura are difficult terrain for nonflying enemies.

Wooden Body
Whenever the treant takes fire damage, it also takes ongoing 5 fire damage (save ends).

STANDARD ACTIONS

⊕ **Slam ✦ At-Will**
Attack: Melee 3 (one creature); +21 vs. AC
Hit: 2d10 + 13 damage.

⁂ **Awaken Forest** (zone) **✦ At-Will**
Attack: Area burst 3 within 10 (enemies in the burst); +21 vs. AC
Hit: 2d10 + 9 damage.
Effect: The burst creates a zone of difficult terrain that lasts until the end of the encounter or until the treant uses this power again.

↩ **Earthshaking Stomp ✦ Recharge** if the power misses every target
Attack: Close burst 2 (creatures in the burst); +19 vs. Fortitude
Hit: 6d6 + 7 damage, and the target falls prone.

Str 24 (+15)	Dex 12 (+9)	Wis 25 (+15)
Con 22 (+14)	Int 14 (+10)	Cha 12 (+9)
Alignment unaligned	**Languages** Elven	

Place a Large creature token inside this ring to create a Huge creature token.

"For ten generations of your kind, you have not been welcome in this wood. What makes you think I have forgotten the wrong you have done?"

—Rallaferanishad, treant of the Wild Grove

Treant Grove Guardian — Level 18 Brute

Huge fey magical beast (plant) | XP 2,000

HP 212; **Bloodied** 106 | **Initiative** +11
AC 30, **Fortitude** 31, **Reflex** 28, **Will** 31 | **Perception** +15
Speed 8 (forest walk) | Low-light vision

Traits

Wooden Body
Whenever the treant takes fire damage, it also takes ongoing 5 fire damage (save ends).

Standard Actions

⊕ Sweeping Slam ✦ At-Will
Attack: Melee 3 (one or two creatures); +23 vs. AC
Hit: 3d12 + 8 damage, and the target falls prone.

⸭ Stump Stomp ✦ Encounter
Effect: The treant moves up to its speed and can move through enemies' spaces during the move. Each time the treant enters an enemy's space for the first time during the move, it can use *slam* against that enemy.

| Str 25 (+16) | Dex 14 (+11) | Wis 23 (+15) |
| Con 22 (+15) | Int 14 (+11) | Cha 12 (+10) |

Alignment unaligned | **Languages** Elven

Place a Large creature token inside this ring to create a Huge creature token.

Blackroot Treant — Level 19 Elite Soldier

Huge fey magical beast (plant, undead) | XP 4,800

HP 368; **Bloodied** 184 | **Initiative** +13
AC 35, **Fortitude** 32, **Reflex** 29, **Will** 31 | **Perception** +13
Speed 6 (forest walk) | Low-light vision
Saving Throws +2; **Action Points** 1

Traits

✪ Killing Roots (healing, necrotic) ✦ Aura 2
Any enemy that ends its turn in the aura takes 10 necrotic damage. Any undead ally that ends its turn in the aura regains 10 hit points.

Wooden Body
Whenever the treant takes fire damage, it also takes ongoing 5 fire damage (save ends).

Standard Actions

⊕ Slam (necrotic) ✦ At-Will
Attack: Melee 3 (one creature); +24 vs. AC
Hit: 2d10 + 6 damage, and ongoing 10 necrotic damage (save ends).
Effect: The treant marks the target until the end of the treant's next turn.

⸭ Double Attack ✦ At-Will
Effect: The treant uses *slam* twice.

Minor Actions

⸭ Entangling Roots ✦ At-Will
Attack: Melee 4 (one creature); +22 vs. Reflex
Hit: The target falls prone. The target is restrained (save ends).

| Str 27 (+17) | Dex 14 (+11) | Wis 18 (+13) |
| Con 24 (+16) | Int 16 (+12) | Cha 22 (+15) |

Alignment evil | **Languages** Elven

TROGLODYTE

Foul-smelling creatures that dwell in the shallow depths of the Underdark, troglodytes are violent, primitive monsters that use force to take what they want.

Considered by many to be the most loathsome of all humanoids, troglodytes are degenerate reptile folk whose subterranean homes are warrens of filth and disease. Troglodytes are characterized by their foul stench and their primitive ways. They possess enough intelligence to speak and make weapons, and they are even more animalistic and barbaric than orcs and gnolls. A troglodyte is governed by instinct and primitive desires; it lacks the rational thought to resolve disputes through diplomacy. The vile reptile creatures take advantage of unwary travelers, eating the people and taking their valuables. Even a seasoned warrior or explorer might run afoul of troglodytes. As a result of such conflicts, a troglodyte lair becomes littered with trophies from kills, the value of which troglodytes remain oblivious of.

Loathsome Primitives: A troglodyte tribe consists of about thirty members. The creatures are xenophobic and war with other troglodyte tribes to guard their territory. Sometimes a conflict between multiple troglodyte warrens spills onto the surface of the world with deadly repercussions. In these cases, the troglodytes might forget about fighting each other and instead turn their attention to new prey. The other races of the Underdark have concluded that reasoning with troglodytes is impossible, so they enslave the creatures and force them to do their bidding. A troglodyte's penchant for wanton violence makes it difficult to control. Slave masters must remain vigilant lest the troglodyte

Troglodyte Mauler	Level 6 Soldier
Medium natural humanoid (reptile)	XP 250

HP 74; **Bloodied** 37	**Initiative** +6
AC 22, **Fortitude** 20, **Reflex** 17, **Will** 18	**Perception** +5
Speed 5	Darkvision

Troglodyte Stench ✦ Aura 1

Living enemies take a -2 penalty to attack rolls while in the aura.

STANDARD ACTIONS

⊕ **Greatclub** (weapon) ✦ **At-Will**

Attack: Melee 1 (one creature); +11 vs. AC

Hit: 4d4 + 4 damage.

Effect: The troglodyte marks the target until the end of the troglodyte's next turn.

⊕ **Claw** ✦ **At-Will**

Attack: Melee 1 (one creature); +11 vs. AC

Hit: 2d4 + 9 damage.

⊙ **Javelin** (weapon) ✦ **At-Will**

Attack: Ranged 10 (one creature); +11 vs. AC

Hit: 2d6 + 4 damage.

MINOR ACTIONS

✦ **Bite** ✦ **At-Will** (1/round)

Attack: Melee 1 (one creature granting combat advantage to the troglodyte); +9 vs. Fortitude

Hit: 3d6 + 4 damage. Until the end of the troglodyte's next turn, the target regains half the normal hit points from healing effects.

Skills Athletics +12, Endurance +12

Str 18 (+7)	**Dex** 12 (+4)	**Wis** 15 (+5)
Con 18 (+7)	**Int** 6 (+1)	**Cha** 8 (+2)

Alignment chaotic evil   **Languages** Draconic

Equipment greatclub, 2 javelins

slaves turn against them or resort to killing each other. Drow and duergar use troglodyte slaves as fodder in battles or as tools for devastating smaller enemy settlements.

Servants of Torog: Troglodytes worship many dark entities, the most prominent of which is Torog, the King that Crawls. Torog is the god of torture and imprisonment, and he dwells in the deepest reaches of the Underdark. The troglodytes' primitive religion calls for them to make sacrifices to Torog in order to earn the god's favor. Because Torog feeds on agony and torture, subjects of troglodyte sacrifices usually endure hours of torment before death comes. Sacrifices are often conducted in the deepest chambers of a lair. These rooms contain unhatched troglodyte eggs that await the blessing of the King that Crawls. A troglodyte tribe rarely conducts a raid for the sole purpose of collecting victims for sacrifice. When a tribe lacks for captives, though, a group gathers to go to the surface to drag back the weakest and most vulnerable individuals it can find.

Raiders from the Underdark: Food and other resources are frequently scarce in the Underdark because of heavy competition between subterranean races. These shortages drive troglodytes to launch raids on surface settlements. These raids are swift and straightforward; troglodytes lack the capacity for trickery or cunning plans. The most shrewdness a tribe exhibits is attacking outlying farms and homes in order to draw out a settlement's defenders, which can then be more easily slaughtered. Otherwise, a troglodyte raiding party distinguishes only between strong settlements and weak settlements. A troglodyte tribe might pillage a small, undefended village to revel in violence, but it will risk an attack on a larger settlement only out of greed for plunder. Troglodytes rarely attack towns or cities, because they tend to have more organized defenses. Occasionally a group of troglodytes emerges into a city through a sewer or a cellar. This advantage can lead troglodytes to launch nighttime raids even in well-fortified locations. Troglodytes rarely take captives, and they don't leave them alive for long. Anyone taken back to a troglodyte warren is either devoured or sacrificed to Torog within a matter of hours or days. A rescuer wishing to find a victim alive must act quickly after a troglodyte raid.

Troglodyte Grunt	Level 6 Minion Skirmisher
Medium natural humanoid (reptile)	XP 63

HP 1; a missed attack never damages a minion.	Initiative +6
AC 20, Fortitude 20, Reflex 18, Will 16	Perception +5
Speed 5	Darkvision

TRAITS

Troglodyte Stench ✦ Aura 1
Living enemies take a -2 penalty to attack rolls while in the aura.

STANDARD ACTIONS

⊕ **Club** (weapon) ✦ **At-Will**
Attack: Melee 1 (one creature); +11 vs. AC
Hit: 7 damage.
Effect: The troglodyte shifts up to 2 squares.

TRIGGERED ACTIONS

Scatter ✦ At-Will
Trigger: The troglodyte is targeted by a close or an area attack.
Effect (Immediate Interrupt): The troglodyte shifts up to 2 squares to a square outside the triggering attack's area of effect.

Str 18 (+7)	Dex 13 (+4)	Wis 14 (+5)
Con 16 (+6)	Int 4 (+0)	Cha 9 (+2)
Alignment chaotic evil	**Languages** Draconic	
Equipment club		

"Once you get past the stench . . . well, little remains but a brutal savage trying to gut you with a bone spear."
—Kalistros of Maelbrathyr

Troglodyte Thrasher

Level 7 Brute

Medium natural humanoid (reptile)

XP 300

HP 100; **Bloodied** 50
AC 19, **Fortitude** 21, **Reflex** 17, **Will** 19
Speed 5

Initiative +5
Perception +6
Darkvision

Traits

Troglodyte Stench ✦ Aura 1

Living enemies take a -2 penalty to attack rolls while in the aura.

Standard Actions

⊕ **Claw ✦ At-Will**

Attack: Melee 1 (one creature); +12 vs. AC
Hit: 4d6 + 5 damage.

† **Tooth and Claw ✦ At-Will**

Attack: Melee 1 (one or two creatures); +12 vs. AC. If the troglodyte targets only one creature, it can make this attack twice against that creature.
Hit: 2d6 + 2 damage. If this attack bloodies the target, the troglodyte uses *claw* against the target.

Str 18 (+7)	Dex 15 (+5)	Wis 16 (+6)
Con 20 (+8)	Int 4 (+0)	Cha 11 (+3)

Alignment chaotic evil   **Languages** Draconic

Troglodyte Impaler

Level 7 Artillery

Medium natural humanoid (reptile)

XP 300

HP 69; **Bloodied** 34
AC 22, **Fortitude** 22, **Reflex** 19, **Will** 17
Speed 5

Initiative +5
Perception +9
Darkvision

Traits

Troglodyte Stench ✦ Aura 1

Living enemies take a -2 penalty to attack rolls while in the aura.

Standard Actions

⊕ **Spear** (weapon) **✦ At-Will**

Attack: Melee 1 (one creature); +12 vs. AC
Hit: 2d8 + 4 damage.

⊗ **Javelin** (weapon) **✦ At-Will**

Attack: Ranged 10 (one creature); +14 vs. AC
Hit: 3d6 + 5 damage.

� **Impaling Shot** (weapon) **✦ Recharge** ⚅ ⚅ ⚅

Requirement: The troglodyte must be wielding a javelin.
Attack: Ranged 10 (one creature); +14 vs. AC
Hit: 3d6 + 5 damage, and the target is restrained (save ends).

Skills Athletics +12, Endurance +13

Str 19 (+7)	Dex 14 (+5)	Wis 13 (+4)
Con 21 (+8)	Int 7 (+1)	Cha 9 (+2)

Alignment chaotic evil   **Languages** Draconic
Equipment spear, 6 javelins

TROLL

The ultimate survivors, trolls can regenerate mortal wounds and regrow lost limbs. They are ugly, stupid creatures, always searching for their next meal.

After securing a lair, a troll spends its days hunting and eating anything edible that lives nearby. A troll is well suited for its lifestyle: Its long, strong arms are perfect for ripping off limbs, its jaws are massive enough to devour large hunks of flesh and bone, and its personality is cruel enough to enjoy every second of the process. Trolls know they have a reputation. People fear them, and trolls are glad to satisfy expectations. A troll believes that a victim paralyzed with terror tastes better, so it seeks out a weak-willed target long before it resorts to hunting a brave foe.

Trolls are notoriously stupid. A smart troll can barely outwit a normal human. Even a small child might be able to trick a troll. Of course, once a troll realizes it has been fooled, it will find the culprit and rip the creature apart. Conversing with a troll is an exercise in futility and frustration (and it requires a person to convince the troll not to eat him or her at first sight). Aside from recalling preferences in what it likes to eat, a troll can remember very little. At best, a troll might be able to recite a couple of short songs or a few phrases as taunts, even if they don't entirely make sense.

Troll	Level 9 Brute
Large natural humanoid	XP 400

HP 120; **Bloodied** 60	**Initiative** +8
AC 21, **Fortitude** 22, **Reflex** 18, **Will** 18	**Perception** +6
Speed 8	

TRAITS

Regeneration
The troll regains 5 hit points whenever it starts its turn and has at least 1 hit point. When the troll takes fire or acid damage, its regeneration does not function on its next turn.

Troll Healing (healing)
Whenever an attack that doesn't deal acid or fire damage reduces the troll to 0 hit points, the troll does not die and instead falls unconscious until the start of its next turn, when it returns to life with 15 hit points. If an attack hits the troll and deals any acid or fire damage while the troll is unconscious, it does not return to life in this way.

STANDARD ACTIONS

⊕ **Claw** ✦ **At-Will**
Attack: Melee 2 (one creature); +14 vs. AC
Hit: 3d6 + 7 damage. If the attack bloodies the target, the troll uses *claw* against it again.

Str 22 (+10)	Dex 18 (+8)	Wis 14 (+6)
Con 20 (+9)	Int 5 (+1)	Cha 9 (+3)
Alignment chaotic evil	**Languages** Common, Giant	

Battle Troll
Large natural humanoid

Level 12 Soldier
XP 700

HP 124; **Bloodied** 62	**Initiative** +12
AC 28, **Fortitude** 26, **Reflex** 24, **Will** 22	**Perception** +8
Speed 7	

TRAITS

Regeneration
The troll regains 5 hit points whenever it starts its turn and has at least 1 hit point. When the troll takes fire or acid damage, its regeneration does not function on its next turn.

Troll Healing (healing)
Whenever an attack that doesn't deal acid or fire damage reduces the troll to 0 hit points, the troll does not die and instead falls unconscious until the start of its next turn, when it returns to life with 15 hit points. If an attack hits the troll and deals any acid or fire damage while the troll is unconscious, it does not return to life in this way.

STANDARD ACTIONS

⊕ **Broadsword** (weapon) ✦ **At-Will**
Attack: Melee 2 (one creature); +17 vs. AC
Hit: 2d12 + 8 damage. If the attack bloodies the target, the troll uses *broadsword* against it again.
Effect: The troll marks the target until the end of the troll's next turn.

↢ **Sweeping Strike** (weapon) ✦ **At-Will**
Attack: Close blast 2 (enemies in the blast); +17 vs. AC
Hit: 2d12 + 5 damage, and the target falls prone.

Str 23 (+12)	**Dex** 19 (+10)	**Wis** 14 (+8)
Con 20 (+11)	**Int** 6 (+4)	**Cha** 10 (+6)

Alignment chaotic evil	**Languages** Common, Giant
Equipment scale armor, broadsword	

Slain by Fire or Acid: Troll flesh regrows at an alarming rate. Only burning a troll with fire or acid can keep the creature down. Anyone familiar with trolls carries a torch when traveling through their lands. When rumors spread that a troll has moved near a settlement, people sometimes leave torches burning on stakes near their doors. Most trolls aren't afraid of fire, though, so the torches just inform a troll that its soon-to-be victims are inside.

Lairs in the Wild: A troll lair is usually a grimy cave or an abandoned building overgrown with vegetation. Trolls prefer cozy lairs, so they pile up leaves, bones, and other filth to make beds. A troll cave can sometimes be located by searching for vultures circling above its lair. Trolls that are fearful of fire and acid might live on islands in foggy lakes, under bridges, or in places where water is accessible. Because trolls are resilient, they can live almost anywhere, from caves in the icy north of the Frostfell to abandoned dwellings in murky swamps.

"I don't care about light. The reason I always carry a burning torch? Trolls."

—Harbek of Hammerfast

Bladerager Troll — Level 12 Brute
Large natural humanoid — XP 700

HP 151; **Bloodied** 75 — **Initiative** +10
AC 24, **Fortitude** 26, **Reflex** 24, **Will** 23 — **Perception** +9
Speed 7

TRAITS

Regeneration
The troll regains 5 hit points whenever it starts its turn and has at least 1 hit point. When the troll takes fire or acid damage, its regeneration does not function on its next turn.

STANDARD ACTIONS

⊕ **Claw ✦ At-Will**
Attack: Melee 2 (one creature); +17 vs. AC
Hit: 3d10 + 9 damage. If the attack bloodies the target, the troll regains the use of *bladerager rend.*

⸸ **Bladerager Rend ✦ Encounter**
Attack: Melee 2 (one creature); +17 vs. AC
Hit: 4d10 + 5 damage, and ongoing 10 damage (save ends).
Miss: Half damage, and ongoing 5 damage (save ends).

TRIGGERED ACTIONS

↢ **Death Burst**
Trigger: The troll drops to 0 hit points.
Attack (No Action): Close burst 2 (creatures in the burst); +15 vs. Reflex
Hit: 4d6 + 7 damage.
Effect: The troll is destroyed.

Str 23 (+12)	**Dex** 18 (+10)	**Wis** 16 (+9)
Con 21 (+11)	**Int** 3 (+2)	**Cha** 8 (+5)

Alignment chaotic evil — **Languages** Common, Giant

The Rank and File: Villains, tyrants, and criminals recruit trolls into their gangs or armies, using the creatures for their muscle, toughness, and ability to inspire fear. Trolls don't always follow orders, though, so they can be undependable thugs and soldiers. Until a battle starts, they're undisciplined and reckless. Once a battle begins, a troll gleefully rips through foes, paying little heed to commands or directions. A troll soldier is content to be paid with a little gold and a lot of food, and it uses whatever gear it is provided with. Heavily armored battle trolls are a mainstay of large armies that fight for evil causes.

Fodder for Experiments: Sinister spellcasters capture trolls in order to tinker with their miraculous healing abilities. These experiments might be aimed at perfecting eternal life, creating the perfect soldier, or fulfilling a sadistic urge. As a result of these profane experiments, many varieties of trolls exist. These creatures, warped in mind and body, fight under the command of the foul spellcasters who spawned them. A bladerager troll, for example, is the result of a ritual that attaches blades and armor plates permanently to the body of a troll. The process typically drives the creature insane, making it even more violent and deadly than a normal troll. When a bladerager troll dies and the magic binding the blades and plates ends, shrapnel hurtles outward, skewering those who managed to slay the creature.

Ghost Troll Render

Level 13 Brute

Large natural humanoid (undead)

XP 800

HP 161; **Bloodied** 80

Initiative +10

AC 25, **Fortitude** 27, **Reflex** 24, **Will** 23

Perception +14

Speed fl y 7 (hover); phasing

Immune disease, poison

TRAITS

Insubstantial

The ghost troll takes half damage from all attacks, except those that deal force damage. When it takes acid, fire, or radiant damage, it loses this trait until the start of its next turn.

STANDARD ACTIONS

⊕ **Spirit Claw** ✦ At-Will

Attack: Melee 2 (one creature); +16 vs. Reflex

Hit: 3d10 + 10 damage.

⊹ **Terror Strike** (psychic) ✦ **Recharges** if the power misses

Attack: Melee 2 (one bloodied creature); +16 vs. Will

Hit: 5d6 + 12 psychic damage, and the target is slowed (save ends).

First Failed Saving Throw: The target is knocked unconscious instead of slowed (save ends). If the target takes damage, the effect also ends.

Str 24 (+13)	Dex 18 (+10)	Wis 16 (+9)
Con 21 (+11)	Int 5 (+3)	Cha 11 (+6)
Alignment chaotic evil	**Languages** Giant	

UMBER HULK

Horrors from the deepest Underdark caverns, umber hulks burrow through the earth in search of prey. When one bursts into a surface realm, its claws rend flesh and its gaze sows chaos among its victims.

Umber hulks are deadly predators that lurk in the dark spaces of the world. With their strange second set of eyes, they confuse, disorient, and madden, leaving creatures defenseless against their claws, which are strong enough to rip through stone.

Burrowing Beasts: An umber hulk uses its tough claws to cut through solid stone. It steadily scoops away rock as easily as a humanoid might shovel snow. As the creature swiftly digs, it hurls crumbling boulders behind it, creating tunnels just large enough to allow its hardened body to pass through.

Burrowing takes a lot of energy, so an umber hulk must eat often to replenish its strength. Although digging through solid stone is a loud and slow process, an umber hulk usually has a purpose or direction in its travels. In most cases, the creature burrows to create connections between existing tunnels. With its tremorsense, an umber hulk might detect an open space in nearby bedrock and then tunnel to discover what lies beyond.

Umber Hulk	Level 12 Elite Soldier
Large natural magical beast	XP 1,400

HP 248; **Bloodied** 124	**Initiative** +11
AC 28, **Fortitude** 25, **Reflex** 23, **Will** 22	**Perception** +13
Speed 5, burrow 2 (tunneling)	Darkvision, tremorsense 5
Saving Throws +2; **Action Points** 1	

STANDARD ACTIONS

⊕ **Claw ✦ At-Will**
Requirement: The umber hulk must not have a creature grabbed.
Attack: Melee 2 (one creature); +17 vs. AC
Hit: 3d6 + 10 damage.

⨑ **Double Attack ✦ At-Will**
Effect: The umber hulk uses *claw* twice. If both attacks hit the same target, the umber hulk grabs the target (escape DC 20).

⨑ **Rending Claws ✦ At-Will**
Effect: Melee 2 (one creature grabbed by the umber hulk). The target takes 40 damage.

MINOR ACTIONS

↢ **Confusing Gaze ✦ At-Will** (1/round)
Attack: Close blast 5 (creatures in the blast); +15 vs. Will
Hit: The umber hulk slides the target up to 5 squares, and the target is dazed until the end of the umber hulk's next turn.

Str 26 (+14)	**Dex** 16 (+9)	**Wis** 14 (+8)
Con 20 (+11)	**Int** 5 (+3)	**Cha** 11 (+6)

Alignment unaligned	**Languages** —	

Creators of Subterranean Passages: Through their tunnels, umber hulks string together caverns and dungeons into local networks of caves. While a purple worm might create a great highway between the grand caverns of the Underdark, umber hulks make the back streets and alleys.

The tunnels that an umber hulk creates are large enough for a creature smaller than it to walk comfortably, but creatures of equal size must squeeze, and creatures larger than the umber hulk cannot fit at all. Drow, duergar, and illithids use trained umber hulks to dig tunnels for them, although they must employ slaves to expand the tunnels to a more comfortable size.

Although an umber hulk leaves behind a passage when it burrows, the tunnel is not necessarily safe or easy to traverse. Debris sometimes chokes the path. An umber hulk has little need to clear or stabilize the tunnel, after all, since it can simply dig itself out.

"Two big bug eyes, two little eyes that can almost make you think there's a brain behind those huge mandibles— it's confusing just to look at the thing. Never mind whatever magic lets it dig into your mind like its claws dig through rock."

—Elior of Harkenwold

FRANCIS TSAI

Umber Hulk Tunneler — Level 15 Skirmisher
Large natural magical beast — XP 1,200

HP 148; **Bloodied** 74   **Initiative** +13
AC 29, **Fortitude** 28, **Reflex** 26, **Will** 25   **Perception** +15
Speed 5, burrow 2 (tunneling)   Darkvision, tremorsense 5

STANDARD ACTIONS

⊕ **Claw ✦ At-Will**

Attack: Melee 2 (one creature); +20 vs. AC

Hit: 1d8 + 7 damage.

† **Snatch and Run ✦ At-Will**

Effect: The umber hulk uses *claw* twice against the same target. If at least one of the attacks hits, the umber hulk shifts up to 5 squares, pulling the target with it to a square adjacent to it.

MINOR ACTIONS

↩ **Rebuffing Gaze** (psychic) ✦ **At-Will** (1/round)

Attack: Close blast 5 (enemies in the blast); +18 vs. Will

Hit: Until the end of the target's next turn, it takes 2d6 psychic damage whenever it enters a square closer to the umber hulk.

Str 22 (+13)	Dex 18 (+11)	Wis 16 (+10)
Con 20 (+12)	Int 5 (+4)	Cha 11 (+7)

Alignment unaligned   **Languages** –

Umber Hulk Bewilderer — Level 15 Controller
Large natural magical beast — XP 1,200

HP 148; **Bloodied** 74   **Initiative** +11
AC 29, **Fortitude** 28, **Reflex** 26, **Will** 25   **Perception** +15
Speed 5, burrow 2 (tunneling)   Darkvision, tremorsense 5

STANDARD ACTIONS

⊕ **Claw ✦ At-Will**

Attack: Melee 2 (one creature); +20 vs. AC

Hit: 1d8 + 6 damage, or 2d8 + 12 against a stunned or dazed target.

↩ **Stunning Gaze ✦ Recharge** ⚄ ⚅

Attack: Close blast 5 (enemies in the blast); +18 vs. Will

Hit: The target is stunned until the end of the umber hulk's next turn.

MINOR ACTIONS

↩ **Staggering Gaze** (psychic) ✦ **At-Will** (1/round)

Attack: Close blast 5 (enemies in the blast); +18 vs. Will

Hit: 1d10 + 5 psychic damage, and the umber hulk slides the target up to 5 squares.

Str 22 (+13)	Dex 18 (+11)	Wis 16 (+10)
Con 20 (+12)	Int 5 (+4)	Cha 11 (+7)

Alignment unaligned   **Languages** –

Ambushers Through Stone: Umber hulks are on a constant search for prey or carrion. Gifted with neither stealth or speed, an umber hulk uses its tremorsense to ambush prey. The monster first finds a road or well-trod passage and then digs a tunnel that comes to within a few feet of the opening. When the umber hulk detects movement through the wall or floor, it bursts through the remaining stone and attacks. By the time a surprised creature reacts, it often finds its body gripped in the monster's enormous claws.

Wild umber hulks do not distinguish between natural stone and that of buildings. They are just as likely to explode into a dungeon chamber as to appear out of the darkness of a cave. Umber hulk incursions into dwarven settlements and the sewers of human cities present a dire threat to those communities.

Unnerving Eyes: An umber hulk possesses two pairs of eyes: a set of small, black ones and a set of large, faceted ones. The large eyes are the source of an umber hulk's dangerous gaze. Depending on the variety of an umber hulk, its gaze might confound a foe, drive an enemy to attack its allies, or assault a creature's psyche. The magical power of an umber hulk's eyes cuts away at a creature's sanity as easily as the monster's claws sever flesh.

Deep Hulk	Level 17 Elite Brute
Large natural magical beast	XP 3,200

HP 404; **Bloodied** 202	**Initiative** +12
AC 29, **Fortitude** 30, **Reflex** 28, **Will** 27	**Perception** +16
Speed 5, burrow 2 (tunneling)	Darkvision, tremorsense 5
Saving Throws +2; **Action Points** 1	

STANDARD ACTIONS

⊕ **Claw ✦ At-Will**

Requirement: The deep hulk must not have a creature grabbed.
Attack: Melee 2 (one creature); +22 vs. AC
Hit: 4d8 + 12 damage.

⊹ **Double Attack ✦ At-Will**

Effect: The deep hulk uses *claw* twice. If both attacks hit the same target, the deep hulk grabs the target (escape DC 23).

⊹ **Rending Claws ✦ At-Will**

Effect: Melee 2 (one creature grabbed by the deep hulk). The target takes 60 damage.

↚ **Maddening Gaze** (charm) ✦ **At-Will**

Attack: Close blast 5 (enemies in the blast); +20 vs. Will
Hit: During its next turn, the target takes a standard action to make a basic attack against its nearest ally. If no ally is within range, the target instead takes a standard action to charge its nearest ally it is able to charge.

Str 26 (+16)	**Dex** 18 (+12)	**Wis** 16 (+11)
Con 22 (+14)	**Int** 5 (+5)	**Cha** 11 (+8)
Alignment unaligned	**Languages** –	

VAMPIRE

Awakened to an endless night, a vampire lusts for the life it lost and sates that hunger by drinking the blood of the living. In their dark and decadent dreams, they live in luxury, ruling over kingdoms of mortals who exist to satisfy their most sinister appetites.

Kings and queens of undeath, vampires rule the night. Some are fiends driven only by their lust for blood. These simple spawn are easily dispatched by those with skill. Other vampires are true lords of darkness, mighty creatures that have achieved a semblance of immortality and have come to control legions of vampires and other undead.

"There's something so pure about a vampire's evil, so perfect in its utter corruption. . . ."

Cloaked in Superstition: Vampires are the subject of many superstitions. Garlic and holy symbols are supposed to repel them. Tales say they cannot cross running water or pass the threshold of a house uninvited. Vampires might even be the source of such falsehoods, though it's likely that fear of the creatures propagates the rumors. Ultimately, few things can protect a person from a vampire other than a sturdy weapon or a powerful implement.

Elder Vampire Spawn	Level 10 Minion Soldier
Medium natural humanoid (undead)	XP 125

HP 1; a missed attack never damages a minion.   **Initiative** +11
AC 26, **Fortitude** 23, **Reflex** 22, **Will** 20   **Perception** +12
Speed 7, climb 4 (spider climb)   Darkvision
Immune disease, poison; **Resist** 10 necrotic

TRAITS

Destroyed by Sunlight
Whenever the vampire starts its turn in direct sunlight, it can take only a single move action during its turn. If it ends that turn in direct sunlight, it turns to ash and is destroyed.

STANDARD ACTIONS

⊕ **Claw ✦ At-Will**
Attack: Melee 1 (one creature); +15 vs. AC
Hit: 8 damage, and the vampire grabs the target (escape DC 18) if it does not have a creature grabbed.

✦ **Bite ✦ At-Will**
Attack: Melee 1 (one creature grabbed by the vampire); +15 vs. AC. If the target is dazed, the attack hits automatically.
Hit: 10 damage, and the target is dazed until the grab ends.

Str 21 (+10)	Dex 19 (+9)	Wis 15 (+7)
Con 18 (+9)	Int 9 (+4)	Cha 12 (+6)

Alignment evil	**Languages** Common

Only a couple of the superstitions about vampires are true: Vampires abhor sunlight, and they cast no shadows or reflections. Not surprisingly, any vampire that wishes to move unnoticed among the living tends to remain in poorly lit areas where mirrors and other reflective surfaces are absent.

Born from Death: Anyone who survives an attack from a vampire might fall prey to the vampire's curse, entering into a deep, deathlike sleep. A person under this curse is often assumed dead and ushered through funeral rites. When that person awakes at the next sunset, he or she is a vampire. If confined within a coffin, this vampire might already be buried or could be awaiting burial in a temple or a family member's home. Most vampires awaken as slavering spawn, but a few retain enough of themselves to emerge from death as true vampires.

> "... It'll tear at your throat like a ravenous beast, then smile at your companions as it dabs its blood-soaked lips with a silk napkin."
> —Terevan of Celduilon

Although a vampire might retain memories of its life, most of the emotional attachments are gone, replaced by the insatiable hunger for warm blood. Only the strongest bonds remain, and often they are negative emotions, such as hate or desire for revenge. Once-pure feelings become twisted by undeath: Love transforms into hungry obsession, and friendship becomes bitter jealousy.

Vampire Night Witch

Level 10 Controller

Medium natural humanoid (undead) — XP 500

HP 98; **Bloodied** 49 | **Initiative** +9
AC 24, **Fortitude** 20, **Reflex** 22, **Will** 24 | **Perception** +12
Speed 7, climb 4 (spider climb) | Darkvision
Immune disease, poison; **Resist** 10 necrotic; **Vulnerable** 5 radiant

TRAITS

Burned by Sunlight (radiant)
Whenever the vampire starts its turn in direct sunlight, it takes 5 radiant damage.

STANDARD ACTIONS

⊕ **Claw** ✦ At-Will
Attack: Melee 1 (one creature); +15 vs. AC
Hit: 4d6 + 4 damage.
Effect: The vampire slides the target up to 3 squares.

✦ **Bite** (healing) ✦ At-Will
Attack: Melee 1 (one dazed, dominated, stunned, or unconscious creature); +15 vs. AC
Hit: 3d10 + 10 damage, and the vampire regains 15 hit points.

⤳ **Dream Lure** (charm, psychic) ✦ At-Will
Attack: Ranged 5 (one creature); +13 vs. Will
Hit: 3d6 + 4 psychic damage, and the target is dazed until the end of its next turn.
Effect: The vampire pulls the target up to 3 squares.

TRIGGERED ACTIONS

Vanish into Shadow (illusion) ✦ Encounter
Trigger: The vampire takes damage while bloodied.
Effect (No Action): The vampire becomes invisible until the end of the encounter or until it attacks.

Skills Acrobatics +14, Athletics +13, Bluff +16, Insight +12, Stealth +14

Str 17 (+8)	**Dex** 18 (+9)	**Wis** 15 (+7)
Con 10 (+5)	**Int** 12 (+6)	**Cha** 22 (+11)

Alignment evil | **Languages** Common

Some sages whisper of rituals that can stop the transformation and awaken a person under the vampire's curse. If the transformation cannot be stopped in this way, then the only way to stop a person from becoming a vampire is to burn or dismember the body. This puts a vampire hunter in the awkward position of slaying a helpless innocent to prevent him or her from becoming a vile creature.

Chained to the Grave: Every vampire remains bound to its coffin, crypt, or grave site, requiring that the vampire rest there every day. Unlike most living humanoids, though, vampires must rest during daylight hours. If a vampire did not receive a formal burial, it must lie under a foot or so of earth at the place of its transition to undeath (a cave or a dungeon chamber beneath the earth also suffices). A vampire can move its place of burial or set up multiple places of burial by transporting a significant amount of grave dirt or a large coffin pieces to another location, where a similar resting place can be crafted.

Master Vampire
Medium natural humanoid (undead)

Level 12 Lurker
XP 700

HP 98; **Bloodied** 49
AC 26, **Fortitude** 25, **Reflex** 24, **Will** 24
Speed 7, climb 4 (spider climb)
Immune disease, poison; **Resist** 10 necrotic

Initiative +15
Perception +14
Darkvision

TRAITS

Burned by Sunlight (radiant)
Whenever the vampire starts its turn in direct sunlight, it takes 10 radiant damage.

Regeneration
The vampire regains 10 hit points whenever it starts its turn and has at least 1 hit point. When the vampire takes radiant damage, its regeneration does not function on its next turn.

STANDARD ACTIONS

⊕ **Claw** ✦ **At-Will**
Attack: Melee 1 (one creature); +17 vs. AC
Hit: 3d6 + 5 damage.

⸸ **Bite** (healing) ✦ **At-Will**
Attack: Melee 1 (one dazed, dominated, stunned, or unconscious creature); +17 vs. AC
Hit: 4d10 + 10 damage, and the vampire regains 20 hit points.

Cloud of Bats (polymorph) ✦ **At-Will**
Effect: The vampire assumes the form of a cloud of bats until the start of its next turn. While in this form, the vampire cannot attack but becomes insubstantial, gains fly 8 (hover), gains a +5 power bonus to Stealth checks, and can move through enemies' spaces.

⤳ **Dominating Gaze** (charm) ✦ **Recharge when no creature is dominated by this power**
Attack: Ranged 5 (one creature); +17 vs. Will
Hit: The target is dominated until the end of the vampire's next turn.

TRIGGERED ACTIONS

Mist Form (polymorph) ✦ **Encounter**
Trigger: The vampire takes damage while bloodied.
Effect (No Action): The vampire becomes insubstantial and gains fly 12. The vampire cannot attack or use *cloud of bats.* This effect lasts for 1 hour or until the vampire ends it as a minor action.

Skills Acrobatics +16, Athletics +17, Bluff +16, Insight +14, Stealth +16

Str 22 (+12)	**Dex** 20 (+11)	**Wis** 17 (+9)
Con 20 (+11)	**Int** 15 (+8)	**Cha** 21 (+11)

Alignment evil   **Languages** Common

A vampire that fails to find rest each day struggles to maintain its strength and sanity. As days without rest go by, a vampire goes mad with hunger for blood, eventually coming to desire the blood of its former race above anything else. Its feeding becomes a strange, externalized self-destruction. A vampire crazed by such bloodlust cannot heal damage to its body until it rests.

WRAITH

Bereft of life and soul, the intangible wraith feels nothing except loss, hate, and wrath.

When a person dies and his or her spirit departs, the animus can remain, clinging to a vestige of life. The animus can become a wraith, an insubstantial creature that emerges amid the vanishing memories of a person's life; it becomes trapped in an endless afterlife, tortured by remembered sensations and driven mad by a hunger to reclaim the life it once had.

Life's Castaways: Life consists of three parts: body, spirit, and will. Without will, the body ceases to function and the spirit leaves. Sages call the will the animus, and they regard it as the shadow of the soul. When a body dies or a spirit departs, sometimes the animus remains in the world. Without the spirit, though, the animus has no purpose, and it runs amok. Like many undead, a wraith is the result of an unfettered animus.

Wraith	Level 5 Lurker
Medium shadow humanoid (undead)	XP 200

HP 53; **Bloodied** 26	**Initiative** +10
AC 19, **Fortitude** 17, **Reflex** 18, **Will** 15	**Perception** +2
Speed 0, fly 6 (hover); phasing	Darkvision
Immune disease, poison; **Resist** 10 necrotic	

TRAITS

Insubstantial
The wraith takes half damage from all attacks, except those that deal force damage. Whenever the wraith takes radiant damage, it loses this trait until the start of its next turn.

Spawn Wraith
When the wraith kills a humanoid, that humanoid becomes a wraith figment at the start of this wraith's next turn. The new wraith appears in the space where the humanoid died or in the nearest unoccupied square, and it rolls a new initiative check. The new wraith acts under the Dungeon Master's control.

STANDARD ACTIONS

⊕ **Shadow Touch** (necrotic) ✦ **At-Will**
Attack: Melee 1 (one creature); +8 vs. Reflex
Hit: 2d6 + 6 necrotic damage, or 4d6 + 14 necrotic damage if the wraith was invisible to the target when it attacked.

TRIGGERED ACTIONS

Shadow Glide (teleportation) ✦ **At-Will**
Trigger: An attack that does not deal force or radiant damage hits the wraith.
Effect (Free Action): The wraith becomes invisible until it hits or misses with an attack or until the end of the encounter. The wraith teleports up to 6 squares and cannot attack until the end of its next turn.

Skills Stealth +11		
Str 4 (-1)	**Dex** 18 (+6)	**Wis** 10 (+2)
Con 17 (+5)	**Int** 6 (+0)	**Cha** 15 (+4)
Alignment chaotic evil	**Languages** Common	

When a wraith slays a living humanoid, another wraith emerges from that person's body within a few minutes, or within a few seconds in areas of intense necrotic energy. Even when powerful magic returns a person to life, his or her wraith remains. A restored cadaver regains its soul and heals fatal wounds, but rather than it regaining its former animus, a new one forms to close the gap between body and spirit. A wraith is consumed by the blackest hate for its twin, and it goes to great lengths to murder the person carrying the new animus.

Bereft of Body: Without the interme-diary of the body, wraiths experience the world as if through a veil of shadow. Although everything has some weight and substance, nothing feels solid, and everything is cold. Colors appear dim, and light is hazy. Nearby sounds seem to come from a great distance away. A wraith can remember the taste and smell of things, but it can no longer experience the physical sensations.

As intangible creatures, wraiths can move through solid objects as easily as a corporeal creature might move through fog. A newly formed wraith might initially avoid passing through walls or doors, recalling them to be solid. As these memories fade, a wraith takes to using its power to pass through barriers in order to find and kill living creatures out of a hunger for the life it lost.

Haunted by the Past: Soulless undead, such as wraiths, retain memories of their previous loves, passions, and interests, but these are dim echoes of the life experiences. Even the strongest emotions from a wraith's life become little more than faint feelings. A wraith might pause to stare at something that fascinated it once, or it might curb its wrath in acknowledgment of a past friendship. Such actions are rare, though. Instead, recognition of something from its past usually provokes mindless fury. The wraith of a caring husband might, for example, deliberately seek out its former wife to exact blind vengeance without ever comprehending why it is angry.

Without a soul, a wraith lacks any true sense of honor, morality, or reason. When it awakens and realizes that all it has lost is now beyond its grasp, a madness sets in, and the wraith slays any around its body. This action does nothing to abate a wraith's anger and usually incites the creature further. The souls of the people a wraith slays rarely tarry, leaving a wraith more alone than before and causing the creature only more anguish at its circumstance.

Many Hateful Forms: Although wraiths do not resemble their former bodies, they still vary widely in form. Some wraiths are shreds of their former selves, harrowing reminders of the horrors of death. Other wraiths gibber insanely, driven mad by their inability to comprehend their situation. A wraith might recall its ambition or leadership in life, acting as commander over a cadre of wraiths. Regardless of its kind, though, a wraith rarely possesses the mental faculties or the charisma to formulate long-term plots. Instead, a wraith is usually content to haunt an area where it can exact revenge on the living, bowing only to the might of powerful undead and necromancers.

Mad Wraith	Level 6 Controller
Medium shadow humanoid (undead)	XP 250

HP 73; Bloodied 36	Initiative +8
AC 20, Fortitude 16, Reflex 19, Will 18	Perception -1
Speed 0, fly 6 (hover); phasing	Darkvision
Immune disease, poison; Resist 10 necrotic	

TRAITS

☼ **Mad Whispers** (psychic) ✦ **Aura 3**

Any enemy that ends its turn in the aura takes 5 psychic damage, and the wraith slides it up to 2 squares.

Insubstantial

The wraith takes half damage from all attacks, except those that deal force damage. Whenever the wraith takes radiant damage, it loses this trait until the start of its next turn.

Spawn Wraith

When the wraith kills a humanoid, that humanoid becomes a wraith figment at the start of this wraith's next turn. The new wraith appears in the space where the humanoid died or in the nearest unoccupied square, and it rolls a new initiative check. The new wraith acts under the Dungeon Master's control.

STANDARD ACTIONS

⊕ **Touch of Madness** (psychic) ✦ **At-Will**

Attack: Melee 1 (one creature); +9 vs. Will

Hit: 2d6 + 7 psychic damage, and the target takes a -2 penalty to all defenses (save ends).

↓ **Touch of Chaos** (charm, psychic) ✦ **Recharge** ⚃ ⚄

Attack: Melee 1 (one creature); +9 vs. Will

Hit: 2d6 + 7 psychic damage, and the wraith slides the target up to 5 squares. The target must then use a free action to make a basic attack against its nearest ally.

Miss: Half damage, and the wraith slides the target up to 2 squares.

Skills Stealth +13		
Str 6 (+1)	Dex 20 (+8)	Wis 3 (-1)
Con 17 (+6)	Int 11 (+3)	Cha 19 (+7)
Alignment chaotic evil	Languages Common	

Wraith Figment — Level 6 Minion Skirmisher

Medium shadow humanoid (undead) — XP 63

HP 1; a missed attack never damages a minion. | Initiative +7
AC 18, **Fortitude** 16, **Reflex** 20, **Will** 17 | Perception +2
Immune disease, poison; **Resist** 10 necrotic | Darkvision
Speed fly 6 (hover); phasing

STANDARD ACTIONS

⊕ **Shadow Caress** (necrotic) ✦ **At-Will**

Attack: Melee 1 (one creature); +9 vs. Reflex

Hit: 7 necrotic damage, and the target is slowed until the end of the wraith's next turn.

MOVE ACTIONS

Shadow Glide ✦ **Encounter**

Effect: The wraith figment shifts up to 6 squares.

Skills Stealth +10

Str 3 (-2)	**Dex** 17 (+5)	**Wis** 10 (+2)
Con 13 (+3)	**Int** 4 (-1)	**Cha** 15 (+4)

Alignment chaotic evil | **Languages** —

Sovereign Wraith — Level 8 Soldier

Medium shadow humanoid (undead) — XP 350

HP 89; **Bloodied** 44 | Initiative +11
AC 24, **Fortitude** 20, **Reflex** 22, **Will** 21 | Perception +6
Speed 0, fly 6 (hover); phasing | Darkvision
Immune disease, poison; **Resist** 10 necrotic

TRAITS

Insubstantial

The wraith takes half damage from all attacks, except those that deal force damage. Whenever the wraith takes radiant damage, it loses this trait until the start of its next turn.

Spawn Wraith

When the wraith kills a humanoid, that humanoid becomes a wraith figment at the start of this wraith's next turn. The new wraith appears in the space where the humanoid died or in the nearest unoccupied square, and it rolls a new initiative check. The new wraith acts under the Dungeon Master's control.

STANDARD ACTIONS

⊕ **Spectral Sword** (necrotic) ✦ **At-Will**

Attack: Melee 1 (one creature); +11 vs. Fortitude

Hit: 2d8 + 2 necrotic damage, and the target grants combat advantage and takes ongoing 5 necrotic damage (save ends both).

Effect: The wraith marks the target until the end of the wraith's next turn.

⨋ **Lonely Death** (illusion) ✦ **Recharge** ⚁ ⚂ ⚃

Effect: The wraith uses *spectral sword*. If the attack hits, all creatures except the wraith are invisible to the target (save ends).

Skills Stealth +14

Str 15 (+6)	**Dex** 20 (+9)	**Wis** 15 (+6)
Con 17 (+7)	**Int** 14 (+6)	**Cha** 19 (+8)

Alignment evil | **Languages** Common

YUAN-TI

Whether they walk on two legs or slither on a scaled tail, the snake-headed yuan-ti plot dominion over all. Their sibilant whispers lurk behind many vile plots and dire calamities, though few discover their machinations until it's too late.

Those who know of this sinister and secretive race of serpentine creatures rarely speak their name above a whisper. The reptilian humanoids seem to come writhing out of myth and bedtime stories. Although rarely seen, yuan-ti have been ubiquitous for generations, their secret existence a nightmarish reality since the end of the Dawn War.

(Left to right) yuan-ti malison sharp-eye, malison stalker, malison chanter

World Domination: When the gods were in the midst of creating the creatures of the world, Zehir found he could not craft his own creature, so he decided to steal one. He appealed to Avandra to teach him how to change the creations of others. At first Avandra refused, but through his silver tongue, Zehir convinced her. Despite being enamored of Zehir, Avandra did attach a condition to his power of alteration: He could change a creature only with its creator's permission. Zehir saw only one way to have his will: to kill humanity's creator so that no one existed to deny him the permission he required.

After the Dawn War ended and the other gods had exhausted much of their strength, Zehir remained strong and vigilant for his opportunity. When the time came, he murdered the now-forgotten creator of humans and laid claim to the race as his own. Under his powers of alteration, countless humans were transformed into members of a serpentine race that became known as yuan-ti. For a time, the other immortals could do nothing to halt the progress of these creatures as they formed the great yuan-ti empire of Zannad. Eventually, when the other gods had regained their strength, they forced Zehir to relinquish control of the human race. The gods squabbled over who should have power over humanity, and in the end, nothing was decided, for the contest continues today. As a result, humans have the potential to be both the most corruptible and most devout of any race.

"Perhaps we once were human, as you say. But what does it matter? Zehir has made us so much more."

—Vastrana, yuan-ti malison

During the time of the empire, yuan-ti lorded over human servants and monstrous slaves, living as royalty. Over time, those who suffered under the yuan-ti united and worked to divide and defeat their former masters. These rebellions led to the first human empires and an end to Zannad. Since then, yuan-ti have schemed to regain their former glory, and they have come close many times. Yuan-ti orchestrate the actions of cultists of Zehir, subtly shifting events in their favor. In a few places, such as the Zahnshahan, the Slithering City, yuan-ti rule openly as in the days of old. For now, these serpentine city-states treat neighbors as friends and allies, at least until the neighboring regions are sufficiently weakened by yuan-ti plots.

Yuan-ti Malison Stalker	**Level 13 Skirmisher**
Medium natural humanoid (reptile)	XP 800

HP 126; **Bloodied** 63	**Initiative** +14
AC 27, **Fortitude** 24, **Reflex** 27, **Will** 25	**Perception** +13
Speed 7	
Resist 10 poison	

STANDARD ACTIONS

⊕ **Morningstar** (poison, weapon) ✦ At-Will
Attack: Melee 1 (one creature); +18 vs. AC
Hit: 2d8 + 7 damage, and the target cannot mark enemies and takes ongoing 5 poison damage (save ends both).

⊙ **Poisoned Dagger** (poison, weapon) ✦ At-Will
Attack: Ranged 10 (one creature); +18 vs. AC
Hit: 3d4 + 6 damage, and ongoing 5 poison damage (save ends).

↓⟩ **Slither Strike** ✦ At-Will
Effect: The yuan-ti ends any marking effect on it and then shifts up to 4 squares. At any point during the shift, the yuan-ti can use *morningstar* or *poisoned dagger*.

Skills Bluff +15, Insight +13, Stealth +17

Str 17 (+9)	**Dex** 22 (+12)	**Wis** 14 (+8)
Con 14 (+8)	**Int** 19 (+10)	**Cha** 19 (+10)

Alignment evil **Languages** Common, Draconic
Equipment morningstar, 5 daggers

Yuan-ti Malison Sharp-Eye
Level 13 Artillery
Medium natural humanoid (reptile)   XP 800

HP 98; **Bloodied** 49
AC 27, **Fortitude** 23, **Reflex** 26, **Will** 24
Speed 7
Resist 10 poison

Initiative +12
Perception +13

TRAITS
Chameleon Defense
The yuan-ti has partial concealment from creatures more than 3 squares away from it.

STANDARD ACTIONS
⊕ **Scimitar** (weapon) ✦ **At-Will**
Attack: Melee 1 (one creature); +18 vs. AC
Hit: 3d8 + 4 damage.

⊗ **Longbow** (poison, weapon) ✦ **At-Will**
Attack: Ranged 20 (one creature); +20 vs. AC
Hit: 3d10 + 6 damage, and the yuan-ti makes a secondary attack against the target.
  Secondary Attack: +18 vs. Fortitude
  Hit: The target is dazed and takes ongoing 5 poison damage (save ends both).

Str 18 (+10)	Dex 23 (+12)	Wis 14 (+8)
Con 14 (+8)	Int 12 (+7)	Cha 18 (+10)

Alignment evil   **Languages** Common, Draconic
Equipment scimitar, longbow, 20 arrows

Yuan-ti Abomination
Level 14 Soldier
Large natural humanoid (reptile)   XP 1,000

HP 140; **Bloodied** 70
AC 30, **Fortitude** 28, **Reflex** 26, **Will** 25
Speed 7, climb 7
Resist 10 poison

Initiative +13
Perception +10

STANDARD ACTIONS
⊕ **Bastard Sword** (poison, weapon) ✦ **At-Will**
Attack: Melee 2 (one creature); +19 vs. AC
Hit: 2d12 + 4 damage, and the yuan-ti marks the target until the end of the yuan-ti's next turn. In addition, the target takes ongoing 5 poison damage (save ends).

↓ **Bite** (poison) ✦ **At-Will**
Attack: Melee 1 (one creature grabbed by the yuan-ti); +17 vs. Fortitude
Hit: 2d12 + 6 poison damage, and ongoing 10 poison damage (save ends).

MINOR ACTIONS
↓ **Grasping Coils** ✦ **At-Will** (1/round)
Requirement: The yuan-ti must not have a creature grabbed.
Attack: Melee 2 (one creature); +17 vs. Reflex
Hit: The yuan-ti pulls the target 1 square and then grabs it (escape DC 21).

Str 22 (+13)	Dex 18 (+11)	Wis 16 (+10)
Con 20 (+12)	Int 12 (+8)	Cha 14 (+9)

Alignment evil   **Languages** Draconic
Equipment bastard sword

Poisonous Plots: Yuan-ti learn well from the lessons of past failures. They are patient, hatching plots that extend for generations. They plan multiple contingencies, so that when one avenue to power becomes blocked, another opens up. Many people of good intention receive encouragement and rewards from yuan-ti or those who serve yuan-ti. A yuan-ti tries to influence people not through force or fear but through the promise of wealth, fame, or helping others. Yuan-ti direct the actions of those who attract their interest, employing more subtlety than mind flayers and more cunning than drow.

Vile Acts and Cruelty: As subtle and cunning as yuan-ti are, they sometimes employ openly evil tactics. A cult of Zehir might infiltrate a city under the guise of a beneficial organization or an elite secret society. Members of the cult, called snaketongue cultists, might be of any humanoid race. They gain serpentine traits and special powers in return for loyalty. Proving one's loyalty usually requires a person to commit a heinous act, such as murder, kidnapping, enslavement, or extortion. Members of the cult perform rituals that force a physical transformation upon a victim. The snaketongue cultists convince a victim that he or she has no option but to serve the yuan-ti, now that the individual is marked by Zehir.

Yuan-ti Malison Chanter	Level 15 Artillery
Medium natural humanoid (reptile)	XP 1,200

HP 118; **Bloodied** 59	**Initiative** +13
AC 29, **Fortitude** 25, **Reflex** 27, **Will** 28	**Perception** +13
Speed 7	
Resist 10 poison	

TRAITS

Bloody Scales
While bloodied, the yuan-ti gains a +2 bonus to speed and a +2 bonus to all defenses.

STANDARD ACTIONS

⊕ **Bite** (poison) ✦ **At-Will**
Attack: Melee 1 (one creature); +18 vs. Fortitude
Hit: 2d6 + 6 damage, and ongoing 5 poison damage (save ends).

⊗ **Mind Warp** (psychic) ✦ **At-Will**
Attack: Ranged 20 (one creature); +20 vs. Will
Hit: 4d6 + 9 psychic damage, and the target takes a –2 penalty to attack rolls until the end of the yuan-ti's next turn.

⊁ **Poisoned Domination** (charm) ✦ **Recharge** when first bloodied
Attack: Ranged 20 (one creature taking ongoing poison damage); +20 vs. Will
Hit: The target is dominated until the end of the yuan-ti's next turn.

TRIGGERED ACTIONS

Deflect Attack ✦ **Recharge** ⚁ ⚂ ⚃
Trigger: A melee or a ranged attack hits the yuan-ti.
Effect (Immediate Interrupt): The triggering attack instead hits one of the yuan-ti's allies adjacent to it.

Skills Bluff +19, Insight +18, Stealth +18		
Str 16 (+10)	**Dex** 22 (+13)	**Wis** 22 (+13)
Con 22 (+13)	**Int** 25 (+14)	**Cha** 25 (+14)
Alignment evil	**Languages** Common, Draconic	

ZOMBIE

These mindless, shambling corpses murder anyone not swift enough to get away.

From somewhere in the darkness comes a thump and a scuffle. As the noise comes again, drawing closer, a gurgling moan can be heard–the rattling wheeze of rotten lungs pressing air out. A form lurches into view, dragging one foot as it raises bloated arms and broken hands like a child seeking an embrace. This creature is a zombie, and it blindly seeks to crush life.

Many Hideous Forms: Fueled by dark magic, malevolent forces, dire curses, or angry spirits, zombies are animate corpses. Any corpse with flesh suffices to make a zombie. It might be a dead warrior from a battlefield, distended from days in the sun, guts trailing from a mortal wound. It might be a muddy cadaver of a woman recently buried and risen again, leaving maggots and worms in her wake. A zombie could wash ashore or rise from a marsh, swollen and reeking from weeks in the water. A zombie could instead appear alive, crafted from a recently deceased corpse.

A zombie need not be the size of a normal humanoid, or even humanoid in form. When a necromancer or a natural phenomenon causes a corpse to rise, the corpse could belong to the smallest beast or the largest giant. When a zombie plague infects a city, any size or kind of creature can be affected–horses, dogs, children, cats–anything that has a pulse.

WAYNE REYNOLDS

Grasping Zombie

Medium natural animate (undead)

Level 1 Brute
XP 100

HP 33; **Bloodied** 16
AC 13, **Fortitude** 14, **Reflex** 11, **Will** 11
Speed 4
Immune disease, poison

Initiative -1
Perception -1
Darkvision

TRAITS

Zombie Weakness

A critical hit automatically reduces the zombie to 0 hit points.

STANDARD ACTIONS

 Slam ✦ At-Will

Attack: Melee 1 (one creature); +6 vs. AC

Hit: 1d12 + 3 damage, or 1d12 + 8 against a grabbed target.

⸸ Zombie Grasp ✦ At-Will

Attack: Melee 1 (one creature); +4 vs. Reflex

Hit: The zombie grabs the target (escape DC 12) if it does not have a creature grabbed.

TRIGGERED ACTIONS

Deathless Hunger ✦ Encounter

Trigger: The zombie is reduced to 0 hit points, but not by a critical hit.

Effect (No Action): Roll a d20. On a 15 or higher, the zombie is instead reduced to 1 hit point.

| Str 16 (+3) | Dex 8 (-1) | Wis 8 (-1) |
| Con 13 (+1) | Int 1 (-5) | Cha 3 (-4) |

| **Alignment** unaligned | **Languages** – |

Shadows of Life: Zombies possess a semblance of life. Sludgelike blood trickles through their veins, and cold, rank breath gusts from their lungs. And yet death has rendered zombies immune to pain, disease, and poison. Although their lungs spasm and stomachs churn, they need not breathe, eat, or sleep. Undeath has given them the power to see in darkness—even without eyes—and the necrotic energy that fuels the creatures makes them tireless.

Zombies do not require food, but some are driven by a hunger for the flesh of the living. These zombies consume their victims while remaining heedless of their struggles and screams. A zombie feasts on a body until another living meal comes along or until the chill of death settles over a body. Some zombies hunger for a particular part of the body, such as the heart or the brain, but such peculiar obsessions are usually the byproduct of a zombie's creator.

"Now zombies, they still have flesh and sinew to hold them in one piece, more or less. It makes them so much more . . . persistent."

—Kalarel,
scion of Orcus

Soulless, Fearless, and Stupid: For a zombie to be animated, a body's soul must have departed. What remains in the corpse is an animus, a vital spark that drives the body without thought or conscience. Without a soul or memories, a zombie has no more humanity or intelligence than a simple animal. As a result, it also lacks a sense of self-preservation. Unless a zombie is properly commanded, a zombie might beat at the door of a home while its residents escape out a nearby window. Despite a zombie's stupidity, the creature remains a dangerous foe due to its resilience. A zombie might step off a ledge to reach a foe and in so doing break its legs. Instead of ceasing its pursuit, though, the zombie will drag its broken legs behind it as it claws toward its target. Another zombie might walk right through a fire and become ignited in flames as it attacks a foe.

A Terrifying Plague: In most cases, a zombie serves its creator or rises in response to the defilement of a sacred location. At rare times, zombies arise in the hundreds. These zombie plagues are provoked by cosmic, magical, or divine events. A zombie plague might be the result of an angry god, a magical experiment gone wrong, a powerful ritual, or a falling star. When the event occurs, the bodies of the dead claw out of their graves and attack the living. Anyone who dies as a result of such an assault soon becomes a zombie after acquiring the disease or curse that the zombies carry. These terrifying plagues can consume an entire civilization if left unchecked.

Hulking Zombie	Level 4 Brute
Large natural animate (undead)	XP 175

HP 70; **Bloodied** 35	**Initiative** +1
AC 16, **Fortitude** 18, **Reflex** 14, **Will** 14	**Perception** +1
Speed 4	Darkvision
Immune disease, poison	

TRAITS

Zombie Weakness
A critical hit automatically reduces the zombie to 0 hit points.

STANDARD ACTIONS

⊕ **Slam** ✦ At-Will
Attack: Melee 2 (one creature); +9 vs. AC
Hit: 2d12 + 2 damage, or 2d12 + 7 against a prone target or one that is grabbed by another creature.

⊕ **Zombie Rush** ✦ At-Will
Effect: The zombie charges and makes the following attack in place of a basic melee attack.
Attack: Melee 2 (one creature); +7 vs. Fortitude
Hit: 2d12 + 2 damage, and the zombie pushes the target 1 square and knocks it prone.

TRIGGERED ACTIONS

Deathless Hunger ✦ Encounter
Trigger: The zombie is reduced to 0 hit points, but not by a critical hit.
Effect (No Action): Roll a d20. On a 15 or higher, the zombie is instead reduced to 1 hit point.

Str 20 (+7)	**Dex** 8 (+1)	**Wis** 8 (+1)
Con 20 (+7)	**Int** 1 (−3)	**Cha** 3 (−2)

Alignment unaligned	**Languages** —

Flesh-Crazed Zombie
Level 4 Skirmisher

Medium natural animate (undead) — XP 175

HP 55; **Bloodied** 27	**Initiative** +6
AC 18, **Fortitude** 17, **Reflex** 16, **Will** 14	**Perception** +3
Speed 6 (8 when charging)	Darkvision
Immune disease, poison	

TRAITS

Flesh-Crazed Charge

While the zombie is charging, its movement does not provoke opportunity attacks.

Zombie Weakness

A critical hit automatically reduces the zombie to 0 hit points.

STANDARD ACTIONS

⊕ **Club ✦ At-Will**

Attack: Melee 1 (one creature); +9 vs. AC

Hit: 1d8 + 6 damage, or 2d8 + 6 if the zombie charged the target.

⊹ **Bite ✦ At-Will**

Attack: Melee 1 (one creature); +9 vs. AC

Hit: 2d6 + 5 damage, and the target is dazed until the end of the zombie's next turn.

TRIGGERED ACTIONS

Deathless Hunger ✦ Encounter

Trigger: The zombie is reduced to 0 hit points, but not by a critical hit.

Effect (No Action): Roll a d20. On a 15 or higher, the zombie is instead reduced to 1 hit point.

Str 18 (+6)	**Dex** 15 (+4)	**Wis** 13 (+3)
Con 15 (+4)	**Int** 1 (-3)	**Cha** 3 (-2)

Alignment unaligned **Languages** –
Equipment club

Zombie Shambler
Level 5 Minion Brute

Medium natural animate (undead) — XP 50

HP 1; a missed attack never damages a minion.	**Initiative** +1
AC 17, **Fortitude** 18, **Reflex** 15, **Will** 15	**Perception** +1
Speed 4	Darkvision
Immune disease, poison	

STANDARD ACTIONS

⊕ **Slam ✦ At-Will**

Attack: Melee 1 (one creature); +10 vs. AC

Hit: 8 damage.

TRIGGERED ACTIONS

Deathless Hunger ✦ Encounter

Trigger: The zombie is reduced to 0 hit points, but not by a critical hit.

Effect (No Action): Roll a d20. On a 15 or higher, the zombie is instead reduced to 1 hit point.

Str 18 (+6)	**Dex** 8 (+1)	**Wis** 8 (+1)
Con 15 (+4)	**Int** 1 (-3)	**Cha** 3 (-2)

Alignment unaligned **Languages** –

Appendix: Animals

This appendix offers statistics for some common animals.

Bear

Bear	Level 5 Brute
Large natural beast	XP 200

HP 80; **Bloodied** 40	**Initiative** +3
AC 17, **Fortitude** 19, **Reflex** 16, **Will** 16	**Perception** +3
Speed 8	

TRAITS

Devour
Any creature grabbed by the bear at the start of the bear's turn takes 1d8 + 5 damage.

STANDARD ACTIONS

⊕ **Claw ✦ At-Will**
Attack: Melee 1 (one creature); +10 vs. AC
Hit: 2d8 + 7 damage.

↯ **Bear Grab ✦ Recharge** when first bloodied
Effect: The bear uses *claw* twice against the same target. If either attack hits, the target falls prone, and the bear grabs the target (escape DC 15) if it has fewer than two creatures grabbed.

Str 20 (+7)	Dex 13 (+3)	Wis 13 (+3)
Con 20 (+7)	Int 2 (-2)	Cha 12 (+3)

Alignment unaligned	**Languages** —

Dire Bear	Level 11 Elite Brute
Large natural beast	XP 1,200

HP 276; **Bloodied** 138	**Initiative** +8
AC 23, **Fortitude** 25, **Reflex** 22, **Will** 23	**Perception** +9
Speed 8	
Saving Throws +2; **Action Points** 1	

STANDARD ACTIONS

⊕ **Claw ✦ At-Will**
Attack: Melee 2 (one creature); +16 vs. AC
Hit: 3d10 + 8 damage.

↯ **Maul ✦ At-Will**
Effect: The bear uses *claw* twice. If both attacks hit the same target, the bear grabs the target (escape DC 19) if it has fewer than two creatures grabbed.

↯ **Ursine Crush ✦ At-Will**
Effect: Melee 1 (one creature grabbed by the bear). The target takes 4d10 + 10 damage.

Str 23 (+11)	Dex 16 (+8)	Wis 18 (+9)
Con 18 (+9)	Int 2 (+1)	Cha 16 (+8)

Alignment unaligned	**Languages** —

"Some bears are pretty peaceful. They'll leave you alone if you don't bother them. These aren't those bears."

—Farren Windhowler, ranger of the Harken Forest

Crocodile

Crocodile	Level 3 Soldier
Medium natural beast (reptile)	XP 150

HP 46; **Bloodied** 23	**Initiative** +4
AC 19, **Fortitude** 16, **Reflex** 14, **Will** 15	**Perception** +3
Speed 4, swim 8	Low-light vision

STANDARD ACTIONS

⊕ **Bite ✦ At-Will**

Requirement: The crocodile must not have a creature grabbed.
Attack: Melee 1 (one creature); +8 vs. AC
Hit: 1d10 + 6 damage, and the crocodile grabs the target (escape DC 13).

↓ **Crushing Jaws ✦ At-Will**

Effect: Melee 1 (one creature grabbed by the crocodile). The target takes 2d8 + 3 damage.

Skills Stealth +7

Str 17 (+4)	**Dex** 12 (+2)	**Wis** 14 (+3)
Con 14 (+3)	**Int** 1 (-4)	**Cha** 7 (-1)

Alignment unaligned	**Languages** —

Horse

Horse	Level 1 Brute
Large natural beast (mount)	XP 100

HP 36; **Bloodied** 18	**Initiative** +1
AC 13, **Fortitude** 15, **Reflex** 13, **Will** 10	**Perception** +5
Speed 10	Low-light vision

TRAITS

Charger (mount)

The horse's rider gains a +3 bonus to damage rolls on charge attacks.

STANDARD ACTIONS

⊕ **Kick ✦ At-Will**

Attack: Melee 1 (one creature); +6 vs. AC
Hit: 2d6 + 4 damage.

↓ **Trample ✦ Encounter**

Effect: The horse moves up to its speed and can move through enemies' spaces during the move. Each time the horse enters an enemy's space for the first time during the move, it makes the following attack against that enemy.
Attack: Melee 0; +4 vs. Reflex
Hit: 2d8 + 4 damage, and the enemy falls prone.

Str 19 (+4)	**Dex** 13 (+1)	**Wis** 11 (+0)
Con 16 (+3)	**Int** 2 (-4)	**Cha** 9 (-1)

Alignment unaligned	**Languages** —

"Sure, you'll strike terror into your enemies' hearts if you ride a manticore or a dire wolf into battle. But a horse is the most likely to carry you back off the battlefield."

—Oakley, knight of Therund

Hyena

War Hyena	Level 8 Minion Soldier
Medium natural beast	XP 88

HP 1; a missed attack never damages a minion. | **Initiative** +9
AC 24, **Fortitude** 21, **Reflex** 20, **Will** 19 | **Perception** +6
Speed 8 | Low-light vision

Traits

✧ **Harrier ✦ Aura** 1
Any enemy in the aura grants combat advantage.

Standard Actions

⊕ **Bite ✦ At-Will**
Attack: Melee 1 (one creature); +13 vs. AC
Hit: 8 damage.

Triggered Actions

⊦ **Savage Response ✦ At-Will**
Trigger: An enemy adjacent to the hyena makes an attack that doesn't include it as a target.
Effect (Immediate Reaction): The hyena uses *bite* against the triggering enemy.

Str 20 (+9)	Dex 17 (+7)	Wis 15 (+6)
Con 16 (+7)	Int 2 (+0)	Cha 5 (+1)

Alignment unaligned | **Languages** –

Rat

Dire Rat	Level 1 Brute
Small natural beast	XP 100

HP 38; **Bloodied** 19 | **Initiative** +2
AC 13, **Fortitude** 13, **Reflex** 11, **Will** 9 | **Perception** +5
Speed 6, climb 3 | Low-light vision

Standard Actions

⊕ **Bite (disease) ✦ At-Will**
Attack: Melee 1 (one creature); +6 vs. AC
Hit: 1d10 + 5 damage. At the end of the encounter, the target makes a saving throw. On a failure, the target contracts dire rat filth fever (stage 1).

Skills Stealth +7

Str 14 (+2)	Dex 15 (+2)	Wis 10 (+0)
Con 18 (+4)	Int 2 (-4)	Cha 6 (-2)

Alignment unaligned | **Languages** –

Dire Rat Filth Fever	Level 1 Disease

Those infected by this disease waste away as they alternately suffer chills and hot flashes.

Stage 0: The target recovers from the disease.
Stage 1: While affected by stage 1, the target loses a healing surge.
Stage 2: While affected by stage 2, the target loses a healing surge. The target also takes a -2 penalty to AC, Fortitude, and Reflex.
Stage 3: While affected by stage 3, the target loses all healing surges and cannot regain hit points. The target also takes a -2 penalty to AC, Fortitude, and Reflex.
Check: At the end of each extended rest, the target makes an Endurance check if it is at stage 1 or 2.
7 or Lower: The stage of the disease increases by 1.
8-11: No change.
12 or Higher: The stage of the disease decreases by 1.

Scurrying Rat Swarm — Level 1 Skirmisher

Medium natural beast (swarm) — XP 100

SWARM

HP 27; Bloodied 13   Initiative +5
AC 15, Fortitude 13, Reflex 15, Will 11   Perception +4
Speed 6, climb 2   Low-light vision
Resist half damage from melee and ranged attacks;
Vulnerable 5 to close and area attacks

TRAITS

⟳ Swarm Attack ✦ Aura 1

Any enemy that ends its turn in the aura takes 4 damage, and the swarm can slide it 1 square as a free action.

Swarm

The swarm can occupy the same space as another creature, and an enemy can enter its space, which is difficult terrain. The swarm cannot be pulled, pushed, or slid by melee or ranged attacks. It can squeeze through any opening that is large enough for at least one of the creatures it comprises.

STANDARD ACTIONS

⊕ Swarm of Teeth ✦ At-Will

Attack: Melee 1 (one creature); +6 vs. AC
Hit: 1d10 + 3 damage, or 1d10 + 8 if the swarm moved at least 2 squares during this turn.
Effect: The swarm can shift 1 square.

Str 12 (+1)	Dex 16 (+3)	Wis 9 (-1)
Con 11 (+0)	Int 1 (-5)	Cha 7 (-2)
Alignment unaligned	**Languages** –	

Shark

Shark — Level 5 Brute

Medium natural beast (aquatic) — XP 200

HP 75; Bloodied 37   Initiative +4
AC 17, Fortitude 18, Reflex 17, Will 17   Perception +4
Speed 1 (clumsy), swim 8   Low-light vision

TRAITS

Aquatic

The shark can breathe underwater. In aquatic combat, it gains a +2 bonus to attack rolls against nonaquatic creatures.

Blood Frenzy

The shark gains a +2 bonus to attack rolls and a +4 bonus to damage rolls against bloodied creatures.

STANDARD ACTIONS

⊕ Bite ✦ At-Will

Attack: Melee 1 (one creature); +10 vs. AC
Hit: 2d8 + 7 damage.

Str 18 (+6)	Dex 15 (+4)	Wis 14 (+4)
Con 15 (+4)	Int 1 (-3)	Cha 8 (+1)
Alignment unaligned	**Languages** –	

"Cold, unfeeling, and brutal. I don't care if you're talking about the sea or the sharks that swim in it."

—Mardred of Hammerfast

Snake

Spitting Cobra
Level 5 Minion Soldier
Small natural beast (reptile)
XP 50

HP 1; a missed attack never damages a minion. | **Initiative** +8
AC 21, **Fortitude** 17, **Reflex** 18, **Will** 17 | **Perception** +4
Speed 6, climb 6 | Low-light vision

Standard Actions

⊕ **Bite** (poison) ✦ **At-Will**
Attack: Melee 1 (one creature); +10 vs. AC
Hit: 6 poison damage, and the cobra marks the target until the end of the cobra's next turn.

⊙ **Blinding Spittle** (poison) ✦ **Recharge** ⚃ ⚄ ⚅
Attack: Ranged 5 (one creature); +8 vs. Reflex
Hit: 6 poison damage, and the target is blinded (save ends).

Str 7 (+0) | **Dex** 18 (+6) | **Wis** 15 (+4)
Con 15 (+4) | **Int** 1 (-3) | **Cha** 10 (+2)
Alignment unaligned | **Languages** —

Deathrattle Viper
Level 5 Brute
Medium natural beast (reptile)
XP 200

HP 75; **Bloodied** 37 | **Initiative** +6
AC 17, **Fortitude** 16, **Reflex** 18, **Will** 16 | **Perception** +7
Speed 4, climb 4 | Low-light vision

Traits

✿ **Death Rattle** (fear) ✦ **Aura** 2
Enemies take a -2 penalty to all defenses while within the aura.

Standard Actions

⊕ **Bite** (poison) ✦ **At-Will**
Attack: Melee 1 (one creature); +10 vs. AC
Hit: 2d6 + 4 damage, and the viper makes a secondary attack against the target.
Secondary Attack: Melee 1; +8 vs. Fortitude
Hit: 1d6 + 2 poison damage, and ongoing 5 poison damage (save ends).

Str 12 (+3) | **Dex** 19 (+6) | **Wis** 10 (+2)
Con 15 (+4) | **Int** 2 (-2) | **Cha** 14 (+4)
Alignment unaligned | **Languages** —

Crushgrip Constrictor
Level 9 Soldier
Large natural beast (reptile)
XP 400

HP 96; **Bloodied** 48 | **Initiative** +9
AC 25, **Fortitude** 23, **Reflex** 20, **Will** 20 | **Perception** +12
Speed 6, climb 6, swim 6 | Low-light vision

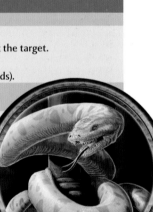

Standard Actions

⊕ **Bite** ✦ **At-Will**
Attack: Melee 1 (one creature); +14 vs. AC
Hit: 2d10 + 6 damage, and the constrictor grabs the target (escape DC 17).

⨎ **Constrict** ✦ **At-Will**
Attack: Melee 1 (one creature grabbed by the constrictor); +12 vs. Fortitude
Hit: 2d12 + 8 damage, and the target is dazed until the end of the constrictor's next turn.

Skills Stealth +12
Str 22 (+10) | **Dex** 16 (+7) | **Wis** 17 (+7)
Con 16 (+7) | **Int** 2 (+0) | **Cha** 10 (+4)
Alignment unaligned | **Languages** —

Snake Swarm	Level 12 Brute
Medium natural beast (reptile, swarm)	XP 700

SWARM

HP 149; **Bloodied** 74   **Initiative** +10
AC 24, **Fortitude** 25, **Reflex** 24, **Will** 23   **Perception** +9
Speed 6, climb 6   Low-light vision
Resist half damage from melee and ranged attacks;
Vulnerable 10 to close and area attacks

TRAITS

☼ **Swarm Attack** (poison) ✦ **Aura 1**
An enemy that ends its turn in the aura takes 10 poison damage.

Swarm
The swarm can occupy the same space as another creature, and an enemy can enter its space, which is difficult terrain. The swarm cannot be pulled, pushed, or slid by melee or ranged attacks. It can squeeze through any opening that is large enough for at least one of the creatures it comprises.

STANDARD ACTIONS

⟲ **Swarm of Fangs** (poison) ✦ **At-will**
Attack: Close burst 1 (enemies in the burst); +17 vs. AC
Hit: 2d8 + 8 poison damage, and the target is slowed (save ends).
Skills Stealth +15

Str 22 (+12)	**Dex** 19 (+10)	**Wis** 16 (+9)
Con 19 (+10)	**Int** 1 (+1)	**Cha** 7 (+4)

Alignment unaligned   **Languages** —

Spider

Spider Swarm	Level 3 Soldier
Medium natural beast (spider, swarm)	XP 150

HP 44; **Bloodied** 22   **Initiative** +6
AC 19, **Fortitude** 13, **Reflex** 16, **Will** 15   **Perception** +3
Speed 6, climb 6 (spider climb)   Tremorsense 5
Resist half damage from melee   **Vulnerable** 5 to close
and ranged attacks   and area attacks

TRAITS

☼ **Swarm Attack** ✦ **Aura 1**
Any enemy that starts its turn in the aura is slowed until the start of its next turn.

Swarm
The swarm can occupy the same space as another creature, and an enemy can enter its space, which is difficult terrain. The swarm cannot be pulled, pushed, or slid by melee or ranged attacks. It can squeeze through any opening that is large enough for at least one of the creatures it comprises.

Web Walk
The spider ignores difficult terrain composed of webs.

STANDARD ACTIONS

⊕ **Swarm of Fangs** (poison) ✦ **At-Will**
Attack: Melee 1 (one creature); +6 vs. Reflex
Hit: 1d6 + 3 damage, and ongoing 5 poison damage (save ends).
Skills Athletics +6, Stealth +9

Str 11 (+1)	**Dex** 17 (+4)	**Wis** 14 (+3)
Con 12 (+2)	**Int** 1 (-4)	**Cha** 7 (-1)

Alignment unaligned   **Languages** —

Deathjump Spider

Level 4 Skirmisher

Medium natural beast (spider)

XP 175

HP 52; **Bloodied** 26
AC 18, **Fortitude** 17, **Reflex** 16, **Will** 15
Speed 6, climb 6 (spider climb)
Resist 5 poison

Initiative +5
Perception +7
Tremorsense 5

TRAITS

Web Walk
  The spider ignores difficult terrain composed of webs.

STANDARD ACTIONS

⊕ **Bite** (poison) ✦ **At-Will**
  Attack: Melee 1 (one creature); +9 vs. AC
  Hit: 1d6 + 3 damage, and the target takes ongoing 5 poison damage (save ends).

↟ **Death from Above** ✦ **Recharge** ⚄ ⚅ ⚅
  Effect: The spider jumps up to 6 squares. This movement does not provoke opportunity attacks.
  After the jump, the spider uses *bite*, knocking the target prone on a hit.

MOVE ACTIONS

Prodigious Leap ✦ **Encounter**
  Effect: The spider jumps up to 10 squares. This movement does not provoke opportunity attacks.

Skills Athletics +9, Stealth +8

Str 14 (+4)	**Dex** 12 (+3)	**Wis** 10 (+2)
Con 12 (+3)	**Int** 1 (-3)	**Cha** 8 (-1)

Alignment unaligned   **Languages** —

Doomspinner Spider

Level 7 Controller

Large natural beast (spider)

XP 300

HP 82; **Bloodied** 41
AC 21, **Fortitude** 20, **Reflex** 19, **Will** 19
Speed 6, climb 6 (spider climb)
Resist 5 poison

Initiative +6
Perception +11
Tremorsense 10

TRAITS

Web Walk
  The spider ignores difficult terrain composed of webs.

STANDARD ACTIONS

⊕ **Bite** (poison) ✦ **At-Will**
  Attack: Melee 1 (one creature); +12 vs. AC
  Hit: 1d8 + 6 damage, and ongoing 5 poison damage, or ongoing 10 poison if the target is immo-bilized, restrained, stunned, or unconscious (save ends).

❋ **Web Casting** ✦ **At-Will**
  Attack: Area burst 1 within 5 (creatures in the burst); +10 vs. Reflex
  Hit: The target is restrained (save ends).
  Effect: Squares in the burst are difficult terrain until the end of the encounter.

MINOR ACTIONS

⤳ **Draw to Doom** ✦ **At-Will**
  Attack: Ranged 5 (one creature); +10 vs. Fortitude
  Hit: The spider pulls the target up to 4 squares.

Skills Athletics +12, Stealth +11

Str 19 (+7)	**Dex** 16 (+6)	**Wis** 17 (+6)
Con 18 (+7)	**Int** 1 (-2)	**Cha** 9 (-2)

Alignment unaligned   **Languages** —

Cave Spider
Level 12 Minion Skirmisher

Medium natural beast (spider)　　　　　　　　　　XP 175

HP 1; a missed attack never damages a minion.	**Initiative** +15
AC 26, **Fortitude** 24, **Reflex** 25, **Will** 22	**Perception** +11
Speed 6, climb 6 (spider climb)	Darkvision, tremorsense 5
Resist 10 poison	

TRAITS
Web Walk

　The spider ignores difficult terrain composed of webs.

STANDARD ACTIONS
ⓐ **Bite** (poison) ✦ **At-Will**

Attack: Melee 1 (one creature); +17 vs. AC

Hit: 10 damage, plus 5 poison damage if the target is immobilized, restrained, stunned, or unconscious.

MINOR ACTIONS
⤳ **Tethering Web** ✦ **At-Will**

Attack: Ranged 10 (one creature); +15 vs. Reflex

Hit: The target is immobilized until the end of its next turn.

Skills Athletics +17, Stealth +18		
Str 22 (+12)	**Dex** 24 (+13)	**Wis** 20 (+11)
Con 19 (+10)	**Int** 1 (+1)	**Cha** 8 (+5)
Alignment unaligned	**Languages** –	

"There's nothing ordinary about a spider with legs as long as I am tall and a body like a cask of ale. Especially when it throws its web to tangle you up or draw you to its fangs."

　—Corrin Riverwander

Wolf

Gray Wolf — Level 2 Skirmisher
Medium natural beast   XP 125

HP 38; **Bloodied** 19   **Initiative** +6
AC 16, **Fortitude** 14, **Reflex** 15, **Will** 13   **Perception** +7
Speed 8   Low-light vision

STANDARD ACTIONS

⊕ Bite ✦ At-Will

Attack: Melee 1 (one creature); +7 vs. AC
Hit: 1d6 + 5 damage, or 2d6 + 5 against a prone target. If the wolf has combat advantage against the target, the target falls prone.
Effect: The wolf shifts up to 4 squares.

Str 13 (+2)	Dex 16 (+4)	Wis 13 (+2)
Con 14 (+3)	Int 2 (-3)	Cha 10 (+1)

Alignment unaligned   **Languages** —

Dire Wolf — Level 5 Skirmisher
Large natural beast (mount)   XP 200

HP 67; **Bloodied** 33   **Initiative** +7
AC 19, **Fortitude** 18, **Reflex** 17, **Will** 16   **Perception** +9
Speed 8   Low-light vision

TRAITS

Pack Harrier

The wolf has combat advantage against any enemy that is adjacent to two or more of the wolf's allies.

Pack Hunter (mount)

The wolf's rider has combat advantage against any enemy that is adjacent to one of the rider's allies other than the wolf.

STANDARD ACTIONS

⊕ Bite ✦ At-Will

Attack: Melee 1 (one creature); +10 vs. AC
Hit: 2d8 + 4 damage, or 3d8 + 4 against a prone target. The target falls prone if the wolf has combat advantage against it.

Str 19 (+6)	Dex 16 (+5)	Wis 14 (+4)
Con 19 (+6)	Int 5 (-1)	Cha 11 (+2)

Alignment unaligned   **Languages** —

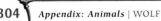

GLOSSARY

This glossary defines some of the game terms used in this book, as well as terms related to them. The material here assumes you're familiar with the basic rules of the game.

aberrant [origin]: Aberrant creatures are native to or shaped by the Far Realm.

acid [keyword]: A damage type. See also **damage type**.

air [keyword]: An air creature is strongly connected to the element of air.

angel [keyword]: Angels are immortal creatures native to the Astral Sea. They don't need to breathe, eat, or sleep.

animate [type]: Animate creatures are given life through magic. They don't need to breathe, eat, or sleep.

aquatic [keyword]: Aquatic creatures can breathe underwater. In aquatic combat, an aquatic creature gains a +2 bonus to attack rolls against nona-quatic creatures.

beast [type]: Beasts are either ordinary animals or creatures akin to them. They behave instinctively.

blind [keyword]: A blind creature relies on special senses, such as blindsight or tremorsense, to see within a specified range, beyond which the creature can't see. The creature is immune to gaze attacks and cannot be blinded.

blinded [condition]: While a creature is blinded, it can't see, which means its targets have total concealment against it, and it takes a -10 penalty to Perception checks. It also grants combat advantage and can't flank.

blindsight: A creature that has blindsight can clearly see creatures or objects within a specified range and within line of effect, even if they are invisible or in obscured squares. The creature otherwise relies on its normal vision.

blocking terrain: A type of terrain that blocks squares, often by filling them. *Examples:* Walls, doors, and large pillars. Blocking terrain provides cover, interferes with movement around it, and blocks line of effect. It also blocks line of sight, unless it's transparent.

burrow speed: A creature that has a burrow speed can move through loose earth at a specified speed, and the creature can move through solid stone at half that speed. The creature can't shift or charge while burrowing.

charm [keyword]: An effect type. A charm power controls a creature's actions in some way. This control is often represented by the creature being forced to attack its ally or being subjected to the dominated condition.

climb speed: A creature that has a climb speed moves on vertical surfaces at that speed without making Athletics checks to climb. While climbing, the creature ignores difficult terrain, and climbing doesn't cause it to grant combat advantage.

clumsy: Some creatures are clumsy while using a specific movement mode (noted next to that mode in the creature's "Speed" entry), and others are clumsy while on the ground (noted next to the creature's speed). While a creature is clumsy, it takes a -4 penalty to attack rolls and all defenses.

cold [keyword]: A damage type. A creature that has this keyword is strongly connected to cold. See also **damage type**.

construct [keyword]: Constructs are not living creatures, so effects that specifically target living creatures do not work against them. They don't need to breathe, eat, or sleep.

damage type: Many attacks deal a specific type of damage. Each damage type has a keyword associated with it. If a power has such a keyword, the power deals that type of damage (the exception is poison, the keyword for which refers to damage, a nondamaging effect, or both).

darkvision: A creature that has darkvision can see in dim light and darkness without penalty. This means the creature ignores the -2 penalty to attack rolls when it attacks a target that has partial concealment as a result of dim light and the -5 penalty to attack rolls when it attacks a target that has total concealment as a result of darkness.

dazed [condition]: While a creature is dazed, it doesn't get its normal complement of actions on its turn; it can take either a standard, a move, or a minor action. The creature can still take free actions, but it can't take immediate or opportunity actions. It also grants combat advantage and can't flank.

deafened [condition]: While a creature is deafened, it can't hear, and it takes a -10 penalty to Perception checks.

demon [keyword]: Demons are chaotic evil elemental creatures native to the Abyss. They don't need to sleep.

devil [keyword]: Devils are evil immortal creatures native to the Nine Hells. They don't need to sleep.

disease [keyword]: Some powers expose a creature to a disease. If a creature is exposed to a disease one or more times during an encounter, it makes one saving throw at the end of the encounter to determine if it contracts that disease. If the saving throw fails, the creature is infected.

dominated [condition]: While a creature is dominated, it can't take actions. Instead, the dominator chooses a single action for the creature to take on the creature's turn: a standard, a move, a minor, or a free action. The only powers and other game features that the dominator can make the creature use are ones that can be used at will, such as at-will powers. For example, anything that is limited to being used only once per encounter or once per day does not qualify. In spite of this condition, the creature's allies remain its allies, and its enemies, its enemies.

In addition, a dominated creature grants combat advantage and can't flank.

dying [condition]: A dying creature is unconscious and must make death saving throws. Monsters normally die when they drop to 0 hit points, so they suffer this condition only in exceptional situations.

dragon [keyword]: Dragons are reptilian creatures. Most of them have wings as well as a breath weapon.

earth [keyword]: An earth creature is strongly connected to earth.

earth walk: A type of terrain walk. A creature that has earth walk ignores difficult terrain that is rubble, uneven stone, or an earthen construction.

elemental [origin]: Elemental creatures are native to the Elemental Chaos.

extra damage: Many powers and other effects grant the ability to deal extra damage. Extra damage is always in addition to other damage. This means an attack that deals no damage, such as the wizard power *sleep*, can't deal extra damage.

fear [keyword]: An effect type. A fear power inspires fright. This fright is often represented by a creature being forced to move, taking a penalty to attack rolls, or granting combat advantage.

fey [origin]: Fey creatures are native to the Feywild.

fire [keyword]: A damage type. A creature that has this keyword is strongly connected to fire. See also **damage type**.

fly speed: A creature that has a fly speed can fly a number of squares up to that speed as a move action. If it is stunned or knocked prone while flying, it falls. See also "Flying" in the *Rules Compendium*.

force [keyword]: A damage type. See also **damage type**.

forest walk: A type of terrain walk. A creature that has forest walk ignores difficult terrain that is part of a tree, underbrush, or some other forest growth.

gaze [keyword]: A kind of attack. Blind or blinded creatures are immune to gaze attacks, and a creature cannot make a gaze attack while blinded.

giant [keyword]: Giants are Large or larger humanoid creatures that trace their origin back to the primordials and the Elemental Chaos.

grabbed [condition]: While a creature is grabbed, it is immobilized. Maintaining this condition on the creature occupies whatever appendage, object, or effect the grabber used to initiate the grab. This condition ends immediately on the creature if the grabber is subjected to an effect that prevents it from taking actions, or if the creature ends up outside the range of the grabbing power or effect.

half damage: When a power or another effect deals half damage, apply all modifiers to the damage, including resistances and vulnerabilities, and then divide the damage in half.

healing [keyword]: An effect type. A healing power restores hit points, usually either by restoring hit points immediately or by granting regeneration.

heavily obscured: A measure of visibility. A creature has total concealment when it is in a heavily obscured square, although it has only partial concealment against an enemy adjacent to it. *Examples:* Heavy fog, smoke, or foliage. Contrast with **lightly obscured** and **totally obscured**.

helpless [condition]: While a creature is helpless, it grants combat advantage and can be the target of a coup de grace.

hidden: When a creature is hidden from an enemy, the creature is silent and invisible to that enemy. A creature normally uses the Stealth skill to become hidden. See also **invisible**.

hindering terrain: A type of terrain that hinders creatures, usually by damaging them. *Examples:* Pits, lava, and deep water. A creature can make a saving throw when it is pulled, pushed, slid, or teleported into hindering terrain. See also **teleportation**.

homunculus [keyword]: Homunculi are animate constructs tasked with guarding a creature, an area, or an object.

hover: If a creature can hover, it can remain in the air if it is stunned. See also **fly speed**.

humanoid [type]: Humanoid creatures vary greatly in how much they resemble humans. Most are bipedal.

ice walk: A type of terrain walk. A creature that has ice walk ignores difficult terrain that is ice or snow.

illusion [keyword]: An effect type. An illusion power deceives the mind or the senses. Illusions often obstruct vision or redirect attacks. If an illusion power deals damage, the damage itself is not an illusion.

immobilized [condition]: When a creature is immobilized, it can't move, unless it teleports or is pulled, pushed, or slid.

immortal [origin]: Immortal creatures are native to the Astral Sea. Unless they are killed, they live forever.

implement [keyword]: An accessory type. This keyword identifies a power that can be used through an implement. A monster's statistics block notes the implements it uses.

insubstantial: When a creature is insubstantial, it takes half damage from any damage source, including ongoing damage. See also **half damage**.

invisible: If a creature is invisible, it has several advantages against creatures that can't see it: It has total concealment against them, it doesn't provoke opportunity attacks from them, and they grant combat advantage to it.

lightly obscured: A measure of visibility. A creature has partial concealment when it is in a lightly obscured square. *Examples:* Dim light, foliage, fog, smoke, and heavy rain or falling snow. Contrast with **heavily obscured** and **totally obscured**.

lightning [keyword]: A damage type. See also **damage type.**

living construct [keyword]: Unlike other constructs, living constructs are living creatures.

low-light vision: A creature that has low-light vision can see in dim light without penalty. This means the creature ignores the -2 penalty to attack rolls when it attacks a target that has partial concealment as a result of dim light.

magical beast [type]: Magical beasts resemble beasts but often behave like people.

marked [condition]: When a creature marks a target, it takes a -2 penalty to attack rolls for any attack that doesn't include the marking creature as a target. A creature can be subjected to only one mark at a time, and a new mark supersedes an old one. A mark ends immediately when its creator dies or falls unconscious.

minion: A minion is destroyed when it takes any damage. If a minion is missed by an attack that deals damage on a miss, the minion doesn't take that damage.

mount [keyword]: A creature that has the mount keyword has at least one mount trait or mount power.

natural [origin]: Natural creatures are native to the natural world.

necrotic [keyword]: A damage type. See also **damage type.**

once per round: Some effects are usable only once per round (sometimes noted as "1/round"). If a creature uses such an effect, it can't use the effect again until the start of its next turn.

ooze [keyword]: Oozes are amorphous creatures.

petrified [condition]: While a creature is petrified, it is unconscious. In addition, it has resist 20 to all damage and doesn't age.

phasing: While phasing, a creature ignores difficult terrain and can move through obstacles and other creatures, but it must end its movement in an unoccupied space.

plant [keyword]: Plant creatures are composed of vegetable matter. They don't need to sleep.

poison [keyword]: A damage and effect type. A poison power delivers a nondamaging poisonous effect, deals poison damage, or both. See also **damage type.**

polymorph [keyword]: An effect type. Polymorph powers change a creature's physical form in some way.

One Polymorph at a Time: If a creature is affected by more than one polymorph power, only the most recent one has any effect. The other powers' effects remain on the creature and their durations expire as normal, but those effects don't apply. However, when the most recent effect ends, the next most recent one that is still active applies to the creature. For example, if a hag is under the effect of change shape and a character uses a polymorph power against the hag, the effect of *change shape* is suppressed until the character's polymorph effect ends on the hag.

Changing Size: If a polymorph power reduces a creature's space, the creature doesn't provoke opportunity attacks for leaving squares as it shrinks.

If a polymorph effect would make a creature too large to fit in the available space, the effect fails against the creature, but the creature is stunned (save ends).

Death Ends: Polymorph effects end on a creature immediately when it dies.

prone [condition]: When a creature is prone, it is lying down. It takes a -2 penalty to attack rolls, and the only way it can move is by crawling, teleporting, or being pulled, pushed, or slid. In addition, it grants combat advantage to enemies making melee attacks against it, but it gains a +2 bonus to all defenses against ranged attacks from enemies that aren't adjacent to it.

If a creature is flying when it falls prone, it safely descends a distance equal to its fly speed. If it doesn't reach a solid surface, it falls.

A creature can end this condition on itself by standing up. A creature can drop prone as a minor action.

This condition can affect limbless creatures, such as fish and snakes, as well as amorphous creatures, such as oozes.

psychic [keyword]: A damage type. See also **damage type**.

radiant [keyword]: A damage type. See also **damage type**.

removed from play [condition]: Some effects can temporarily remove a creature from play. While a creature is removed from play, its turns start and end as normal, but it can't take actions. In addition, it has neither line of sight nor line of effect to anything, and nothing has line of sight or line of effect to it.

reptile [keyword]: Reptiles are cold-blooded creatures that have scaly skin.

restrained [condition]: While a creature is restrained, it can't move, unless it teleports. It can't even be pulled, pushed, or slid. It also takes a -2 penalty to attack rolls, and it grants combat advantage.

save: A successful saving throw. A save ends an effect that includes one of the following notations in parentheses: "save ends," "save ends both," or "save ends all."

shadow [origin]: Shadow creatures are native to the Shadowfell.

shapechanger [keyword]: Shapechangers have the ability to alter their form, whether freely or into specific forms.

slowed [condition]: When a creature is slowed, its speed becomes 2 if it was higher than that. This speed applies to all of the creature's movement modes (walking, flying, and so on), but it does not apply to forced movement against it, teleportation, or any other movement that doesn't use the creature's speed. The creature also cannot benefit from bonuses to speed, although it can take actions, such as the run action, that allow it to move farther than its speed.

spider [keyword]: Spider creatures include spiders as well as creatures that have spiderlike features: eight legs, web spinning, and the like.

spider climb: A creature that can spider climb can use its climb speed to move across overhanging horizontal surfaces (such as ceilings) without making Athletics checks. See also **climb speed**.

stunned [condition]: While a creature is stunned, it can't take actions. It also grants combat advantage and can't flank.

surprised [condition]: While a creature is surprised, it can't take actions. It also grants combat advantage and can't flank.

swamp walk: A type of terrain walk. A creature that has swamp walk ignores difficult terrain that is mud or shallow water.

swarm [keyword]: A swarm is composed of multiple creatures but functions as a single creature. A swarm can occupy the same space as another creature, and an enemy can enter a swarm's space, which is difficult terrain. A swarm cannot be pulled, pushed, or slid by melee or ranged attacks.

A swarm can squeeze through any opening large enough for even one of its constituent creatures. For example, a swarm of bats can squeeze through an opening large enough for one of the bats to squeeze through.

swim speed: A creature that has a swim speed moves through water at that speed without making Athletics checks to swim.

telepathy: A creature that has telepathy can communicate mentally with any creature that has a language, even if they don't share the language. The other creature must be within line of effect and within a specified range. Telepathy allows for two-way communication.

teleportation [keyword]: An effect type. A teleportation power transports creatures or objects instantaneously from one location to another.

threatening reach: A creature that has threatening reach can make an opportunity attack against any enemy within its reach that provokes an opportunity attack.

thunder [keyword]: A damage type. See also **damage type**.

totally obscured: A measure of visibility. A creature has total concealment when it is in a totally obscured square. *Example:* Total darkness. Contrast with **heavily obscured** and **lightly obscured**.

tremorsense: A creature that has tremorsense can clearly see creatures or objects within a specified range, even if they are invisible, obscured, or outside line of effect, but both they and the creature must be in contact with the ground or the same substance, such as water or a web. The creature otherwise relies on its normal vision.

tunneling: A creature that has tunneling leaves tunnels behind it as it burrows. The creature, as well as smaller creatures, can move through these tunnels without any reduction in speed. Creatures of the same size as the tunneling creature must squeeze through these tunnels, and larger creatures cannot move through them at all. See also **burrow speed**.

unconscious [condition]: While a creature is unconscious, it is helpless, it can't take actions, and it takes a -5 penalty to all defenses. It also can't flank and is unaware of its surroundings. When a creature is subjected to this condition, it falls prone, if possible. See also **helpless** and **prone**.

undead [keyword]: Undead are not living creatures, so effects that specifically target living creatures don't work against them. They don't need to breathe or sleep.

water [keyword]: A water creature is strongly connected to water.

weakened [condition]: While a creature is weakened, its attacks deal half damage. However, two kinds of damage that it deals are not affected: ongoing damage and damage that isn't generated by an attack roll. See also **half damage**.

weapon [keyword]: An accessory type. This keyword identifies a power that is used with a weapon, which can be an unarmed strike. Monster attacks don't use proficiency bonuses.

zone [keyword]: An effect type. Powers that have the zone keyword create zones, magical areas that last for a round or more.

Fills an Area of Effect: A zone is created within an area of effect and fills each square in the area that is within line of effect of the origin square.

Unaffected by Attacks and the Environment: A zone cannot be attacked or physically affected, and terrain and environmental phenomena have no effect on it. For example, a zone that deals fire damage is unaffected by cold damage.

Movable Zones: If the power used to create a zone allows the zone to be moved, it's a movable zone. At the end of its creator's turn, the movable zone ends if it is not within range of at least 1 square of it (using the power's range) or if the creator doesn't have line of effect to at least 1 square of it.

A zone can't be moved through blocking terrain.

Overlapping Zones: If zones overlap and impose penalties to the same roll or game statistic, a creature affected by the overlapping zones is subjected to the worst penalty; the penalties are not cumulative. For instance, if a creature is affected by three overlapping zones that each impose a -2 penalty to attack rolls, the creature takes a -2 penalty, not a -6 penalty.

Death Ends: A zone ends immediately when its creator dies.

MONSTERS BY LEVEL

Every monster in the book appears on this list, which is sorted alphabetically by level and monster role.

Monster	Level and Role	Origin	Page
Kobold Slinger	1 Artillery	Natural	180
Dire Rat	1 Brute	Natural	298
Grasping Zombie	1 Brute	Natural	293
Horse	1 Brute	Natural	297
Lesser Water Elemental	1 Controller	Elemental	109
Lesser Air Elemental	1 Lurker	Elemental	108
Stirge	1 Lurker	Natural	259
Dwarf Warrior	1 Minion Artillery	Natural	100
Goblin Sniper	1 Minion Artillery	Natural	152
Decrepit Skeleton	1 Minion Skirmisher	Natural	255
Kobold Tunneler	1 Minion Skirmisher	Natural	179
Goblin Beast Rider	1 Skirmisher	Natural	153
Goblin Cutthroat	1 Skirmisher	Natural	154
Kobold Quickblade	1 Skirmisher	Natural	180
Lesser Fire Elemental	1 Skirmisher	Elemental	109
Scurrying Rat Swarm	1 Skirmisher	Natural	299
Dwarf Clan Guard	1 Soldier	Natural	101
Fledgling White Dragon	1 Solo Brute	Natural	64
Elf Archer	2 Artillery	Fey	110
Guard Drake	2 Brute	Natural	82
Elf Hunter	2 Minion Skirmisher	Fey	113
Human Goon	2 Minion Soldier	Natural	170
Common Bandit	2 Skirmisher	Natural	170
Dragonborn Mercenary	2 Skirmisher	Natural	80
Elf Scout	2 Skirmisher	Fey	112
Gray Wolf	2 Skirmisher	Natural	304
Halfling Thief	2 Skirmisher	Natural	169
Kobold Dragonshield	2 Soldier	Natural	181
Lesser Earth Elemental	2 Soldier	Elemental	108
Spitting Drake	3 Artillery	Natural	83
Poisonscale Brawler	3 Brute	Natural	187
Goblin Hex Hurler	3 Controller (Leader)	Natural	155
Greenscale Trapper	3 Controller	Natural	189
Hobgoblin Beast Master	3 Controller (Leader)	Natural	156
Ochre Jelly	3 Elite Brute	Natural	220
Halfling Trickster	3 Lurker	Natural	169
Imp	3 Lurker	Immortal	51
Pseudodragon	3 Lurker	Natural	83
Poisonscale Needler	3 Minion Artillery	Natural	187
Doppelganger Sneak	3 Skirmisher	Natural	61
Hobgoblin Spear Soldier	3 Skirmisher	Natural	157
Scurrying Wererat	3 Skirmisher	Natural	194

Monster	Level and Role	Origin	Page
Battletested Orc	3 Soldier	Natural	225
Crocodile	3 Soldier	Natural	297
Elf Noble Guard	3 Soldier	Fey	113
Greenscale Raider	3 Soldier	Natural	188
Hobgoblin Battle Guard	3 Soldier	Natural	157
Spider Swarm	3 Soldier	Natural	301
Town Guard	3 Soldier	Natural	171
Young White Dragon	3 Solo Brute	Natural	67
Hobgoblin Warmonger	4 Artillery (Leader)	Natural	158
Orc Archer	4 Artillery	Natural	226
Bugbear Thug	4 Brute	Natural	159
Hulking Zombie	4 Brute	Natural	294
Duergar Scout	4 Lurker	Natural	94
Green Slime	4 Lurker	Natural	221
Duergar Thug	4 Minion Brute	Natural	96
Orc Savage	4 Minion Brute	Natural	226
Deathjump Spider	4 Skirmisher	Natural	302
Flesh-Crazed Zombie	4 Skirmisher	Natural	295
Greenscale Raider	4 Skirmisher	Natural	189
Bloodseeker Drake	4 Soldier	Natural	84
Duergar Guard	4 Soldier	Natural	95
Young Black Dragon	4 Solo Lurker	Natural	68
Blazing Skeleton	5 Artillery	Natural	255
Duergar Raid Leader	5 Artillery (Leader)	Natural	96
Gnoll Huntmaster	5 Artillery	Natural	142
Bear	5 Brute	Natural	266
Deathpledged Gnoll	5 Brute	Natural	144
Deathrattle Viper	5 Brute	Natural	300
Rage Drake	5 Brute	Natural	84
Ravenous Ghoul	5 Brute	Natural	128
Shark	5 Brute	Natural	299
Beholder Gauth	5 Elite Artillery	Aberrant	25
Gelatinous Cube	5 Elite Brute	Natural	222
Dryad Recluse	5 Lurker	Fey	91
Gargoyle Rake	5 Lurker	Elemental	122
Gnome Spy	5 Lurker	Fey	148
Wraith	5 Lurker	Shadow	284
Zombie Shambler	5 Minion Brute	Natural	295
Stirge Suckerling	5 Minion Lurker	Natural	259
Spitting Cobra	5 Minion Soldier	Natural	300
Bugbear Backstabber	5 Skirmisher	Natural	159
Carrion Crawler Scuttler	5 Skirmisher	Aberrant	32
Dire Wolf	5 Skirmisher	Natural	304
Orc Reaver	5 Skirmisher	Natural	227
Dragonborn Soldier	5 Soldier	Natural	81
Ghoul	5 Soldier	Natural	126
Hobgoblin Commander	5 Soldier (Leader)	Natural	158
Tiefling Fury	5 Soldier	Natural	262
Young Green Dragon	5 Solo Skirmisher	Natural	69

Monster	Level and Role	Origin	Page
Gnome Illusionist	6 Artillery	Fey	149
Orc Storm Shaman	6 Artillery	Natural	229
Blackscale Crusher	6 Brute	Natural	191
Frenzied Werewolf	6 Brute	Natural	195
Ogre	6 Brute	Natural	216
Orc Rampager	6 Brute	Natural	228
Greenscale Bog Mystic	6 Controller (Leader)	Natural	190
Orc Pummeler	6 Controller	Natural	228
Mad Wraith	6 Controller	Shadow	286
Troglodyte Grunt	6 Minion Skirmisher	Natural	270
Wraith Figment	6 Minion Skirmisher	Shadow	287
Ambush Drake	6 Skirmisher	Natural	85
Death Husk Stirge	6 Skirmisher	Natural	260
Rust Monster	6 Skirmisher	Natural	251
Gnoll Blood Caller	6 Soldier	Natural	144
Troglodyte Mauler	6 Soldier	Natural	269
Young Blue Dragon	6 Solo Artillery	Natural	70
Troglodyte Impaler	7 Artillery	Natural	271
Gnoll Gorger	7 Brute	Natural	145
Troglodyte Thrasher	7 Brute	Natural	271
Doomspinner Spider	7 Controller	Natural	302
Human Transmuter	7 Controller	Natural	172
Demon-Eye Gnoll	7 Lurker	Natural	146
Dire Stirge	7 Lurker	Natural	261
Young Bulette	7 Lurker	Natural	29
Eladrin Bow Mage	7 Minion Artillery	Fey	114
Human Thug	7 Minion Skirmisher	Natural	182
Skeletal Legionary	7 Minion Soldier	Natural	257
Dryad Hunter	7 Skirmisher	Fey	92
Fang of Yeenoghu	7 Skirmisher (Leader)	Natural	145
Gnome Assassin	7 Skirmisher	Fey	150
Ogre Hunter	7 Skirmisher	Natural	218
Carrion Crawler	7 Soldier	Aberrant	33
Eladrin Fey Knight	7 Soldier (Leader)	Fey	114
Otyugh	7 Soldier	Natural	231
Young Red Dragon	7 Solo Soldier	Natural	71
Gnoll Far Fang	8 Artillery	Natural	146
Gnome Entropist	8 Artillery	Natural	151
Ettin Thug	8 Brute	Natural	119
Gluttonous Rust Monster	8 Brute	Natural	252
Shambling Mummy	8 Brute	Natural	212
Young Owlbear	8 Brute	Fey	264
Dryad Witch	8 Controller	Fey	93
Eladrin Twilight Incanter	8 Controller	Fey	115
Gnoll Pack Lord	8 Controller (Leader)	Natural	147
Tiefling Occultist	8 Controller	Natural	163
Black Pudding	8 Elite Brute	Natural	223
Owlbear	8 Elite Brute	Fey	235
Ettin Wrath Chanter	8 Elite Controller (Leader)	Natural	119

Monster	Level and Role	Origin	Page
Black Pudding Spawn	8 Minion Brute	Natural	223
War Hyena	8 Minion Soldier	Natural	298
Human Duelist	8 Soldier	Natural	173
Minotaur Soldier	8 Soldier	Natural	208
Ogre Mercenary	8 Soldier	Natural	218
Sovereign Wraith	8 Soldier	Shadow	287
Gnoll Demon Spawn	9 Brute	Natural	147
Troll	9 Brute	Natural	272
Minotaur Magus	9 Controller (Leader)	Natural	210
Succubus	9 Controller	Immortal	52
Bulette	9 Elite Skirmisher	Natural	30
Gargoyle	9 Lurker	Elemental	122
Displacer Beast	9 Skirmisher	Fey	57
Eladrin Battle Dancer	9 Skirmisher	Fey	115
Minotaur Charger	9 Skirmisher	Natural	209
Crushgrip Constrictor	9 Soldier	Natural	300
Trained Owlbear	9 Soldier	Fey	236
Young Rust Monster Swarm	9 Soldier	Natural	253
Beholder	9 Solo Artillery	Aberrant	26
Ettin Hunter	10 Artillery	Natural	120
Venom-Eye Basilisk	10 Artillery	Natural	22
Ogre Juggernaut	10 Brute	Natural	219
Skeletal Tomb Guardian	10 Brute	Natural	257
Stirge Suckerling Swarm	10 Brute	Natural	261
Vampire Night Witch	10 Controller	Natural	282
Charnel Otyugh	10 Elite Soldier	Natural	232
Ettin Marauder	10 Elite Soldier	Natural	121
Impaling Roper	10 Lurker	Elemental	247
Moldering Mummy	10 Minion Brute	Natural	213
Elder Vampire Spawn	10 Minion Soldier	Natural	281
Bog Hag	10 Skirmisher	Fey	165
Manticore Striker	10 Skirmisher	Natural	198
Mesmeric-Eye Basilisk	10 Soldier	Natural	21
Bramblewood Treant	10 Soldier	Fey	265
Hydra	10 Solo Brute	Natural	174
Gargoyle Rock Hurler	11 Artillery	Elemental	123
Manticore Impaler	11 Brute	Natural	198
Demonic Savage Minotaur	11 Brute	Natural	211
Savage Displacer Beast	11 Brute	Fey	58
Wilt-Eye Basilisk	11 Controller	Natural	22
Dire Bear	11 Elite Brute	Natural	296
Neo-Otyugh	11 Elite Controller	Aberrant	233
Wind-Claw Owlbear	11 Elite Controller	Fey	237
Doppelganger Infiltrator	11 Lurker	Natural	62
Legion Devil Hellguard	11 Minion Soldier	Immortal	53
Chain Devil	11 Skirmisher	Immortal	53
Mummy Tomb Guardian	11 Soldier	Natural	213

Monster	Level and Role	Origin	Page
Medusa Venom Arrow	12 Artillery	Natural	202
Bladerager Troll	12 Brute	Natural	274
Earth Archon	12 Brute	Elemental	18
Snake Swarm	12 Brute	Natural	301
Basilisk	12 Controller	Natural	23
Green Hag	12 Controller	Fey	166
Flesh Golem	12 Elite Brute	Natural	160
Cave Roper	12 Elite Controller	Elemental	248
Royal Mummy	12 Elite Controller (Leader)	Natural	214
Umber Hulk	12 Elite Soldier	Natural	276
Master Vampire	12 Lurker	Natural	283
Dretch Lackey	12 Minion Brute	Elemental	44
Drow Stalker	12 Minion Lurker	Fey	116
Cave Spider	12 Minion Skirmisher	Natural	303
Battle Troll	12 Soldier	Natural	273
Githyanki Warrior	12 Soldier	Natural	138
Medusa Bodyguard	12 Soldier	Natural	201
Flamekiss Hydra	12 Solo Brute	Natural	176
Deathbringer Dracolich	12 Solo Controller	Natural	72
Abyssal Basilisk	13 Artillery	Elemental	23
Drow Arachnomancer	13 Artillery (Leader)	Fey	117
Githyanki Mindslicer	13 Artillery	Natural	139
Hill Giant Hunter	13 Artillery	Natural	132
Manticore Spike Hurler	13 Artillery	Natural	199
Yuan-ti Malison Sharp-Eye	13 Artillery	Natural	290
Ghost Troll Render	13 Brute	Natural	275
Hill Giant	13 Brute	Natural	132
Hill Giant Earth Shaman	13 Controller (Leader)	Natural	133
Medusa Spirit Charmer	13 Controller	Natural	203
Displacer Beast Pack Lord	13 Elite Skirmisher	Fey	59
Githyanki Legionary	13 Minion Soldier	Natural	141
Babau	13 Skirmisher	Elemental	45
Drow Venomblade	13 Skirmisher	Fey	116
Fire Archon	13 Skirmisher	Elemental	18
Githyanki Raider	13 Skirmisher	Natural	140
Vrock	13 Skirmisher	Elemental	46
Yuan-ti Malison Stalker	13 Skirmisher	Natural	289
Ice Archon	13 Soldier	Elemental	19
Manticore Sky Hunter	13 Soldier (Leader)	Natural	199
Abyssal Eviscerator	14 Brute	Elemental	47
Arena-Trained Ogre	14 Brute	Natural	219
Cyclops Crusher	14 Brute	Fey	36
Drider Fanglord	14 Brute	Fey	89
Water Archon	14 Controller	Elemental	19
Lich Necromancer	14 Elite Controller	Natural	183
Mind Flayer Thrall Master	14 Elite Controller (Leader)	Aberrant	205
Winterclaw Owlbear	14 Elite Soldier	Fey	237
Night Hag	14 Lurker	Fey	167
Cyclops Guard	14 Minion Brute	Fey	38

Monster	Level and Role	Origin	Page
Cyclops Rambler	14 Skirmisher	Fey	38
Drider Shadowspinner	14 Skirmisher	Fey	88
Angel of Protection	14 Soldier	Immortal	13
Drider	14 Soldier	Fey	87
Yuan-ti Abomination	14 Soldier	Natural	290
Adult Purple Worm	14 Solo Brute	Natural	240
Rakshasa Archer	15 Artillery	Natural	244
Yuan-ti Malison Chanter	15 Artillery	Natural	291
Umber Hulk Bewilderer	15 Controller	Natural	278
Crag Roper	15 Elite Soldier	Elemental	249
Bough Dryad	15 Minion Skirmisher	Fey	93
Angel of Battle	15 Skirmisher	Immortal	14
Umber Hulk Tunneler	15 Skirmisher	Natural	278
Carrion Crawler Putrefier	15 Soldier	Aberrant	33
Rakshasa Warrior	15 Soldier	Natural	243
Rakshasa Mage	16 Controller	Natural	245
Earth Titan	16 Elite Brute	Elemental	133
Treant	16 Elite Controller	Fey	266
Abyssal Ghoul Devourer	16 Lurker	Elemental	129
Lich Remnant	16 Minion Artillery	Natural	184
Angel of Valor Veteran	16 Minion Soldier	Immortal	15
Legion Devil Veteran	16 Minion Soldier	Immortal	54
Abyssal Ghoul	16 Skirmisher	Elemental	128
Cyclops Hewer	16 Soldier	Fey	39
Fire Giant Flamecrusher	17 Brute	Elemental	136
Frost Giant	17 Brute	Elemental	134
Duergar Infernal Consort	17 Controller	Natural	97
Deep Hulk	17 Elite Brute	Natural	279
Death Knight	17 Elite Soldier	Natural	42
Enormous Carrion Crawler	17 Elite Soldier	Aberrant	35
Stone Golem	17 Elite Soldier	Natural	162
Frost Giant Marauder	17 Skirmisher	Elemental	134
Elder White Dragon	17 Solo Brute	Natural	73
Venom-Maw Hydra	17 Solo Brute	Natural	177
Fire Giant Forgecaller	18 Artillery	Elemental	137
Treant Grove Guardian	18 Brute	Fey	267
Death Knight Blackguard	18 Elite Skirmisher	Natural	43
Dire Bulette	18 Elite Skirmisher	Natural	31
Mind Flayer Unseen	18 Lurker	Aberrant	206
Nabassu Gargoyle	18 Lurker	Elemental	124
Abyssal Ghoul Hungerer	18 Minion Soldier	Elemental	129
Devil-Bred Duergar	18 Minion Soldier	Natural	98
Fire Giant	18 Soldier	Elemental	136
Elder Black Dragon	18 Solo Lurker	Natural	74